STIGMA

STIGMA

HOW WE TREAT

OUTSIDERS

GERHARD FALK

PB **Prometheus Books**
59 John Glenn Drive
Amherst, New York 14228-2197

Published 2001 by Prometheus Books

Inquiries should be addressed to
Prometheus Books
59 John Glenn Drive
Amherst, New York 14228–2197
VOICE: 716–691–0133, ext. 207
FAX: 716–564–2711
WWW.PROMETHEUSBOOKS.COM

05 04 03 02 01   5 4 3 2 1

Library of Congress Cataloging-in-Publication Data

Falk, Gerhard, 1924–
    Stigma : how we treat outsiders / Gerhard Falk.
        p. cm.
    Includes bibliographical references and index.
    ISBN 1–57392–880–1 (alk. paper)
    1. Stigma (Social psychology) 2. Marginality, Social. I. Title.

HM1131 .F35 2001
302.5—dc21   2001019035

Printed in the United States of America on acid-free paper

CONTENTS

PART THREE. ACHIEVED STIGMA

ACKNOWLEDGMENTS

I want to thank my wife, Ursula Adler Falk, and my son, Clifford J. Falk, for the many hours they spent proofreading this manuscript and defeating the vagaries of the computer.

PREFACE

This book seeks to exhibit a social phenomenon first explored scientifically by the French sociologist Émile Durkheim in 1895. Stigma has of course been known and discussed long before Durkheim as visible among the playwrights and novelists of earlier years.

Shylock, the Jew in Shakespeare's *Merchant of Venice*, is only one example of stigmatization as practiced for 2,000 years among Christians. Dickens in *Oliver Twist* powerfully depicts the stigma attached to poverty in the eighteenth century, and Shaw's *Pygmalion*, written in the early twentieth century, deals with the stigma attached to social class in Victorian England. The American writer Theodore Dreiser depicts the fate of single women in the nineteenth century in his novel *Jennie Gerhardt*. Stigma engulfing a whole family is a theme which Steinbeck forcefully explores in the twentieth-century novel *The Grapes of Wrath*.

Innumerable examples of a concern with the stigmatized of this world are also visible in non-English literature. Tolstoy uses *Anna Karenina* to treat the topic of stigma most dramatically, and the French writer Balzac repeats Shakespeare's story of *King Lear* in his powerful novel *Le Père Goriot*.

A great number of other writers have dealt with the issue of stigma as have opera composers and painters.

It is my purpose here to discuss how stigma affects present-day Americans and to feature those who are most frequently the targets of stigma, earned or not. Such a review of the stigmatized among us may serve to reflect upon the participation of many well-meaning people in the stigmatization of others and thereby help those who view others in a negative light to overcome their aversions, prejudices, and indifference.

This book is dedicated to those most despised and driven to their deaths by a stigma that has lasted 2,000 years and caused unending misery to millions because they were Jews. May they rest in peace.

INTRODUCTION

Every human society establishes boundaries between those considered "insiders" and those who carry with them a "stigma" or label, often one of disapproval, but in modern times there are also many positive examples. This book describes a number of people who are stigmatized in American society at the beginning of this new century. Included are those whose stigma derives from a condition which the target of the stigma either did not cause or over which he has little control. Such a stigma is called "existential." Included in existential stigma are the mentally ill, homosexuals, retarded people, those who are exceedingly obese, the old, single women, and Native Americans.

There are also people who have earned a stigma because of their conduct and/or because they contributed heavily to attaining that stigma. We call this an "achieved" stigma and include those who have achieved more than most others in American society. Such excessive achievement leads to resentment. Immigrants are included because they usually made a great effort to achieve entry into the United States. The homeless, prostitutes, addicts of various sorts, and certainly criminals all contribute to the stigma which their status implies.

Mental illness carries a severe stigma in American life. This is mainly true because we live in a scientific, secular society which has little room for irrational conduct. While in earlier years the mentally ill were mainly cared for in mental hospitals, efforts at cost cutting have led to the deinstitutionalization of the mentally ill in recent years.

Homosexuality has provoked a great deal of condemnation in still Puritan America. Although that orientation continues to arouse anger and rejection among many Americans, more acceptance of homosexuality is gaining ground in the United States and elsewhere. Nevertheless, recent efforts by homosexuals to gain the right to marry have been rejected by the courts, by the legislatures, and by the voters.

Unusually obese people have also been rejected by most Americans although there is good reason to believe that exceptionally fat people have little chance of changing their situation. Therefore the obese have developed a number of survival strategies including diet and exercise. Such strategies are of course not available to the retarded. The retarded are easily exploited and their stigma tends to involve their families as well. This is also true of the old, who are frequently rejected because so many Americans suffer from "gerontophobia." Fear and hatred of the old is a social construct which was useful in pioneer days but serves no purpose now when the proportion of the old to the entire American population is on the increase. Also on the increase is the number of single adults. The single life is generally viewed as acceptable for men but not for women. Hence single mothers as well as divorced and widowed women are the subjects of a good deal of rejection and stigmatization, a fate shared by native Americans on or off the reservation.

Until the most recent past the United States government did all it could to eradicate native American culture. Today a more positive policy toward American "Indians" has developed although the popular image of the drunken savage continues to plague the original settlers of this hemisphere.

It may seem incongruous to some that high achievement is also stigmatized among Americans. This is particularly surprising because individualism is the bedrock of American beliefs. Yet, resentment against achievement is found in all strata of American life and creates a dilemma for those driven to work hard and follow the "American Dream" which is best understood by following the obstacles immigrants have had to face here over two centuries.

Immigrants are of course by definition outsiders. However, not all immigrants are equally stigmatized. In the past those who were other than Anglo-Saxon Protestants were commonly rejected by the native majority. Such rejection is still practiced but appears to be more often the province of extremists. In view of the worldwide acceptance of English as a second language, and because of the needs of our technological society, immigrants in the new century face far less difficulty than was the case in the past.

Instead the homeless have become the targets of a great deal of antagonism by those more fortunate than they. Because a good number of the homeless are substance abusers there are many Americans who believe that the homeless want to be in that situation. This overlooks the fact that there are homeless people who cannot pay rent because they earn too little while working full-time jobs. Only recently has Congress attempted to help the homeless by legislation designed to improve affordable housing opportunities.

Among the homeless are prostitutes whose occupation was at one time seen as a religious obligation. In light of the rise of the Judeo-Christian ethic in the ancient world prostitution was condemned then and remains a sin, despite the efforts of prostitutes to relabel their occupation "sex work" and to unionize. There are male as well as female prostitutes. Most are the children of dysfunctional families as are so many alcohol and drug addicts. Although alcohol addiction was at one time viewed with great disdain in America because it was associated with foreigners and immigrants, that view has changed. After Prohibition it became evident that the use of alcohol could not be suppressed in this country. Subsequently drugs other than alcohol became the targets of the prohibitionists, with the same consequences. The stigmatization of drug users has led to the current "war on drugs" with the consequence that there are now over 2 million Americans in our overcrowded prisons. This immense rate of incarceration has benefited politicians, prison employees, and business people but has not reduced the use of illicit substances. There are of course numerous inmates in American prisons who are indeed criminal predators although the rate of violent crime in America has declined because of the great decline in the birthrate in recent years.

The lesson learned from this review of stigmatized people in American life is that we and all societies will always stigmatize some conditions and some behavior because doing so provides for group solidarity by delineating "outsiders" from "insiders." We begin therefore with a review of the works of sociologists from Durkheim to Goffman whose research has given us a great deal of insight into the conditions and uses of stigma in human culture.

SOCIAL PSYCHOLOGY IN EVERYDAY LIFE

PART ONE

THE PRODUCTION OF STIGMA | 1

THE USES OF STIGMA AND DURKHEIM'S INSIGHT

In ancient Greece, we are told, only 43,000 residents of Attica and Athens were citizens out of a population of 315,000. Of the noncitizens 115,000 were slaves. The others were manual workers and were considered unfit for citizenship on those grounds. Hence, slaves constituted 37 percent of the total population. Slaves were usually prisoners of war or, in some cases, the product of slave raids on various countries in the Mediterranean area. In an effort to ensure that their valuable property would be safe and that runaway slaves would be returned, the Greeks tattooed their slaves with a pointed instrument. Such an instrument pricked the skin and made a mark called a "stigma." Hence, the term "stigmatization," because the ancient Greek word for "to prick" is "stig."[1] Modern American usage of the words "stigma" and "stigmatization" refers to an invisible sign of disapproval which permits insiders to draw a line around "outsiders" in order to demarcate the limits of inclusion in any group. That type of demarcation permits "insiders" to know who is "in" and who is "out" and allows the group to maintain its solidarity by demonstrating what happens to those who deviate from accepted norms of conduct.

The European Jews were "outsiders" in Christian Europe for two thousand years and were the perpetual example to which Christian clergy pointed when seeking to insure the loyalty of their followers. Thus, Christian clergy would preach to Christians that the misery of the

17

Jews was the consequence of Jewish failure to accept Christian doctrine and that Christians who refused to agree to church teachings would risk the fate of the Jews for themselves.[2]

This is what one of the founding fathers of sociology, Émile Durkheim, meant when he wrote in 1895 that the establishment of a sense of community is facilitated by a class of actors who carry a stigma and stigmatization and are termed "deviant." Unity is provided to any collectivity by uniting against those who are seen as a common threat to the social order and morality of a group. Consequently, the stigma and the stigmatization of some persons demarcates a boundary that reinforces the conduct of conformists. Therefore, a collective sense of morality is achieved by the creation of stigma and stigmatization and deviance.[3] Durkheim wrote: *"Imagine a society of saints, a perfect cloister of exemplary individuals. Crimes or deviance, properly so called, will there be unknown; but faults which appear venial to the layman will there create the same scandal that the ordinary offense does in ordinary consciousnesses. If, then, this society has the power to judge and punish, it will define these acts as criminal (or deviant) and will treat them as such"* [4] (italics added).

Examples of the power of stigma and stigmatization to designate some members of a community as dangerous "outsiders" are the witchcraft trials in seventeenth-century New England and the McMartin Preschool trial in twentieth-century California.

In the winter of 1692 a number of young girls, aged nine and eleven, in Salem Village, Massachusetts, "got down on all fours and ran about under the furniture, barking and braying, and sometimes fell into convulsions when (they) writhed and screamed as if suffering the torments of the damned."[5] In addition to these "fits" the "victims" suffered loss of hearing and memory and believed they were being suffocated. These symptoms became contagious so that soon numerous other girls also developed these traits. A number of physicians were consulted who could find no physical cause for these difficulties and therefore concluded that "the evil hand is on them." Thereupon the clergy was consulted. They saw at once that "supernatural" forces were tormenting these girls and that "witchcraft" was at work. Induced to name the witches who were causing all these horrors, the girls named three women who were already outsiders in the community. One was a West Indian woman said to know all about magic, a second woman was a beggar viewed as neglectful of her children, and a third had lived with a man before marrying him. These three women were of course found to fly around the room, pinching and otherwise tormenting their victims. That meant they were witches. In view of all the attention they received the girls now accused two hundred additional citizens of witchcraft.

Nineteen of these "witches" were hanged, one was crushed to death, two died in jail, and another remained in jail. This hysteria ended, however, when the girls accused some of the town's most respected citizens.[6]

In 1983, almost three hundred years after these events, a similar hysteria gripped the town of Manhattan Beach, California. On August 12 of that year, Judy Johnson, who had been diagnosed as suffering from acute paranoid-schizophrenia, complained to the police that her son had been molested by a part-time aide of the preschool he was attending. Raymond Buckey, the accused, was the grandson of the owner, Virginia McMartin. Peggy Buckey, her daughter, was co-owner of the school.

In view of this complaint the chief of the Manhattan Beach police circulated a letter to two hundred parents with children enrolled at the school. Parents were urged to question their children as to whether they had been sexually abused at the preschool. A local TV station broadcast that the preschool was associated with a "pornography ring." The panic resulting from these reports led to the appointment of the Children's Institute International (CII) to interview the affected children. CII is a group of child psychologists and social workers. They came into Manhattan Beach and diagnosed 360 children as having been sexually abused. No physical evidence could be found for these allegations. Nevertheless, medical examiners also asserted that 150 children had been sexually abused. As the panic spread, St. Cross Episcopal Church in Hermosa Beach, California, was included in the schools reputedly abusing children. The pastor of that church became a victim of so much harassment and so many death threats that he closed his church and moved to another part of the country.

A six-year criminal trial followed these accusations. The state of California spent $15 million on this trial which led to the acquittal on most of the counts against them of the seven people then working in the McMartin Preschool. On other counts the juries were "hung" so that no one was finally found guilty of any offense. Prior to the trial a telephone survey in the southern California area discovered that 97 percent of those questioned thought the defendants guilty of "satanic ritual abuse" and other offenses. During these trials the accused were said to have murdered small children and were also accused of drinking baby's blood. There were of course no missing children or dead bodies discovered in connection with these accusations.[7]

One consequence of the McMartin trial was that more than one thousand other innocent persons were convicted of similar "satanic rituals" in other parts of the United States and some European countries. Today, these accusations are no longer as popular as they were in the 1980s, although it is certain that other forms of hysterical accusations will, from time to time, be injected into our communities and revive the old "witchcraft" accusations.[8] We need to ask, therefore, just why a scientific community such as America continues to stigmatize innocent people on such grounds even as we embark upon the twenty-first century.

There are, of course, in every community some discredited people who already carry the label of deviant. This was certainly true of the three women first accused of witchcraft in Massachusetts. It was also true, however, of Raymond Buckey, the young man originally accused of sexually abusing children in the McMartin Preschool. Men who work in child care or nursing or other caring occupations are suspect in America. It is generally believed by Americans that men who are engaged in child care play a female role and that they are probably homosexuals. These beliefs therefore place such men outside the expectations of the community so that they are stigmatized by occupation.[9] It is, of course, by no means certain that men engaged in a "caring occupation" are therefore homosexuals. However, an unpopular label can be conferred on some citizens by others so that the stigmatized person will then suffer the consequences of the label in a manner similar to that which has been attributed to someone who is indeed engaged in unpopular behavior. This then leads to what psychologist Erving Goffman called "a spoiled identity," meaning that the stigma and stigmatization have disqualified the stigmatized individual from full social acceptance.[10] This "spoiled identity" is easily recognized in the lives of homosexuals in American culture. It is for this reason that homosexual Americans who announce their sexual preference publicly call this announcement "coming out of the closet." Such a "coming out" is risky for all "gay" women and men because the assumption of a new identity in the case of homosexuals risks rejection and in addition has "financial and career implications."[11]

Several national opinion polls since 1992 have shown that there is widespread fear and hatred of homosexuals in the United States and that 59 percent of Americans do not consider homosexuality an acceptable lifestyle. Since homosexual "deviance" is practiced by 3 percent of American women and 5 percent of American men, a total of 3,975,000 women and 6,625,000 men or more than ten million Americans are affected by these common beliefs.[12]

All homosexuals do not at once reveal themselves to others and are therefore *discreditable* but not necessarily *discredited*. Hence, homosexuals, mental patients, prostitutes, drug abusers (including alcoholics), and ex-convicts know that they cannot reveal their condition without running the risk of rejection. Knowing this, they must "pass" as conventional people lest they be the victims of scorn and contempt. This kind of scorn and contempt also affects the old and is called "ageism."

Here we have an excellent example of what sociologists call *labeling*. This means that the old in American society and in some other capitalist societies possess potentially discrediting characteristics because negative judgments are imposed upon them. Thus, the old have an audience of younger people who *label* them as incompetents who cannot work because they are mentally ill or psychotic. The label "old" further implies that the old cannot learn because they are all in a state of mental decline and that being old they are, of course, sexually defunct. These views and other negative attitudes concerning the "old" are social disabilities and are the product of cultural transmission and diffusion and are not inherent ipso facto in any chronological condition.[13] Nevertheless, the "old" are stigmatized in American life to such an extent that there exists a widespread attitude in the United States that social psychologists have called *gerontophobia*, or the "unreasonable fear and/or irrational hatred of older people by society and themselves."[14]

This unreasonable fear is in part related to the American obsession with youth and the manner in which death is hidden from view in our culture. The truth is that the population of the United States is older now than it has ever been and that 13 percent of the American population is more than sixty-five years of age in 2001, the first year of the twenty-first century. Because we were once a pioneer and immigrant country we did indeed have a very young population before the twentieth century. Consequently, old age became stigmatized, not only because the old could hardly do the physical labor required in an unexplored continent, but also because the old were an easily dismissed minority. Culture lag dictates that these attitudes continue even as the population of the United States includes more old people than ever before.

Death, however, is the most stigmatized event in the life cycle of Americans. This is not true everywhere and it was not true everywhere in earlier American experience. Then, most people died at home and death was a well-known event in every family. Now, however, most Americans die in a hospital or a hospice so that death has become largely invisible to most of us. In fact, "by the 1950s in America, the sole watchers at the deathbed were heart monitors and oxygen tanks."[15]

Death is therefore stigmatized as are the dying. Yet, contrary to the demands by many patients and their relatives that "scientific" methods must be used to combat death even in extremis, hospices acknowledge that this cannot be successful and that death should not be denied when a terminal prognosis is clear. Thus, the hospice movement reaffirms the prescientific attitude that death is part of the life continuum. Death is stigmatized because it is a condition and not a label.

It is significant that *stigma* and *stigmatization* not only create negative reactions in the audience that perceives the feature that defines the outsider, but that the stigma and stigmatized are themselves part of that negative audience.

The existence of stigma and stigmatization depends largely on language as Edward Sapir has shown. Sapir was a professor and author in linguistics. Together with his colleague Benjamin Whorf he developed the Sapir-Whorf hypothesis, which holds that we know the world only in terms that our language provides. Therefore, those who speak different languages live in different worlds. Sapir called stigma and stigmatization-producing language "inventive thought," which means that people who have little or even no experience will nevertheless express opinions on a subject they do not know by using language which then constructs the reality that is thereafter perceived.[16]

We must here distinguish between those stigmatizations which are the product of *societal* deviance and those which are the product of *situational* deviance. *Societal* deviance refers to a condition widely perceived, in advance and in general, as being deviant and hence stigma and stigmatized. Homosexuality is therefore an example of societal deviance because there is such a high degree of consensus to the effect that homosexuality is different, and a violation of norms or social expectations. *Situational* deviance refers to an actual deed by the person who thereafter is stigmatized. A robber or other street criminal is an excellent example. It is the crime which leads to the stigma and stigmatization of the person so affected.[17] Therefore, situational deviance cannot be stigmatized unless it is discovered, while societal stigma and stigmatization exist as potential labels to be attached to those who identify themselves or are so identified. False accusations are an example of how a stigma and stigmatization can be attached to someone who is associated with a behavior that does not exist. Someone falsely accused is stigmatized because the attribution of deviance exists even if no behavior of any kind can be found to support the attribution.

There may therefore be no difference between the way a person is treated who is falsely accused and someone who is justifiably accused. Conversely, there are many people who deal in "secret" deviance and are not accused because their behavior is unknown to anyone but themselves. Such people are not recognized as deviants because no stigma and stigmatization can attach to them.

Even more bizarre are efforts to stigmatize people who do not exist and who therefore could not possibly have done anything deviant. The best example is the frequent denunciation of "the government." We do of course have a government. However, those who make blanket denunciations of the government usually include comments about "them" and say that "they" are doing this or that. "They" are never identified. In fact, "they" don't exist. Of course, racial and religious minorities are also stigmatized "en masse" even where they are not to be found. An excellent example is the denunciation of Jews in Poland. There are no Jews in

Poland because all 3.5 million Jews who once lived there were murdered by the Poles and the Germans during the occupation of Poland by the German army between 1939 and 1945. Nevertheless, political opponents who are by no means Jewish are stigmatized as Jews in Polish elections even as anti-Jewish graffiti is as common in Poland today as it was in Nazi Germany during the 1930s.[18] This illustrates that a whole group of persons can be stigmatized by means of legends which generally have no basis in fact and which are independent of anything that the stigmatized group has done, could have done, or will do. The believers in legends need only to know that the target of their hostility deserves to be stigmatized for something he could have done even if it is evident that he did none of the deeds of which he is accused.[19]

The issue that any discussion of stigma and stigmatization must confront is whether these terms are only social constructs or whether all phenomena in the world have an essence that places them in unalterable categories. Plato and many other Greek philosophers believed the latter. This view is called *essentialism* and claims that all phenomena in the world have an indwelling essence that automatically places them into a specific and unchanging category. This is illustrated by the well-known Platonic dialogue between Glaucon and Socrates concerning the task of science, which Plato thought consisted of finding the true and unchanging nature of things, i.e., "their hidden reality or essence."[20] Essentialists believe they can discover "true" alcoholism or "real" homosexuality. Essentialists would therefore call a biological parent the "real" parent even if a child has been adopted by someone else on the first day of his life. Adoptive parents are never "real" to an essentialist. Essentialists defend their view by demonstrating that an apple is not an orange, water is not dry land, and a ruby is not a diamond. They say that a tomato is not a vegetable but a fruit; rape isn't sex, it is violence; and abortion is murder. Hence, essentialists insist that "homosexuality is biologically derived and therefore immutable, appearing in all societies at about the same rate."[21]

Constructionists view deviance differently. In this view, indwelling traits, if they exist at all, do not classify someone or something. Constructionists hold that even if something is biologically determined this does not classify anyone. People classify other people, say constructionists, because evidently all phenomena can be classified in many ways. Hence the constructionist will argue that the "real" parent of an adopted child could well be the adoptive parent *or* the biological parent depending on how one wants to construct the relationship. Alcohol can be a drug or a medicine. Abortion is not murder, say the constructionists, if we consider that a zygote is not a human being. Yet, it could be construed to be murder for those who choose to label the zygote human.

In short, the constructionist defines the world around him as being the product of various perspectives that can change all the time.

Stigma and stigmatization therefore attach to conduct that is viewed by an audience as deviant even as deviance may be "in the eye of the beholder" and not in the essence of the "deviant." There are a good number of situations in every society which are labeled reprehensible and which lead to condemnation and stigmatization of the person(s) seen as outsider(s). This is true even among scientists. An excellent example is the stigmatization of the archeologist Tom Dillehay who discovered that the earliest inhabitants of the Americas were *not* the Clovis people who came across the Bering Strait 11,000 years ago. His excavations in the hills of Monte Verde in Chile led to the conclusion that humans were already living in those hills 12,500 years ago, long before the arrival of the Clovis people. This claim has now been accepted by archeologists as sound and proved. Yet, "for years at scientific conferences others would be introduced as doctor this and doctor that. I was always the guy who is excavating Monte Verde. Some people wouldn't even shake my hand." Here we have a clear case of stigmatization based on deviance derived from the view that scientific orthodoxy is the absolute truth.[22]

It is noteworthy that the scientific community has always stigmatized "outsiders" who had the gall to deviate from various orthodoxies. Joseph Lister, a British surgeon, "was roundly denounced by his fellow surgeons when, in 1865, he promoted 'antisepthis.' Antisepthis is a means of defeating infection in wounds and consists of the use of chemicals which cleanses such wounds."[23]

Cardiac surgery is commonplace today. Yet, earlier in the twentieth century, i.e., in 1929, Dr. Werner Forssman was "dismissed as a charlatan by the dictator of German surgery of the time, Ferdinand Sauerbruch, who claimed that Forssman had conducted a 'circus trick' when he inserted a uriteral catheter into his antecubital vein, directed it toward his heart, walked to the X-ray room, and had a radio photograph taken." At that time it was absolute truth and final orthodoxy that the heart could not be touched without provoking certain death and that an operation on the heart was utterly out of the question. Sauerbruch therefore prevented Forssman from gaining any appointment at any "decent German hospital." Yet, in 1956, Forssman was awarded the Nobel Prize in medicine for his immense courage of experimenting on himself and therefore making cardiac surgery possible.[24]

So far we have seen that stigma and stigmatization can occur whenever and wherever some people find behavior or characteristics of other people offensive and/or reprehensible. In addition, stigma and stigmatization occurs whenever those labeled offensive are sanctioned by hostility, disapproval, and even punishment. Therefore, stigma and stigmatization is everywhere because almost any conduct or any characteristic can be seen as deviant by some audience.

Stigma also has a temporal quality. This means that something stigmatized at one time may not be stigmatized at another time. For example, in 1950 only 5 percent of American children were born to an unmarried mother. By 1997, however, one-third of all American children were born to an unmarried mother. At that time and since then more than 27 percent of all American families are headed by a single parent, including 4 million never-married women. Evidently, the stigma and stigmatization of unmarried motherhood were not nearly as great in the year 2000 as it was fifty years earlier although there can be no doubt that there are those who would most definitely condemn unmarried parenting.[25]

There are those who hold that women are ipso facto stigmatized in American culture. This argument has come to the forefront of public attention as the women's liberation movement became prominent in the 1960s and has continued with ever greater force to the present. Efforts at liberation from the traditional stigma and stigmatization of being a woman were already successful in the 1920s when suffragettes finally succeeded in gaining the vote for women with the addition of the Nineteenth Amendment to the U.S. Constitution in 1920. Nevertheless, women continued to be stigmatized for some time thereafter. For example, in 1930 a survey of 1,500 school systems showed that 77 percent of them would not hire married female teachers while 63 percent fired female teachers who married while already employed. A 1936 Gallup poll revealed that 82 percent of Americans thought that married women should not work if their husbands were employed. These attitudes persisted well into the 1950s.[26]

In the 1970s, however, "feminists" began to reject the traditional stigmatization of women as incompetent breeding boxes and demanded to develop themselves while rejecting the expectations of others. Most important in launching this new women's movement was Betty Friedan, whose book *The Feminine Mystique* argued that women were defined exclusively in terms of their relationship to men as mothers, daughters, wives, girlfriends, or concubines, leaving women with "the problem that has no name." Thereafter, Friedan founded the National Organization of Women which today has a membership of half a million. As a consequence of these efforts, the median income of women has risen sharply. In 1970, American women earned only 59 percent of male earnings, but in 1980, that figure had risen to 60 percent, and in 1990 to 71 percent. At the beginning of the year 2001 it is anticipated that female income will be about 76 percent of male income in this country. It was 73 percent of male income in 1999. That statistic alone demonstrates that female stigma and stigmatization persists eighty years after women first voted in a federal election.

These examples serve to show that stigmatization depends on an audience whose members sit in judgment of a person or group of persons. This means that although social reaction does not create the behavior or condition that is negatively evaluated or stigmatized, it does lend itself to such a status. Evidently, being female is not reprehensible on its face. Nevertheless, women earn less than men. Women are also treated differently within the criminal justice system than are men. Women receive fewer resources and are treated with more paternalism in the criminal justice system than are men. Female homosexuality is also viewed in a harsher light than is the homosexual conduct of men. Even today, women are expected to be more circumspect, less direct, and more accommodating than men in American culture and throughout the world. These gender boundaries function to maintain the privileges of men by restraining women and holding them in a subordinate condition.[27]

Being female remains a societal stigma. This is the basis of the argument made by feminists who view the entire condition of women in America at the turn of the century as resting on the process of devaluation. This means that the real indicator of stigmatization is *imputed* deviance, not actual behavior. Such imputed deviance can be seen in religion-inspired myths such as the story of Adam and Eve, which clearly demonstrates an effort to have women remain subservient to men ad infinitum. Such religious designation may be called *formal* labeling because it is written and supported by the institution of religion.

Since Christianity is the religion practiced by the overwhelming majority of Americans it cannot be a surprise to note that together with its spiritual mother, Judaism, the Judeo-Christian tradition devalues women. This is known to anyone who has only a cursory understanding of these religious traditions because the most elementary Bible stories include the tales concerning Adam and Eve and other pronouncements holding women in contempt and labeling them dangerous. This therefore indicates that "women don't even have to engage in 'behavior' in order to face devaluation."[28]

Studies of deviance ascribed to women lead to the conclusion that more than formal labeling, *informal* labeling is much more significant in creating stigmatization in everyday life.

Deviance labeling can be either formal or informal. Formal labeling is achieved by subjecting someone, anyone, to formal agencies of social control such as the police, the courts, or a school. A formal agency of social control is a permanent institution which uses a bureaucracy to enforce its decisions. Formal agencies of social control have legal power.

Informal labeling is applied to offenses that do not appear in the law books but which are enforced by interpersonal responses. Such labels can be designations such as "aggressive," "bitchy," "hysterical," "fat," "homely," "masculine," or "promiscuous."[29]

We have recognized the difference between societal deviance and situational deviance. Women, like blacks, suffer from societal deviance and are also vulnerable because both groups are highly visible and are, therefore, not only discreditable but also discredited.[30]

Stigmatized people, women included, often display what Gordon Allport called "traits due to victimization." These include various kinds of defensiveness, passivity, in-group hostility, identification with the oppressor, and, of course, seriously impaired self-esteem. This may also be called self-hatred, a condition not only found among some women but also among European Jews and some of their imitators such as the former prime minister of Israel, Shimon Peres.[31]

Women tend to view their gender as their "master status" so that everything they do and everything that happens to them appears to have a relationship to their sex and not to their achievements, family and friends, or occupational standing. A study by Martina Horner revealed that female college students at the end of the 1960s feared that academic success would lead to their exclusion from a normal social life and that women then feared being maligned for their success.[32]

Some women have therefore used contrived helplessness, seductiveness, flattery, eagerness to please, and excessive deference in their relationships with men so as to accommodate themselves to the stigmatization they assumed existed. All of this has declined considerably during the last twenty years of the last century as the rebirth of feminism as "consciousness raising" has come to the forefront of the women's liberation movement. That movement is primarily interested in a shift of power from men to women or, at the very least, a mutual arrangement in which power is shared, as both sexes have common interests.

WOMEN AS DEVIANTS

Many men fear women. This means that there are numerous men who are frightened of female characteristics per se and who view women as a category which cannot be explained in terms applying to men and regarded as normal or meeting expectations. This anxiety on the part of men has sometimes been interpreted to mean that women are sexually threatening in that some men reputedly fear that they cannot satisfy women sexually. Dorothy Dinnerstein has discussed this "archtypical nightmare vision of the insatiable female," as understood in nineteenth-century America. At that time the demands for sexuality were widely seen as undermining men's work energy and economic success. Nineteenth-century marital advisors actually suggested that a man who gives in to too many sexual encounters would fail in business.[33]

This belief totally ignores that the reverse could also be the case because it never occurred to nineteenth-century American men that women could be "in business" in the first place. This despite the evidence that in the nineteenth-century large numbers of poor women worked outside the home. These women, however, were not viewed as "respectable" and therefore became invisible to the writers, politicians, and opinion makers of the day.

Historically, of course, the most stigmatized women were unmarried mothers, as illustrated by Nathaniel Hawthorne's famous novel *The Scarlet Letter.* That story, together with a large array of other warning tales dealing with "sexual morality," depicts a most profound hostility to women based on the most elementary, biological female function, i.e., reproductive capacity. In nineteenth-century America this hostility to women was linked to a general anxiety concerning the large number of immigrants who entered this country every year. "Many social leaders and molders, doctors, clergymen, popular novelists and politicians, saw America as a beleaguered island of WASP righteousness, surrounded by an encroaching flood of dirty, *prolific (proles* = "children" in Latin) immigrants and sapped from within by the subversive practices of women."[34]

That rate of immigration into the United States was indeed immense in the nineteenth century and in the early decades of the twentieth century. For example, during the decade 1831–1840, more than 599,000 immigrants entered this country. That constituted a rate of 3.9 per 1,000 in the population. In the next decade, that rate had increased to 8.4 only to increase to 9.3 between 1851 and 1860. Yet, the largest increase in immigration was still to come. In the decade 1901–1910, the United States welcomed 9,003,295 individuals as permanent immigrants. Therefore, 11 percent of the American population were recent immigrants in 1910. That level of immigration was never again reached in any subsequent decade.[35]

These "hordes" of immigrants were viewed with fear and alarm by the largely white, Protestant, Anglo-Saxon population already established here. In an anxiety-driven "search for order," blacks were segregated and lynched, the Ku Klux Klan rose to national prominence, anti-Catholic and anti-Jewish sentiment became widespread, riots against Italian immigrants gripped New Orleans and other cities, nativism became a national obsession, and "advocates of female castration [clitorectomy] saw themselves as reimposing order of the kind conventionally expected of female behavior."[36]

The need to "reimpose order" was incited by the increasing demands of women to participate in politics and their demands to gain the vote, commonly called the "suffrage movement." Since voting and other political activities had always been restricted to men, women who now demanded the right to vote were viewed as insane and criminal. In the words of Dr. William Goodell, professor of clinical gynecology at the University of Pennsylvania, "an insane woman is no more a member of the body politic than a criminal."[37]

Common consensus held that nineteenth-century American women were to be dependent, submissive, supportive, smiling, and entirely predictable. Sex was viewed as something women disliked but had to endure. Any woman seeking to alter this rigid imprisonment was seen as abnormal and as an indication that such a woman sought to become a man. Therefore, female castration was used to eliminate such a threat. Dr. David Gilliam wrote in 1896 that female castration would return a woman to her erstwhile condition of subservience so that she would thereafter be "improved, . . . some of them cured . . . the moral sense of the patient is elevated . . . she becomes tractable, orderly, industrious, and cleanly."[38]

While such a view of women is outdated and utterly unsupportable in end-of-the-century America it is noteworthy that female castration is still widespread in all Arab and African countries although that has seldom come to the attention of the Western world.

In any event, women who wanted to vote were seen as rebellious and unpatriotic and unwilling to perform their primary duty, i.e., the raising of children. In fact, women were told that they did not need to vote since they had the opportunity to raise boys to be patriots and publicly engaged citizens so that their mothers had an indirect influence on the vote in any case. Women, it was believed, could do indirectly what men had an opportunity to do directly. That attitude best depicts how being a woman became a stigma ipso facto in the Victorian age.[39]

The Victorian family pattern that supported these arrangements was ideally a nuclear household in which a father left for work every morning so that the money he earned could support a loving wife/mother and their children. Marriage in this Victorian scheme was forever and divorce was seldom employed and generally regarded with contempt. Children were said to obey their parents in these pre–world war families in which companionship and relationships were of principal importance while sex was never mentioned and indeed played a minor role in the expectations of women and men. Women were expected to raise moral, respectful, healthy, and competent children and to take great satisfaction in the approbation given them in the community if they succeeded in that task. This ideal family became dominant in the 1840s and remained unchallenged until the 1920s. Thereafter such families continued their relative dominance until the 1960s. Since then the Victorian family has declined sharply and constitutes a minority of living arrangements today.

This meant that despite Victorian beliefs which served a predominantly male dominated economic system, the traditional patriarchal household was gradually disappearing at the end of the nineteenth century. The principal reason for this decline in patriarchy was that the workplace became separated from the home in about 1900, so that men lost the total control over their family which they had always practiced before the industrial age came upon us. One consequence of this separation was that women now became more identified with the warmth of the home and men became identified with the cold and impersonal economic world.[40] Indeed, the independent "self-made" businessman became the cultural hero of America in the nineteenth century. However, the vast majority of men, immigrant and native alike, were underpaid laborers in a sweatshop or factory.[41]

About 20 percent of women also worked outside the home. These women were generally single. It was assumed that white women would cease employment as soon as they were married, particularly because the work available to women was either domestic, isolating such women in the homes of their employers, or in unsafe and brutal factories. Black married women did not benefit from such an assumption. They worked endless hours in filthy sweatshops and stayed there for a lifetime because racial discrimination gave them no other opportunities to earn a livelihood.[42]

The dominant white, Protestant, Anglo-Saxon culture which governed social life in the United States until the First World War was seriously challenged once the war ended. This challenge developed from the entrance of a large number of immigrants into the United States who were not WASPs, by the attainment of federal female suffrage in 1920, and by the ever-increasing participation of women in the economy and in higher education.

Free public education was the first of a series of events that led to the gradual emancipation of women from drudgery to self-fulfillment. This can be seen by noting that between 1900 and 1920 the population of the United States increased by 50 percent while the number of high school diplomas awarded increased 500 percent for both women and men. In addition, the Progressive Party, mainly anchored in Wisconsin politics, proclaimed the right of every person to seek meaning and direction for his or her own life. Translated into political terms this meant the demand for direct primaries, the short ballot, initiative, referendum and recall, the eight-hour workday and, above all, the right of women to vote.[43] Augmented by Freudian psychoanalysis, new interpretations of art and literature, and behavioral psychology, the Progressive Era promoted a new kind of family that sociologists have described as "a unity of interacting personalities."[44]

Although this model of family life became popular in the 1920s, the economic sphere continued to be reserved for men so that gender roles remained quite distinct as well-illustrated by the study of Muncie, Indiana, undertaken by sociologists Robert and Helen Lynd in the 1920s. Their study revealed that companionship did not matter much to the people of "Middletown" at the beginning of the century, and/or there wasn't much discussion between the sexes. Women were regarded by both sexes as more emotional and less practical than men. There was little communication between men and their children. In the working class a good minority of Muncie wives were employed outside the home. However, among the business and professional classes it was unheard of for married women to work in paid employment. Such women volunteered or participated in club life.

At the end of the twentieth century, however, great changes in the relationship between the sexes had taken place. These changes came about slowly. While the Victorian order weakened considerably during the 1920s, the Great Depression of 1929–1940 revived many of the old views concerning the employability of women outside the home. This was evidently the product of the huge male unemployment rate. After the Second World War, the rearmament of which helped end the Great Depression, the economic status of women improved marginally. To some extent women continued to be tied to the house because of the "baby boom" of the 1950s, which increased the American birthrate from 18.7 per 1,000 in the population in 1935 to 25.3 in 1957. Thereafter, the birthrate declined sharply, reaching a low of about 16 per 1,000 at the end of the century.[45]

Added to this decline in childbearing is the high divorce rate experienced by Americans with increasing frequency during the past fifty years. This is best understood by noting that only 10 percent of marriages begun in 1900 ended in divorce while 50 percent of marriages begun in the 1970s have resulted in divorce. All this has led to the "two-career family" as more and more women have entered the labor force and become less and less dependent on men.

Subsequently, Pres. John F. Kennedy appointed a Commission on the Status of Women in 1963 and Betty Friedan founded the National Organization of Women, which demanded civil rights for women, including a ban on sexual harassment, among other things.

Therefore, at the end of the 1990s fully one-fourth of all lawyers, doctors, and accountants were women, up from about 4 percent in the 1970s. Women now constitute 52 percent of undergraduate students and

45 percent of graduate students entering such professions as engineering, law, medicine, and pharmacy.[46]

As the economic power of women has increased, single parenthood has also increased. In 1999 one-third of all American children lived in a household headed by a single parent. In 1970 only 13 percent of families were headed by a single parent. Eighty-three percent of these single-parent families in 1999 were headed by women. Furthermore, the number of married couples without children was greater than the number with children.[47]

This brief review of great changes in the American family during the twentieth century indicates that the stigmatization of women on the whole is far less than it was at the beginning of the century and that the "Age of the Woman" is upon us.

SUMMARY

The word "stigma" refers to the branding of slaves in ancient Greece. In American usage, however, it has come to mean the rejection of numerous individuals, and often entire groups of people, on various grounds. For example, the Jews living in Christian Europe were viewed for two millennia as stigmatized outsiders. Similarly, the physically disabled, mental patients, homosexuals, ex-convicts, and a host of others are also labeled "deviant" as are so many others who deviate from the expectations of a group.

The French sociologist Émile Durkheim has shown that the function of creating a boundary in any human group is group solidarity. This, therefore, explains the "witch-hunt" in seventeenth-century Massachusetts and the child abuse scare in twentieth-century California. Techniques of designating some folks as outsiders include labeling or discrediting those who appear different.

Some deviance is therefore societal and other forms of deviance are situational. Stigma may also be temporal in that behavior labeled deviant at one time may be acceptable at another time. This is well illustrated by the changing position of women in American life during the past fifty years.

Prior to that time, and in many societies outside of the United States, such changes in the position of women were nowhere in evidence. Instead, many societies are still guided by biblical legends that devalue all women, an attitude generally supported by religion. The consequences of such informal labeling are, among others, self-hatred and self-doubt.

At the end of the twentieth century, many changes have occurred in the relationship between the sexes and the subsequent decline of the patriarchy that had governed American families for so long. Increasingly we have families that are based on the equality principle. Women therefore earn more and more while some have already amassed a great deal of wealth. It is therefore to be predicted that the total equality of women with men will be reached in a few years. No doubt economic and educational traditions have been shattered forever with respect to keeping women in the labor force. Women are gaining more and more income and therefore more political power. It is therefore certain that the stigma of being a woman, per se, has just about come to an end.

Women in American society are the largest stigmatized group in that women even at the end of the twentieth century still have not attained the same rights and opportunities as devolve on men. Feminists call this condition "devaluation." Evidently, "devaluation" is imputed deviance and is not the product of sexual differences. Instead, devaluating women is part of the Judeo-Christian tradition and has led to "labeling" and self-hatred.

During the century now past there has been a great deal of feminine consciousness raising as evidenced by a tremendous increase in female economic power, the suffragette movement giving women the right to vote, the increase in unmarried motherhood, and the weakening of the American patriarchy. All this has militated in favor of ending the erstwhile "stigma" of being born female.

This is not so with respect to mental illness, erstwhile called insanity, and mental retardation. Those who suffer from these conditions are viewed with considerable ambivalence by many Americans. Indeed, the mentally ill and the retarded have the semistatus of patients in this country. Nevertheless, many Americans reject psychiatric illness or retardation when they see it or it becomes a public issue. Therefore we shall use the next chapter to fully explore the issue of mental illness and retardation and show that the stigma attached to both of these conditions has had a cyclical history from the most ancient times to the present.

NOTES

1. *Random House Dictionary of the English Language* (New York: 1983).

2. John Knox, *The Works,* ed. David Lang (1854; reprint, New York: AMS, 1966), p. 456.

3. Émile Durkheim, *The Rules of the Sociological Method* (New York: Free Press, 1964).

4. Ibid., pp. 68–69.

5. Marion L. Starkey, *The Devil in Massachusetts* (New York: Alfred A. Knopf, Inc., 1949), p. 40.

6. Ibid.

7. Paul and Shirley Eberle, *The Abuse of Innocence: The McMartin Preschool Trial* (Amherst, N.Y.: Prometheus Books, 1993).

8. American Broadcasting Co., "Turning Point" (November 16, 1996).

9. Michael Galbraith, "Attracting Men to Nursing: What Will They Find Important in Their Career?" *Journal of Nursing Education* 10, no. 4 (1991): 182–86.

10. Erving Goffman, *Stigma and Stigmatization: Notes on the Management of Spoiled Identity* (Englewood Cliffs, N.J.: Prentice-Hall, 1963), pp. 41–43.

11. Sue Levin, *In the Pink: The Making of Successful Gay and Lesbian-Owned Businesses* (Binghamton, N.Y.: Harrington Park Press, 1999), p. 109.

12. Gerhard Falk, *Sex, Gender and Social Change: The Great Revolution* (Lanham, Md.: University Press of America, 1998), p. 292.

13. Ursula Adler Falk and Gerhard Falk, *Ageism, the Aged and Aging in America* (Springfield, Ill.: Charles C. Thomas Publishing Co., 1997), p. 5.

14. Joseph H. Bunzel, "Concept, Meaning and Treatment of Gerontophobia," *Zeitschrift für Alternsforschung* 25, no. 1 (January 25, 1971): 15–19.

15. Vicki Goldberg, "Looking Straight Into the Eyes of the Dying," *New York Times,* March 31, 1996, B34, B37.

16. Edward Sapir, *Language: An Introduction to the Study of Speech* (New York: Harcourt, Brace and World, 1949). See also Benjamin L. Whorf, *Language, Thought and Reality* (New York: Wiley, 1956).

17. Kenneth Plummer, "Misunderstanding Labeling Perspectives," in David Downes and Paul Rock, *Deviant Interpretations* (London: Martin Robertson, 1979), pp. 85–121.

18. Robert S. Wistrich, "Once Again, Anti-Semitism Without Jews," *Commentary* 94 (August 1992): 45–49.

19. Patricia A. Turner, *I Heard It Through the Grapevine: Rumor in African-American Culture* (Berkeley: University of California Press, 1993).

20. Karl Popper, *The Open Society and Its Enemies* (New York: Harper Torchbooks, 1963), p. 31.

21. Frederick L. Whitam and Ronin M. Mathay, *Male Homosexuality in Four Societies: Brazil, Guatemala, the Philippines and the United States* (New York: Praeger (1986), p. 182.

22. Sharon Bagley and Andrew Murr, "The First Americans," *Newsweek* (April 26, 1999): 56.

23. Allen B. Weisse, *Conversations in Medicine: The Story of Twentieth-Century American Medicine in the Words of Those Who Created It* (New York: New York University Press, 1984), pp. 1–2.

24. Werner Forssmann, *Experiments on Myself: Memories of a Surgeon in Germany* (New York: St. Martin's Press, 1964).

25. U.S. Bureau of the Census, "U.S. Statistics at a Glance—Social Indicators" (Washington, D.C.: Census Bureau On Line Service, 1996).

26. Gerhard Falk, *Sex, Gender and Social Change: The Great Revolution* (Lanham and New York: University Press of America, 1998), p. 25.

27. Ibid., p. 11.

28. Edwin M. Schur, *Labeling Women Deviant: Gender, Stigma and Social Control* (New York: Random House, 1983), p. 236.

29. Ibid., p. 3.

30. Helen M. Hacker, *The Feminine Protest of the Working Wife* (Garden City, N.Y.: Adelphi University, Department of Sociology), 1968.

31. Gordon W. Allport, *ABC's of Scapegoating* (New York: Anti-Defamation League of B'nai B'rith, 1969).

32. Matina Horner, *The Challenge of Change; Perspectives on Family, Work and Education* (New York: Plenum Press, 1983).

33. G. C. Barker-Benfield, *The Horrors of the Half-Known Life* (New York: Harper and Row, 1976), p. 196.

34. Ibid., p. 122.

35. John W. Wright, ed., *The New York Times Almanac* (New York: Penguin Books, 1998), p. 292. See also U.S. Department of Justice, Immigration and Naturalization Service, "Immigrant and Nonimmigrant Aliens Admitted to the U.S.," in *The 1993 Information Please Almanac* (Boston: Houghton Mifflin & Co., 1994), pp. 821–30.

36. Barker-Benfield, *The Horrors of the Half-lived Life*, p. 122.

37. William Goodell, "Clinical Notes on the Extirpation of the Ovaries for Insanity," *American Journal of Insanity* 38 (January–April 1882): 295.

38. David T. Gilliam, "Oophorectomy for the Insanity and Epilepsy of the Female: A Plea for Its More General Adoption," *Transactions of the American Association of Obstetricians and Gynecologists* 9 (1896): 320.

39. Nina Baym, "At Home with History: History Books and Women's Sphere before the Civil War," *Proceedings of the American Antiquarian Society* 101, no. 2 (1992): 275–95.

40. Francesca M. Cancian, *Love in America: Gender and Self-Development* (New York: Cambridge University Press, 1987), pp. 15–29.

41. Arthur Schlesinger Jr., *The Age of Roosevelt: The Crisis of the Old Order 1919–1933* (Boston: Houghton-Mifflin Co., 1957), p. 96.

42. Sara M. Evans, "Women in Twentieth-Century America: An Overview," in *The American Woman 1987–1988: A Report in Depth*, ed. Sara E. Rix (New York: W. W. Norton & Co., 1987), p. 42.

43. Selig Adler, *The Isolationist Impulse* (New York: Collier Books, 1961), p. 70.

44. Cancian, *Love in America*, p. 34.

45. Wright, *The New York Times Almanac*, pp. 483–85.

46. Falk, *Sex, Gender and Social Change*, p. 30.

47. Wright, *The New York Times Almanac*, p. 284.

EXISTENTIAL STIGMA

PART TWO

MENTAL ILLNESS 2

THE ULTIMATE
STIGMA

MENTAL ILLNESS IN A RATIONAL SOCIETY

On July 13, 1972, U.S. Sen. Thomas F. Eagleton of Missouri was nominated for the vice presidency of the United States by the Democratic Party. The presidential candidate was Sen. George McGovern of South Dakota. Yet, only a few days later, on July 31, Eagleton withdrew his nomination at the request of the presidential candidate. The reason for the withdrawal was the stigma that attaches to emotional distress in America. Eagleton had admitted that he had been hospitalized for "nervous exhaustion" on three occasions and had twice received electric shock therapy. That admission led to tremendous pressure from the media and party leaders to relinquish the nomination in a clear demonstration that even the hint of mental instability provokes the "ultimate stigma" in American life.[1]

Episodes of mental illness have often been considered sources of shame and a stain on families and are therefore hidden from others. Similarly, cancer was at one time cause for ostracism because it was frequently incurable and equated with death. Today, such a stigma no longer attaches to cancer since there are many who have been cured of one or another type of that disease. Therefore, even as cancer still arouses much fear and anxiety, cancer patients are now willing to discuss their condition and to express themselves. Likewise, AIDS patients are stigmatized because that disease is communicated through sex or other exchanges of body fluids and because it is viewed as leading to certain death.

Mental illness is of course not very often fatal, and it is not spread by means of physical contact. Nevertheless, the stigma attached to mental illness is severe because we live in a world in which the ability to think and act rationally and in a meaningful fashion has been declared mandatory by public opinion since the Age of Reason began in the early eighteenth century. Included in this demand is the necessity in a postindustrial society for each of us to perform independently those daily tasks assigned to us by our occupation, family obligations, and community membership. This attitude was by no means new when Isaac Newton (1642–1727) proclaimed the world a machine abandoned by its creator.[2]

However, the secular philosophy of Socrates (427–347 B.C.E.) and Aristotle (384–322 B.C.E.), the atheism of the historian Thucydides (d. ca. 401 B.C.E.), and the theism of Epicurus (341–270 B.C.E.) all had considerable influence on the early American rationalists Thomas Jefferson, Ralph Waldo Emerson, and Henry David Thoreau. Added to the Greek influence were such Roman writers as Lucretius (145–30 B.C.E.), whose famous phrase "*Tantum religion potuit suadere malorum*" or "Religion has caused so many evils" could not have escaped the attention of the classically educated Americans who wrote our Constitution after undoubtedly reading his book *On the Nature of Things* (*De Rerum Natura*). We could easily extend our list of classical secularists by including Horace (Quintus Horatius Flaccus, 65–8 B.C.E.), Ovid (Publius Ovidius Nasso, 43 B.C.E.–17 C.E.), Cicero (Marcus Tullius Cicero, 106–43 B.C.E.), and others. Suffice it to show that secularization and the demand for a life based on reason is as ancient as Greek civilization.

Then, when the Greco-Roman experience was "reborn" during the Renaissance beginning with Durante Alighieri or Dante (1265–1321) and Francesco Petrarca or Petrarch (1304–1374) a virtual flood of writings rebelled against all the ancient orthodoxies and produced René Descartes (1596–1650), whose insistence that we doubt everything summarized the work of his great contemporary, Baruch Spinoza (1632–1677) and served as a precursor to the teachings of Immanuel Kant (1724–1804).

The final victory of secularization of the Western world became visible in the work of the philosopher Voltaire (François Marie Arouet, 1694–1778). Together with the French encyclopedists he secured a secular, rational attitude for all the years since he launched his sarcasms upon the literate public.

Added to philosophy is the whole history of science which was summarized by Georgia Harkness in her 1952 book, *The Modern Rival of the Christian Faith,* in the phrase that "secularization is the organization of life as if God did not exist." If we substitute the word "nonreason" for "God" then we can appreciate that the Western, technological, American world is founded on reason to the extent that that is possible.

Evidently, then, unreasonable people including the mentally ill are viewed not only as a danger to themselves and others, but also as outsiders who challenge the very basis on which American civilization rests, i.e., rational thinking, reasonable conduct, and scientific progress.[3]

For many centuries death was pronounced upon those whose heart had stopped beating. Today, that measure is no longer in use. In American medicine death is pronounced when the brain no longer functions. Therefore, those whose mental capacity appears impaired and confused remind us of that thin line between rational and irrational thinking and of the even thinner line between life and death. This is the second reason for the stigmatization of the mentally ill.

Third, many people view the mentally ill as potential suicides who have lost control over their own lives and are tormented by inner demons. Many people view mental illness with fear and rejection. It is of course true that many mentally ill people will exhibit an apathy for living which is frightening and which demonstrates that mental illness can rob us of our will to survive.

Yet another reason for the stigmatization of the mentally ill in American life has been the ever-increasing release of patients from mental hospitals during the past thirty years. This has made mental patients far more visible than they were when most were incarcerated for life or a long period of time. This can be seen in the numerous homeless persons who inhabit the streets of American cities and who are often former psychiatric patients. Lacking medication and resources of any kind, these homeless people roam about aimlessly and thereby reinforce the stigma concerning the mentally ill, who were hidden from the public before 1960 when deinstitutionalization became popular with the rise of social psychiatry.[4]

The stigma concerning mental illness resulting from all these causes is so strong in America today that psychiatrist Stefan Lerner tells his patients "that they would be ill advised to talk frankly about their illness (psychiatric condition) . . . since disclosing such information may be injurious to their reputations or careers." Every psychiatrist in the country should give his patients the same advice. The evidence is that someone diagnosed as mentally ill or having any psychiatric complaint may well discover that he cannot get life, health, or disability insurance in the future. Because patients referred to psychiatrists usually have no organic problems they are seen as "second-class patients" by doctors and insurance companies. In part the stigma associated with the label "mental illness" is responsible for the stigmatization of those affected. However, the argument that we should therefore eliminate the phrase from our language is tautological because any other phrase used will soon lead to the same stigma as "mental illness" does now. Consider that "mentally retarded" has been eliminated in favor of the phrase "mentally challenged" with the result that the latter conjunction is now stigmatized as well.[5]

THE DEMONOLOGY OF
MENTAL ILLNESS

The current view of mental illness may in part be replicated in other civilizations and at other times. Nevertheless, opinions concerning mental illness have had a long history in the Western world. Therefore, as is true of all culture, views of mental illness have changed over many years because social change is a certain and ubiquitous human condition. Hence it can be said with confidence that stigma has always attached to mental illness, whatever its supposed cause.

Early Greek and Hebrew sources assigned conduct that we call "mental illness" to demons. The word "daemon" originally referred to any god or divinity. It was only in later Greek and Latin usage that the word became associated with an evil spirit or the devil. The word "devil" meant "slanderer" in Greek. It was used to translate the Hebrew word *Satan,* meaning "accuser," into Greek as the Bible and the whole Judeo-Christian tradition engulfed the Greco-Roman world.

The belief that a person who behaves in an irrational fashion is inhabited by demons has by no means been abandoned in the United States at the beginning of the twenty-first century despite our emphasis on reason. The difference between the view that a person is mentally ill or inhabited by demons lies in the assertion that the ill person can be cured by scientific means from a temporary setback while those in the grip of demons cannot really be cured. The person in the grip of a demon is forced, against his will, to do the bidding of the demon. Hence, irrational conduct is not in the control of the person so afflicted because the victim of the demon is forced from the outside into conduct foreign to him. By contrast, our mental patients are what they seem to be: crazy. The ancient Greeks, then, viewed peculiar conduct as an inherent aspect of his "luck," good or bad, which he could not control and which instead controlled him. Such beliefs became particularly popular in times of crises, such as famines, depressions, defeats of all kinds, and in connection with illness. The anthropologists Ralph Linton and Bronislaw Malinowski have shown in separate studies that the effects produced by grave economic or other crises lead to a great increase in superstition and the emergence of beliefs in evil spirits and demons where such beliefs were previously absent.[6]

Plato (427–348 B.C.E.) discusses mental illness in his *Republic,* in which he argues that the structure of the state and of the *psyche* or mind are parallel. The principal argument in the *Republic* is that injustice is madness or disease and justice is health. Sickness of the psyche is also equated with vice in Plato as is cowardice, intemperance, and injustice. In addition, self-deception or ignorance of the self are viewed by Plato as mental illness. Even the drive for power, great pride, and overwhelming passion are viewed as mental illness in Plato's scheme. Plato attributed emotional illness to the influence of the family and called for its abolition in favor of a guardian class.[7] If the family causes mental illness, then abolishing the family will eliminate mental illness.

More important to this discussion is the *Hippocratic Corpus,* attributed in part to the most ancient of Greek doctors Hippocrates (460–377 B.C.E.), but also to many of his successors who developed an entire code of medical ethics as well as descriptions of numerous diseases they treated over the years and called the *Hippocratic Corpus.* Included in the *Hippocratic Corpus* is an essay *On the Sacred Disease* or, in our terms, epilepsy. The author, whether Hippocrates or someone else, asserts that the "Sacred Disease" is no more sacred than any other and that the phrase "sacred" was invented by charlatans who would not admit they could not cure the disease and therefore preferred to consign it to the supernatural. The "scientific" argument in the *Hippocratic Corpus* is that when the veins that carry air to the brain are blocked, disease results. The brain is here described as the source of mental and emotional activity. It is significant, however, that the *Hippocratic Corpus* cannot be seen as influencing public opinion very much. Public opinion continued to view epilepsy and other indications of mental dysfunction as both holy and accursed and those who exhibited these symptoms as stigmatized and to be avoided. The *Hippocratic Corpus* includes an assertion that those who suffered from epilepsy and other alleged mental illnesses in ancient Greece were subject to fear, shame, and guilt and that it was the author's wish to combat these feelings in the patient and those who witnessed his distress.[8]

The Greek medical texts completely rejected supernatural factors as satisfactory explanations of disease. Therefore ancient Greek medicine affirmed that mental disorders were psychological reflections of physiological disturbances. This is confirmed by the *Hippocratic Corpus*, which holds that the locus of mental disorders is in the brain, thus contradicting Aristotle's cardiocentric views and the popular idea that mental disorders can be explained by supernatural factors. Even today, and certainly among the ancient and medieval peoples, it was popular to attribute mental illness to demons, spirits, or the devil.

One of the best-known explanations for disease among the ancients was the assumption that there are four "humors" in the human body—

blood, yellow bile, black bile, and phlegm—each of which was thought to be in the ascendancy in one of the seasons, i.e., spring, summer, fall, and winter. Bile is a liquid secreted by the liver. Black bile was held chiefly responsible for mental disease by Galen (Claudius Galenus, 130–201), a Greco-Roman physician. It was thought by him and others that mental illness was most common in the fall because the brain was then affected by the manner in which the "black bile" was influencing the mind. Celsus, a Roman encyclopedist and medical writer, continued the reliance of the "black bile" explanation of mental illness, influencing the views of Rufus of Ephesus who lived during the reign of Trajan at the beginning of the Common Era. His views on mental illness are said to have influenced medieval thought "for more than 1,500 years." He, too, attributed mental illness to black bile, giving examples of mentally ill persons who believed themselves to have no head, to be an earthenware pot, or who thought that their skin had dried up and was now a parchment. Such behavior caused the ill-educated and mainly illiterate population who witnessed it to view the mentally ill with fear and rejection, attaching to such persons not only a social stigma but also an otherwordly connection.[9]

During and after the rise of Christianity in the Roman Empire, beginning in 325 when Constantine designated it the official religion of his empire, supernatural beings began to speak to some people. These persons were called "prophetai" from the Greek *phetai* meaning "to speak" and *pro*, meaning "before." Hence a prophet is someone who sees the future. People who claim such foresight may well be considered "demon-ridden" or, in our terms, psychotic. This is not to deny that the future can be made intelligible by reasonable people engaged in scientific work or by extrapolating experience or mathematical inference.

Even the ancients, however, called persons who believed that they could make predictions based on mental disturbance "belly talkers." Early Christians thought such persons were "filled with the spirit." All of these expressions, however, describe people who suffer from dissociation, a state in which the patient hears voices, sees supernatural beings, or witnesses occult powers. This kind of conduct is by no means extinct despite the stigma that may attach to it. Not long ago, the Virgin Mary allegedly appeared in the sky above the parking lots at LaGuardia Airport in New York City, leading to a huge traffic jam as thousands of motorists stopped their cars to see this apparition. Such behavior is seldom stigmatized, however, because one function of religion is to permit the expression of psychotic ideas by means of religious symbolism. A good example of such visionary conduct was the proclamation of a Cappadocian prophetess in 235 who "took it upon herself to administer the sacraments, claimed she could produce earthquakes and offered to lead God's people back to Jerusalem."[10] Likewise, Sabbatai Zvi, a Greek Jew, claimed in 1648 to be the long-awaited Messiah (Hebrew-smeared or anointed from "unguere," i.e., "to smear"). He led a group of believers to Constantinople on his way to the Holy Land only to be arrested by the Turkish sultan and forced to convert to Islam.[11]

These and many more events attributed to religious beliefs are indeed delusions normally originating in a sense of hopelessness and despair. Nevertheless, such delusions are generally rejected as gross nonsense by educated observers and were stigmatized by such people then as much as belief in flying saucers is stigmatized now. Yet, the European "man in the street" throughout the Middle Ages believed that mental illness, whatever its manifestations, was supernatural in origin. The belief in the existence of Satan was strong and therefore many thought that mental illness was proof of a pact with the devil. There were many, as late as the seventeenth century, who thought that Satan had earthly agents called witches. Mentally ill people were generally accused of witchcraft, leading to their torture, exorcism, or both.[12]

RELIGION AND THE TREATMENT OF THE "INSANE"

There were evidently some who denied the demonological assumptions of the majority. For that reason there were a few hospitals for the mentally ill as early as the sixteenth century. Notable among those who pioneered the treatment of the mentally ill was Johan Weyer, who is credited with being the founder of psychiatry. He had some support from a few writers such as von Hohenheim (1493–1541) who used the pen name Paracelsus (nearly Celsus) after the Roman medical writer Celsus.

In general, however, these advanced thinkers were ridiculed or ignored by their contemporaries so that the demonological explanation of mental illness remained dominant well into the seventeenth century both in Europe and America and certainly in other parts of the world. Nevertheless, the English tradition with reference to the mentally ill was a good deal more enlightened than common belief would suggest. In England the Court of Chancery administered the affairs of persons deemed incompetent by reason of mental illness although no distinction was made between the mentally ill and retarded individuals, generally called idiots (idios is Latin for "peculiar").

Subsequently a Court of Wards was founded in England. That court examined persons thought to be incompetent. Such examinations were called de lunatico inquirendo (the lunatic inquiry). These courts, including a jury of twelve men, attempted to assess the subject's judgment so that those who were adjudicated "naturally ill" (mentally ill at birth) were then subjected to exorcisms.[13]

Apparently, then, both the demonic and the natural explanations for mental illness were used to deal with this phenomenon, although undoubtedly, then as now, those who favored supernaturalism had a large following. Supernatural explanations of mental illness, as we have seen, centered on the view that there were witches in the world and that witchcraft or demonology was indeed practiced by those who appeared to be "sorcerers" or in Greek, *daimones.* It is significant that the Greek word *theos*, meaning "God," is of the same origin. Likewise in Hebrew, the word *Malach,* meaning "messenger," was at one time meant to describe a messenger from God to men. Translated into Greek and Latin, the word became *angelos* or "angel" in English. Influenced by both Jewish and Zoroastrian sources, Christians transferred some of the *angelos* into evil spirits, once more identified with the Greek *daimones,* thereby dividing the angels into two groups, those obedient to God and those obedient to the devil or Satan. Thus, the idea of the sorcerer was born. The sorcerer, male or female, became a witch in the late Middle Ages and the early modern age, i.e., the sixteenth and seventeenth centuries. Such witches were said to ride out at night, blowing horns and striking down all human beings who had the bad luck of meeting them. Christian believers thought that witches had made a "pact with the devil," repudiated Christ, met secretly at night (as in Macbeth), desecrated the crucifix and the Eucharist (Greek from *eu* or "good" and *charisma* or "gift"), engaged in sexual orgies, sacrificed children, and ate human flesh (i.e., conducted cannibalism). These beliefs were used by the Romans to persecute Christians and later by the Inquisition to destroy all "heretics" until they became the standard means of dealing with "witches" during the European and American witch craze lasting from about 1450 to 1700. In 1486 a book by two Dominican inquisitors detailed all of the proceedings by reputed witches. That book, the *Malleus maleficarum* or *Hammer of Witches*, was widely read by both Catholic and Protestant Christians so that followers of both traditions equally feared the end of Christian civilization unless something was done about the witches in their midst.

Those accused were mostly women, as indicated by the record of such accusations during the Salem witchcraft craze in Massachusetts where the first hanging of a "witch" occurred in 1647. In 1692 the craze had reached such heights that in that year alone nineteen persons were executed for witchcraft. The objects of these accusations and killings were unpopular persons and in particular those whom we would call mentally ill or who suffered from the dementia of old age. Interpreting everything and everyone in religious terms, the Puritans of New England thought they discerned Satanic influences in the mentally ill and ascribed their peculiar conduct to demonic forces that were believed to be "in league with" the devil.[14]

At the beginning of the eighteenth century the witchcraft obsession had abated in New England so that mentally ill citizens were no longer persecuted thereafter. No real attempt was made during that century to either confine the mentally ill or to cure mental illness, because mental illness was not understood and no "cure" existed. In fact, the literature reveals that a number of people whose conduct exhibited severe mental disturbance were left alone and no attempt was made to understand or treat their bizarre behavior. Among these individuals was James Otis, who reputedly "raved, jumped out of windows" and otherwise behaved in a manner indicating real "madness" but nevertheless continued as a member of the provincial assembly of Massachusetts. Samuel Coolidge, who "wandered about in a dazed condition, often half-dressed and occasionally with no clothes at all," nevertheless taught school for years in that state. Joseph Moody, a minister in the town of York, wore a handkerchief over his face. Yet, his congregation "tolerated his behavior" until he could no longer speak in public. Likewise, Samuel Checkley, another minister, was allowed to deliver his sermons in gibberish. There were others whose conduct was indeed bizarre, such as one of the five Smith brothers in Brampton, Massachusetts, who wore a sign saying, "I am God," while in Taunton, Charles Leonard "wandered the streets of the town day and night as he laughed in a wild, insane manner."[15]

Because there were no facilities for housing or treating the "insane" in eighteenth-century America, some were boarded out with families who were paid by the public treasury. The majority of the "insane" stayed with their own families. It was 1770 before the first private "madhouse" was opened in Hull, Massachusetts. This then indicates that families had little alternative but to deal with the "insane" themselves, although Boston sent some of its "insane" to the town almshouse together with all the poor who needed public assistance. An almshouse was so named because the Latin word *alma* means "nourishment." It was indeed a poor house.

Early in the eighteenth century, mental illness was still regarded as a "punishment from God" or a "test from God." Yet, at the middle of the century a physical explanation for "madness" came into vogue: the spleen was regarded as the organ causing mental "disease." Well into the nineteenth century some towns in New England began to place the "insane" in cages in the town almshouses while others put them in jails. There the mentally ill were "confined in chains" and treated with great brutality. One man had been confined for thirty years and others were equally mistreated. When the Massachusetts legislature asked the towns to report on the "mad in their midst" this report led a number of reformers to establish the first "insane asylums" in America: Blooming-dale in New York City in 1821, McLean Asylum in Massachusetts in 1818, and the Hartford Retreat in Connecticut in 1824. Then, in 1833 Massachusetts opened the Worcester State Lunatic Hospital. This led to a new and more benevolent attitude toward those with mental illness, although the stigma associated with being a mental patient was in no way alleviated by such confinement. In fact, the stigma associated with mental illness after the establishment of the first mental hospitals was related to Protestant religious thought[16] because Puritans viewed mental illness as a sign of divine disapproval.

Some thought that the "insane" should be given "moral treatment" in order to recover. The belief that "moral treatment" influenced the mentally ill coincided with a religious movement called "The Second Great Awakening," which consisted of daily Protestant religious worship and a repudiation of the Calvinist doctrine of predestination. Good works and community volunteerism were stressed by the Protestant community of the nineteenth century so that the superintendents of the early "insane asylums" practiced the Protestant faith in light of these beliefs. In sum, prayer and Bible reading together with a reliance on Gall's phrenology and various philosophers such as Locke and Condillac gave asylum managers the foundation for their approach to mental ill-ness and governed the view of "insanity" thereafter for some years.[17] It was believed that Bible reading would return the ill person to sanity.

It was commonly believed by the superintendents of asylums in the eighteenth and nineteenth centuries that mental disease affected one or a few faculties at a time and that the other faculties remained in a healthy state. These "healthy" faculties were to be reawakened by reli-gious treatment as they were believed to be dormant during bouts of insanity. Therefore, chaplains were routinely hired to live on the grounds of the asylums unless there was opportunity for patients to attend a nearby church. The chaplains employed at these asylums were urged to study phrenology and the organization of the brain and how "the whole moral character changed by slight disorder of the brain."[18]

Emphasis was placed on patients attending religious services because such worship was believed to inspire self-control and rational behavior. The "religious faculty" was thought to remain healthy when the other faculties were diseased so that "religious truth" could still be received by those who were mentally ill.

Although religious views were predominant in American treatment of the mentally ill, these views were intermingled with the beginnings of psychological insights derived from much observation on the part of those in charge of "insane asylums." Nevertheless, incarceration in an "asylum" led to considerable ostracism and stigmatization in the American community in the eighteenth and nineteenth centuries even as it does today.

It is argued by some that the stigma of mental illness is in fact the consequence of incarceration in an "asylum" or mental hospital and is not the product of the symptoms of mental illness. This is disputed by others who claim that any stigma associated with mental illness is not the outcome of association with mental hospitals or mental health professionals but is the result of the bizarre behavior of the mentally ill. This dispute is as old as the "asylums" themselves and continues to this day. Hence in the era of religious intervention into mental illness there were those who thought that it was not "melancholia" or "insanity" that was responsible for the poor self-esteem of the mentally ill but general rejection and a devaluation of such persons as "not quite human." In fact, at the end of the nineteenth century there were those who thought that excessive religious zeal was more to blame for insanity and its consequences than the disease itself. Hence D. Hack Tuke claimed that there is a disease he called *melancholia religiosa* and which he attributed to "great despondency as to his (the patient's) future salvation," a state which the great German psychiatrist Richard Krafft-Ebing also observed.[19]

Therefore, Krafft-Ebing describes *melancholia religiosa* in these terms: "A patient, naturally religious, that has fallen a victim to melancholia takes refuge from his depression and fear in prayer. The failure to obtain the uplifting and comforting feeling that prayer formerly gave makes prayer seem ineffectual. The patient realizes this with horror and falls into despair. He sees that he is abandoned by God and has lost eternal happiness. He deserves this fate because he is a sinner, has prayed too little, and not honored God enough."[20] Such preaching no doubt provoked a stigma that must have weighed most heavily on the minds of Christian believers. Yet, despite Krafft-Ebing's great influence on psychiatry at the beginning of the twentieth century, religious melancholia disappeared from clinical consideration by the time of the First World War, which saw the permanent secularization of the United States.

GOFFMAN, SZASZ, AND THE DEINSTITUTIONALIZATION OF THE MENTALLY ILL

Secularization is a process which reappeared in the seventeenth century with the philosopher Benedict Spinoza (1632–1677) and became the daily gospel of Americans after the country turned from a chiefly agricultural community into an industrial one around the time of the Treaty of Versailles. Since then (1919), secular, scientific language has been used to explain mental illness and almost everything else.

Among the explanations of mental illness is the sociological argument that mental illness is perpetuated by the labeling engaged in by psychiatrists and others. This view holds that a psychiatric label sets into motion cultural stereotypes and negative images that result in the devaluation of those labeled. Others contend that labeling helps patients to gain access to needed treatment and that therefore labeling is both necessary and important to assure those with mental problems that they can improve their lives with the help of services not otherwise available to them. Observation indicates that both arguments have merit and that both the receipt of services and social stigma are the outcome of negative labeling. It is easy to understand that the stigma of mental illness damages the patient's self-esteem and becomes his "master status." The most socially important status we have is called our "master status." It is the status with which we are most identified and which has a generalized symbolic value. Thus, a mental patient may also be a son, a daughter, an accountant, and a thirty-five-year-old member of the Knights of Columbus. However, the most visible status of a mental patient is being a mental patient, so that all other statuses of such a patient are ignored or interpreted in light of his master status. Therein lies the principal stigma that a mental patient must endure and that is undoubtedly responsible for at least some of the difficulty many mentally ill persons have in attempting to recover.

Evidence links stigma to self-esteem: mental patients often feel that they are ruled by forces over which they have no control. For that reason, and because the stigma associated with mental patients is so all-pervasive, life satisfaction is lowest among those Americans who feel most stigmatized.[21]

Sociologist Fred E. Markowitz studied the effects of stigma on the psychological well-being and life satisfaction of persons with mental illness. He found that persons with mental illness are more likely to be unemployed, have less income, experience a diminished sense of self, and have fewer social supports than "normal" people. Markowitz found a strong relationship between symptoms of depression and anxiety as mentally ill persons often experience rejection because they view themselves negatively. This leads to a state of anticipated rejection and consequently to the rejection that the anticipation itself provokes. For example, mentally ill persons frequently fail to greet people they know for fear of being rejected if they do so. They pretend not to see someone they should be greeting. This behavior is in turn viewed as unfriendly and hostile by others, and therefore leads to the very rejection the mentally ill person already expected.[22]

Mental illness is viewed as a negative trait, therefore it discredits those to whom it is ascribed. Ascription is therefore more important than the condition itself as the same behavior may be regarded as having a positive interpretation in one place and at one time while being seen as negative at another time and in another place. While there were (and are) societies where mental illness was (and is) given the interpretation of spiritual superiority or relationship to supernatural "beings," in American society at the beginning of a new millennium mental patients receive less sympathy and are viewed with more distaste than any other disabled group among us. Mental patients, therefore, are delivered into a terrible and vicious circle. Like ex-convicts, former mental hospital patients find that the label of "mental patient" stays with them long after they have been discharged from a mental hospital. Like other minority groups, former mental patients face enduring discrimination in housing, employment, and even in legal situations. Even individual "quirks" in normal people are attributed to mental illness if they occur among former mental patients so that the stigma is perpetuated. The stigma dictates that the mentally ill person is inferior and incapable of handling his own affairs. Psychologists A. Farina and K. Ring discovered that in an experimental situation those who revealed some personal information including the remark that they had been in a mental hospital were rated as inadequate. Yet, when these same individuals told another group of subjects nothing that would lead to the conclusion they had ever been mental patients, which they were not, they were given a far better rating than when they posed as mental patients. In short, the stigma, not the condition, was evaluated by the observers.[23]

The most devastating stigmatization of mental illness is imposed on those who are patients in a mental hospital. The very phrase "mental hospital" has a negative connotation. According to sociologist Erving Goffman, who published his most influential book *Asylums* in 1961, inmates of mental hospitals are humiliated and abused. Goffman claims that this abuse leads to the depersonalization of the inmates by the staff until the patients accept the staff's view of them. This then is the ultimate stigma. Goffman speaks here of the "moral career" of the mental hospital inmate. This "moral career," according to Goffman, consists of the realization by the inmate that he has been deserted by society and is now subject to any mortifying experience imposed by the staff. It leads to the recognition by the inmate that he is a failure and a "mental case." Goffman claimed that psychiatrists could not help mental patients because they did not understand that behavior seen on a hospital ward was quite different from behavior in the community. He also argued that psychiatrists see those patients who need help the least and that incarcerated mental patients reject the services offered by psychiatrists. Goffman's scathing criticism along with the publication that same year of psychiatrist Dr. Thomas Szasz's *The Myth of Mental Illness,* concerning mental hospitals, led to the deinstitutionalization of thousands, which regrettably led to unforeseen consequences for many of America's mental patients.[24]

Szasz denies that psychiatry is a branch of medicine and calls psychiatry and mental illness a "double impersonation." Szasz means that mental patients impersonate the "sick role" and that physicians who say they can treat the "illness" of mental patients are impersonating physicians and "play the role of a medical therapist." His principal ire, however, was aroused by mental hospitals that he believed were to be condemned and rejected because some patients were held there involuntarily even while psychiatry could do them no good.[25]

Mental patients who have been incarcerated do indeed have to deal with stigma. This is particularly true because mental hospitals have generally been isolated from the community so that patients who have been discharged from such a facility become "marginal." A marginal patient is someone who is involved in two or more cultures, shares the life of two different groups, feels he or she is not at home in either culture, and is stigmatized. A stigma in this connection is a sign or social attribute that so devalues a person's social identity that it disqualifies the person from social acceptance. That definition, better than any other, fits the mentally ill. It is precisely that stigma which causes many a former mental hospital patient to fail on the outside with the result that he or she must return to the hospital. Therefore, hospital aftercare needs to involve the family of the mental patient. [26]

THE MENTALLY ILL
AND THEIR FAMILIES

It is widely believed that families are responsible for the mental illness of their members. This may be in part true since a predisposition to mental illness may well be part of the genetic makeup of some people. Whatever the merits of such a belief, it can be said with certainty that the families of the mentally ill are also the victims of the stigma that attaches to the mentally ill themselves. This is particularly true in cases of schizophrenia but is also visible in patients with all sorts of diagnoses.

First it must be understood that a family which includes a mentally ill person risks the possibility of other members becoming emotionally distraught, if not mentally ill, because of the behavior of the patient now living with them. While it is well understood that stressful events, such as a major illness or an accident, can have long-ranging effects on the emotional condition of the victim, it is less often understood or even discussed that when "a close relative has become mentally ill (it) is one of the most devastating and catastrophic events that they (the family) can experience."[27]

The stress that the stigma of mental illness places on a patient's family has become much more common during the twenty years since deinstitutionalization was implemented. Two kinds of burdens are carried by the families of the mentally ill. There is the objective burden of financial hardship due to medical bills and the patient's economic dependency. There is also the curtailing of social activities and the altered relationship with friends and relatives due to the excessive demands the patient places on the family. In addition, the time and effort expended on the mentally ill person leads to the neglect of others in the family. Because deinstitutionalization places the burden of care on the family this is really a feminist issue since in our culture women are the prime caregivers for ill persons who remain at home. This may mean that a woman's career will be disrupted or destroyed by the chronic mental illness of a family member. It is of course true that *all of this is also involved when physical illness affects a family member.* Nevertheless, the stress families experience as a result of mental illness includes the patient's abusive and even assaultive behavior, offensive incidents in public places, conflicts with neighbors, loss of money, poor physical hygiene, property damage and fire hazards, insomnia that keeps families awake all night, and rejection of medication needed to control such conduct. This kind of situation also leads to the agony of deciding whether or not to institutionalize the loved one who may have become the hated one. It should be understood that many patients are aware of the losses they have incurred. Mental patients generally know that they have failed in their life aspirations, that they are a burden to others, and that their lives are extremely restricted. In addition there is the emotional pain that the stigma of mental illness places on all concerned.[28]

Social barriers are generally erected against the families and households of persons evaluated in a negative fashion. This is true of stigmatized persons of any category. Generally, outsiders, including professionals, let it be known that the family is responsible for the mental illness of the patient and that parents in particular are responsible for the condition of their children. Many parents worry all their lives over the contribution they may have made to the mental illness of one or more of their children and feel guilty because of this. Yet, the parents of such mentally ill people are generally at a loss to explain the mental illness of their offspring, particularly if they have other children who are not so afflicted. Many such parents have had to face the mental illness of their adult children for decades even as the media and so-called mental health professionals blame them for the illness of their child. The message here is that "the patient's illness was their fault and they should go away and leave the professional to undo the damage."[29]

Because professionals are often unable to explain mental illness and are also reluctant to deal with families of the mentally ill, such families are frequently sent to family therapy sessions. This increases the stigma already suffered by the family since the advice that the family also needs counseling implies they, too, are mentally ill or at least responsible for the illness of their relative. Generally the treatment plan developed by professionals cannot be followed by the mother of the mentally ill person at home because many of these treatment plans are unrealistic in terms of money, energy, and demands on the family. Psychologist Kathleen G. Terkelson claims that some clinicians convey to the patient that his symptoms are somehow useful to others and fulfill some function in his family. Added to these burdens and the stigma they carry are the popular media who preach parental responsibility for childhood deviance, leading to self-stigmatization by the family, especially by mothers.[30]

Recently, support groups for families of adults with mental illness have been organized. Such groups are not unique to the families of the mentally ill. Self-help support groups have arisen in the last twenty years in connection with many kinds of illness, disability, and loss. There are now self-help groups for the retarded, for parents of dead children, for heart and lung disease issues, and for a host of other life circumstances.

As we have already seen, the stigma of mental illness attaches to family members and is most visible among the 40 percent of mentally ill people who live with their families all or part of their lives. These groups differ from the traditional groups organized by mental health professionals in that they seek to discover how the family can cope with present circumstances rather than deal with the "cause" of it all. Support groups allow families of mentally ill persons to share information, resources, and understanding. Furthermore, such groups are of great help in dealing with the stigma associated with mental illness everywhere else. Again, we recognize that support groups are needed among all who suffer the consequences of perceived deviance, be they immigrants, homosexuals, ethnic minorities, or the mentally ill.[31]

There is in America a National Alliance for the Mentally Ill (NAMI) that represents families who feel devalued by mental health professionals and those who are angered by government priorities that shortchange persons with severe mental illness. As a lobbying group, NAMI has succeeded in transferring mental health research programs to the National Institute of Mental Health and in establishing a new mental health agency, called the Substance Abuse and Mental Health Services Administration. This alliance seeks to promote support groups among those whose family members are so stigmatized.[32]

Psychiatrist Sheldon Norton et al. studied the benefits accruing to the members of the National Alliance for the Mentally Ill and compared these outcomes with families of the mentally ill who were not members of the alliance. These researchers found that members of the alliance received significant benefits from their association with others facing the same problems. First, such membership permits the members to gain more knowledge about mental illness. In turn, this increases their ability to cope with a mentally ill relative and in getting help for such a patient and hence living with the stigma derived from that illness.

Norton and his colleagues found that the vast majority of those who utilize such self-help groups are white, female, and well educated. This is no doubt the case because those with a higher socioeconomic status have solved the problems of basic survival and can therefore deal more with the psychological issues involved in the stress they face each day.[33]

This then invites consideration of those who are not able to deal with their own mental illness or that of their relatives, some of whom are people who were sent out of mental hospitals at the end of the 1970s and 1980s and who are now found wandering the streets of American towns and cities because they are homeless. This does not mean that all of the homeless are mentally ill. It does mean, however, that the mentally ill are overrepresented among the homeless.

Estimates concerning the number of the homeless in the United States vary a great deal. The major reason for this variance is that there are a number of definitions of what constitutes homelessness and how to count the homeless. *Point-in-time* counts deal with the number of homeless on any one day or during one week. *Period-prevalence* counts examines the number of people who are homeless over a given period. Therefore, the latter includes people who are intermittently homeless. It should also be considered that by definition the "homeless" cannot easily be counted because they are not in any one place or house or shelter where they can be found. Keeping in mind all of these considerations, it has been estimated by the National Law Center for Homelessness and Poverty that in 1999 there were no fewer than 500,000 but no more than 600,000 homeless people in this country. Of these around 25 percent are believed to be mentally ill. This number is sometimes updated by using a projected rate of increase of 5 percent a year to produce an estimate of over 700,000 people homeless on any given night and up to 2 million people who experience homelessness in any one year.[34]

The following is a succinct statement of the relationship between mental illness and homelessness: "Mental disorders prevent people from carrying out essential aspects of daily life, such as self-care, household management, and interpersonal relationships. Homeless people with mental disorders remain homeless for longer periods of time and have less contact with family and friends. They encounter more barriers to employment, tend to be in poorer physical health, and have more contact with the legal system than homeless people who do not suffer from mental disorders."[35]

Because homelessness has recently been recognized as a major social problem in this country, a steady growth of the professional literature concerning it can be recorded. Psychologists Charles W. Bellavia and Paul A. Toro have shown that these studies diverge widely in their estimates as to the number of homeless, the proportion of the homeless who are mentally ill, and the definition of mental illness. The problem hinges largely on whether or not substance abuse is a form of mental illness or merely creates it. If drug and alcohol abuse are included in the estimate of mentally disordered persons among the homeless, then the proportion rises from about 25 percent to 61 percent of all who are homeless. There are other problems with estimating the number of the mentally ill whether with or without a home. For example, it can be argued that a mentally ill person is only someone who has spent time in a mental hospital or institution for the emotionally disturbed. If that definition is used, then the number declines a great deal. However, the numbers included in any estimate change in conjunction with other indicators of mental illness such as current symptoms of mental illness or a lifetime history of mental illness or incarceration in a mental hospital or substance abuse.[36]

In any case, research reveals that the mentally ill among the homeless suffer the most stigmatization and are the most isolated. Because of the stigma associated with mental illness, the homeless among them have usually alienated their families and have lost touch with them. Instead, the mentally ill homeless, and surely others as well, develop dependence on a small set of formal services and on other homeless people.[37]

Psychiatrists Julie A. Lam and Robert Rosenheck found that Americans of African descent who are homeless have significantly more family members to whom they feel close than is true of other ethnic groups. This may be a reflection of the strong kin networks attributed to inner city blacks and to the fact that blacks are more tolerant of the mentally ill than whites because of their own victimization and the stigma that attaches to being black in American society.[38] Lam and Rosenheck also found that the older homeless persons have significantly fewer relationships with their families of origin. Older homeless people also have less contact with their children than is true of the general population. This finding is by no means surprising since the condition of homelessness would hardly occur among those who have adult children with the resources and the will to keep their parents off the streets.[39]

LABELING THE MENTALLY ILL

The stigma of mental illness is the product of labeling. This means that mental patients and former mental patients suffer social rejection because they have acquired a label that appears to indicate that they are dangerous. In addition to the phrase "mentally ill," which leads to a great deal of social distance, the behavior of mental patients or former mental patients also contributes to the social distance they encounter so often. Former mental patients know this and fear that their erstwhile status may be revealed.

Social distance is best understood by reviewing the following social distance scale first invented by sociologist Emory Bogardus.[40] Such a measure of social distance would include answers to such questions as these: 1. How would you feel about renting a room in your house to a former mental patient? 2. How about on the same job as a former mental patient? 3. How would you feel about having a former mental patient as a neighbor? 4. How about having a former mental patient take care of your children for an hour or two? 5. Would you care if one of your children married a former mental patient? 6. Would you introduce a former mental patient to a single person of the opposite sex? 7. Would you recommend a former mental patient for a job working for one of your friends or relatives?[41] According to psychologists Bruce G. Link, Frances T. Cullen, James Frank, and John F. Wozniak, these questions are answered by most people in a negative fashion. That means that most people want to distance themselves from those labeled mentally ill because most people view the mentally ill as dangerous.

There has been some dispute between observers of former mental patients concerning the effects of labeling. There are those who insist that it is the behavior of the former mental patient and not labeling that leads to social rejection. It is of course true that some people, on learning that someone has been a mental patient, will consider this an invitation to help the former mental patient by giving him or her an "extra break" and thereby help the person live in the community once more. Yet, even a helping attitude concerning the mentally handicapped is frequently the product of stigma as is the case when a blind person is praised for moving about his apartment or when great capacity is attributed to a crippled person. Former mental patients and all who have suffered a handicap resent special attention or exceptional attention because they see such "special kindness" as a definition based on stigma. Those affected by these stigma are of course unable to distinguish between increased kindness based on the stigma of mental illness or on a genuine effort to help reintegrate a former mental patient into the circle of friends and relations. Former mental patients as well as others who have been stigmatized worry over the motives of those showing exceptional interest in them. Is the extra kindness motivated by the religious belief that one must be helpful to those less fortunate? Because of the ambiguity that all stigmatized persons face, there are many who seek to conceal their history by withdrawing from social interaction. This withdrawal is not limited to mental patients but can be seen among the old, among the physically handicapped, and among stigmatized ethnic groups such as the European Jews. The fears of the stigmatized groups are based on reality. Former mental patients know that there is a substantial group of citizens in every community who are afraid to interact with them.

In an interesting study, psychologists Stephanie Cormack and Adrian Furnham found that the same conduct and the same problem was judged more serious by the American public when given a psychiatric label than when not given such a label. For example, a person who was said to be "paranoid" or "schizophrenic" was judged far more dangerous than someone whose behavior was described in the same terms but without any psychiatric terminology.[42] Likewise, Kelly E. Piner and Lynn R. Kahle found that "the label of mental illness is stigmatized even in the absence of bizarre behavior."[43]

Stigma has long-term and pervasive effects. This is mostly seen in depressive symptoms among those who are stigmatized even in the context of effective mental health and substance abuse intervention. Both perceived devaluation and discrimination and real discrimination experiences affect the stigmatized person, and particularly the mentally ill. Stigma, then, has important consequences for the mentally ill even when people improve while participating in a treatment program. In addition there is a good deal of evidence that even when the rejection by others has largely disappeared it is difficult for the stigmatized mental patient and others to shake off the mark and the meaning attached to it.[44]

Mental illness is a social role. The societal reaction to mental illness and its symptoms determines the outcome of the "illness" for the mentally ill person who can seldom escape the stigma attached to his condition and its consequences.

SUMMARY

The mentally ill are the victims of stigmatization because the Western world, since the ancient Greeks, has sought to rest on reason and scientific observation. Since mental illness leads to irrational conduct it is viewed with disdain and with fear, particularly after the release of many mental patients from psychiatric hospitals in the 1970s and 1980s. This does not mean that the mentally ill were always treated in a rational manner. Instead, numerous explanations for mental illness have been in fashion over many years. These include the ancient Greek view that mental illness is bad luck, the view that mental illness and particularly epilepsy is a "sacred" disease, and a variety of religious explanations for mental illness. In the sixteenth and seventeenth centuries ancient Greek and Hebrew fears of demons were revived in Europe and America and led to witch-hunts and the condemnation of numerous mentally ill people on the grounds they were "in league with the devil." After the seventeenth century "moral treatment" consisting of religious exercises and readings were promoted as "cures" for mental illness. This kind of "moral treatment" coincided with the rise of mental hospitals or asylums. After many years of hospitalizing the mentally ill that strategy was abandoned at the end of the 1980s so that families once more became the main support for people suffering from mental illness. The need to take care of mentally ill family members has led to the stigma-tization of entire families.

A good number of the mentally ill are homeless. This is largely due to the closing of so many hospitals for the emotionally ill and mentally disturbed. Consequently, such former mental patients are subject to labeling that designates mental illness as the master status of those afflicted. That the interpretation of deviant behavior is crucial in attaching a stigma to some conduct and not to other types of conduct is best illustrated by viewing the status of homosexuals in America at the end of the twentieth century. That will be the topic of our next chapter.

NOTES

1. Frank Eagleton, *The Columbia Encyclopedia*, 5th ed. (New York: Columbia University Press, 1993).

2. Herbert M. Morais, *Deism in Eighteenth-Century America* (New York: Russell and Russell, 1960), pp. 54–84.

3. Georgia Harkness, *The Modern Rival of the Christian Faith* (New York: Abbington-Cokesbury, 1952).

4. John P. Docherty, *Inpatient Psychiatry in the 1990s* (San Francisco: Jossey-Bass, 1994), pp. 5–6.

5. Stefan Lerner, "On the Words 'Mental Illness,'" *American Journal of Psychiatry* 52, no. 11 (November 1995): 62.

6. Abram Kardiner, *The Individual and His Society: The Psychodynamics of Primitive Social Organization* (New York: Columbia University Press, 1939), p. 287.

7. Bennett Simon, *Mind and Madness in Ancient Greece* (Ithaca, N.Y.: Cornell University Press, 1978).

8. Ibid., p. 222.

9. Stanley W. Jackson, *Melancholia and Depression: From Hippocratic Times to Modern Times* (New Haven and London: Yale University Press, 1986), pp. 29–43.

10. E. R. Dodds, *Pagan and Christian in an Age of Anxiety* (New York: Cambridge University Press, 1990), p. 66.

11. Solomon Grayzel, *A History of the Jews* (Philadelphia: Jewish Publication Society, 1947), p. 514.

12. Gegory Zilboorg, *A History of Medical Psychology* (New York: W. W. Norton & Co., 1941), p. 153.

13. Jerome Kroll, "A Reappraisal of Psychiatry in the Middle Ages," *Archives of General Psychiatry* 29 (1973): 276–83.

14. Jeffrey B. Russell, "Concepts of Witchcraft," in *The Encyclopedia of Religion,* ed. Mircea Eliades (New York: Macmillan Publishing Co., 1989), pp. 417–23.

15. Mary Ann Jimenes, "Madness in Early American History: Insanity in Massachussetts from 1700 to 1830," *Journal of Social History* 20, no. 1 (1986): 25–26.

16. Ibid., pp. 36–37.

17. Tanaquil Taubes, "Healthy Avenues of the Mind: Psychological Theory Building and the Influence of Religion During the Era of Moral Treatment," *American Journal of Psychiatry* 155, no. 8 (1998): 1003–1008.

18. Ibid., p. 1003.

19. D. Hack Tuke, *A Dictionary of Psychological Medicine* (1890; reprint, New York: Arno Press, 1976), pp. 1091–92.

20. Richard von Krafft-Ebing, *Textbook of Insanity* (Philadelphia: F. A. Davis, 1904), pp. 301–302.

21. Howard S. Becker, *The Other Side* (New York: Free Press, 1964), p. 3.

22. Fred E. Markowitz, "The Effects of Stigma on the Psychological Well-Being and Life Satisfaction of Persons with Mental Illness," *Journal of Health and Social Behavior* 39, no. 4 (1998): 335–47.

23. A. Farina and K. Ring, "The Influence of Perceived Mental Illness on Interpersonal Relationships," *Journal of Abnormal and Social Psychology* 70 (1965): 47–51.

24. Raymond M. Weinstein, "Goffman's *Asylums* and the Total Institution Model of Mental Hospitals," *Psychiatry* 57, no. 4 (November 1994): 348–67.

25. Thomas S. Szasz, *The Myth of Mental Illness* (New York: Dell Publishing Co., 1961), p. 306.

26. William Michaux, *The First Year Out* (Baltimore: Johns Hopkins University Press, 1969), pp. 153–60.

27. N. C. Angermeyer, "Normal Deviance—Changing Norms Under Abnormal Circumstances," in P. Pichot et al., *Psychiatry, The State of the Art,* vol. 7. *Epidemiology and Community Psychiatry* (New York: Plenum Press, 1983), pp. 473–79.

28. Harriet P. Lefley, "The Families Response to Mental Illness in a Relative," in *Families of the Mentally Ill: Meeting the Challenges,* ed. A. Hatfield (San Francisco: Jossey-Bass, 1987).

29. Morris J. Goldstein, "Editor's Notes," in *New Developments in Interventions With Families of Schizophrenics,* ed. M. J. Goldstein (San Francisco: Jossey-Bass, 1981), p. 2.

30. Kathleen G. Terkelson, "Schizophrenia and the Family: Adverse Effects of Family Therapy," *Family Process* 22 (1983): 191–200.

31. Sheldon Norton, Albert Wandersman, and C. R. Goldman, "Perceived Costs and Benefits of Membership in a Self-help Group: Comparisons of Members and Non-members of the Alliance for the Mentally Ill," *Community Mental Health Journal* 29, no. 2 (1993): 143–60.

32. David Mechanic, "Establishing Mental Health Priorities," *Milbank Quarterly* 72, no. 3 (1994): 150.

33. Ibid.

34. National Law Center on Homelessness and Poverty, *Out of Sight—Out of Mind? A Report on Anti-Homeless Laws, Litigation and Alternatives in Fifty United States Cities, 1999* (Washington, D.C.: National Law Center on Homelessness and Poverty, 1999).

35. "NCH Fact Sheet #5" National Coalition for the Homeless (Washington, D.C.: National Center on Homelessness and Poverty, April 1999).

36. Charles W. Bellavia and Paul A. Toro, "Mental Disorder Among Homeless and Poor People: A Comparison of Assessment Methods," *Community Mental Health Journal* 35, no. 1 (February 1999): 57–67.

37. Julie A. Lam and Robert Rosenheck, "Social Support and Service Use Among Homeless Persons with Serious Mental Illness," *International Journal of Social Psychiatry* 45, no. 1 (1999): 13–28.

38. Clifford M. B. Galanis and Edward E. Jones, "When Stigma Confront Stigma: Some Conditions Enhancing a Victim's Tolerance of Other Victims," *Personality and Social Psychology Bulletin* 12, no. 2 (June 1986): 169.

39. Ibid., p. 22.

40. Emory S. Bogardus, "Measuring Social Distance," *Journal of Applied Sociology* 9 (1925): 299–308.

41. Bruce G. Link et al., "The Social Rejection of Former Mental Patients: Understanding Why Labels Matter," *American Journal of Sociology* 92, no. 6 (May 1987): 1461–1500.

42. Stephanie Cormack and Adrian Furnham, "Psychiatric Labelling, Sex Role Stereotypes and Beliefs About the Mentally Ill," *International Journal of Social Psychiatry* 44, no. 4 (1998): 235–47.

43. Kelly E. Piner and Lynn R. Kahle, "Adapting to the Stigmatizing Label of Mental Illness: Foregone But Not Forgotten," *Journal of Personality and Social Psychology* 47, no. 4 (October 1984): 811.

44. Bruce G. Link et al., "On Stigma and Its Consequences," *Journal of Health and Social Behavior* 38, no. 2 (June 1997): 77–190.

SEXUAL IDENTITY AS STIGMA | 3

HOMOSEXUALS AS

"DEVIANTS"

On October 7, 1998, Russell Henderson and Aaron McKinney attacked Matthew Shepard. Matthew Shepard was a twenty-one-year-old student at the University of Wyoming. He was known to be gay and was lured from a bar by Henderson and McKinney who told him they were also gay. He was tied to a split-rail fence, tortured, beaten, and pistol-whipped by Henderson and McKinney. He was then left for dead in the freezing temperature. Eighteen hours later he was found by a cyclist who called for help. Shepard was still alive at that time but died on October 12, 1998, at Poudre Valley Hospital in Fort Collins, Colorado. This crime was labeled a "vile and senseless crime" by District Court Judge Jeffrey Donnell when he sentenced Henderson to two consecutive life terms in April of 1999.

While the gross cruelty of Henderson and McKinney may have seemed "senseless" to the judge, sociological analysis explains such conduct on several levels. First, the brutality of the actions taken by Henderson and McKinney are such that both killers evidently believed that their actions were legitimate. It is not certain that it was their intention to murder their victim. There can be no doubt, however, that it was their intent to injure and utterly degrade Shepard solely because he was a homosexual.[1]

Another seemingly "senseless" murder involving a homosexual victim occurred in March of 1999 when Charles Butler Jr. and Steven Eric Mullins killed Billy Jack Gaither in Alabama. Earlier, Butler and Mullins had abducted Gaither from the textile mill in which he was working, beat him to death with an ax handle, and stuffed his body into a car trunk. Both killers plead guilty in the hope of avoiding the death penalty. The pleas were accepted as Alabama is hostile to gay issues; it is one of nineteen states in which hate crime laws do not cover discrimination based on sexual orientation.[2]

A third example of such a hate-driven murder was the killing of Pvt. Barry Winchell by Pvt. Calvin Glover on the Fort Campbell, Kentucky, army base in July of 1999. Winchell, a homosexual, had bested Glover in a fight two days before the killing. Glover felt that losing a fight to a homosexual was particularly humiliating because he held the common prejudice that homosexuals are "sissies" and can't fight. To avenge his loss he killed Winchell while his victim was asleep.[3] Glover was convicted and sentenced to life in prison.

Behavior which may seem utterly senseless to some will appear legitimate to those who believe that they have the support of a significant reference group in committing almost any crime against a perceived "out-group." This was certainly the case in the murder of Shepard, which was weakly condemned even by Christian conservatives who nevertheless oppose all hate-crime laws designed to protect homosexuals. According to the opponents of such "hate-crime" laws, these laws are designed to "silence political opposition." There are also groups who believe that murder (and other unlawful acts) should not be viewed as a hate crime. It should just be murder.

Steven A. Schwalm, representing the Family Research Council which claims to defend "faith, family, and freedom," argues that hate-crime laws are politically inspired and seek to prevent disagreement with the homosexual community. Likewise, a Christian group located in Colorado Springs argues that "because we are standing up and opposing the homosexual agenda, we are being looked upon as advocating violence against homosexuals, when we categorically reject violence against homosexuals."[4]

Despite these protestations, it appears to many American men that their masculinity is reaffirmed by using violence against "outsiders." It is therefore not surprising that Henderson and McKinney "picked a street fight with two Hispanic men" on a street corner in Laramie, Wyoming, shortly after they killed Shepard. The principle of legitimacy operates here again, as Hispanics are also "outsiders," as are a host of others in American culture.[5]

HOMOSEXUAL MARRIAGE

Because legitimacy is so important in creating a climate of acceptance for those who, for any reason, are "different," homosexual Americans have tried for some years to gain legal equality with heterosexuals with particular reference to the right to marry someone of the same sex. Same-sex marriages are not a new arrangement in human history. John Boswell, the best-known historian of homosexuality and author of a large number of articles and books on that subject, has shown that the history of marriage includes same-sex couples, almost all male, so that ceremonies and liturgy for same-sex marriages existed in Europe throughout the medieval period.[6] In this country and elsewhere some folks hid their true sex in order to marry someone of the same sex. The prominent New York politician Mary Anderson, who called herself Murray Hall, "masqueraded as a man over twenty-five years and married women twice."[7]

More recently, various religious groups have endorsed same-sex marriages. Among these have been some Buddhists; some Christian denominations including Episcopalians, Presbyterians, Quakers, and Unitarians; and some Jewish groups including Reform and Reconstructionists. Despite these efforts on the part of some religious groups to legitimize such marriages, no American state has to date accepted such unions as legitimate marriages. Therefore, a nearly thirty-year struggle has been undertaken by homosexual groups and their defenders to attain legally recognized same-sex marriages in the United States and elsewhere.

The first legal challenge to the refusal of states to recognize same-sex marriage came in 1971 when Richard J. Baker and James McConnell were turned down by the Minnesota State Supreme Court in their effort to have their same-sex marriage legally recognized. In that decision the court relied on Genesis and "fundamental differences in sex" to reach its verdict. Similarly, John Singer and Paul Barwick lost in their effort to marry in Washington State because of "the nature of the marriage itself" and because "two males cannot produce children." Likewise, two female partners, Donna Berkett and Manonia Evans, were refused a marriage license in Milwaukee in 1971.

Not discouraged by these rebuffs, a female couple argued before the U.S. Supreme Court in *Jones* v. *Hallahan* in 1973 that Kentucky's refusal to issue them a marriage license constituted violation of the First and Eighth Amendments. The Court rejected this argument on the grounds that marriage exists between two persons of opposite sexes and that therefore a marriage license was refused on the grounds of "their own incapability of entering into a marriage as that term is defined." Additional suits by two lesbian mothers in 1974 met the same fate.

Then, in 1975 two men from Phoenix, Arizona, were granted a legal marriage license by a county clerk only to have the license voided by the Arizona Supreme Court which cited the Bible as grounds for that decision. In addition, the Arizona legislature passed a bill that year banning same-sex marriage. Also in 1975 a county clerk in Boulder, Colorado, issued marriage licenses to five same-sex couples only to find that the state attorney general revoked all same-sex marriage licenses. The attorney general of Maryland supported the Montgomery County clerk that year in issuing a marriage license to two women. However, this license was revoked by the courts later that year. In 1976 two Chicago lesbians were arrested for the fourth time after a five-hour sit-in at the county's marriage license bureau. They insisted on receiving a marriage license even though they had spent a year in prison for an earlier offense of the same nature.

Such legal efforts were continued in the 1980s, including 1987 when a mass ceremony and demonstration was held in front of the Internal Revenue Building as part of the March on Washington on October 10 of that year. There, about two thousand couples participated in a "recommitment" ceremony which had no legal impact. In 1989 the San Francisco Bar Association issued a statement in support of same-sex marriage and the District of Columbia Human Rights Commission testified on behalf of Craig Dean and Patrick Gill that failure of the district to grant these men a marriage license constituted violation of the district's human rights laws. Nevertheless, the courts ruled against these partners in 1995.

In 1990 a New York man sued under that state's inheritance law as "surviving spouse" of a partner who had died. However, the court ruled *In the Matter of Estate of Cooper* that "persons of the same sex have *no* constitutional rights to enter into a marriage with each other."[8] Numerous other efforts to legalize same-sex marriages were attempted during the 1990s, only to fail in the courts. However, in Hawaii, Judge Kevin S. C. Chang ruled on December 3, 1996, that three same-sex couples could legally marry. Their case, known to lawyers as *Baehr* v. *Lewin*, challenged the right of Hawaii to reject their applications for marriage licenses on constitutional grounds. After the state refused to issue such licenses, Judge Chang rejected the state's argument that it was in the best interest of children to bar same-sex marriages. This ruling in turn led to a near-panic reaction by opponents of same-sex marriages, particularly because the Hawaii Supreme Court had ruled in 1993 that it is unconstitutional to deny marriage licenses to same-sex couples.[9]

Because a similar effort to permit same-sex marriages seemed to succeed in Alaska as well, the U.S. Congress passed the Defense of Marriage Act on September 10, 1996. This was followed by the inclusion on the ballots of Alaska and Hawaii on November 4, 1998, of provisions for same-sex marriages in both states. In Alaska 68 percent of voters rejected same-sex marriages and in Hawaii 69 percent rejected a similar provision.[10]

Finally, on April 25, 2000, Vermont became the first and only state in the Union to approve legal benefits and protection to homosexual couples. The law, as passed by the Vermont legislature, creates civil unions of homosexuals who can now get a civil union license from a town clerk and then have their union certified by a judge or a member of the clergy. Dissolutions of such union will be handled by a family court in a manner similar to a divorce on the part of heterosexual married couples. It should be noted that these unions are not called marriages.[11]

THE CIVIL RIGHTS OF HOMOSEXUALS

The Defense of Marriage Act of 1996 was promptly signed by President Clinton after it passed both houses of Congress. This act had two purposes. First, "to defend the institution of traditional heterosexual marriage" and second, "to protect the right of the States to formulate their own public policy regarding the legal recognition of same-sex unions. . . ."[12]

The first of these purposes seems spurious since the effort of same-sex couples to gain the right to marry cannot in any fashion threaten the institution of heterosexual marriage.

Despite the announced purpose to defend the institution of heterosexual marriage, the legislative history associated with this law goes directly to the "particular development in the State of Hawaii." The "particular development" cited refers to the possibility that Hawaii would indeed allow same-sex marriages and that therefore all states in the Union would be obliged to recognize such "marriages" under the "Full Faith and Credit Clause" of the U.S. Constitution (Article IV, Section 1):

> Full Faith and Credit shall be given in each State to the public Act, Records, and judicial Proceedings of every other State. And the Congress may by General Laws prescribe the Manner in which such Acts, Records and Proceedings shall be proved, and the Effect thereof.[13]

This could be interpreted to mean that all states must allow the same-sex marriages of any state to be valid. In fact, the Lambda Legal Defense Fund, which supports homosexual activities around the country, announced that it would support every effort to bring the announced universal recognition of homosexual unions to a successful conclusion.

Furthermore, it seemed to the majority of House members that federal benefits that depend on marital status would become available to same-sex couples married in Hawaii and that therefore large numbers of same-sex couples would go to Hawaii to marry and gain these benefits. Hence, the Defense of Marriage Act is not only an effort to express hostility to same-sex marriage but also an effort to save a great deal of the taxpayers' money which marriage benefits imply.[14]

Another interest of government in heterosexual marriage is the interest of the state in child rearing and in children generally. The argument set forth by opponents of same-sex marriage is that a long-term relationship between heterosexual partners is not only a private affair but also a public concern.

Proponents of same-sex marriage therefore point out that heterosexual marriage is indeed embattled since one-half of all who use their marriage license get divorced within one decade of their marriage and that about a third of all American children are born to unwed mothers. They therefore hold that same-sex marriages in which children are secure are better for children than heterosexual marriages in which couples fight, divorce, or have illegitimate children. Despite the rather ubiquitous homophobia prevalent in this country, there are some gay and lesbian couples who have succeeded in adopting children or who have natural-born children whom they are raising in their own homes. While such families have not been adequately assessed there is not now any evidence that children raised by gay or lesbian couples are damaged in any fashion by having such a family.[15]

Congress, in passing the Defense of Marriage Act, also argued that the voters in every state have turned down every effort to permit same-sex marriages and therefore the Congress could do no less.[16] In a vehement defense of same-sex marriages, the American Psychological Association (APA) made several arguments that group claims are not motivated by political considerations but only by scientific findings. Such an argument is of course hardly supportable, as Immanuel Kant has shown sufficiently and the APA has yet to learn.

Nevertheless, the position of the American Psychological Association is important because it summarizes most arguments in favor of same-sex marriage and also bolsters the rights of gays and lesbians to lead a normal life. The APA first demonstrates that homosexuality is surely not a mental illness as some homophobics would like to believe. Instead, the APA defines homosexuality by listing four characteristics which meet the APA's definition of homosexuality. These are: (1) that there is an ongoing attraction to persons of the same gender, (2) that there is a private personal identity or self-concept as homosexual, (3) that there is a public identity based on sexual orientation, and (4) that there is identification with a "community" which shares the same sexual orientation.[17] It is further the contention of the American Psychological Association that homosexuality is not a matter of choice. That is undoubtedly true, just as it is true that all of us are constrained by biology and inheritance to live within the limits of our body and our abilities. Therefore it is reasonable to support same-sex marriage for those who cannot be heterosexual. However, in connection with the Civil Rights Act of 1964 the defense of homosexual rights is contentious.

The reason for this is that the Civil Rights Act deals with groups which have distinguishing characteristics making them easy targets for discrimination. Examples are women, blacks, Native Americans, or Hispanics. Homosexuals, of course, have no such distinguishing physical characteristics. Homosexuals suffer discrimination and rejection because of something they do. It is only in their performance that their stigma becomes an issue. Therefore, some would argue that the Civil Rights Act does not apply to homosexuals. Yet, the Civil Rights Act does protect religious and ethnic groups who exhibit no visible stigma. An excellent example are Jews. Despite the oft-repeated canard that all Jews have large noses, the fact is that it is not possible to distinguish Jews from other Americans except by such behavior as attending Jewish worship, eating or failing to eat certain foods, or using Jewish phrases in their speech. Therefore, like homosexuals, behavior, not an essential condition or characteristic, determines the minority status of some ethnic and religious groups. In defining homosexuality, therefore, we are once more faced with the issue of *essentialism* versus *constructionism*. If, as the APA contends, homosexuality is *essential*, then this places homosexuals in a category to be defended by the Civil Rights Act. If, however, homosexuality is a matter of choice as constructionists would have it, then neither same-sex marriage nor civil rights protection would apply to them.[18]

It is in part the belief that homosexuality is a matter of choice that has led to such a long history of persecution for those who are homosexually inclined. No better example of such persecution can be found than the atrocities committed against the famous British poet Oscar Wilde (1854–1900), who was publicly humiliated and then imprisoned for the "crime" of homosexuality. In fact, Wilde was "chained and forced to stand for half an hour on the center platform at Clapham Junction from 2 P.M. to 2:30 P.M. on the rainy afternoon of November 20, 1895." It is therefore gratifying that one hundred years after his death the British finally erected a statue to one of their most excellent poets, who was in fact an Irishman, as were so many of England's best.[19]

Oscar Wilde's fate is of course well known particularly because he wrote *The Ballad of Reading Gaol,* while spending two years in prison. There is little doubt that his early death at the age of forty-six was hastened by that terrible experience.[20] Oscar Wilde was of course not the only one so abused because of his sexual inclination. In fact, thousands of others were equally mistreated by those who cannot accept differences based on choice or essence. However, those who seek to push homosexuals clearly into an out-group prefer to label homosexual conduct voluntary. This permits the Family Research Council, for example, to advertise on television that religious conversion will "heal" homosexuality.[21] The Family Research Council is a Washington, D.C., nonprofit organization which "promotes the traditional family unit and the Judeo-Christian value system."

THE FEAR OF AIDS

In view of the foregoing we need now to review whether or not, at the beginning of the twenty-first century, stigmatization of homosexuals has significantly decreased as compared to the middle of the century. We have already seen that the 1950s experienced a resurgence of Victorian attitudes concerning the relationship between the sexes. At the end of the century, however, the status of homosexuals in America was greatly complicated by the AIDS crisis, which affected health-related workers a good deal more than the general population, although the fear of that disease became widespread among all Americans beginning about 1980.

No doubt, the fear of AIDS was linked to homosexuality almost as soon as the disease was given widespread publicity in the mid-1980s. This became visible when the *New York Times* published the result of a poll which found that as a result of AIDS 37 percent of adults were less favorably disposed toward homosexuals than before they heard of that disease. Nevertheless, 59 percent of those polled said then that the AIDS epidemic made no difference in the way they felt about homosexuals, 2 percent said they were more sympathetic, and 2 percent were undecided. The Gallup poll, which had made that survey, reported that those whose attitudes had worsened because of AIDS were most likely to be over sixty-five years of age, non-high-school graduates, and those with lower incomes.[22] Another survey taken in 1985 by the National Opinion Research Center also showed that by the mid-1980s the number of respondents who thought that homosexual relations between two adults is always wrong was on the increase—from 67 percent in 1974 to 73 percent in 1985. In addition, attacks on homosexuals seemed to be increasing as a result of the AIDS epidemic.[23] Yet, a study conducted in 1991 revealed a decrease in negative attitudes toward homosexuals in the five-year time span between 1986 and 1991. Again, males who lived in rural areas had a greater antihomosexual attitude than others. It is significant, however, that the forty-and-over age group, as well as college students, expressed a significant decrease in antihomosexuality during that five-year time span.

Because social workers, psychologists, physicians, and nurses are specifically trained to deal with illness and its consequences, it is worthwhile to review how those associated with these professions react toward homosexuals in general. A review of the healthcare literature for the years 1983 to 1987 may be divided into literature that revealed a positive

attitude, literature that revealed a negative attitude, and neutral literature. Evidently, positive literature is very limited so that only a few positive articles were discovered in nursing journals, general medicine journals, and psychiatric journals. Negative images of homosexuality were
far more common than positive images in the healthcare literature.
Three themes emerge from a review of the literature that tends to support a negative view of homosexuals. The first is the frequent reference
to AIDS patients as a "stigmatized" group. Of course, all homosexuals are
by no means AIDS patients, and not all AIDS patients are homosexuals.
However, the literature tends to ignore nonhomosexual AIDS sufferers.
A second theme that emerged from the negative literature concerning
homosexuals again linked AIDS to homosexuality, with the outcome that
physicians and medical students both tended to hold AIDS patients more
responsible for their illness than leukemia patients, more deserving to
die, to lose jobs, and to be isolated. A third negative theme deals with the
psychological needs of AIDS patients and the healthcare staff. The principal concern here is the need to deal with an unsympathetic public who
frequently voice the opinion that AIDS is a "punishment from God." A
good number of writers in psychiatric journals address homosexuals as
"borderline psychotics," and homosexuality as an "illness."[24]

A truly neutral effort to deal with homosexuality is found in the
work of historian Vern L. Bullough and nurse Bonnie Bullough. Their
study is significant because it is statistically sound, examines three
sexual minorities, and concludes that homosexuals "as a group distinguish themselves from the others not by feminine characteristics but by
fewer traditional masculine characteristics."[25]

Social workers are now the most frequently employed psychotherapists. Trained to put aside biases and to respect cultural diversity and to
resist popular bigotry, it is to be expected that social workers would
exhibit far less hostility toward homosexuals than is common among the
American population as a whole. Social workers Cathy S. Berkman and
Gail Zinberg investigated homophobia among social workers in a cohort
of 187 social workers. That study concluded that the overwhelming
number of social workers were not homophobic. Compared with the
general adult population of the United States, social workers were significantly less homophobic than a national sample studied in 1993. It is
of interest in this connection that men were more homophobic than
women in every study.[26]

In 1996, social workers Thomas O'Hare, Cynthia L. Williams, and
Alan Ezoviski surveyed 175 students at a Rhode Island liberal arts college with a population of approximately 9,700 using the Index of Attitudes toward Homosexuality Scale and the Fear of AIDS Scale. (These
scales were invented by psychologists Marc Pratarelli and Jennifer Don-

aldson to test attitudes toward homosexuality.) This study dealt with students' general attitude toward homosexuality with these conclusions:

1. Over two-thirds of the respondents indicated that they knew a gay or lesbian;
2. Only about one-fifth said they knew someone infected with HIV;
3. About one-half considered same-sex couples a family;
4. More than 67 percent endorsed the right of same-sex couples to marry;
5. More than 48 percent endorsed the right of same-sex couples to adopt children;
6. Seventy-six percent believed that same-sex couples should share life insurance benefits; and
7. Eighty-four percent endorsed equal rights for gays and lesbians.[27]

Whatever one may think of the level of homophobia still present in the United States today, it is nevertheless encouraging that a representative sample of New England college students is generally favorably disposed toward homosexuals and homosexual issues. It is also important to recognize that attitudes toward homosexuals are greatly determined by the beliefs any population may have concerning the cause of homosexuality. This means that those who believe that there is a biological basis for homosexual conduct are far more likely to hold positive views concerning homosexual conduct and homosexual rights than those who believe homosexuality is a matter of choice.[28]

A study by physicians Brian McGrory, David McDowell, and Phillip Muskin of medical students' attitudes toward homosexuals was conducted at the College of Physicians and Surgeons of Columbia University and at the University of Mississippi Medical School in 1988. This revealed that markedly negative and prejudiced attitudes toward homosexuals and AIDS patients existed in Mississippi at that time. Mississippi medical students stated that they would not be willing to befriend persons with AIDS, found them deserving of death, less deserving of compassion than patients with other diseases, and less "likeable." Mississippi medical students had a negative view of all homosexuals at the time of the study.

At the same time, medical students at Columbia University in New York City believed that a patient with AIDS was more responsible for his disease than patients with other diseases. Nevertheless, New York City students did not believe that AIDS patients should lose their jobs, objected to discrimination against AIDS patients and homosexuals, and generally had a far more sympathetic view of homosexuals than Mississippi students. The more positive attitude of New York City medical students toward homosexuals than Mississippi medical students lies in part in the fact that some of the medical teachers at Columbia University were and are homosexuals and that students came in contact with homosexuals during their schooling. This was true of students who had come to New York from all parts of the country.

It is noteworthy that the attitudes of professors toward homosexuality play a considerable role here in shaping the bias that future doctors will carry with them throughout their careers. Therefore it is safe to conclude that New York City medical students at Columbia University experienced a less prejudiced environment than was true in Mississippi and were therefore more willing and able to resist the bigotry of the general population concerning homosexuality.[29]

A study published in 1999 shows that approximately one-fourth of medical students at "a large Midwestern university" believed homosexuality to be immoral and dangerous. Nine percent even held that homosexuality is a mental disorder. The vast majority of those questioned had different views. They thought that homosexuals should have equal opportunity in employment, that they should be allowed to work with children, and that they themselves felt comfortable working alongside homosexuals and had no inclination to avoid them.[30]

Medical study resulting in the M.D. degree is normally followed by a period of a postdoctoral practicum called residency. Since upward of 20 percent of practicing physicians, residents, and medical students have expressed an unwillingness to treat AIDS patients, we have here an attitude directly contrary to the Hippocratic Oath, which demands that physicians treat all patients regardless of self-interest and/or personal risk.

According to health science researchers Michael Yedidia, Carolyn Berry, and Judith Barr, there is a significant impact of socialization during residency on physicians' attitudes toward patients with AIDS as well as toward homosexuals. This means that training and education do have an impact on changes in physicians' willingness to treat AIDS and in mediating the negative effects of homophobia. Such training needs to center on medical ethics, which require that "all medical decisions and actions should be guided by the intention to do good and no harm." That is of course the core of the Hippocratic Oath.[31]

As the AIDS crisis continued into the 1990s, homosexuals became more willing to demand the right to live their lives without fear of harassment and in accord with the basic principles of American justice. The landmark event that forced the criminal justice system to recognize these rights and which led to the developing concept of a "lesbian/gay pride" attitude was the so-called Stonewall Rebellion of 1969. That rebellion refers to the three-day violent protest against the routine rousting of homosexuals at the Stonewall Inn on Christopher Street in New York City. Shouting "gay power," the crowd demonstrated that unwarranted arrests of homosexuals would no longer be tolerated. Consequently, marches were held in New York and Los Angeles annually to celebrate that milestone in the history of American freedom.[32]

On June 28, 1994, tens of thousands of homosexuals or "gay" people came to New York to celebrate the twenty-fifth anniversary of the "Stonewall Riots." Carrying a mile-long rainbow flag, the international symbol of the "gay" civil rights movement, 100,000 people marched on the United Nations that day demanding that the Universal Declaration of Human Rights be extended to male and female homosexuals.[33]

Some studies concerning public opinion toward homosexuals in 1985, 1987, and 1994 show a gradual liberalization of public attitudes. Professor of political science Richard Seltzer shows that in 1987 there was a somewhat less irrational attitude as compared to 1985. This is evident from a study showing that by 1987 fewer respondents wanted to support repressive measures against homosexuals than was true in 1985. In sum, those who disliked homosexuals were willing to have homosexuals repressed in both years.[34]

A study of public opinion published by political scientist Alan Yang in 1997 indicates that 70 percent of those polled persisted for nearly two decades, from 1973 to 1991, in the view that sexual relations between two adults of the same sex is wrong. After 1991, however, there was a clear drop in the number willing to call such conduct "always wrong." In fact, in 1994 there was a 20 percent drop in disapproval despite the persistent belief that homosexual conduct is "immoral." In that same year the public was evenly divided over whether "homosexual relations between consenting adults" should be legal. Furthermore, a majority of the public believed that homosexuals faced a great deal of discrimination. Consistent with that finding is the decline of those feeling "very unsympathetic" to the homosexual community, which was 46 percent in 1983 but only 30 percent in 1994. Similarly, there was a rise in the number willing to permit homosexuals to be teachers, although that liberalization did not extend to the clergy. The most dramatic rise in acceptance of the homosexual community came about in the area of civil rights. More than 80 percent of those polled said in 1994 that they thought gays and lesbians should have the same protection against discrimination in jobs and housing accorded to everyone else. In the 1970s only a slim majority believed this.[35]

HOMOPHOBIA AND ITS CONSEQUENCES

In an interesting study published in 1998, Paul Cameron and Kirk Cameron of the Colorado Family Research Institute found that about 40 percent of child molestation stories in the nation's newspapers involved homosexuals. In a companion study of *Newsweek* magazine the Camerons found that 60 percent of stories about child molestation involved homosexuals. This raises the important question as to whether or not the common belief that homosexuals are more likely to molest children than heterosexuals is valid. If we are to take the word "valid" literally and apply its Latin origin, *valere,* meaning "strong," then we must conclude that the evidence concerning the charge that homosexuals are disproportionately involved in child molestation is not only not strong, but very weak.

The reasons for this weakness are not hard to find. First, and foremost, it is well known and evident that newspapers print only stories that attract readers by their sensational aspects and that fit into the preconceived notions of the readers. Because homosexuals are already socially stigmatized by the belief that they must be child abusers, stories involving homosexuals and child abuse are given wide circulation by the media. Stories concerning child abuse by heterosexuals are not that interesting unless they concern such media icons as Susan Smith of South Carolina who killed her two young sons in 1994, or the so-called David Koresh (of Branch Davidian notoriety).

A favorite target of media accusations of child abuse are child-care workers and teachers. Innumerable accusations have proved false but are particularly instituted against homosexual suspects. As we have already seen in the McMartin Preschool case, there are numerous accusations concerning child abuse that are attributed to homosexuals even when the abuse never occurred and when the "abuser" is not a homosexual.[36]

It is noteworthy that the American Psychological Association and the American Psychiatric Association together with the National Association of Social Workers submitted an *amicus* brief to the U.S. Supreme Court in 1995 in which they asserted that, although "gay men have been stigmatized with the allegation that they are disproportionately responsible for child sexual abuse, *there is no evidence of any positive correlation between homosexual orientation and child molestation*"[37] (italics added).

Lesbian mothers are also frequent targets of stigma associated with the belief that their children must inevitably be stigmatized, too. This belief is used by many judges to refuse lesbian mothers the right to raise children. Yet, a study by psychologists Beverly King and Kathryn Black has shown that the assumption that children of lesbian mothers will be stigmatized is unrealistic. King and Black found that the stigmatization of children of lesbian mothers is less than stigma associated with being lesbians. Moreover, between 80 and 100 percent of college students who participated in the King/Black study were willing to be acquaintances, friends, or best friends with children of lesbian mothers. In addition, it was found that persons who believed that homosexuality is caused by environmental factors were less willing to deal with lesbian mothers than those who believed this to be an inherited "disease."[38]

Among those ready to believe in any accusation against homosexuals are those Americans who follow biblical teachings without question. For example, Gen. 9:22 has been interpreted by some as an allusion to homosexual conduct by Ham, the son of Noah. In Gen. 19:1–11 we read the story of Lot, a resident of Sodom, whose house was surrounded by men seeking to "know" his male guests leading to their instant blindness, if we are to believe that biblical account. Although there is no explicit mention of homosexuality in Genesis, Lev. 18:22 commands that "Thou shalt not lie with mankind, as with womankind: it is abomination." Lev. 20:13 also makes "no bones" about the aversion of biblical teaching to homosexuality and adds the punishment of death to its injunction. "And if a man lie with mankind," we are told, "as with womankind, both of them have committed abomination: they shall surely be put to death: and ye shall slay the beast." Additional negative comments concerning homosexuality may be found in Rom. 1:18–32.[39]

This and other phrases concerning the "abomination" of homosexuality have surely contributed immensely to homophobia in Western culture for centuries. Now, Jews and Christians have used these biblical passages as "evidence" that homosexuals, lesbians included, could not properly live within their religious communities. There is considerable evidence that gay male Christians are denied full acceptance by the Christian community. There can be little doubt that "most Christians consider being gay and Christian incompatible owing to the perceived straightforward prohibition against it in the Bible."[40]

Therefore, some Christians encounter extreme guilt when they first discover their sexual orientation. This in turn leads those who feel such guilt and shame to experience great anxiety about the possible exposure of their sexuality. This leads to a great deal of alienation and low self-esteem. There are also homosexual Christians who attempt to change from their homosexuality to heterosexuality. Living Water and Exodus International are two groups of former homosexuals who are committed to the view that homosexual conduct is religiously unacceptable. Both groups promote abstinence or a heterosexual marriage.[41] In addition, a number of conservative Christian groups, fearing the influence of what they see as a "powerful homosexual lobby," have decided to convert homosexuals to heterosexuals by prayer and the help of "ex-gay" Christian ministers. To achieve this aim, Janet L. Folger, the national director of the Center for Reclaiming America, raised a considerable amount of money for the purpose of advertising in leading newspapers with combined circulation reaching into the millions. These advertisements called on Christians to renounce homosexuality and feature people who are former homosexuals or lesbians. The assumption here is that homosexuality is not immutable or genetically based and that fundamentalist Christians can "save" the sinners.[42]

In an effort to help the victims of homophobia, the state of Colorado legislature proposed to pass an "Ethnic Harassment" bill in 1991. This bill added "sexual orientation" to the list of protected statuses. A group of Christian fundamentalists protested this bill at a judicial committee hearing and also organized an effort to prevent the inclusion of sexual orientation as a protected status under the Colorado statute. The Christian group was greatly helped in its effort when it won the endorsements of former senator Bill Armstrong and Bill McCartney, the "legendary" University of Colorado football coach who founded the Christian men's movement called "Promise Keepers" and who called homosexuality "an abomination." Nevertheless, Amendment 2 won in Colorado by 53.4 percent.[43]

Some organizations devoted to the conversion of homosexuals go further than advertising in newspapers or pressuring legislatures. There are homosexuals who accuse the Family Research Council, a Christian fundamentalist group, of "gay bashing" by publishing the names of homosexuals on their Internet site with the implication that something needs to be done about gays. According to a homosexual couple who adopted an HIV-positive crack baby, the language used on the Internet is threatening and an invitation to violence.[44]

The vast majority of homosexual Christians do not of course accept the view that they are sinners, nor do they believe they can be "converted" to a different, heterosexual, lifestyle. Therefore, feeling rejected by Christian churches, many homosexuals engage in a strategy of "counterrejection." This "counterrejection" is the consequence of attitudes expressed by Christian churches toward the homosexual community. Some churchers have shown more leniency in that respect in recent years. Thus, the Church of England and its American counterpart, the Episcopal Church, published *Issues in Human Sexuality* in 1991. Authored by the House of Bishops, this document asks Christians to respect the choice of lesbians and homosexuals who have decided to remain in a relationship including genital sexual activity. This recommendation was made only in favor of the laity and was not to apply to clergy, thereby complicating the situation for those who are priests in the Anglican-Episcopal tradition.[45]

The Roman Catholic Church issued its first official document concerning homosexuality in 1975. That year the church published a *Declaration on Certain Questions Concerning Sexual Ethics* in which homosexuality was briefly mentioned. In 1986, however, the church published its *Letter on the Pastoral Care of Homosexual Persons* leading to considerable controversy because the document labeled homosexual inclination an "objective disorder" indicating personal pathology and thus the theoretical possibility of being "cured." Genital acts by homosexuals are called "intrinsically disordered" in that "letter" because they contradict biblical teaching and are incapable of producing new life. These statements led to a great deal of anger and indignation among homosexual Catholics and a climate of stigmatization, alienation, and marginalization of gay Christians.[46]

Jewish views concerning homosexuality are also rooted in the Bible with particular reference to the several prohibitions of homosexual conduct already cited. The Hebrew Torah consists of twenty-four books including the Five Books of Moses. Christians have divided these books into thirty-nine books. These books constitute the basis of Judaism. Included in the Torah concept are also the other books, particularly the Talmud, which was codified in about 200 C.E. This huge compilation of oral law consists mainly of rabbinical commentary on the Torah and includes legends, stories, and proverbs all designed to teach religious principles. Therefore, current Jewish views concerning homosexuality are based largely on talmudic interpretations as understood by present-day American rabbis who also consult such major Jewish scholars as Joseph Caro, Maimonides, Akiba Ben Joseph, and Hillel.*

Accordingly, the Rabbinical Assembly of the United Synagogue of Conservative Judaism adopted a resolution concerning homosexuality in May 1992. That resolution sought to make "gays and lesbians welcome in synagogues" and recommended several means of achieving that stance in American synagogues. The resolution of that assembly also holds that homosexuality is involuntary and that therefore, "homosexuality should no longer be considered an abomination." Nevertheless, the Rabbinical Assembly did not condone or condemn homosexual activity.[47]

Orthodox, or Torah True Judaism, holds that "Jewish values do not change from generation to generation since they are divinely established and human nature remains the same." Therefore, the Orthodox hold that homosexual activity is an abomination and deserving of death as clearly enunciated in Leviticus. Nevertheless, Orthodox Judaism seeks to distinguish the sin from the sinner and views the sinners as part of the Jewish community. It is even conceded that should homosexuality be proven to be involuntary then homosexuals would not be morally responsible for homosexual acts. However, according to Jewish orthodoxy homosexuality has not been proven to be involuntary at this time so that homosexuals cannot now be excused for their "sins."[48]

---

*Among these authorities are Yehezkel Kaufman, Moshe Greenberg, Hayim Donin, Louis Jacobs, Jacob Neusner, and others, all of whom contributed to the *Jewish Encyclopedia of Moral and Ethical Issues.*

CHANGING ATTITUDES TOWARD HOMOSEXUALITY

One of the major issues in the lives of gay and lesbian people is the problem of dealing with the hostility this lifestyle arouses in so many Americans. Among those who often express anger, disappointment, and hostility to the "coming out" of homosexuals are parents and other relatives whom we may collectively call "significant others." That term was coined by the social-psychologist George Herbert Mead and is defined as "those persons whose care, affection, and approval are especially desired—and who are most important in the development of the self." Evidently, parents, siblings, and other relatives and close friends are "significant others."[49]

It is therefore a task of considerable magnitude for a dyad of gays or lesbians to maintain their relationship in the face of the hostility so many experience from those who mean the most to them. A number of studies are available concerning the interaction between coupled gay men and their parents and in-laws. All of these studies conclude that gay men are almost certain to face parental and in-law antipathy regarding their homosexuality and their relationships with their partners. A study by Michael La Scala, professor of social work at the State University of New Jersey, made at the end of 1998 is quite representative of all the studies made in this connection. La Scala interviewed numerous homosexual men and found that all agree on the importance of maintaining a sense of independence, which La Scala calls "a thick skin," as a means of protection from parental hostility. Some "gay" men are evidently strengthened against parental hostility by their relationship to other "gays." Others crumble. In fact, a sense of independence and emotional self-protection is necessary for all gays and lesbians in our homophobic society.[50]

Homophobia is not only visible in the American family; it is also entrenched in government, industry, education, and the military. In fact, gays and lesbians are much more likely to be discharged from the military than is true of heterosexual service personnel. The principal reason for this is that prosecutors are much more likely to seek out homosexuals and lesbians in the military than is true of heterosexual offenders. In fact, homosexuality is treated as an offense in and of itself. In the military this is particularly problematic because the majority of each corps prides itself on being real men. Therefore the military, and largely all American men, suffer from a masculine terror of being thought of as less than a man or a "sissy." Therefore, endless jokes about "queers" are part of the daily fare among men in the armed services as well as in factories, offices, and gymnasiums.[51]

Such homophobic expressions are taught early in American culture, leading to "cultural stigma" for homosexuals. These individuals are rejected on the grounds that they belong to a stigmatized group. For example, American children can be heard shouting "faggot" as a pejorative before they know what that word means. Parents and others are constantly making remarks describing homosexuality in unfavorable terms so that most gays learn that homosexuality is stigmatized long before they recognize that they themselves are homosexuals. Seen from the viewpoint of symbolic interactionists it is easy to understand that many homosexuals suffer from a low self-esteem imposed by the negative reactions they encounter every day. Therefore, it is reasonable to agree that those homosexuals who are least visible have more positive self-perceptions than those who are more visible. This should be kept in mind by those who organize parades and "gay power" rallies.[52]

It is assumed in much of American culture that homosexual acts such as kissing and holding hands should not be seen in public. Where such conduct is visible it is severely criticized and can lead to both verbal and/or physical assault. Therefore fear of discovery governs much homosexual behavior in public. Heterosexual behavior, by contrast, is very much visible in public places. Indeed there are the bounds of "public decency." Nevertheless, holding hands, kissing, and hugging at airports and other public places is so common as to arouse no comment whatever. Hence, heterosexual conduct is viewed as normal, that is, expected while the same behavior by two women and particularly two men is viewed as unexpected and abnormal. Therefore, homosexuals behave in a "normal" manner in public and consequently participate in making their sexual interests invisible. This invisibility in turn perpetuates the belief that homosexuality is unacceptable and must remain "in the closet."[53]

Seeking to discover how attitudes toward homosexuals may be changed, Pratarelli and Donaldson investigated whether such attitudes are immediately affected by reading written educational material containing information that supports a biological explanation for homosexuality. It was predicted that participants would respond more favorably to survey items after being presented a biological explanation for homosexuality. Administered to male and female college students, the survey concluded that contrary to most studies by other researchers, acceptance or rejection of homosexuals does not depend on whether a social or biological explanation for homosexuality is presented. However, physical presence and acquaintance with homosexuals has positive results and brings about more acceptance.[54]

As early as 1949 sociologist Samuel Stouffer showed in the famous study of *The American Soldier* that both prejudice and discrimination were best allayed by proximity and authority. This means that those who are personally acquainted with someone stigmatized as an "out-group" are far more likely to learn to accept a member of such a stigmatized group than those who know nothing about the "out-group" from personal experience. In addition, however, the promotion of an "out-group" member reduced bigotry and stigma immeasurably. Therefore, the gradual introduction of black officers into the U.S. armed services did more to reduce stigmatization of blacks than any other measure tried. It is precisely powerlessness that incurs contempt and stigmatization.

Recognition of the need to manage one's own life and escape the stigma associated with homosexuality is therefore in part responsible for the greater proportion of homosexually owned businesses as compared to heterosexually owned enterprises. Eighteen percent of homosexuals have taken the risk of running their own business as compared to only 11 percent in the heterosexual community. This means that homosexuals are 64 percent more often their own bosses than is true among the general population. Author Sue Levin explains this as the consequence of prejudice against homosexual employees in the corporate structure, which, however, is expressed only in a "subtle" fashion and is "not something organizations exactly write into their handbooks." She writes that many gays and lesbians leave the corporate world and establish their own businesses because they know they cannot "fit in" in the corporate structure. The failure to "fit in" has always been reason to exclude various minorities from gaining promotion in corporate America and affects gays and lesbians to the same extent today as it affected others in the past. Evidently, then, self-direction is one of the best solutions to the limitations otherwise imposed on any minority by the hostility that differences have always provoked.[55]

For example, it can be said with certainty that it was the weakness of European Jews that invited their mass murder even as it is the strength of their Israeli descendants that earned the Jews of Israel the respect of the world. Likewise, it is absolutely vital that homosexuals assume positions of influence and power in American life in order to fulfill the promises of our democracy.[56]

That democracy and its basic American values are embodied in the Declaration of Independence and in the Constitution. The Declaration "holds these truths to be self-evident, that all [people] are created equal." If that is so, then surely gays and lesbians are equal to heterosexuals. The Declaration further promises that all people are "endowed by the Creator with certain inalienable Rights, that among these are Life, Liberty and the pursuit of Happiness." Again, this must apply to all who live in America or it cannot apply to anyone. In addition, the preamble of the Constitution claims that the Constitution seeks to "establish justice." Obviously, then, all this must apply to people of every sexual persuasion even as it has been expanded to include women as well as men, blacks as well as whites, minority religions as well as Protestants.[57]

Surely these promises should also apply to those who, by reason of physical condition or appearance, whether social or biological, appear "different." Yet, we find that such differences can lead to severe stigma in our culture. Therefore, the stigma based on physical condition will be the subject of our next chapter.

SUMMARY

The murder of homosexuals by homophobes illustrates the fear that homosexuality arouses in some people. Viewed as outsiders, homosexuals have recently made an effort to be legally married. This effort has so far been largely defeated by the courts, by legislation, and by popular votes.

Nevertheless, the American Psychological Association holds that homosexuality is not a matter of choice so that rejection of homosexual attachments is a gratuitous cruelty. There are those who seek to associate AIDS exclusively with homosexuals. Despite these attitudes a gradual shift in public opinion in favor of homosexuals is discernible. Public opinion polls indicate that there is a definite drop in disapproval of homosexual activity. Only religious fundamentalists continue to cling to the view that homosexuality is to be utterly rejected. Such rejection is not only directed against homosexuals but affects others as well. Among these are obese people. Their situation is the subject of our next chapter.

NOTES

1. Tom Kenworthy, "Gay Student's Attacker Pleads Guilty, Gets Two Life Terms," *Washington Post*, April 6, 1999, p. A2.

2. Sue Ann Pressley, "Two Accused of Killing, Burning Gay Man," *Washington Post*, March 5, 1999, p. A24.

3. Mark Thompson, "Why Do People Have to Push Me Like That?" *Time* 154 (December 13, 1999): 56.

4. James Brooke, "Gay Man Dies from Attack, Fanning Outrage and Debate," *Washington Post*, March 5, 1999, p. A1.

5. Ibid., p. A2.

6. John Boswell, *The Marriage of Likeness: Same-Sex Unions in Pre-modern Europe* (London: Harper Collins, 1995).

7. Martin B. Duberman, Martha Vicinius, and George Chauncey Jr., *Hidden From History: Reclaiming the Gay and Lesbian Past* (New York: Meridian/Penguin Books, 1990).

8. *Legal Marriage Court Cases—A Timeline* (Seattle: Partners Task Force for Gay & Lesbian Couples, 1999).

9. Carey Goldberg, "Hawaii Judge Ends Gay-Marriage Ban," *New York Times*, December 4, 1996, p. 1. See also "Hawaii Gives Gay Couples Marital Benefits," *New York Times*, July 10, 1997, p. B7.

10. "Same-Sex Marriage Loses in Alaska, Hawaii Elections," *Marantha Christian Journal* (November 4, 1998): 1.

11. Ross Sneyd, "Vermont Gay Union Bill Is Approved," http:dailynews.yahoo.com/h/ap/2000425/ts/vermont-gay-marriage.htm.

12. House of Representatives, *Congressional Record* 42 (1996): 2905–47.

13. Constitution of the United States, Article IV, sec. 1.

14. *Congressional Record*, 2906.

15. Editorial, *Spectrum* 46, no. 41 (December 6, 1996): 4.

16. Ibid., p. 2919.

17. Ray W. Johnson, "APA, Science and the Defense of Marriage Act," *Psychological Reports* 81, no. 3, pt. 1 (December 1997): 1010.

18. Ibid., p. 1014.

19. Neil McKenna, "Diary," *New Statesman* 127 (December 4, 1998): 7.

20. Patricia F. Behrendt, *Oscar Wilde: Eros and Aesthetic* (New York: St. Martin's Press, 1991).

21. Brooke, "Gay Man Dies from Attack," p. A17.

22. "Thirty-seven Percent Say AIDS Altered Their Attitude to Homosexuals," *New York Times*, December 15, 1985, p. 41.

23. John Rudolph, "The Impact of Contemporary Ideology and AIDS on the Counseling of Gay Clients," *Counseling and Values* 33 (1989): 97–108.

24. Sandra L. Schwanberg, "Attitudes Towards Homosexuality in American Health Care Literature 1983–1987," *Journal of Homosexuality* 19, no. 3 (1990): 117–36.

25. Vern Bullough, Bonnie Bullough, and R. Smith, "Masculinity and Femininity in Transvestite, Transsexual and Gay Males," *Western Journal of Nursing Research* 7, no. 3 (1985): 317–32.

26. Cathy S. Berkman and Gail Zinberg, "Homophobia and Heterosexism in Social Workers," *Social Work* 42, no. 4 (July 1997): 319–32. See also G. M. Herek and E. K. Glunt, "Interpersonal Contact and Heterosexuals' Attitudes Toward Gay Men: Results from a National Survey," *Journal of Sex Research* 30 (1993): 239–44.

27. Thomas O'Hare, Cynthia L. Williams, and Alan Ezoviski, "Fear of AIDS and Homophobia: Implications for Direct Practice and Advocacy," *Social Work* 41, no. 1 (January 1996): 51–58.

28. Marc E. Pratarelli and Jennifer Donaldson, "Immediate Effects of Written Material on Attitudes Toward Homosexuality," *Psychological Reports* 81, no. 3 (December 1997): 1411–45.

29. Brian J. McGrory, David M. McDowell, and Phillip R. Muskin, "Medical Students' Attitudes Toward AIDS, Homosexual, and Intravenous Drug-Abusing Patients: A Re-evaluation in New York City," *Psychosomatics* 31, no. 4 (fall 1990): 426–33.

30. Debra L. Klamen, Linda S. Grossman, and David R. Kopacs, "Medical Student Homophobia," *Journal of Homosexuality* 37, no. 1 (1999): 54–63.

31. Michael J. Yedidia, Carolyn A. Berry, and Judith K. Barr, "Changes in Physicians' Attitudes Toward AIDS During Residency Training: A Longitudinal Study of Medical School Graduates," *Journal of Health and Social Behavior* 37, no. 2 (June 1996): 179–91.

32. "The Stonewall Rebellion," *New York Times*, June 29, 1969, p. 33.

33. International Gay and Lesbian Association, "Being Gay and Lesbian: The Legal and Social Situation of Gay Men—A Country by Country Survey," *Los Angeles Times*, December 1, 1992, p. H–6.

34. Richard Seltzer, "AIDS, Homosexuality, Public Opinion, and Changing Correlates Over Time," *Journal of Homosexuality* 26, no. 1 (1993): 85–97.

35. Alan S. Yang, "Attitudes Toward Homosexuality," *Public Opinion Quarterly* 61, no. 3 (fall 1997): 477–88.

36. Paul Cameron and Kirk Cameron, "What Proportion of Newspaper Stories about Child Molestation Involves Homosexuals?" *Psychological Reports* 82 (June 1998): 863–971.

37. *Romer* v. *Evans* et al., Amendment 2, U.S. Supreme Court (October 1995).

38. Beverly R. King and Kathryn R. Black, "Extent of Relational Stigmatization of Lesbians and Their Children by Heterosexual College Students," *Journal of Homosexuality* 17, no. 2 (1999): 65–81.

39. Gen. 9:22 and 19:1–11; Lev. 18:22 and 20:13; Rom. 1:18–32.

40. Andrew K. T. Yip, "The Politics of Counter-Rejection: Gay Christians and the Church," *Journal of Homosexuality* 37, no. 2 (1999): 51.

41. Charles M. Ponticelli, "The Spiritual Warfare of Exodus: A Positivist Research Adventure," *Qualitative Inquiry* 2, no. 2 (1996): 198–219.

42. Laurie Goodstein, "The Architect of the 'Gay Conversion' Campaign," *New York Times*, August 13, 1998, p. A10.

43. Nancy D. Wadsworth, "Reconciliation Politics: Conservate Evangelicals and the New Race Discourse," *Politics and Society* 25, no. 3 (September 1997): 350–52.

44. Rank Rich, "Family Values Stalkers," *New York Times*, January 30, 1999, p. A19.

45. Yip, "The Politics of Counter-Rejection," p. 51.

46. Congregation for the Doctrine of the Faith, *Letter to the Bishops of the Catholic Church on the Pastoral Care of Homosexual Persons* (London: Catholic Truth Society, 1986).

47. Rabbinical Assembly's Commission on Human Sexuality, *Pastoral Letter on Human Sexuality* (New York: United Synagogue of Conservative Judaism, 1998), pp. 19–23.

48. Nachum Amsel, *The Jewish Encyclopedia of Moral and Ethical Issues* (Northvale, N.J.: Jason Aronson, 1994), p. 95.

49. George Herbert Mead, *Mind, Self, and Society* (Chicago: University of Chicago Press, 1934).

50. Michael C. La Scala, "Coupled Gay Men, Parents, and In-Laws: Intergenerational Disapproval and the Need for a Thick Skin," *Families in Society: The Journal of Contemporary Human Services* 79, no. 6 (November/December 1990): 585–95.

51. David D. Gilmore, *Manhood in the Making* (New Haven, Conn.: Yale University Press, 1990), p. 17.

52. Deborah E. S. Frable, Camille Wortman, and Jill Joseph, "Predicting Self-Esteem, Well-Being, and Distress in a Cohort of Gay Men: The Importance of Cultural Stigma, Personal Visibility, Community Networks, and Positive Identity," *Journal of Personality* 65, no. 3 (September 1997): 599–624.

53. Gary Smith, Susan Kippax, and Murray Chapple, "Secrecy, Disclosure and Closet Dynamics," *Journal of Homosexuality* 35, no. 1 (March, 1998): 53–73.

54. Marc Pratarelli and Jennifer S. Donaldson, "Immediate Effects of Written Material on Attitudes Toward Homosexuality," *Psychological Reports* 81 (1997): 1411–15.

55. Sue Levin, *In the Pink; The Making of Successful Gay- and Lesbian-Owned Businesses* (Binghamton, N.Y.: Harrington Park Press, 1999), p. 25.

56. Samuel A. Stouffer, *The American Soldier: Adjustment during Army Life* (Princeton, N.J.: Princeton University Press, 1949).

57. Declaration of Independence; Constitution of the United States.

OBESITY | 4

APPEARANCE AS STIGMA

IN A RICH SOCIETY

OVERWEIGHT: THE "SELF-INFLICTED" PROBLEM

"Let me have men about me that are fat; Sleek-headed men and such as sleep o'nights: Yon Cassius has a lean and hungry look; He thinks too much: such men are dangerous."

So wrote William Shakespeare (1564–1616) in 1601, exhibiting the common belief, current then and now, that weight and appearance have behavioral origins and consequences. Shakespeare was born seventeen years after King Henry VIII (1491–1547) died. It is therefore possible, but unlikely, that Shakespeare had not heard of the fat, yet most dangerous king, or that he could have foreseen the hugely fat, yet dangerous Hermann Göring (1893–1946), Hitler's friend who never had a "hungry look" but was sentenced to death by hanging as a mass murderer in 1946. We could list numerous other fat men far more dangerous than many thin men. Suffice it to say that Shakespeare believed what many people believed, then and now, so that obesity is not only a health issue in America but is also a sociopsychological issue that the obese population of this country must confront every day of their lives.[1]

On a widely publicized sound cassette, published in 1999, the television performer Camryn Mannheim discussed her overweight condition and the prejudices she had to confront since childhood. She calls her cassette *Wake Up! I'm Fat* thereby sounding a note of defiance against the daily "butt of the joke" position which her appearance regularly provoked.[2]

THE TELEVISION PERFORMER

Camryn Mannheim is not the only overweight woman to have published an account of her experiences as stigmatized by those whom Charlotte Cooper has called "fatphobic." Because "fatphobia" is so widespread, everyday life impacts negatively and painfully on the overweight. Cooper has identified several concerns of "fat" people which normal-sized people never notice. First, the oversized physically do not "fit in." This means that at work, in social situations, in public transportation, at turnstiles, cubicles of all kinds, theaters, and restaurants the bodies of the "fat" will not be accommodated.

Fat people also have trouble finding clothing to fit. Few clothing stores stock supersized clothing. Therefore, oversized people must pay more to specialty stores to get clothes that fit them. Even mail-order catalogues use slim models. Hence fat people feel stigmatized because they do not have nearly the choice of clothing thin people have. In fact, many fat people resort to the dictum: "If it covers me up, I'll take it." In addition to finding clothing that fits, overweight people also consume more clothing because their size causes them to tear or wear out their clothes more often than is true of normal-sized people. Furthermore, oversized people perspire more than normal-sized people and that, too, causes clothes to deteriorate faster than is common among people of normal size.

Difficulties in adjusting to one's physical surroundings are of course not the only problems faced by those who are overweight. American culture has made fat people either invisible or the object of ridicule. This "invisibility" is mainly practiced by the media whose use of overweight actors or announcers is extremely limited. In addition, reporters, columnists, and other performers write such comments as this: ". . . this woman, frightened to leave her home, is so fat that if she did come outside she would be the only man-made object outside of the Great Wall of China visible from outer space." Those most affected by this kind of negative imagery believe that the media contribute a great deal to the rejection the overweight must confront.[3]

Even in their private lives, overweight persons are confronted with comments and assumptions intolerable to them. Many overweight persons grow up with fat-related nicknames or, far worse, fat-hating and punitive attitudes. Such attitudes are often clothed in "kind" remarks that are nevertheless hurtful, for example, "Why don't you go on the Dr. XYZ Diet?" or "Let me give you the name of a doctor who specializes in obesity," or "Too bad you're so heavy—you have such a pretty face." In other families, one person's fatness is considered a shameful and embarrassing subject so that the fat person will incorporate a body-hating attitude into his own psyche. This in turn leads the overweight into all kinds of efforts to deal with this private and public ignominy and opprobrium.

Fat people also suffer a great deal in their public lives. Teachers and other students frequently make hostile or insulting remarks concerning overweight even as many job openings are refused fat people by those who believe that those who are overweight are not fit and healthy enough to do the job. In many companies fat employees are used only in areas where they are not visible to the clients. In situations where such policies are not followed and fat people are indeed visible to customers they generally receive a great deal of unwanted attention. This is particularly the case in restaurants, food stores, and social occasions involving the serving of food.

Eating in public can occur every day at work as employees eat lunch in the workplace even as children eat lunch in school cafeterias. Many overweight people do not use these restaurants for fear of becoming the targets of all kinds of remarks and even insults while eating there. Professor of social science Dawn Zdrodowski contacted five hundred overweight women concerning their experiences when "eating out." Many of those interviewed pointed out that other people would call attention to what the fat person was eating. Space presents another problem for the excessively fat when visiting a public eating facility. So many restaurants have booths or furniture screwed into the floor that very large people either cannot get in or out of these areas without "taking the table cloth with you" and without calling attention to their weight. While normal-sized persons can eat anything anywhere, fat people must carefully consider where to eat, where to sit, and what to order. Fat people try to sit near the door or at the counter so that they need not walk about too much in the restaurant. Most disconcerting for fat people are the remarks strangers will make. Here are some examples: "I was having an ice cream once while sitting on a wall with my young granddaughter. A young couple went past, she looked and said: 'That's disgusting.' Even my granddaughter heard her. I was mortified"; "I heard my nephew's friend say, 'Let's eat before she does or there'll be none left.' . . . They laughed . . . I cried"; "In the hot weather we sometimes eat our sandwiches in the park. I used to enjoy that but one day a boy said: 'Feed the ducks with your dinner. They look hungry and you obviously haven't experienced hunger.' I laughed along with everyone else, but it hurt"; "We were all women having a night out. I didn't want to go on for a meal so I said I had already eaten. One of the women said: 'It doesn't look like that would usually stop you having another one.' It was turned into a joke but I felt uncomfortable after that"; "One waiter leered at me and asked: '. . . The sixteen-ounce [steak], madam?' Even if I'd considered the idea I changed my mind and ordered the four-ounce.

At any rate it wasn't (what) I was going to have." These and many other examples of situations faced by the overweight when eating in public describe the stigma to which the overweight are subject every day.[4]

This however, raises the question of self-consciousness. No doubt many overweight people are so concerned with their body that they perceive and interpret the actions and words of others as directed at them even when these "others" had no such intentions. Sociologist Erving Goffman, as we mentioned in chapter 1, holds that body idioms involve the shared understanding of meaning, including body management, among strangers where individuals pay attention to the careful positioning of their bodies in everyday life. Obviously, all individuals are concerned with the impression they create when interacting with others. However, for the overweight person there is the added dimension of how much space it is acceptable for anyone to occupy. If we concede that "excess body fat is probably the most stigmatized physical feature," we can also agree that fat people "push the bounds of acceptability."[5]

There is little or no support for overweight people because it is seen as a self-inflicted problem that can easily be solved. The victim is blamed. Therefore the overweight person is stigmatized, which in turn leads to a "self-fulfilling" condition whereby the fat person sees himself as deviant. Once more we quote Goffman, who defines a stigma as "any attribute that deeply discredits or spoils the identity of its holder by indicating an undesirable distinctiveness from others."[6]

This distinctiveness then leads to a great deal of anxiety which is in turn alleviated by yet more overeating, particularly as the overweight feel that they must eat alone to escape the stigma placed on them by the general hostility they encounter everywhere.

In addition to some subtle comments, fat people, like homosexuals or anyone else who is "different," are the targets of overt aggression. Such comments as "she is fat but has such a pretty face" are commonplace. Even efforts to be complimentary toward fat people can be painful reminders that many observers view fat people as being all alike. Such assumptions as the belief that fat people are more "fun to be with" or are emotionally more stable than thin people create the warranted impression that the commentator does not recognize the person but only the appearance of the overweight. It can be said with equal assurance, however, that this is true of thin people as well and that this affects women more than men. Hence, well-shaped, beautiful women and men often find that they too are treated as if they had only a body and no mind or personality.[7] This comes about because "beautiful people" can indeed expect to perform poorly in school and in many jobs as teachers and employers "take it easy" on those they like to have around. This is particularly true of men employing young women.

OBESITY IN THE MINORITY COMMUNITY

Overweight, as well as so many other personal and social difficulties, has become universalized in recent years. This means that child abuse, alcoholism, drug addiction, teen pregnancy, domestic violence, and of course overeating are all described by the media as being "a problem for most Americans." *The Surgeon General's Report of 1988* includes this statement: "We must fight the prevalence of obesity which crosses all lines of American society."[8]

The truth is, of course, that overeating is not evenly distributed throughout American society and the public knows that. In fact, stigmatized behavior generally clusters among the least affluent Americans. Social scientists therefore have difficulty in collecting data concerning stigmatized behavior because of the justifiable fear of any potential subjects. In addition, sociologists have repeatedly called attention to the fact that behavior and conditions that are stigmatized lend themselves to discrimination. This is particularly true of obesity because it cannot be hidden as may be the case with alcoholism, homosexuality, or criminal behavior.[9]

It is also evident that obesity is not stigmatized in the same fashion in all social classes, ethnic groups, and subcultures. This is best seen when we inspect the view of obesity as understood by African Americans, who are most often members of the lower class. Self-reporting clearly demonstrates these cultural differences which assign differential status-roles to obese Americans depending on the subculture which various obese people use as their reference groups. A reference group is any group whose expectations we follow. This could be your family, your religious group, or even your bowling league.

A number of investigations have shown that the virulent and institutionalized form of fat hatred present in white America is not replicated in the black community. Evidence for this difference can be found in the fact that 48 percent of all adult black men and 60 percent of all adult black women between forty-five and seventy-five years of age are obese. Among all American adults, of whom 83 percent are white, only 26 percent are overweight by medical standards. Women, however, exceed this average. About one-third of all white women are obese by medical standards. The phrase "medical standards" refers to 120 percent of recommended weight for height.[10]

We have featured the problems of obese women because women are judged on their appearance much more than is true of men. Women also experience the stigma of obesity much more severely than do men. Thus, obese women tend to be lower in socioeconomic status than nonobese women. This is the case because some obese women make less money than their nonobese sisters. Obese female applicants are also victimized in the college selection process. These and so many other difficulties encountered by obese women cause them to be very much more preoccupied with weight issues than are men.[11]

Several studies have been made to assess the attitudes of nonwhites or non-Anglo-Americans concerning obesity. Social psychologists Charles Crandall and Robert Martinez report that compared with Mexican students, American students report significantly greater negative attitudes toward obese individuals. In fact, typical American ideologies concerning belief in a just world, self-determination, and conservatism were found to be correlated with antifat attitudes.[12]

In the African American community larger body sizes were also viewed more positively than is true in the white community. In a study conducted among first- through third-grade students, black girls chose for themselves significantly larger ideal body figures than did white girls.[13] In another study, psychologist Daniel Dawson found that when women are compared within categories of relative weights, proportionately fewer African American women than either white or Hispanic women consider themselves overweight. This is so because African American women do not evaluate their weight in relation to a health-based ideal but in relation to other women of their race who are, on the average, heavier than white women.[14]

Further confirmation of this more positive attitude toward larger body size by black girls can be seen in the diet eaten by blacks and whites. Cultural attitudes play a decisive role in diets consumed by various groups in the American population. Thus, the National Food Consumption Survey discovered that African Americans eat a good deal more salt pork, bacon, and luncheon meats than is true of whites. These foods have a high-fat, high-cholesterol, low-fiber content. Further, the manner of food preparation in the African American community increases the risk of obesity and obesity diseases. Consequently, overweight is a good deal greater among members of this racial group than it is among those who do not eat in that manner.[15]

Culture is of course most important in influencing our judgment as to attractive or unattractive body parts. Michael Cunningham found that black men found large female buttocks attractive whereas white men were more interested in smaller or "firm" body parts. Similarly, Charlotte Cooper reports that in London, England, "big bottoms and thighs are desirable amongst young, working-class Afro-Caribbean people."[16] There are several reasons for this cultural diversity. First, the greater statistical frequency of obesity among blacks makes that condition less deviant than is true among whites. Furthermore, the stigma of obesity carries a different meaning for whites than blacks. The stigma of obesity is related to a more conservative white ideology than is generally found among blacks. That ideology holds that fat people are fat because they are morally weak and have little self-control and that obesity implies sloth and lazy self-indulgence. It was therefore common for white advertisers, playwrights, producers, and actors to portray large black women as the common stereotype of black appearance. This can be seen in such productions as *Show Boat, Gone with the Wind, I'm No Angel,* and many others. These productions always include slim, white, beautiful women. Black overweight women by contrast appeared unattractive, largely incompetent, and certainly nonthreatening in comparison. Blacks generally do not subscribe to the puritanical outlook still so frequent among European Americans as is also indicated by a more liberal black voting record than is generally true of whites.[17]

Body image is also related to socioeconomic status. Kristin Flynn and Marian Fitzgibbon studied the body image ideals of low-income African American mothers and daughters and found that middle-income African American females "are more satisfied with their current weight" when compared to their white counterparts. According to Flynn and Fitzgibbon, African American females also have less drive for thinness and have heavier body image ideals than was true even among those African American women who were attending health-education classes.[18]

Rural Americans also differ in body mass from urban Americans. Jeffrey Sobal found that rural areas tend to have a different social-class structure than urban places, typically containing a higher proportion of low-income individuals with lower educational levels. Thus, despite the evidence that obesity is an important social and health issue in contemporary society, lower socioeconomic status women tend to be more obese than urban women. Evidently, then, social class is a major influence on the weight of rural and urban residents. That this is the case is visible because urban areas "enforce" thinness by mores, i.e., social norms that demand a thin appearance at work, in social situations, and even in private life. This is not true in rural areas where slim appearance is less important and obesity is not nearly as penalized. This is in part caused by the greater economic opportunities enjoyed by slim people who can therefore find work in urban areas and move away from the farm, leaving fat people behind. It is also reasonable to suggest that those who run their own business—farming—do not need to keep up a slim appearance in order to hold their job. Farm women need not worry about much competition for the fidelity of their husbands from better-looking females in the economic sphere.[19]

It is also vital to consider that the American ideal of body shape, particularly for women, reflects a condition only the rich or affluent can afford. It requires effort, money, and time to eat mainly protein, join health clubs or hire trainers, prerequisites which the white community can afford much more often than the black community. Given that 51.2 percent of all African American women live below the poverty level, it is evident that this alone contributes heavily to their obesity.[20]

Then, there are also blacks who deliberately ignore white values and standards and use obesity to affirm their sense of self-esteem. There are a number of studies that show that many blacks reverse the valued characteristics of the mainstream white culture and do precisely the opposite. Therefore it is entirely reasonable to see excessive weight among blacks as a challenge to the racial oppression which blacks confront every day.[21]

There is also a good deal of evidence to suggest that the effect of obesity in the labor market and the "marriage market" is less for black women than for white women. This does not ignore that black women earn less and have more difficulty finding a husband than is true of white women. It means, however, that although obese women of both races have lower wages and lower income compared to their needs than slim women, these effects are smaller for black women. This is true because black female marriage opportunities are less likely to be influenced by obesity. Among white women, however, "the bulk of the income differences of obese women and women of recommended weight, stems from marriage market factors rather than labor market factors."[22]

The marriage market is of course dominated by beliefs concerning attractiveness in each culture and subculture. First, therefore, is the evident fact that weight is an important criterion in selecting romantic partners, a priori and in maintaining a romantic and/or sexual interest in the partner after marriage, especially among men. Surely it is common knowledge that in the United States today obese people are stigmatized in dating relationships. Therefore, obese people have more difficulty attracting a marital partner than is true of slim people and hence marry later than the non-obese. Obese people are also forced to marry less desirable partners and therefore marry heavier partners.[23]

Because many people gain a good deal of weight after they marry, married people tend to be heavier than single people. This may in part be true because generally, married people are older than single people. Furthermore, many couples gain weight together in what has been described as "marital synchrony." Nevertheless, married men are more often fatter than married women. This is true because married women continue to worry about their weight because appearance is more important to women than to men. Of course married and single men may consider overweight very important but this is decidedly not as important to men than to women because appearance is less emphasized among men. Furthermore, married men eat more regularly and eat better than single men because food preparation continues to be a female duty even today. Married men are also less likely than single men to engage in sports and other physical activities.[24]

We have reviewed some aspects of adult obesity. There are, however, also children who are overweight. In fact, pediatric obesity is the most prevalent nutritional problem in the United States. Children who appear obese earlier in childhood appear to persist in obesity longer. They have little chance of losing that weight later as the severity of the overweight affects its persistence. There is a direct relationship between persistence of overweight and its severity. Hence childhood obesity is a significant risk factor for obesity in adulthood. In girls, obesity in childhood results in early menses and in boys it is associated with better than average height. These biological outcomes would be of minor significance if it were not for the psychosocial consequences of childhood obesity. The work of sociologists Norman Goodman, Sanford Dornbush, and Stephen A. Richardson demonstrates, however, that children as young as five associate obesity with negative characteristics. No doubt the media, particularly television, reinforce the images of thinness among children since fat people are virtually absent from television.[25]

Children who are obese also suffer from the rejection of obese people so common in American society. Among children this rejection is largely based on the belief that obese people are weak and hence vulnerable. Fat children, and obese adults, but particularly fat adolescents, are less likely to make friends or to feel they belong or are socially integrated. This is not only threatening the health of the obese but also their emotional life, as children and adolescents must also daily endure insults and cruelties derived from the interpretation of their appearance.

The stigma of overweight is particularly burdensome to children and adolescents. As Émile Durkheim showed more than one hundred years ago, one's relative position in the social structure and degree of integration into the social system have substantial effects on health and well-being. Therefore it is not surprising that the children of unmarried mothers or fathers and those with little emotional support are at greater risk of obesity. Another way of saying this is that the presence of social ties for the caretakers of children can have positive health effects, not only for the adult but also for her children. Therefore, we can reasonably conclude that the increase in childhood obesity observed in the United States during the thirty years ending in 1995 can be in part attributed to a truly dramatic increase in single female-headed households during that same period. For example, in 1994 a total of 1,007,000 unmarried women aged fifteen to forty-four gave birth to 1,290,000 children. This constituted 26 percent of all women who gave birth. This also means that the proportion of children born to an unmarried mother has increased from 18.4 percent in 1980 to 32.6 percent in 1994.[26] The number of teenagers who gave birth also increased during those years. In sum, the number of children living in a one-parent household has more than doubled since 1970 and therein lies a good deal of the childhood overweight just observed.[27]

Among adolescents an increase of obesity of 18 percent for boys and 21 percent for girls has been observed in the United States, western Europe, and Canada. This is mainly attributed to dietary intake, that is, overeating and to a decrease in the physical activity of large numbers of adolescents in all countries affected. A study by professor of obstetrics Jennifer O'Dea and professor of education Suzanne Abraham confirms these findings because these researchers found that contrary to popular belief, young male and female students, when asked how they felt about themselves, labeled athletic and sports ability as the least of their concerns. Close friendships, doing well at school and work, and being romantically appealing were considered the three most important factors determining how the sample in the O'Dea/Abraham study feel about themselves. In that connection it was found that overweight male students felt that their job skills and ability to do well at part-time work were poor. Overweight students also considered their scholastic ability to be less important than was true of "lean" students. Of course, the overweight students also considered their athletic ability to be poor and believed themselves to be socially less acceptable than other students.[28] This is the case because our weight-obsessed society teaches us to despise our own overweight bodies.

In that estimate especially girls are indeed quite right. In fact, a good number of adolescent girls who are not overweight nevertheless believe that they are fat while many who think they are "just right" are in fact 5 percent below average. Adolescent overweight is important not only because children of that age are vulnerable to the kind of stigmatization already discussed, but it is also important because overweight in adolescence has consequences in adult life. Obese girls are much more likely than slim girls to remain unmarried and remain in poverty because of employer discrimination.[29]

OBESITY AND THE SELF: THE OUTCOME OF STIGMA

We have explored the sociology of obesity which deals with the situations in which obesity is observed and adjudicated. There is however also a psychological aspect of obesity concerning the relationship of obesity to the emotional adjustments of obese persons under the conditions we have just outlined.

Obesity begins in childhood. Therefore students of childhood obesity have found in numerous studies that *obese children have less positive self-perceptions* than slim children. This finding refers first and foremost to physical competence. However, obese children do not suffer only from negative body esteem. The evidence is that children who are dissatisfied with their personal appearance are also dissatisfied with other aspects of their lives, not related to looks.[30]

This indicates that the discrimination suffered by the obese has important consequences in childhood, adolescence, and adulthood. Among children this can be measured because the obese have more behavioral problems in school and at home than slim children. Much of children's lives centers around physical activities and sports. This means that physical activity with other children is closely related to popularity and social relations. Therefore a feeling of self-worth is also related to these variables so that children with a low physical self-image will view themselves in a negative fashion in areas other than sports.

The condemnation of the obese is of course not new or the product of the twentieth century alone. In societies adhering to theological norms, gluttony was and is viewed as a sin. American society relinquished religious explanations of behavior for secular explanations after the eighteenth-century psychiatric explanations for obesity were promoted with the rise of interest in psychology and psychoanalysis at that time. Professional psychotherapists therefore viewed the obese as suffering from emotional disturbance and failed impulse control.

Hence it was widely accepted that obesity resulted from an emotional disorder in which food intake, particularly excessive food intake, relieved the anxiety and depression to which obese persons were usually susceptible. Psychoanalytic theorists went further and traced the origin of obesity to the oral stage of libidinal development. Psychoanalysts claim that the obese are fixated at the oral stage of life so that conflicts and frustrations suffered by those so fixated would lead to overeating or, in psychoanalytic language, using an excess of "oral supplies."[31]

There are those who continue to support the psychoanalytic point of view concerning obesity because psychoanalysis seems to explain the compulsive eating problems as acts derived from early childhood experiences. According to classical psychoanalysis female fatness was diagnosed as an obsessive-compulsive symptom related to narcissism and insufficient ego development. All of this meant that overeating was reduced to a character defect by the psychoanalysts as well as other psychologists. Efforts to treat obesity by psychological means of any kind have proved largely unsuccessful. When this became clear to both the obese and those treating them, experimentalists sought to discover biological reasons for obesity.[32]

Such biological roots of obesity do indeed exist and affect a few obese people. However, biological explanations can hardly suffice to account for the 30 percent increase in overweight people in the United States since 1991, and biological explanations cannot be used to explain why 20 percent of American children were overweight in 1999. Instead it is more reasonable to attribute overweight to behavior. This may be illustrated by showing that the message of health professionals to avoid fatty foods is easily drowned out by the $33 billion annual advertising campaigns of those who promote sugary drinks, fast food such as hamburgers, candy, and other "junk." As a result, and at present, the average American woman is 5'4½" tall and weighs 143.4 pounds. The average American man is 5'10" tall and weighs 177.2 pounds. Therefore, between 24 percent and 26 percent of American adults are obese depending on the definition of "obese" among various observers.[33] According to the Metropolitan Life Insurance Company, the average woman should weigh only 124 to 138 pounds depending on "frame." The average man should weigh 151 to 163 pounds at 5'10".

"Observers" of anything are of course culture-bound. Therefore, as we have already seen, there is considerable criticism of overweight among whites but not among blacks. At least one reason for this discrepancy is the relative condition of obesity to the significant reference group in which obesity is evaluated. This means that blacks are more willing to accept obese persons than is true of whites. This finding is corroborated by the discovery that college graduates and others with high earnings are less willing to accept obesity than is true of those not well educated and those earning only average or less than average incomes. Since the well educated write and speak about obesity, it may well be that the "issue" is class-related and therefore does not concern the majority of those affected.

Compulsive eating is largely attributed to women in American society. Therefore it is reasonable to conclude that there is something about being female in America that induces some women to become fat. Journalist Susie Orbach argues that "fat is *not* about lack of self-control or lack of will power but is about protection, sex nurturance, strength, boundaries, mothering, substance assertion, and rage." Orbach then details all of the disadvantages from which women in American culture have traditionally suffered. These complaints can of course be well documented and are indeed substantial. However, there are also a good number of obese men who, by definition, do not suffer the disadvantages women suffer. Therefore, it is hard to support the view that fat is a feminist issue. It is also a masculine issue despite the indisputable fact that women suffer more than men from the definition of the situation surrounding fat.[34]

This then raises the question of whether overweight is emotionally distressing because of the negative consequences it has in our society or whether it is so distressing because of its physical implications. The first interpretation refers to the stigma associated with overweight already discussed. If that stigma is internalized then theories of the "looking-glass self" would explain depression, negative self-evaluations, and self-rejections as we evaluate ourselves in the light of the manner in which others see us.[35]

The second interpretation concerning overweight is that constant dieting, endless efforts to lose weight, and the frequently reported poor health of the overweight are more responsible for emotional distress than the social consequences of obesity. Catherine Ross, professor of sociology at Ohio State University, has examined this issue in detail. She found that "dieting to lose weight as an attempt to fit norms (expectations) that equate attractiveness with thinness is more distressing than being overweight per se." Being overweight is also associated with poor physical health. That, in turn, is associated with depression. Therefore 92 percent of depression among the obese is the result of endless efforts to diet and of poor physical health.[36]

Evidently then, exercise is the method that the obese need to use to lose weight, maintain good health, and avoid depression. Activity is the direct antithesis of depression. Therefore, it is exercise that has at least a moderate and often a large beneficial effect on depression, self-esteem, and psychological adjustment so that we can conclude that dieting and exercise must go together to be effective.[37]

Dr. David Jenkins, University of Toronto professor of medicine and nutrition sciences, holds that "sloth and gluttony" are the roots of obesity. In his view the problems stem from the fact that humans are equipped with biological systems adapted for survival in the feast-or-famine world of humanity's hunter-gatherer ancestors. Body cells are by nature capable of storing energy for periods of scarcity. In the major industrialized nations such as the United States such scarcity is rare so that more people overeat than starve. Hence, the abundant food supply linked to a sedentary lifestyle is the core of the problem. It is for this reason that physical activity is regarded as the prime method of controlling weight. Unfortunately, only one-half of Americans ever join exercise programs. Furthermore, one-half of those who do indeed join an exercise program drop out during the first three to five months. This indicates that many of those who do join exercise programs do not stay with it long enough to gain any advantage from it.[38]

Undoubtedly emotional well-being is one positive outcome of exercise. A number of studies confirm this view and indicate that regular exercise has an effect on self-reported measures of anxiety. Exercise also has a beneficial effect on depression and improves self-esteem and mood. Exercise has also been shown to improve various aspects of personality and psychosocial adjustment. Cognitive functioning also improves with exercise as does a decline in antisocial behavior. Several other lesser benefits may also be associated with regular exercise, making dieting easier and weight loss more likely.[39]

Because the well educated write and lecture on the obesity issue while the poorly educated do not, there is a possibility that the limited view of obesity attributable to the educated has been unjustifiably universalized. In fact, fat people do not deviate nearly as much from the norm among the poor and the less educated than they deviate from the norms of the high-earning well-educated population. Therefore, it is possible that as more and more Americans become overweight, fat will become the norm and will lose its stigma among most Americans.

There are those who claim that about half the American and Canadian population, including a large number of children, weighs too much. Canada, with a population no larger than that of California, nevertheless faces medical costs of $15 billion a year or more to deal with obesity-related medical problems. Obesity is viewed by public-health officials as the cause of at least two-thirds of all diabetes cases; a third of all cardiovascular problems, including many strokes; gall bladder disease; and joint problems.[40]

The Metropolitan Life Insurance Company has developed a weight table used by the U.S. Department of Health and Human Services. That table seeks to define "obese" or "desirable" weight in terms of a height/weight ratio. Accordingly, a 5'7" man should weigh between 140 and 152 pounds and a woman of the same height should weigh between 133 and 147 pounds. The same table announces that a man who is six feet tall should weigh between 155 and 169 pounds and a woman 5'10" tall should weigh between 142 and 156 pounds.[41]

No height/weight chart alone can determine what constitutes overweight. The reason for this is of course that two or more people of the same height and same weight may be overweight or not depending on bone structure, musculature, and other factors. Therefore, Body Mass Index is now used to determine overweight. BMI is defined as truncal circumference. To measure body fat several methods have been devised. Among these are underwater weighing which deals with water replacement, bioelectrical impedence which measures the length of time needed to send an electrical impulse through the muscles, and a "skin fold" test which calibrates fat at seven sites. These methods circumvent the dispute concerning mere height-weight ratio. In the words of Shauna Stisser, a specialist in exercise science: "It is not the weight, it is the body fat."[42]

To rid oneself of that fat is so all-encompassing that many fat people feel all their lives that they are physically but also emotionally starving. It is of course true that for some people a propensity for putting on weight comes with their genetic inheritance. This is, however, very rare. Doctors estimate that only a fraction of 1 percent of the obese are afflicted by one of the thirty diseases associated with flawed genes. Yet, even among those so affected, good eating habits and exercise will still control weight and the body's energy balance. Therefore, the anxiety, emotional pain, social handicaps, and physical danger associated with obesity really affect everyone involved.[43]

DIETS, PANACEAS, AND THE WEIGHT-LOSS INDUSTRY

The stigma of obesity is so pervasive that those suffering from its effects will use numerous methods to deal with their difficulty even as they try to avoid the one method that is absolutely crucial to losing weight. That crucial method is regular exercise. Regular exercise not only helps to reduce weight, it also prevents the return of the pounds lost. Yet, the abhorrence of exercise is such that many have turned to mechanical means in the hope of having machines do for them what they will not do for themselves. For example, in the 1960s it was popular to use a motorized contraption with a large canvas belt which "jiggled" the rear end of the obese user on the grounds that this would "break up" the fat cells. The only result of using such machines was red and irritated skin. The more current version of this contraption is the Electrical Muscle Stimulation machine. This device sends a weak current into the muscles causing them to contract and relax in quick succession. The manufacturers claim that a forty-five-minute use of such a machine is the equivalent of 880 sit-ups. According to Barbara Wickens, writing in *Maclean's* magazine, the machine does nothing for its users other than spend their money.[44]

There are some fat people who are considered "morbidly obese." These are people whose Body Mass Index is 40 or greater. For example, a man 6 ft. tall who weighed 300 lbs. would have a Body Mass Index of 40. A woman 5'5" tall and weighing 235 lbs. would also have a Body Mass Index of 40. At the other end of the BMI scale would be a man 5'7" tall, weighing 152 lbs. He would have a BMI of 25, which is in the "ideal" zone. Yet, a woman only 5'2" tall and weighing only 105 lbs. would have a Body Mass Index of only 19 and hence may weigh too little. Because women are more anxious to deal with their appearance than is true of men there are some women who suffer from bulemia, an eating disorder consisting of a cycle of bingeing and purging that can be truly dangerous for those affected.

Those, however, who suffer from the stigma of extreme fat have sometimes turned to surgery as a means of dealing with their problem. At one time such surgery consisted of wiring the patient's jaws shut so that he/she could ingest only through a straw. Recently doctors have used stomach stapling in order to reduce the size of the stomach. Other patients have had a balloon inserted in the stomach to accomplish the same thing. There is also liposuction, which involves the use of a subcutaneous tube connected to a high-vacuum device. This then sucks out fat deposits through a tiny incision. This method of reduction works at once but, like all surgery, involves some risks of infection or reactions to the anesthetic. The most popular effort to reduce weight is dieting. Yet, dieting and all other methods depend of course on the ability of the obese person involved to resist regaining excessive weight.[45]

Because that resistance is seldom present within the psyche of the overweight, millions have turned to diet pills, which constitute a $60 billion industry in North America at the beginning of this century. Diet pills have been used in this country for nearly a century. In 1910, doctors began to prescribe diet pills including arsenic and strychnine. Then, in the 1940s, amphetamines became popular because they were used to keep fighter pilots alert with the observed side effect of also suppressing their appetites. In the 1990s, "fen-phen" was widely used as a diet pill. This consisted of fenfluramine and phentermine. Studies revealed, however, that fenfluramine led to heart-valve abnormalities, so it was withdrawn. Other drugs have been used—either prescriptive or over the counter—with varying degrees of success.

There are of course all kinds of diet or low-calorie foods on the shelves of American food stores. Health-food stores sell reducing teas, diet drinks of all kinds, and vitamin supplements. These foods generally include oat fiber or cayenne pepper because "hot" foods increase the basal metabolic rate which is the rate at which the body burns calories. There are also diet foods that contain ingredients such as ephedrine, a caffeinelike stimulant, or uva-ursi, a diuretic. All of these pills, beverages, and foods are consumed in large quantities every day despite great doubt concerning their efficacy.

Then there are of course the endless "guru" diets promoted by authors of diet books. These authors are generally doctors who claim to have finally found the "true" answer to obesity and therefore the key to weight loss. For example, the best-selling book *Dr. Atkins' New Diet Revolution* led numerous obese people into a messianic zeal of dieting according to Dr. Robert Atkins's prescription. This consisted of eating pork rinds and limiting broccoli while Dr. Dean Ornish, another author of a diet book, told his readers to push the high-fiber, low-fat diet to such an extreme that he would allow only 10 percent of all intake to be fat when standard recommendations permitted a 30 percent fat intake. Finally, there are those diet "gurus" who approach all this from a religious point of view and seek to bring obese people to weight reduction by means of prayer.[46]

Wherever there is a need, fraud cannot be far behind. So it is with the diet industry. There are of course honest, reasonable, and reliable people associated with that industry. Nevertheless it is appropriate to call attention here to deception and fraud in the diet industry as it has been uncovered at congressional hearings, in the media, and by those seeking to escape the pain of obesity and the stigma it provokes.

In 1992 during the 102nd Congress, the Subcommittee on Regulation, Business Opportunities and Energy of the Committee on Small Business, etc. held hearings concerning fraud and deception in the diet industry.

Most of the hearings were used to allow representatives of the Federal Trade Commission (FTC) to advise Congress and hence the public to resist the practices of numerous enterprises that make unsubstantiated weight-loss claims. These claims receive a large audience. It is estimated that at least one-third of adult American women and nearly one-fourth of adult men are always trying to lose weight while 28 percent of both sexes try to maintain their weight.

To counter the fraudulent efforts of the weight-loss industry the Federal Trade Commission has used "consent agreements," court-ordered redress judgments and permanent injunctions to prevent profit seekers from selling deceptive products to the stigmatized. Included in the concerns of the Federal Trade Commission are safety claims which do not reflect the risks associated with the products or programs advocated. A second fraudulent effort made by diet and/or mechanical device sellers are claims that their product will lead to weight loss without exercise or reduction in calories. Testimonials concerning the results of using diets or mechanical devices may also be investigated by the Federal Trade Commission. These testimonials are often fraudulent or misleading. Furthermore, the FTC seeks to determine whether claims concerning weight maintenance made by manufacturers are true or fraudulent. We know that overweight people not only have to deal with the problem of obesity per se but must also struggle with remaining at a lesser weight once that has been attained. The truth is that dieters usually regain all of the weight they once lost within five years.[47]

One example of widespread fraud in the diet industry was the claim by Nu-Day that users of their diet program would lose weight without exercising. A consent agreement with the FTC led to the cessation of this claim. Telemarketing Industries was forced to sign a consent decree leading to the cessation of a Spanish-language advertisement on their part which claimed in Spanish that the user of their product would lose weight without reducing caloric intake or exercising. Then there was Slender You, Inc., which claimed that their exercise table would lead to weight loss without any effort on the part of the user. The Amerdream Corp. of Arizona was forced to pay $675,000 for consumer redress after the Federal Trade Commission found that they sold a product called Ultimate Solution with the false promise of a 100 percent money-back guarantee and a $1,000 Treasury Bond just for buying and testing a two-month supply.[48]

These efforts that take advantage of those stigmatized by obesity are not new. In 1910, so-called Professor Frank Kellogg sold Kellogg's Safe Fat Reducer by inserting an ad in the magazine *Woman Beautiful* which drew 135,000 replies despite the fact that it was worthless.[49]

Today, there are thousands of journal articles, books, and technical works published each year concerning obesity. There is even an *International Journal of Obesity,* the *International Journal of Eating Disorders, Appetite,* and others all designed to deal with the stigma of fat on the human body. Innumerable low-fat diet cookbooks are also very popular as are "dieter's specials" on restaurant menus. There are also organizations such as Weightwatchers of America and Overeaters Anonymous. There is also Thin Forever, an organization that uses "rap sessions" and assertiveness training to deal with obesity. One advertiser even claimed that his product would "melt the fat off your body—like a blow torch would melt butter."

Evidently, then, the stigma of overweight is being exploited by those who see a profit in the discomfort of others. We see therefore that the obese among us must not only deal with the rejection that the very word "stigma" implies, but must also be on their guard against exploitation related to their desperate efforts to lose weight. The obese are the willing victims of charlatans selling miracle cures, "cranky" diets, pills, potions, and quick fixes. Once more we underscore that many of these methods do indeed lead to weight reduction but that none of these methods lead to permanent weight loss. Almost always, the overweight returns because the obese, like all of us, must eat. Therefore, the ultimate responsibility for weight loss lies with the individual. Unlike other conditions which may be entirely curable by a health professional, the maintenance of normal weight can only be achieved by each person who needs no doctor to tell him what he already knows and what the world has been "rubbing in" for years.

Furthermore, it is most unlikely that a doctor would know anything about weight loss that the patient doesn't know himself. In addition, a good number of doctors are overweight themselves and are evidently as unable to cope with their problem as the patients who come to them for advice.[50]

COPING WITH STIGMA

We have seen that those who are stigmatized by obesity feel that stigmatization affects every aspect of their lives. Obese people cope with job discrimination, social exclusion, public ridicule, trouble finding clothing, mistreatment by doctors, and even denial of health benefits. There is therefore an organization called the National Association of Fat Acceptance. Their purpose is explained in their name. A survey of 445 of their members found that 98 percent reported verbal harassment from family, friends, and even health professionals. On the job, 75 percent reported teasing by supervisors and fellow workers, and one-half reported that they had been refused jobs because of size discrimination. Similar reports are made all the time by obese people involved in other studies.

Therefore it is important to discuss briefly some coping mechanisms used by the victims of size discrimination and stigmatization. The first and most common method used by the obese to deal with the stigma attached to their size is to make positive self-statements intended to "head-off" negative remarks, such as the "Wake up. I'm fat" comment used by actress Camryn Mannheim. Another method used by the obese, and for that matter all who are stigmatized, is to use faith, religion, and prayer for self-consolation. This method was of course used for many centuries by the Jews of Europe who succeeded in surviving nearly two thousand years of persecution based on the grossest of stigmatization by "living" in the unseen world of supernatural ideology.

There are a few other methods used by the obese to deal with their stigmatization. These methods are employed infrequently because they are difficult to use. One such method would be to educate people about the nature of obesity and the stigma that surrounds it. Sometimes becoming rude and insulting toward the stigmatizer is a defensive reaction. Physical violence has been resorted to as well, but it is rare. Finally, there are those who seek psychiatric treatment to deal with the pain they experience.[51]

Sondra Solovay has written the only book which deals with the legal aspects of weight discrimination. *Tipping the Scales of Justice: Fighting Weight-Based Discrimination*[52] describes the pain suffered by the overweight in our society every day. To remedy this and to cope with this discrimination Solovay seeks to use the antidiscrimination laws of this country which, she says, rest on three premises: (1) it is wrong to discriminate against a person for a characteristic they cannot control; (2)

capable people should not be prevented from contributing to the economy and society; and (3) it is "wrong to discriminate when the result is an impingement on fundamental rights, freedoms, and human dignity."

Solovay shows that even children are affected by our fat-hating society so that a study of San Francisco children showed that one-half of nine-year-old girls are already dieting.

"It is possible," says Solovay, "to participate in virtually any form of mainstream culture for a twenty-four-hour period and not find several examples of fat prejudice."

To cope with this injustice Solovay lists several resources such as the National Association to Advance Fat Acceptance. However, as a lawyer, Solovay refers to a number of statutes which she believes can be invoked on behalf of fat people who have suffered discrimination. Included are the Americans with Disabilities Act and a number of local statutes.

The methods used by the obese to live with the bigotry they encounter everywhere are not unique. Of course, the obese and the public generally believe that the fat have only themselves to blame. Yet, we have seen that the causes of obesity are such that they cannot be exclusively attributed to the willful overeating of the overweight population. There are, however, a good number of Americans who are the victims of stigmatization entirely because of their condition, which they cannot help or influence in any fashion. These are the mentally retarded, whose situation we shall examine in the next chapter.

SUMMARY

The obese population of America is indeed stigmatized in many ways. They are the butt of daily harassment, including unwarranted remarks, jokes, insults, and even assault. The obese are also handicapped by the limited choices available in clothing, and the difficulties encountered with furniture and travel conveyances. There are cultural differences concerning the perception of overweight by black or white Americans and between urban and rural people.

Among whites, the marriage market stigmatizes women considerably so that fat women are generally poorer than slim women because the overweight are forced to marry poorer men. There are also numerous psychological consequences associated with the stigma of overweight.

Overweight people have developed several strategies for coping with their stigmatized existence which includes dieting and exercise. Because most methods seldom succeed in keeping weight down, fat people must use stratagems that defend their situation in face of a great deal of hostility. This is also true for those who are mentally retarded, a phrase now changed to "developmentally handicapped." Therefore, mental retardation is the subject of our next chapter.

NOTES

1. William Shakespeare, *Julius Caesar* 1.2.191.
2. Camryn Mannheim, *Wake Up! I'm Fat* (New York: Soundelux Cassette, 1999).
3. Charlotte Cooper, *Fat and Proud: The Politics of Size* (London: Women's Press, 1998), pp. 18–20.
4. Dawn Zdrodowski, "Eating Out: The Experience of Eating in Public for the Overweight Woman," *Women's Studies International Forum* 19, no. 6 (November–December 1996): 665–64.
5. Esther Rothblum, "The Stigma of Women's Weight: Social and Economic Realities," *Feminism and Psychology* 2, no. 1 (1992): 61–73.
6. Erving Goffman, *Stigma: Notes on the Management of Spoiled Identity* (Englewood Cliffs, N.J.: Prentice-Hall, 1963), pp. 41–43.
7. Ibid., p. 26.
8. United States Public Health Service, *1988 Surgeon General's Report on Nutrition and Health* (Washington, D.C.: U.S. Department of Health and Human Services, 1988), p. 242.
9. David Wagner, *Checkerboard Square: Culture and Resistance in a Homeless Community* (Boulder, Colo.:Westview Press, 1993).
10. U.S. Department of Health and Human Services, National Center for Health Statistics, *DHHS Publication No. PHS 85-1232* (Washington, D.C., 1985).
11. Robert Pingitore et al., "Bias Against Overweight Job Applicants in a Simulated Employment Interview," *Journal of Applied Psychology* 79 (1994): 909–17.
12. Charles Crandall and Robert Martinez, "Culture, Ideology and Anti-fat Attitudes," *Personality and Social-Psychology Bulletin* 22 (1996): 227–43.
13. M. E. Collins, "Body Figure Perceptions and Preferences among Pre-adolescent Children," *International Journal of Eating Disorders* 10 (1991): 199–208.
14. Daniel A. Dawson, "Ethnic Differences in Female Overweight: Data from the National Health Interview Survery," *American Journal of Public Health* 78 (1988): 1326–29.
15. Albert Frisancho, William Leonard, and L. Bollenteno, "Blood Pressure in Blacks and Whites and Its Relationship to Dietary Sodium and Potassium Intake," *Journal of Chronic Diseases* 37 (1984): 515.
16. Cooper, *Fat and Proud*, p. 28.
17. Michael Cunningham et al., "Consistency and Variability in the Cross-cultural Perception of Female Physical Attractiveness," *Journal of Personality and Social Psychology* 68 (1995): 261–79.
18. Kristin Flynn and Marian Fitzgibbon, "Body Image Ideals of Low-Income African-American Mothers and Their Preadolescent Daughters," *Journal of Youth and Adolescence* 25, no. 5 (October 1996): 615–51.

19. Jeffrey Sobal, Richard T. Tropiano, and Edward A. Frongillo Jr., "Rural-Urban Differences in Obesity," *Rural Sociology* 61, no. 2 (summer 1996): 289–305.

20. Bureau of the Census, *1990 Census of Population: Social and Economic Characteristics* (Washington, D.C.: U.S. Government Printing Office, 1990).

21. Albert Fallon, "Culture in the Mirror: Socio-cultural Determinants of Body Image," in T. F. Cash and Ted Pruzinsky, *Body Images: Development, Deviance and Change* (New York: Guilford Press, 1990), pp. 60–109.

22. S. Averett and S. Korenman, "Black-White Differences in Social and Economic Consequences of Obesity," *International Journal of Obesity* 23 (February 1999): 173.

23. John Sobal, Victor Nicolopoulos, and J. Lee, "Attitudes about Weight and Dating among Secondary School Students," *International Journal of Obesity* 19 (1995): 376–81.

24. Jeffrey Sobal, Barbara S. Rauschenbach, and Edward A. Frongillo Jr., "Marital Status, Fatness and Obesity," *Social Science and Medicine* 35, no. 7 (October 1992): 915–23.

25. Norman Goodman, Sanford Dornbusch, and Stephen A. Richardson, "Variant Reactions to Physical Disabilities," *American Sociological Review* 28 (1963): 429.

26. John W. Wright, ed., *The New York Times Almanac* (New York: Penguin Putnam, 1998), p. 282.

27. L. B. Gerald et al.,"Social Class, Social Support and Obesity Risk in Children," *Child Care, Health and Development* 20, no. 3 (May–June 1993): 145–63.

28. Jennifer A. O'Day and Susan Abraham, "Association between Self Concept and Body Weight," *Adolescence* 34, no. 133 (Spring 1999): 69.

29. Mary E. Pritchard, Sondra L. King, and Dorice M. Czajka-Narins, "Adolescent Body Mass Indices and Self-Perception," *Adolescence* 32, no. 128 (winter 1997): 863–80.

30. B. K. Mendelson and D. R. White, "Development of Self-body-esteem in Overweight Youngsters," *Developmental Psychology* 21 (1985): 90–96.

31. H. J. Kaplan, "The Psychosomatic Concept of Obesity," *Journal of Mental Disorders* 125 (1957): 181.

32. Susie Orbach, *Fat Is a Feminist Issue* (New York: Berkley Publishing Group, 1988), p. 5.

33. "A Weighty Problem," *American Institute for Cancer Research Science News* 11 (March 1999).

34. Orbach, "Fat Is a Feminist Issue," p. 6.

35. Chares H. Cooley, *Human Nature and the Social Order* (New York: Schocken Books, 1964).

36. Catherine E. Ross, "Overweight and Depression," *Journal of Health and Social Behavior* 35, no. 1 (March 1994): 63–78.

37. Gerhard Falk, *Hippocrates Assailed: The American Health Delivery System* (Lanham, Md. and New York: University Press of America, 1999), chap. 10.

38. Bess H. Marcus et al., "Self-efficacy, Decision Making and Stages of Change: An Integrative Model of Physical Exerise," *Journal of Applied Social Psychology* 24, no. 6 (March 1994): 489.

39. Stuart Biddle, "Exercise and Psychosocial Health," *Research Quarterly for Exercise and Health* 66, no. 4 (1995): 292–97.

40. Mark Nichols, "The Obesity Epidemic," *Maclean's* 112, no. 2 (January 11, 1999): 55.

41. J. E. Manson et al., "Body Weight and Longevity," *Journal of the American Medical Association* 257 (1987): 353–58.

42. Interview with Shauna Stisser, Exercise Science Specialist, Buffalo Jewish Community Center, July 20, 1990.

43. Nichols, "The Obesity Epidemic," p. 58.

44. Barbara Wickens, "Extreme Acts: Drastic Shortcuts to Slimness Carry Their Own Risks," *Maclean's* 112, no. 2 (January 11, 1999): 60–61.

45. Ibid.

46. Robert Atkins, *Dr. Atkins' New Diet Revolution* (New York: Avon Books, 1997); Dean Ornish, *Stress, Diet and Your Heart* (New York: Holt, Rinehart and Winston, 1982).

47. Darla Danforth, "Statement Before the House Committee on Small Business Subcommittee on Regulation, Business Opportunities and Energy" (May 21, 1992). Danforth was the director of the Division of Nutrition Research Coordination of the National Institutes of Health at the time of her testimony.

48. Ibid., supplemental attachments from *FTC News* on several dates.

49. Hillel Schwartz, *Never Satisfied* (New York: Free Press, 1986), p. 238.

50. Elizabeth Evans, "Why Should Obesity Be Managed?" *International Journal of Obesity* 23, no. 4 (May 1999): 53–55.

51. James Rosen, "Obesity Stigmatization and Coping," *International Journal of Obesity* 23 (March 1999): 221–30.

52. Sondra Solovay, *Tipping the Scales of Justice: Fighting Weight-based Discrimination* (Amherst, N.Y.: Prometheus Books, 2000).

THE MENTALLY RETARDED OR DEVELOPMENTALLY HANDICAPPED 5

LIVING WITH STIGMA

FEEBLEMINDED, MORON, AND OTHER LABELS

"**A** man was driving through the grounds of a mental hospital when one of the tires on his car had a flat. The driver removed the hubcap from the affected wheel, took off the lug nuts, and placed them in the hubcap. He then took the spare wheel and tire out of his trunk in the hope of securing the spare wheel where it was needed. In the course of working he kicked the hubcap and all the lug nuts fell into a drainage hole. The driver was desperate. He now could not secure the spare wheel and tire. As he stood there worrying, an inmate from the mental hospital walked by. Seeing the driver's dilemma he said: 'I see you can't secure that wheel because you lost the lug nuts. So take one lug nut from each of the other wheels and drive to the nearest garage with the lug nuts you now have left on each wheel.' The driver was elated and said to the mental patient: 'I am astonished that you understood the solution to my problem right away. I thought you were crazy.' 'I *am* crazy,' said the mental patient, 'but, I'm not stupid.'"

This story illustrates the common misconception that there is no difference between mental retardation and mental illness. Yet, the difference is profound because the mentally ill can recover and often do recover. Mental retardation, however, does not permit the assumption of a "normal" intelligence but is a permanent attribute of some Americans who must live with that stigma as long as others care to maintain it.

From the view of the mentally retarded, "two worlds exist. The mentally retarded world and the normal world." This does not mean that there is a physical separation between these two "worlds." As psychologist James Dudley shows, the retarded do indeed have complete access to all the facilities and events involving normal people. This is so because the vast majority of the mentally retarded exhibit no obvious impairments.[1]

There are, however, some retarded people who have physical handicaps that are visible. These may include speech impairments, physical deformities, and uncontrollable body movements such as "rocking." Such body motions are deemed "stereotypic" by investigators and are common among individuals diagnosed with mental retardation. A definition of "stereotype" is that it is performed repetitively, with little variation, and without apparent purpose. Another definition of "stereotype" is "a coordinated repetitive rhythmic and patterned movement, posture, or vocalization that is carried out virtually the same way during each repetition." In addition to "rocking," other "stereotypes" associated with the mentally retarded are hand-waving, head-banging, facial-grimacing, and tongue-thrusting. Body-rocking is the most common of these visible traits.[2]

Some of the mentally retarded also conduct themselves in a manner that may be annoying to others. For example, they may intrude themselves into the "private sphere" of others with uninvited physical contact or conversation. Furthermore, most mentally retarded people have no access to sex and almost all of them have never had sexual intercourse because they are rejected by normal members of the opposite sex.

It is generally agreed by professional observers that despite these difficulties the greatest problem faced by the mentally handicapped is the stigma associated with their deficiency. We have already defined a stigma as a "negative social meaning" and can therefore recognize that the mere appearance of the mentally handicapped can lead to rejection in a society like ours, which values good looks and intelligence.

All stigma and all beliefs are subject to circular reaction. This concept refers to the evidence that those who are accosted in a negative manner assume that they are somehow at fault so that they become "stigma carriers." As such they behave in a fashion that reflects their beliefs about themselves. They are caught in the cycle of rejection. They experience rejection all the time. Then they also anticipate rejection, which leads to behavior inviting further rejection. In short, the mentally retarded are fully aware of the negative interpretation given their handicap in American society and therefore actually look for evidence that they will be rejected and that their suspicions are justified.[3]

From the beginning of the twentieth century to about 1930, retarded people were called "feebleminded" by the medical profession and everyone else. This led the developmentally handicapped, or retarded, to feel that they belong to a different category of humanity than the normal majority who impose the stigma of abnormality upon them. In fact, the use of the term "feebleminded" was associated with the belief that the "feebleminded" are a threat to society and that the "feeble-minded" deserve to be treated with indignities of various kinds. Like an enemy in war, the "feebleminded" were dehumanized during the first part of the twentieth century. This dehumanization was achieved by the use of the "organic metaphor," which has been in use since the days of Plato and became a principal argument used by English sociologist Herbert Spencer in promoting social Darwinism in the early years of the twentieth century. Spencer was widely read and cited. He taught that the social system was a living organism in a very real sense. Therefore it became popular to argue that it is possible for the unhealthy segments of society to contaminate the healthy segment of society. If society is to survive it must either remove the contamination or adapt to it. The language used in this connection is that of immunology to the effect that "foreign" elements must be rejected from the "healthy body" of society. Such views were of course the foundation of the eugenics movement in this country and involved the belief that "undesirables" should be prevented from "breeding." The most extreme eugenic views of the 1930s were held by the Nazi theorists in Europe. However, even in this country such views were popular with an emphasis on the "danger" that morons constituted. In 1927 the U.S. Supreme Court decided in *Buck* v. *Bell* (274 U.S. 200) to uphold the enforced sterilization of poor black women. Justice Oliver Wendell Holmes wrote in that decision that "three generations of imbeciles are enough."

The stigmatized label "moron" was attached to those "feebleminded" with the highest intelligence among all the feebleminded. They were believed to pose the greatest threat to society because they could "pass as normal and were therefore not subject to the measures of social control such as sterilization." It was then also believed that feebleminded-ness was hereditary. Therefore the children of the feebleminded were expected to be feebleminded as well.[4]

In light of all this, sexual expression in retarded individuals was viewed with great misgivings early in the twentieth century. It was feared that retarded adults would have very large families and that this would have the effect of depressing the average level of intelligence in the general population. This fear led to the passage of laws in many states pertaining to marriage of the retarded and to sterilization. These fears gradually abated. Nevertheless sterilization continued until the 1950s. Prior to the 1950s sterilization had usually been a prerequisite before an institutionalized retarded person was allowed to return to the community. After 1950 these compulsory sterilization procedures gave way to voluntary procedures or to judicial approval when the individual was not capable of giving his consent.[5]

Yet, the stigma attached to the sexuality of the retarded continues to be a problem for the retarded today. This is in part true because sex is generally stigmatized in our puritanical community. Among the retarded this unspoken prohibition is even greater than among normal people. When, prior to 1980, most retarded were institutionalized, sex was seldom an issue because institutions are usually segregated by gender. After 1980 many retarded were released from institutions so that their sexual needs became visible at home and in the community. This aroused a good deal of hostility among those who saw the retarded engage in quasi-sexual activities such as holding hands or merely walking together. Evidently, the stigma of mental retardation is particularly strong in connection with any attempt by the retarded to show an interest in the opposite sex. This phenomenon is also observable when old people exhibit any sexual interest. It is popular to believe that sex is only for the young and good-looking and never for anyone without either of these attributes. In any case, before the 1950s "feeblemindedness" was thought to be dangerous and needed to be curbed by placing sexual restrictions on those who suffered from it.[6]

In her important book *White Trash* geneticist Nicole H. Rafter shows that those who believed in the foregoing "causes" of "feeblemindedness" also thought that the "feebleminded" would hardly notice that they were being treated inhumanely or that they were the victims of such harsh stigmas. The "feebleminded" were compared to a disease so that one author wrote: "It would by no means be a misnomer to call the American Eugenics Society a Society for the Control of Social Cancer."[7]

Additional beliefs concerning mental retardation were that the "feebleminded" suffer from too much "bad" blood and that such "bad blood" can destroy "good blood" if not held in check. There was also talk about "defective germ plasm," "decadent stock," and the "contamination of sound strains." All this was given the cloak of legitimacy when the Supreme Court ruled in the *Buck* v. *Bell* decision of 1927 that sterilization was a rightful and constitutionally permitted procedure similar to vaccination. That decision was in part related to the view that crime and delinquency keep on increasing because new defectives are born and the additional opinion that "we have become so used to crime, disease, and degeneracy that we take them as necessary evils." In 1938 hysteria concerning all of this led to the formation of the National Society for the Legalization of Euthanasia (a Greek term meaning *good death*) whose goal was "to allow incurable sufferers to choose immediate death rather than await it in agony."[8] They evidently believed that mental defectives would die of this condition. William McDougall, Henry Goddard, and Leon Whitney, all famous writers and scholars, were on the board of directors of the society.

Although such extreme statements and beliefs are not commonly held today, the mentally retarded continue to be the targets of injustices promoted by the criminal justice system. The retarded become ready victims of such injustices when a particularly brutal crime is committed and the police feel pressured to find the offender quickly. Such pressure, mainly generated by the media, lead the police to seize upon anyone who is viewed as "peculiar" or "abnormal." That almost always includes the mentally retarded, who can easily be persuaded to waive their right to remain silent, who do not request a lawyer, and who are likely to sign any confession placed before them. Few juries would fail to convict someone who has confessed because juries, drawn from the average American population, cannot believe that anyone would confess to a crime he or she did not commit. The police know better, of course, and therefore some unscrupulous officers and prosecutors like to "railroad" mentally retarded people into the electric chair or prison because in many instances that is far easier to accomplish than to find someone who does not want to be found.

The mentally retarded and others who have been institutionalized are taught to trust authority figures such as parents, teachers, and the police. This kind of behavior modification is called "learned helplessness" in which compliance with authority becomes "second nature." The mentally retarded are either unaware of their rights or do not have the inner strength to stand up for their rights. The mentally retarded and those with brain injuries are generally isolated. They bear the brunt of jokes and are called "morons" and "retards," leaving them vulnerable to anyone pretending to be their friends. This permits criminals to have a mentally retarded person take the blame for their criminal deeds. It also allows the police to exploit the mentally retarded. Furthermore, the mentally retarded usually go to great lengths to "cover up" their disability to avoid the stigma attached.

Therefore, numerous retarded people have been convicted of "capital" crimes to which they had no connection or while they were under the influence of a career criminal who used them to gain his objectives.[9]

STIGMA AND SOCIAL ISOLATION

The very label *mentally retarded* is evidently viewed with great anxiety by those who are so designated. Therefore, *slow learner* is far more acceptable to them because a slow learner need not necessarily suffer from mental retardation. It is therefore of great importance to recognize that mental retardation is stratified in that some who are mildly retarded will resemble normal people a great deal more than other retarded people. Those who are severely handicapped are those whose intelligence does not lend itself to achieving nearly as many tasks as is true of those who are suffering from only a minimum of retardation. The labeling issue needs to be clarified by dealing with two questions. The first is, whether or not to label people with mental retardation and the second is exactly which label to use. It is of course well known that labels have deleterious effects on the persons so labeled if the label involves unpopular attributes such as "schizophrenic" or "retard." This is illustrated by the study made by sociologist Daniel Rosenhahn called "On Being Sane in Insane Places." Rosenhahn and other volunteers succeeded in getting themselves admitted to psychiatric hospitals by complaining of "hearing voices." This was not the case. Despite the fact that these volunteers neither displayed nor complained of any such symptoms after their admission the participants were not discharged for some time and even then were labeled "schizophrenic in remission" by the professional staff in those hospitals.[10]

The question as to which label to use has never been resolved. In earlier years the word *idiot* was used. This is derived from the Latin word *idios* meaning "peculiar." That was then followed by *imbecile,* meaning "without support" and "mentally deficient" followed by "mentally retarded." This illustrates that the current effort to use "developmentally handicapped" will probably solve nothing since the term will either not be accepted or come to have the same negative connotation that all the other words have had in the past. The only term that has so far not been devalued has been the word "exceptional." It is of course true that retarded persons are exceptional. The connotation of the word is, however, that the exceptional person is superior. For that reason "exceptional" can still be used although it can be foreseen that any close association between "exceptional" and mental retardation will have the same consequences as all other label changes.

There has been some research showing that people who have been primed with descriptions of people with positive connotations led to later judgment of those people being significantly more positive. The research concerning this is quite old and should be duplicated at the beginning of the present century.[11]

James Dudley has listed a number of experiences common to almost all who suffer from retardation. These experiences lie at the heart of the stigma issue and consist of such events as having to listen to an announcement that: "Here comes a retardate" or "You look like a truck rolled over you" or being told "You are stupid." Childlike treatment, denying a retarded person the right to present his views, ignoring the retarded person, staring, and even open ridicule are all part of the daily experiences of the retarded.[12]

The outcome of this kind of treatment is social isolation. This has become particularly acute during the decades since 1963 when many institutions for the retarded were closed and their inhabitants began to appear in public in greater numbers than ever before.[13]

Because the mentally retarded are aware of their stigmatization they, like so many other stigmatized people, derogate each other in order to minimize their fragile sense of self-acceptance. Sociologist Erving Goffman has shown that *stigma* is the difference between one's actual and virtual identity. This means the difference between how one actually is and how one is expected to be. Among others who are the victims of stigma such a difference is generally considerable, for example, the old. As we shall see in chapter 6, the old are very much stigmatized in this country. It is commonly believed that the old are asexual, demented, and cantankerous. Yet, the facts concerning the old do not coincide with these beliefs as research has shown.[14]

Retarded persons, however, are indeed not as competent as normal people. The differences between belief and reality are smaller than is the case with the old or other stigmatized people. Therefore, neither ignoring the stigma nor attempting to "pass" will help the retarded. "Passing" is of course also quite difficult. This can be attested to by Jews who seek to "pass" as non-Jews but who suffer a great deal of guilt concerning their erstwhile affiliation. A far better option for someone stigmatized for any reason is to acknowledge and "own" the stigma. This is achieved by developing a strong group identity as has been done by blacks who use the rallying cry "Black is beautiful!" and by some homosexuals who have used the phrase "It is great to be gay!"[15]

MENTAL RETARDATION AND THE SCHOOLS

Another way in which stigmatized people, including the mentally retarded, can face the stigma associated with their condition is to use the *loss paradigm* as developed by Dr. Elizabeth Kübler-Ross in connection with death and dying. Kübler-Ross claims that those of us who know we are dying need to pass through several stages of emotion before we can accept our own death. She designates these emotions as shock, denial, anger, sadness, and acceptance. If this is so and it can help the dying then it should also help parents who must suddenly deal with the birth of a retarded child. This feeling of shock is particularly devastating if the retardation is severe such as in the case of Down's syndrome, usually caused by the presence of an extra chromosome resulting in the child having an abnormally small head and a flat face exhibiting a "Mongolian slant." There are numerous other symptoms including a protruding tongue, heart problems, and failure to reach adult height and the maximum attainment of a mental age of eight.[16]

Because Down's syndrome is so visible and causes the Down's patient to deviate dramatically from normal individuals, the impact of stigma is greater among the retarded with Down's syndrome than with others. Usually, as we have already seen, stigma attaches to persons who fail to meet the expectations of the group among whom they live. Avoidance is of course one of the most common reactions to stigmatized persons and particularly those who are physically different from the expected average. Every society makes two decisions concerning stigma. The first is to designate what kind of deviance shall be stigmatized. The second societal decision deals with the manner in which members of that society may react toward the stigmatized, be they religious minorities, street people, or the mentally retarded. Added to the inducement afforded all of us by our community to avoid those who are different, there is additional inducement to avoid a retarded person with Down's syndrome because major physical disabilities remind all of us of our own mortality and the possibility that we may get sick. Hence the handicapped are often treated as if they were not quite human.

In every culture, the American culture included, people learn how to respond to individuals with disabilities by watching and listening to others in their social group. These responses often include the termination of social relations. Family members are of course also subjected to the same negative social responses as the handicapped persons. Such negative responses are elicited from professionals as well as lay observers. As one doctor said regarding the retarded: "I don't really enjoy a really handicapped child who comes in drooling, can't walk, and so forth . . . . Medicine is geared to the perfect human body. Something you can't do anything about challenges the doctor and reminds him of his own disabilities."[17]

Despite the evidence that stigma attaches to families who harbor a retarded child, Mary E. Hannah and Elizabeth Midlarsky report "that being in a family that also has a child with mental retardation does not lead to a greater degree of mental distress or pathology than is found in families without a child who has mental retardation." The same researchers found that the brothers and sisters of mentally retarded children are no less happy than siblings of normal children and that their self-esteem is not affected by the disability of their brothers and sisters. It is important to mention here that the study by Hannah and Midlarsky was conducted with families who *volunteered* for the research. It is therefore not unreasonable to assume that those who do have difficulty living with a retarded family member are less likely to volunteer for a research project than those who have no such difficulties.[18]

Social theorist George Herbert Mead wrote that all of us are subject to meanings and expectations taught by the society in which we live and that we learn the meaning of events in our lives through symbolic interaction with others. Therefore, during the prenatal period parents construct an image of their infant. The mental image thus constructed is produced through interaction with friends, coworkers, and family and is reflective of self and significant others. Since our society values health, beauty, and wholeness, an infant born with Down's syndrome will be viewed as deviating immensely from the fantasy infant thus constructed. To reemphasize this issue we may say that mental images or expectations regarding the birth experience are *socially constructed during the prenatal period.* The media also portray birth as a beautiful and exciting experience. Perfect and gorgeous babies are portrayed in the advertisements sent to prospective parents and childbirth classes prepare parents for the "happy event" when they will receive a perfectly formed infant. Therefore, the birth of a child with Down's syndrome symbolizes shattered dreams regarding the child and the future of the family.[19]

Parents who are confronted with the news that their child has Down's syndrome are often disappointed and feel inadequate. Here are two comments made by parents of such children. One mother wrote: "When we received the news that she had Down's syndrome, it was as if the child of our dreams had died." Another mother wrote: "When he [her husband] finally broke it to me, I felt the whole world crumbling in around me. All my dreams for my little girl were shattered in that very instant. My husband and I held each other and cried."[20]

Initially, then, many parents of retarded children view this as a tragedy. Yet, numerous parents also report that as they become more acquainted with their child and get to know the child as a person first and disabled second, they can learn to redefine their situation and accept the condition of the child.

Likewise, the retarded person must also learn to accept his or her condition and go through the stages outlined by Kübler-Ross. Whether the retarded use one or both of these methods, benefits result from either method. Consciousness raising by using a group identity has the advantage of talking openly about the stigma, in this case mental deficiency. This permits the affected persons to shift the "blame" to others. The second method, the *loss paradigm,* allows the retarded person to accept his condition and drop his defensive behavior.[21]

It is also evident that any group of like-minded people, stigmatized or not, lends support to its members and improves the status of the "in-group" vis-à-vis the "out-group." An "in-group" is a sociological term referring to a social group "commanding a member's esteem and loyalty." Such a group is even more important among retarded and other stigmatized people as the "in-group" permits stigmatized retarded persons to achieve more positive self-acceptance than would be possible alone and without group support.[22]

The fact is that group support or the lack of it is positively related to psychopathology among all of us. For those with mental retardation, however, social support is of even greater importance than it is for normal people. Since social support is more often lacking among those with mental retardation, it is to be expected that psychopathology is also more common among the retarded than among normals. Social interaction is of course not always positive. Negative or stressful interaction is quite common. However, normal persons can easily minimize stressful interactions by avoiding such contacts in favor of persons who do not cause them stress. People with mental retardation are less capable of avoiding social strain. This is so because mentally retarded persons lack the social skills of normal people and are not usually capable of articulating that they wish to be left alone. This issue has been investigated by psychiatrists Yona Lunsky and Susan Havercamp who found that those among the retarded who suffered a good deal of "social strain" were also more likely to be diagnosed as suffering from psychopathology. It is of course unclear whether social strain is a direct cause or effect of psychopathology. In any case the retarded depend largely on the social support they gain from each other.[23]

It is therefore of interest to know how the retarded view others who are also retarded since that group is their chief support in a rejecting world and because the view the retarded have of others with the same affliction tells us a good deal about the self-image of the retarded. Frederick Gibbons, professor of psychology at Iowa State University, conducted two studies to determine the opinions retarded persons have of each other. He found that the retarded see other retarded persons as less socially desirable and less physically attractive than nonretarded persons. Further analysis led Gibbons to the conclusion that the retarded have fairly pessimistic opinions of their chances for success at social behavior. This belief is sufficient to limit the social behavior of the retarded even if the retardation is too mild to be understood by the average person.[24]

Sociologists have known for some time that stigmatized persons engage in downward comparisons with other stigmatized persons because it helps them feel better about their own situation. This phenomenon is seen among the retarded as well. Hence, retarded persons with higher intelligence like to "self-aggrandize" by comparing themselves with retarded people of lesser intelligence.[25]

Now, stigma is not confined to those who exhibit the deviance that provokes it. Instead, those associated with a deviant person, such as the parents of the mentally retarded, are also stigmatized by the fate of their child. Therefore the American Association of Mental Retardation receives numerous letters and other communications from parents who are distressed about the pejorative connotation of the phrase *mental retardation*. Both those labeled "mentally retarded" and their relatives have for years demanded that this terminology be eliminated from the language. This has led some professionals to diagnose the same condition as *mental deficiency*. The outcome of that effort has not been satisfactory for those affected because the word "retarded" has not been abandoned, and because "deficiency" is as much despised by those affected as is "retarded." If the term "deficient" is used long enough it will have the same meaning as "retarded" does now.

"Retarded" is a label so very much despised because our culture places so much emphasis on "intelligence" by giving children "intelligence" tests on numerous occasions during their school career. We can even take an intelligence test on the Internet and in popular magazines. Those who read and deal with this concept are seldom aware that intelligence tests are dubious instruments that may or may not measure innate ability. Instead, public opinion admires the "intelligent" person and therefore holds so-called retards in contempt.[26]

It is of course through the schools that almost all retarded people learn their status. This does not mean that parents and their children do not know that a child may be retarded even before coming to school. It is, however, the school that finally creates the label "retarded" because the school permits comparison of children with one another. Furthermore, America's schools are based on competition. Evidently, then, a child who is a permanent loser in the competitive world of American education will soon acquire the label associated with mental retardation whether or not that or some other phrase is finally used. It makes no difference to the target of the label which label is used. Learning disabilities can be caused by many things other than retardation.

Psychologist Jane R. Mercer has isolated six stages in the labeling process which permits schools to place various labels on children who are enrolled. Mercer writes: "The first step in becoming retarded in the public schools is to enroll in the public school system. . . ." This may seem a strange conclusion if we hold that mental retardation is an innate condition. However, we have already seen that low intelligence is not the only aspect of mental retardation. The reaction of others to the revelation that someone is of low intelligence and hence a "retard" is the other part of the interactive situation that produces the status of retardation. Therefore, where the stigma is absent because the mental deficiency is not known, retardation does not result. Mercer and associates studied children who attended the public schools and others who attended private schools in a medium-sized American city. She found that because public schoolchildren come significantly more from lower-status homes than is true of private schools, religion controlled or not, the chances of being labeled "retarded" are far greater among those who attend public schools than those who attend private schools. Mercer wrote: "Children attending Catholic schools (and other private schools) incurred relatively little risk of being labeled as mental retardates unless they were visibly and severely deviant." Mercer further found that children in private schools are more likely than public schoolchildren to come from higher-status Anglo-European families. Therefore, the first stage in being labeled mentally retarded is usually the decision of parents to enroll a child in a public school and not in a private school. The second stage in attaining the status of "retarded" is the decision of a classroom teacher to send a child for psychological evaluation by a school psychologist. Our schools are competitive. Therefore it is one of the functions of a classroom teacher to distribute rewards and punishments in the classroom. Hence, every class is divided by the teacher into "excellent readers" or "average readers" or "slow readers." Others are called "the fast group in mathematics" or the "slow group in history." Yet, all of the children in any of these groups are considered "normal," including the child who "flunks." Those, however, who cannot learn anything or who conduct themselves in a bizarre fashion in the classroom will be placed in a "special education" class and then descend to the status of "retarded." Therefore the third stage in achieving the status of "retarded" after failing the role expectations of the teacher is to be retained for a grade. Mercer reports that holding a "retained student" status is the first step on the path to retardation in the public schools. Furthermore she observed that "children who are held back have the distinctive social characteristics that are very similar to the characteristics of children who are eventually labeled retarded and placed in special classes."[27]

Referral by the principal is the fourth stage on the road to mental retardation. Principals have a considerable amount of choice in either giving a child a so-called social promotion on the grounds he is a "late bloomer" or sending him for psychological testing and evaluation. Since large schools usually have as many days of psychological services available to them as smaller schools, referrals in larger schools are less likely than in smaller schools which seek to fill up the time of the psychologists sent them by referring as many children as possible. Therefore, the size of a school impacts on the chances of becoming "mentally retarded." Stage five in that process begins when the psychological testing and evaluation procedure leads to the conclusion that a child has failed the tests. Having already been selected for such a test and then failing it leads to placement in a special-education class and therefore to the establishment of an IQ score. If that score is quite low, for example, 67, then the label of "retarded" is almost sure to follow. It is significant in this connection that Mercer found that children from low-status homes run twice the risk of being labeled mentally retarded as do children from higher-status homes.[28]

THE THREE DIMENSIONS OF LEARNING DISABILITY

We have repeatedly shown that the burdens of impairment itself are aggravated by the negative perceptions added to that burden by the stigma associated with these impairments. This means that the impaired are double burdened. Acknowledging then that mental impairment is a disability we find that mental impairment affects every aspect of daily life. Professionals have labeled these activities ADLs or "Activities of Daily Living" such as washing, shaving, dressing, cooking, and using public transportation. Inability to perform even these tasks makes some retarded persons trainable but not educable. Yet, those who can learn but have an IQ in the vicinity of 70 find that even in its mildest forms mental disability seriously impedes school and economic achievements.

In the past, when unskilled labor was still needed, it was often possible for people with limited intelligence to earn their living though unskilled work and thereby escape the stigma of "retarded," particularly since those whose disability is minimal do not give a "retarded" impression to "normal" people. However, with the advent of the postindustrial, technological society which all of us must now learn to face, the skills needed for occupational effectiveness are not available to the slow learner or mentally disabled person or retarded individual. We use all of these terms to show that the label may change, but the condition continues to impair its sufferers no matter the label used. Schools have now begun to use the term "learning disability" for all children whose IQ is above the 60s while retaining "mentally retarded" for those whose IQ is below 65.

As a consequence the number of children served by school systems under the label "mentally retarded" has decreased by 38 percent between 1977 and 1996 while there has been a fourfold increase in the number of children designated by schools as suffering from "learning disability."

Learning disability has three dimensions: the social, the practical, and the conceptual. In the area of the social and the practical, the retarded person will not be able to lead a fully independent life as an adult. The conceptual, however, deals with learning. Now it is evident that learning disabilities are not limited to retarded children or adults. For example, foreigners who face language difficulties may also exhibit learning disabilities. Then there are children with attention deficit disorder. There are also children and adults who have speech or motor problems or suffer from autism or cerebral palsy. All of these have been designated as "cognitive disabilities" by the U.S. Department of Education. These "cognitive disorders" have been divided into Specific Academic Learning Disorder or learning disordered; Broad Academic Learning Disorder or slow learner; and General Learning Disorder or mentally retarded. The first two of these designations are of an academic nature and concern only schools and are not necessarily visible to the average citizen who has no training in recognizing these conditions.[29]

The Department of Education became involved in the issue of "cognitive disabilities" with the passage by Congress of the Americans with Disabilities Act in 1990. That act includes the Individuals with Disabilities Education Act (IDEA) designed to provide "free appropriate public education" to all "eligible" children with disabilities. Fifty-one percent or 2.7 million American children identified by schools as needing assistance under the IDEA were classified in 1997 as having a learning disability. In addition, 11 percent or 600,000 children were classified as being mentally retarded. In 1999 the federal government allocated $702 per child to a school district for special education for the 62 percent of children so affected. That sum is of course also spent on children whose disability is of a purely physical nature.

It may be speculated whether the increase in learning disabilities by 37.8 percent from 1987 to 1997 was the product of this federal generosity. In any case this is a significant increase in learning disabilities leading to the need for more special education teachers who are fully certified in their positions. The purpose of all these expenditures and efforts is of course the alleviation of the consequences of mental retardation of which at least one half or more is the stigma attached to it.[30]

One major consequence of mental retardation is the inability of most retarded persons to earn their own livelihood. Because the economic world is so competitive it is understood that the retarded cannot ordinarily compete for jobs with normal people. That is at least one social consequence of mental retardation. Other disabilities that have social consequences include the "courtesy stigma." Erving Goffman has defined a "courtesy stigma as a stigma acquired as a result of being related to a person with a stigma" and that is most significant.[31]

It is of great importance to those who suffer a "courtesy stigma" to find some way of dealing with the devaluation a retarded child places on them. Evidently, parents develop strategies that make an unmanageable problem manageable for them. In short, they learn how to play an *unwanted* role.

Early in our lives we learn the norms of social life. A *norm* is an expected behavior. People who do not conform to what is expected of them by their reference group soon find that they have been stigmatized in that they become the object of all kinds of secondary rejections such as silence or primary aggression such as verbal abuse and even physical aggression.

Every human group decides what it means to be a member and who is eligible. Hence there are rules that are violated at the risk of discrediting the actor. Such discreditation calls into question the actor's actual identity and the validity of the rules of social engagement. This means that an actor who violates the rules must either be expelled from the group or the group expectations—its *norms*—need to be changed. Yet, it frequently happens that those who cannot sustain competency may still claim to be group members and thereby make uncertain and problematic all membership in a group. If a retarded person or a mentally disabled person can claim group membership then the membership of normal persons seems diminished and less valid.

A good deal of embarrassment results from the discrepancy between what is expected and what turns out. The discrepant person, the retarded, or in other situations the criminal or the homosexual, or the obese or the mentally ill, *needs to be defined in a permanent way* if the disruption to organized social life is to end. Either the discrepant person can be included or he can be designated as outside the conventional social order so that members of the group can rest secure in their learned beliefs concerning outsiders.[32]

When a child is diagnosed as having a permanent disability it becomes necessary for those affected to accept the stigma that results from such a diagnosis. That stigma of course adds something to the biographies of the parents. They become carriers of stigma by association. It has been speculated whether "marked" individuals, i.e., those who are stigmatized, gain in status and acceptance if they are seen in the company of "normals." Several outcomes of such association are possible. The first would be the destigmatization by association of marked individuals; the second would be the stigmatization by association of normal individuals, or no influence of such associations whatever. Psychology professor Steven Neuberg et al. studied this issue and found that stigmatized people were *not* destigmatized by their association with well-regarded others. This means that we cannot expect a reduction of stigma concerning the mentally retarded or anyone else by merely associating them in school or elsewhere with normal people. On the contrary, Neuberg found that "targets," as he calls the stigmatized, were increasingly rejected by such an association because they were viewed as particularly untrustworthy and dishonest when associated with high-status persons. Furthermore, Neuberg and his colleagues found that "normals" were being derogated as a consequence of their association with stigmatized "targets." This last finding demonstrates our ambiguity toward "high-status" persons. While our most admired "winners," whether in sports, business, or academics, may serve as role models whom we would like to emulate, we also seem to seek opportunities to "cut them down to size" by finding flaws in them. Therefore, the association of a high-status person with a retarded person or anyone else who is stigmatized shows as a "chink in their armor" and allows us to derogate the powerful or the role models in any society. Because this is so there are many people who choose not to volunteer for organizations devoted to helping stigmatized people. Many "normals" ask themselves whether they would suffer status degradation if it became known that they help the retarded or people with AIDS or invite homosexuals to their home.[33]

Sociologist Arnold Birenbaum studied the adaptation of mothers of children with mental retardation who lived at home. These mothers were all subjects of "courtesy stigma" but sought to maintain a normal-appearing round of life. Since the "courtesy stigma" is not inherent in the person so affected because she is not retarded, we can say that the "courtesy stigma" is a situationally induced social construct rather than a constant attribute of a person. Therefore, all of the mothers studied by Birenbaum met approval as well as discreditation. Approval was gained by these mothers when they maintained relationships with people who showed "consideration" while limiting their involvement with voluntary associations that worked on behalf of individuals with mental retardation.[34]

It is of course certain that the stigma of mental retardation does not impact in the same fashion on all family members or on all families. For example, it has been observed that in middle-class families who are very much concerned with status placement of their children in schools and colleges there is only limited contact between "normal" children and their retarded siblings. By avoiding contact with retarded brothers or sisters, children who have retarded siblings succeed in participating in the adolescent subculture which is in any event stressful and precarious to maneuver.[35]

This clearly demonstrates that the definition "mental retardation" is a social attribute as is the attribute "normal." Hence, parents of retarded children can, through activities, maintain a normal-appearing life and retain contact with family and friends. British sociology professor Margaret Voysey has called this "impression management" because it seeks to lessen the hidden injuries of daily contact with strangers and neighbors. The shock of first learning about the retardation of one's child leads at once to concern about how the family appears to others. Hoping to conform despite differences, many parents retreat from involvement with others. Furthermore, parents experience that approval of the larger community hinges on bearing their burden "lightly." This means that parents are expected not to complain too much or even mention their problem. This need to seek the approval of others may translate into failure of families to work very hard at assisting their mentally retarded child to become established in school, work, or neighborhood. In short, the stigma imposed on the family by outsiders reduces the aid the family would furnish the retarded if the stigma were not present.[36]

All retarded persons are by no means living with families or in institutions. An estimated 887,000 retarded Americans live on their own. These are the retarded who struggle the most to develop the skills others take for granted—holding down a job, using public transportation, and dealing with money. Because the retarded are generally trusting individuals they are becoming more and more the targets of the credit-card industry whose junk mail, telephone tactics, and barrage of television advertisements are difficult to fend off even for normal people. Often, the retarded believe that a telemarketing call is an act of friendship. One consequence of this is the increasing indebtedness of the retarded which can easily lead to the loss of the independent life they have so carefully constructed for themselves.

In part, this increase in debt is the product of the impersonality which prevails in business. Prior to the advent of massive media credit campaigns bankers and credit union employees would meet the credit applicant face to face. This permitted them to determine that someone was a poor credit risk, particularly if he read at a fourth-grade level, spoke in a monotone, and indicated otherwise that he might not be able to pay back his debt.

The credit industry is also faced with the problem of discrimination. It is illegal to discriminate against the disabled. In addition, mental retardation occurs in a hierarchy. There are those whose IQ is 90 and who are only mildly and unrecognizably retarded. There are others evidently retarded and incompetent. Hence, the credit industry has trouble drawing a line below which credit will not be granted. Can it be determined that someone with an IQ of 94 is creditworthy but someone with an IQ of 89 is not?[37]

Because of the problems facing the retarded, there are today both public and private organizations available to give retarded persons opportunities to gain access to financial, educational, recreational, and vocational programs. Included in these organizations are high schools that offer vocational programs designed to give the retarded vocational opportunities. In addition there are agencies in most larger cities that follow graduates of such programs as they enter the job world and help them adjust to paid employment. One of the most important differences between the experience of the mentally retarded in high school as compared to employment is that in school such students are given six times more direction than is ever offered "on the job." Therefore it is obvious that employment requires a good deal more self-reliance than schooling because schools do not truly duplicate employment experiences. The consequences for the employed mentally retarded is that their failure to follow directions can lead to a good deal of rejection ranging from ridicule and anger to loss of employment.[38]

Agencies that support the mentally retarded on the job help individuals with mental retardation to find and hold jobs in the competitive workplace. Because of the stigma that surrounds mental retardation those who are so burdened often find that they cannot develop the kinds of friendship and social relations that ordinarily accrue to other employees. Yoshi Ohtake and Janis G. Chadsey investigated the long-term social support which the nature of friendship promotes on the job for retarded workers. They found that a variety of factors threatened the continuity of employment for the retarded, including arguments with customers, disagreements with coworkers, low productivity, and failure to understand directions. When the retarded enter employment they are generally visited on the job by job counselors representing helping organizations. These professional visitors are "job coaches." Typically, these coaches must withdraw and fade out direct intervention once a retarded person has worked in a setting for a while. At that point the support of the retarded worker becomes the responsibility of a supervisor and of coworkers. A number of investigators have shown, however, that social interaction between retarded workers and others is rare. Mentally retarded workers seldom interact socially with other workers and few have social friends. Coworkers without disabilities generally do not want to deal with retarded workers except when necessary on the job. Investigation by numerous researchers show what common experience shows as well, namely, that "nearly all coworkers without disabilities had work acquaintances, work friends and social friends in their employment setting." Yet, among employees supported by outside agencies, because of their retardation, very few interact socially after work with coworkers who have no disabilities. The principal reason for this is that the stigma of mental retardation prevents even a minimum of self-disclosure between normal and retarded workers. Since self-disclosure is a prerequisite for social friendship it is obvious that stigma reduces contacts between normal and retarded coworkers to a minimum.

From this it can be seen that the organizations furnishing support for the retarded on the job and in addition help in other ways to give the retarded an opportunity to live outside institutions have not been able to do much about the stigmatization of retarded workers in employment situations.[39] While these organizations do indeed lessen the burden of caring for a retarded family member, the stigma management problems that accompany retardation do not go away with the quality programs available. In fact, it is possible that the burden of the stigma associated with using these services may make the stigma even more intense, as utilization of such services makes it impossible to hide the condition of a family member from public view. Because so many services are available to the family with a retarded member, their difficulties in dealing with outsiders will be less understood than was true before these services were available. The inability of the family to be "normal" when they do not have to bear the burden of a retarded member alone permits their community to be less understanding of family pain and fears.

All of us convey social information about ourselves to others. Generally we can manipulate this "presentation of self in everyday life." However, the "rituals of adversity" lead to continued social derogation.

This derogation may at one time affect only those who appear "different" because of their retardation, obesity, mental illness, or sexual orientation. It needs to be kept in mind, however, that those who are considered "normal" may find themselves the target of stigma at other occasions, particularly in old age.

SUMMARY

There are distinct differences between the mentally ill and the mentally retarded which are frequently overlooked. While most of the mentally retarded have access to the normal world, some show physical and behavioral signs of mental retardation that lead to their rejection.

In earlier years the organic metaphor and the eugenics movement led to the belief that the mentally retarded should be sterilized. It was thought that procreation among the mentally retarded would "contaminate" American society and that therefore the mentally retarded should not be allowed any sexual expression, or at least they should not be permitted to have children.

The stigma of mental retardation has led to the exploitation of the mentally retarded by criminals and the criminal justice system. This stigma is felt most heavily by the parents of children with Down's syndrome but is also the product of labeling in schools. Families of the retarded are also stigmatized by the "courtesy stigma."

Employment is possible for those who are mildly retarded, but even in these situations the retarded are generally rejected as are the old in American culture. Therefore we shall discuss the ubiquitous old age stigma in our next chapter.

NOTES

1. James R. Dudley, *Confronting the Stigma in Their Lives: Helping People with a Mental Retardation Label* (Springfield, Ill.: Charles C. Thomas, 1997).

2. Karl M. Newell et al., "Variability of Stereotypic Body-Rocking in Adults with Mental Retardation," *American Journal of Mental Retardation* 104, no. 3 (May 1999): 279–88.

3. Ibid., p. 29.

4. Gerald Vincent O'Brien, "Protecting the Social Body: Use of the Organism Metaphor in Fighting the Menace of the Feebleminded," *Mental Retardation* 37, no. 3 (June 1999): 190.

5. George S. Baroff, *Mental Retardation* (New York: Harper & Row, 1986), p. 393.

6. Ibid., p. 396.

7. N. H. Rafter, *White Trash: The Eugenic Family Studies 1877–1919* (Boston: Northeastern University Press, 1988).

8. O'Brien, "Protecting the Social Body," p. 192.

9. Fred Pelka, "Unequal Justice: Preserving the Rights of the Mentally Retarded in the Criminal Justice System," *Humanist* 57, no. 6 (November–December 1997): 28–32.

10. Daniel L. Rosenhahn, "On Being Sane in Insane Places," *Science* 179 (1973): 250–58.

11. Samuel E. Asch, "Forming Impressions of Personality," *Journal of Abnormal and Social Psychology* 41 (1946): 258–90.

12. Ibid., p. 60.

13. Elinor Gollay et al., *Coming Back: The Community Experiences of Deinstitutionalized Mentally Retarded People* (Cambridge, Mass.: Abt Books, 1978).

14. Ursula A. Falk and Gerhard Falk, *Ageism, the Aged and Aging in America* (Springfield, Ill.: Charles C. Thomas, 1997), chap. 2.

15. Daniel Kravetz, "Consciousness Raising and Self Help," in *Women and Psychotherapy: An Assessment of Research and Knowledge,* ed. A. M. Brodsky and R. T. Hare-Mustin (New York: Guilford Press, 1981), pp. 267–83.

16. "Disease, Condition and General Health Topic: Down Syndrome" (*Yahoo Health* on Internet).

17. Richard Darling, "Parental Entrepreneurship: A Consumerist Response to Professional Dominance," *Journal of Social Issues* 44 (1988): 148–58.

18. Mary E. Hannah and Elizabeth Midlarsky, "Competence and Adjustment of Siblings with Mental Retardation," *American Journal on Mental Retardation* 104, no. 1 (January 1999): 33.

19. Milton Seligman and Rosalyn Darling, *Ordinary Families, Special Children: A Systems Approach to Childhood Disabilities* (New York: Guilford Press, 1989).

20. M. M. Quinn, "Attachment Between Mothers and Their Down's Syndrome Infants," *Western Journal of Nursing Research* 13 (1991): 382–96.

21. S. E. Szivos and Edward Griffiths, "Group Processes Involved in Coming to Terms with a Mentally Retarded Identity," *Mental Retardation* 28, no. 6 (December 1990): 333–41.

22. John J. Macionis, *Sociology*, 7th ed. (Upper Saddle River, N.J.: Prentice-Hall, 1999), p. 178.

23. Yona Lunsky and Susan M. Havercamp, "Distinguishing Low Levels of Social Support and Social Strain: Implications for Dual Diagnosis," *American Journal of Mental Retardation* 194, no. 2 (March 1999): 200–204.

24. Frederick X. Gibbons, "Stigma Perception: Social Comparison Among Mentally Retarded Persons," *American Journal of Mental Deficiency* 90, no. 1 (July 1985): 98–106.

25. S. E. Taylor, J. V. Wood, and R. R. Lichtman, "It Could Be Worse: Selective Evaluation as a Response to Victimization," *Journal of Social Issues* 39 (1983): 1940.

26. Robert Edgerton and Steven Bercovici, "The Cloak of Competence: Years Later," *American Journal of Mental Deficiency* 80 (1976): 485–97.

27. Jane R. Mercer, *Labeling the Mentally Retarded* (Berkeley: University of California Press, 1973), pp. 96–108.

28. Ibid., p. 117.

29. U.S. Department of Education, *Seventeenth Annual Report to Congress on the Implementation of the Individuals with Disabilities Education Act* (Washington, D.C.: U.S. Government Printing Office, 1995).

30. U.S. Department of Education, *Twentieth Annual Report to Congress on the Implementation of the Individuals with Disabilities Education Act* (Washington, D.C.: U.S. Government Printing Office, 1999).

31. Erving Goffman, *Stigma: Notes on the Management of Spoiled Identities* (Englewood Cliffs, N.J.: Prentice-Hall, 1963).

32. Harold Garfinkel, "The Encounters Where Individuals Are Conferred the Stigmatized Status Have Been Called 'Degradation Ceremonies,'" *American Journal of Sociology* 61 (1956): 420–24.

33. Steven L. Neuberg et al., "When We Observe Stigmatized and 'Normal' Individuals Interacting: Stigma by Association," *Personality and Social Psychology Bulletin* 20, no. 2 (April 1994): 196–209.

34. Arnold Birenbaum, "The Recognition of Acceptance of Stigma," *Sociological Symposium* 7 (1971): 15–22.

35. Gerald Miller, "An Exploratory Study of Sibling Relationships in Families with Retarded Children," *Dissertation Abstracts International* 35: 2994B–2995B.

36. Margaret Voysey, *A Constant Burden: The Reconstitution of Family Life* (Boston: Routledge and Kegan Paul, 1975).

37. Joseph B. Cahill, "Credit Cards Invade a New Market Niche: The Mentally Disabled," *Wall Street Journal,* November 10, 1998, p. 1.

38. Janis Chadsey-Rusch and Patricia Gonzalez, "Analysis of Directions, Responses, and Consequences Involving Persons with Mental Retardation in Employment and Vocational Settings," *American Journal of Mental Retardation* 100, no. 5 (March 1996): 481–92.

39. Yoshi Ohtake and Janis G. Chadsey, "Social Disclosure Among Coworkers Without Disabilities in Supported Employment Settings," *Mental Retardation* 37, no. 1 (February 1999): 25–35.

PUNISHMENT WITHOUT CRIME 6

THE STIGMA OF
BEING OLD

THE AGING OF AMERICA AND
THE LANGUAGE OF AGEISM

The stigma that attaches to the very word "old" and hence to old people in America and other technological cultures is "ageism." That word was coined by Robert N. Butler, M.D., in 1968. Butler defines ageism as: "a process of systematic stereotyping of and discrimination against people because they are old."[1]

Like all stigmas, "old age" influences the self-image and behavior of its victims. This means that the old among us tend to adopt negative definitions of themselves, thereby perpetuating the negative stigma against them and reinforcing the beliefs that promote the stigma in the first place.

The most common method used by the old is to proclaim that there must be something very wrong with old age. This comes about as many of the old refuse to identify themselves as old at all. This self-sabotaging behavior can be seen among those who are indeed old but affect the dress of the young, deny their age to others and even to themselves, and refuse to deal with others of equal age. Such conduct is of course not surprising in our youth-worshiping society. Yet, the reasons for the stigmatization of the old and the adoration of all who are young almost disappeared from American society during the second part of the twentieth century. The principal reason for the rejection of the old in earlier American history was that the young and not the old constituted most of the immigrants who came here. This is true in all immigrant countries because only the young, and not the old, are willing to risk moving

129

far away from home and coming to an unexplored continent as was true of those who came to America before 1900.

Another reason for the stigmatization of the old and the elevation of the young is that the tremendous rate of change our postindustrial, electronic society now experiences permits the young to learn a great number of things that the old, who are no longer in school, do not usually know. Hence, it appears to many young people that they know more than their elders and therefore hold the "ignorant" older generation in contempt.

American society became an ageist society shortly before the First World War, thus the stigma of old age is only about a century old. Prior to the twentieth century many people did not even know how old they were because they lacked a birth certificate. Furthermore, age was not important to Americans then living in a preindustrial, predominantly rural society, a condition still common in many parts of Africa, South America, and Asia.

Preindustrial, rural societies lack the schools and hence the education that is so important in age-grading all Americans. Any technological society, which needs educated people to grow and prosper, will include all of its children in some education scheme that is normally age-graded. This then produces age consciousness as most children never see anyone in any other class, either younger or older than themselves.

There are many other cultural features in American life that make people age conscious. These features include such aspects as a minimum drinking age, a retirement age, a minimum age for drivers, and the targeting of different age groups by advertisers. These advertisers are very influential in developing media messages for different age groups and in influencing attitudes toward the aged.[2]

In view of the great changes in the age structure of the American population these attitudes are an example of culture lag. Culture lag occurs when a belief, behavior, or material object in a culture lags behind in its development compared to all other aspects of that culture. Hence, the belief that only the young are valuable and that the old are to be viewed negatively is burdened by the fact that the American population is getting older and older all the time.

Thus, in 1990, the number of Americans over sixty-five years of age was 12.5 percent. This rose to 12.7 percent in 2000. It is anticipated by the Bureau of the Census that in 2010 the number of Americans sixty-five years of age or older will be 13.2 percent, in 2020 the figure for seniors will reach 16.5 percent, and by 2030 more than one-fifth of all Americans (20.2 percent) will be senior citizens as it is now defined. In 2000 at least seventy-five thousand Americans were centenarians (one hundred years of age). It is noteworthy that 80 percent of the old in America are women.[3]

One of the consequences of this growth of the old population in the United States is the contradiction that the stigma against the old creates. For even as those still working complain that too many old people hold jobs that should really be given to the young and unemployed, the tax-paying public also complains that the old are retired and are using too many benefits for themselves. Here is an example of how prejudice will have it both ways as the old are condemned for holding jobs the young seek for themselves even as the old are also condemned for not working and thus using retirement benefits.

Since these contradictions are the product of stigma and not of an understanding of the facts concerning aging, it is reasonable to expect that the stigma of old age may disappear or at least become reduced as the life expectancy of Americans increases. This increase is easily discerned by comparing the life expectancy of an American born in 1916 to someone born in 1999. During that time life expectancy rose from fifty-two years to seventy-eight years.[4]

Because "old" is a "dirty word" in American culture the old often act out the role expected of them. Hence some of the old return to a "second childhood" by repeating the same stories over and over again, or telling jokes that belittle them or include in their speech such overly friendly forms of speech and gesture that their fear of rejection by reason of the age stigma becomes obvious.

Psychologists Charles Purdue and Michael Gurtman undertook two experiments to verify the hypothesis that in the United States hardly anyone can escape stigmatizing the old. Using an unannounced memory test, Purdue and Gurtman found that more negative traits were recalled when they had been encoded with reference to an "old" person while more positive traits were recalled when encoded with reference to a "young" person. These experiments support the view that there is an unintentional and unconscious stigma among Americans against the old. Thus, the same trait is seen as negative when attributed to an old person and positive when attributed to a young person. In fact, these researchers found that the word "old" with its strong negative prior association causes distortions in the evaluation of any information in which the word "old" appears.[5]

Additional evidence for the stigmatization of the old in American popular culture and in Western technological societies generally is the ageist language used even in social science research and among social work and psychology professionals. Psychologist K. Warner Schaie found that psychological research usually assumes that age is the cause of differences or changes in behavior even when other explanations are readily available. He further found a failure of psychology and social-work researchers to recognized reciprocity between the old and the young. Hence, much emphasis is given in such research to the care of the old by the young, even as care given to the young by the old is ignored. It is expected that grandparents take care of grandchildren if parents are not available. Yet, it is generally believed in America that a middle-aged child who takes care of an old parent is doing a great deed, is "sacrificing" himself and carrying a great burden.[6]

Social-science research includes the assumption, according to Schaie, that the old are sick and that there are no individual differences in that respect. All of these beliefs are visible in the ageist language used by the various helping professions so that the textbooks used by students reflect this ageist language if the aged are mentioned at all. Human development texts deal almost entirely with children and adolescents and rarely with the middle-aged. The aged are totally excluded from such books. An examination of 139 textbooks in psychology published over forty years revealed that there are numerous negative messages conveyed by text writers about old age which are labeled "scholarly research" for young readers.[7]

Language revealing the stigmatization of old age is not limited to social-science research, of course. Instead, ageist language is in common use in America and is first seen in the euphemisms or sanitized terms describing the old and the aging process. A "euphemism" is a Greek word meaning "good words." Examples are such phrases as "pass away" for "die," or "senior citizen" for "old man" or "old woman."

In addition to these efforts to circumvent mention of old age, there are also a good many English words that directly attack the old. *Old goat, fossil, old bag,* and *dead wood* are only a few of the words intended to insult and humiliate old age. Some of these terms reveal a considerable amount of sex stigma and age stigma at the same time such as *old maid, dirty old man,* and other forms of condemnation.

The function of such stigmatizing language is oppression. By oppression is meant that the victims of such language are subject to lower incomes; violence, sometimes called "elder abuse"; and lack of power in that the old cannot influence the outcome of events affecting them while they are frequently deprived of any credit for their contributions to the community.

It is true that those among the old and retired who are exceedingly active may be able to escape some of these difficulties. Productivity, whether by acting, writing, painting, engaging in business, or working in any occupation to one's liking, defeats some of the stigma of old age because one of the central themes of that stigma is that the old are unproductive and wasteful. Hence, the master status of those who are old and not productive is their age. Yet, the master status of the old who are productive is their output and their creativity. In short, the stigma of old age can be reduced somewhat by working in a productive enterprise.

OLD AGE AND DENIAL: THE COSMETIC INDUSTRY HARVESTS THE STIGMA

Because language is so pervasive there are those who now seek to promote the view that old age is only a social construct and that the stigmatization of old age can only be eliminated if that social construct is eliminated. This argument is in itself a form of stigmatizing old age since childhood, adolescence, or middle age are not mentioned by those seeking to eliminate old age from our consciousness. In his book *Ageism*, English gerontologist William Bytheway states that "it is indisputable that a rethinking of ageism cannot be based upon the presumption that old age exists. Old age is a cultural concept that has certain popular utility in sustaining ageism within societies that need scapegoats."[8]

This extreme view overlooks that the mere elimination of the phrase "old age" does not eliminate the dynamics that the stigma of old age include. Surely no one would seriously suggest that sexism and racism would disappear if we eliminated these words from the English language.

It is of course true that ageism differs from sexism and racism in the important respect that it includes a great deal of self-hatred. Racists and sexists can rest securely on the assumption that they will never be of the opposite sex or become members of another race. Ageism, however, is unique in that those who practice it will inevitably become old themselves if they experience longevity. The great contradiction within ageism is that many of those who practice ageism do all sorts of things to prolong their lives and thereby insure that they will join the stigmatized group of seniors whom they reject. It would seem on the surface that it would be in the self-interest of the young to eliminate ageism before they themselves reach old age. Yet, this is not so. Few people see old age as their own future. Instead they view the old as apart from themselves.

In her most important analysis of old age, French social theorist Simone de Beauvoir writes: "When we look at the image of our own future provided by the old we do not believe it: an absurd inner voice whispers that *that* will never happen to us—when *that* happens it will no longer be ourselves that it happens to . . . ."[9]

It is of course nonsense to view the old and the young or the not-so-old as disparate groups. The fact is that aging is a gradual process and therefore there is a continuity between ages without a definable beginning or end other than birth and death. Therefore the stigma attached to old age can also be attached to other ages although perception often precludes this. For example, depression is believed to be a symptom of aging. The antidote to depression is activity. This may be perceived as a means of achieving "successful" aging although there are innumerable old people who are not depressed while there are indeed vast numbers of depressed people who are not old. This can be seen by the very large sale of antidepressant drugs such as Prozac, Paxil, Zoloft, and Sersone. These drugs reputedly raise the serotonin level in the blood and that in turn is thought to block depression.[10]

The belief that the old must be depressed or must be instructed as to how to lead their lives is commonplace. In fact, the very language used by the not-yet-old toward those perceived as old includes the stigma associated with ageism. Numerous studies have shown that caregivers and others who come in contact with the old use more questions and repetitions than they do with younger people. A simpler syntax is also used by such caregivers when speaking to the old since it is *expected* that the old have less intellect than the young. This stigma, the belief in a lowering of the intellect in old age, is utterly unfounded but is widely assumed.[11]

There are those who seek to escape the stigma of old age by claiming that there is a dichotomy between the outer appearance of the old and their inner self. Some old people say that although they look old they feel young inside. Such an assertion implies that there is a mind/body split. This view has been dubbed the "mask of ageing theory." The major aspects of this theory are that aging is a state of mind and that therefore people who don't feel old are not old on some level. According to this view those who resist being called old have overcome the common self-hatred that results from living in an ageist society and have attained a positive identity instead.

The visible fact is, however, that many old people living in an ageist society are ageists themselves and seek to distance themselves from other old people. In a desperate effort to escape the stigma of old age many old people claim to be an exception to the ageist stereotype. Such folks, as ageists, will concur that all the other old people do indeed fit into the categories that ageists assign to them. They themselves, however, seek to establish their separate identity by claiming that they do not see themselves as old.[12]

The internalization of self-hatred is not unique to the old. It is a common feature among all who are outsiders and who are the targets of stigma. Many who experience self-hatred seek to "pass" by pretending that they belong to the majority. This is possible in some situations. The European Jews, for example, were quite facile at adopting the pose of non-Jews during all the years of their persecution on that continent. For the old, however, this is hardly possible. "Passing" in the case of the old is built on a pretense that visible evidence denies. Furthermore, all efforts to deny what we really are affirms stigmatization since denial would evidently not be necessary if the stigma were not present in the first place. Trying to "pass" leads to the undignified condition of self-denial and a secret self-hatred. Such self-denial may well be based on the hope of belonging to a group to whom one can never belong. This is particularly true of the old because age cannot be reversed despite the advertisements of the cosmetics industry. That $50 billion American industry literally lives by selling to those who dread old age and who have swallowed whole the principle that one can somehow escape the stigma of old age by the use of face-lifts, makeup, and diets.[13]

The entire cosmetics industry is based on the view that there is a discrepancy between body and self when in fact such a view is the very essence of the stigma imposed on the old. Surely, the opposite view is far more supportable. Instead of denying aging induced by the ageist stigma, the old and others need to celebrate differences in age just as differences in race, nationality, gender, and religion are constantly celebrated in American culture. The denial of the old implies that everything the old have learned during all the years they have lived is meaningless. Such expressions as "I am seventy-five years young" are offensive because they confirm the stigma of old age and deny the experiences that have accumulated in seventy-five years. Old age is not only the absence of youth. Old age is a status in itself and it is an achievement in which the old person is what he has always been, only more so. Hence, old age is a continuation of the life that has been lived up to that point and an affirmation that we are as old as we are without apology. Albert Einstein reputedly said that "the only constant is change." This is evidently the case. The old have changed because change is a universal law of nature. Yet, we remain the same because age occurs in a continuity from birth to death so that distinct epoch of change cannot be discerned. There is of course a great deal of value in old age, which is obscured by the youth and future orientation of our culture. Because of that future orientation many old people in America are always depressed since they do not have a future. Yet, the old agree that life is ongoing. It is not categorized and does not come in compartments. The old-age stigma insures that the young are segregated from the old, the old are divided among themselves while failing to understand that body, mind, and soul are one.[14]

THE EXCLUSION OF THE OLD

Old-age stigma is of course related to chronological conditions. It is also, as we have seen, a social status. The stigma of old age is also situational. The chronological aspect of aging is understood when we use such age criteria as "over fifty-five" or "over sixty-five" to indicate the age at which someone may attain some privilege such as a pension or some penalty such as job loss. Chronological age is of course not social age. This is experienced every day by people who are indeed "senior citizens" although they do not have the physical characteristics associated with that status. Some people do not look their age and therefore are socially younger than their years.

From the viewpoint of social stratification age is ranked along a hierarchy of values in which old age in American culture is seldom very high. This is noticeable in the relative absence of old people from the media, specifically television. In that medium the old are disproportionately underrepresented both in programs and in advertisements. However, the increasing economic power of the old has relaxed their exclusion somewhat, as advertisers want to sell their products to the huge senior citizen market.

The stigmatized, including the old, are an embarrassment to those with whom they come in contact. Therefore, the stigmatized, including the old, are expected to withdraw as much as possible from social situations and thereby protect the non-old from such embarrassment. That embarrassment at being in the company of the old is an aspect of social stratification. It is always an embarrassment for people in the upper echelons of any hierarchy to be in the presence of those who have been devalued. Stigma helps those who observe the stigmatized to view the stigmatized as a category who all the members of which have the same characteristics. Not only the old, but other groups as well are assumed to share the same characteristics if they appear to belong to the same category. People of the same race, national origin, religion, education, or occupation are believed to have similar origins or characteristics. It comes as a shock to many to learn that Geraldo Rivera is a Jew; that a general of the First World War, Pavel von Rennenkampf, was in fact a Russian and not a German; and that JoAnn Faletta is the conductor of a major symphony orchestra. Stigmatized thinking seeks to overlook all of these exceptions to the general rules that deny the prejudices on which stigma rest.

Likewise, an ageist employer may discard all applications of job seekers over age forty in the belief that all those over forty cannot perform. All of this is dependent on thinking in terms of social stratification, which places men above women, whites above blacks, and the young above the old.

Stigma related to old age refers to one's social identity. Psychologist Paul C. Luken has presented four types of situations which confront the old and which confirm anyone's social identity. The first is comprised of daily situations such as cleaning, bathing, dining, reading, walking, watching TV, or cooking. Most of the old can perform all of these tasks and therefore will not be stigmatized in situations in which these activities take place.

Social identity is more compromised for the old in situations that involve physical and mental activities they may not be able to perform. Examples are athletic competition, shoveling snow, and strenuous exercise or preparing one's income tax, playing chess, or writing. These are all situations in which failure and hence stigmatization are likely.

Then there are numerous administrative situations in which age becomes a factor leading almost always to stigmatization. Such situations include using senior discounts for transportation or attending movies, or using tuition-free education, or being rejected for insurance or in employment. Such situations almost always lead to stigmatization and its concomitant rejection.[15]

It is of course true that aging is a universal phenomenon and that all of us suffer deterioration of our bodies until we die. That fact does not, however, mean that the social practices concerning age must always and everywhere be the same. The evidence is that every human society transforms biological conditions and needs into social events. Therefore, sex differences become gender differences as each society promotes a particular cultural view as to what constitutes female or male behavior and what females or males may expect in their specific culture. Likewise, old age is socially constructed despite the fact that there is of course a biological and chronological old age. This means that the shape of social relations between people of different ages and the life experiences of the old differ from time to time and from culture to culture.

It is certain that groups of people born in the same year and called a "cohort" by sociologists experience similarities in the aging process. This is true because social relations are manifest in specific geographical and historical contexts. One of these contexts is the stigmatizing of old age, also called ageism, as practiced in the United States today.

The old, and everyone else, can acquire their identity from the stereotype imposed on them by their society. Many old people accept these stigmas and act accordingly. Yet there are those who reject the stereotypes of the old and, together with their advocates, make every effort to transform the stigma of old age into a more supportive image. This is the reason why, as we have already reviewed, age, gender, and class shape the experiences of the old concerning old-age stigma and the oppression of the old derived from that stigma.

Ageism is a form of prejudice. Like all prejudices, ageism limits the people who are its objects and shapes the perception of those who hold such a prejudice. As we get older our experiences with aging change as does our experience with the stigma of old age. The real function of prejudice and discrimination is oppression. This can be seen with reference to ageism even as it can be seen with reference to sexism and racism. Oppressed people, including the old, are marginalized. Because old age carries a stigma, the old are deprived of their work by being pushed into retirement. In some instances the old are physically abused ("elder bashing"). The old are made powerless by having others, such as adult children, make decisions that affect an old person's life. The old are also subject to exploitation when they give their money to adult children or are used to baby-sit or otherwise work in enterprises benefiting others. The knowledge of the old is actively denied because the stigma of old age denies that the old know anything worth hearing.[16] For example, I am acquainted with a middle-aged woman who regards anything expressed by an old person as "psychobabble." I have also repeatedly seen old people ignored by younger people who talk only to those of their own age. For example, at funerals or during visits to a bereaved widow, the visitors generally talk only to each other and ignore the widow. There is also the situation in which an old person walking with someone younger meets a third person who then asks about the younger companion of the old person about the senior's health, etc., without once addressing the old person. In these situations the stigma of old age is so great that the younger persons speak only to each other and act as if their old companion were not there. Patricia Moore, in her twenties, dressed as a sixty-year-old, wore opaqued contact lenses, and taped her joints to imitate the effects of arthritis. In that condition she attended a conference on building for an aging population. Despite the subject matter of the conference nobody spoke to her. During her flight the flight attendant spilled coffee on her but was hardly bothered. Taxi drivers would not stop for her fearing she would take too long to get in and out and that she would tip badly. Evidently, ageism is a form of oppression.[17]

The stigma of old age became most severe in the United States at the time of World War I when the old were unable to meet the requirements of industry. Prior to the First World War this country was principally engaged in agriculture in which family farms predominated. After the First World War industrial production became the major theme in the American economy as the family farm declined in importance. In 1910, before the First World War, 31 percent of Americans were engaged in farming. In 1920 only 27 percent of Americans earned their living in agriculture, and at the end of the twentieth century only 1.6 percent of Americans were so employed.[18]

Therefore, retirement was promoted as an appropriate transition from work and as a pleasant and leisurely stage of life. This occurred even as American culture became a consumer culture from which the old were excluded because their reduced income marginalized them both materially and socially.

Now, at the beginning of the century, the old are no longer the poor. Large numbers of the old are now affluent or at least financially independent. This makes it possible for the old to assert themselves in the economy so that their rising affluence and their growing numbers force many businesses to accede to their demands. This includes a redrawing of the image of the old and a lessening of the stigma attached to old age. Therefore, real-estate companies depict the old as active participants in golf, tennis, and other sports. Employers seek out the old to work in part-time jobs not wanted by younger people even as various volunteer programs develop an image of the old as productive and active "senior citizens." The result, at the beginning of the twenty-first century, was an ambiguous and even contradictory image of the old. They are invested by popular culture with the stigma of Alzheimer's disease and incompetence generally even as billboard and the media portray the old more and more as self-sufficient, active, and competent individuals.[19]

AGEISM AND ECONOMIC DISCRIMINATION

The stigma of old age is institutionalized in the United States. This means that each of the social institutions that serve our daily and recurrent needs are so organized as to stigmatize the old who must use these institutions as much as those who are not old. Most important among these institutions is the economy. Here the stigma of old age makes itself manifest in work rules, production quotas, and the belief that the old are physically incompetent. These rules drove older workers from the economy at the beginning of the twentieth century.

At the end of that century manufacturing jobs and factory work generally had declined somewhat with service occupations increasing considerably. This shifted the ageism in the economy to the service sector with the result that in some industries the old, although quite competent to do the nonphysical labor required, were the target of stigma and prejudice as much as before. An excellent example of the economic stigmatization is "gray listing" of actors and screenwriters in the movie and television industry. In the belief that "big money" can only be made by catering to young audiences, Hollywood screenwriters over the age of forty have been "gray listed" and are not employed on the grounds that they could not possibly know the interests of the young. The writers and directors excluded from employment are generally victimized by executives in their twenties or early thirties. Reminiscent of the McCarthy era when anyone labeled a "Communist sympathizer" was "blacklisted," the refusal of agents to even consider the "over-forty" writers now excludes Academy Award winners and Emmy winners, sending them into permanent unemployment. This includes a thirty-five-year-old writer who was very successful when she claimed to be nineteen years old. As soon as the studios discovered her true age she was excluded from writing further material for studios who believe that the simple-minded material they seek for their young ticket buyers can only be written by those in their teens.[20]

A second example of using the age stigma to exclude the older person is found in the legal profession. Recently, the United States Equal Opportunity Commission investigated the manner in which New York law firms hire junior-level attorneys. This investigation challenged the old and encrusted practice of hiring only new graduates as "associates" who will then move up the ranks until they make "partner" in about eight to nine years.

By hiring from among new law school graduates or advertising for those with a limited number of years of experience the system recruits only young people and eliminates the older job seeker in advance. The stigma of age is so well accepted among lawyers it is never in doubt.

The same applies to academics. Ageism is so entrenched in academic employment that no one can even be considered for employment as an assistant professor unless he is less than forty years of age. Even that age is often considered "too old" for a junior position. This practice is particularly destructive in the academic setting because most first-time appointees are about twenty-eight years old, since it takes seven years to attain "tenure" those who are not given that promotion are then roughly thirty-five years old when looking for another job. This means that they are competing with a new group of just graduated Ph.D.s who are of course seven years younger. Now the stigma of age is invoked almost everywhere so that the applicant in the middle thirties or older is eliminated from all consideration.[21]

The claim of those who refuse to appoint anyone over forty is always the same. It is said that the older employees have no new ideas, that they are "deadwood," that they "don't fit in," and that the old are probably sick.[22]

The stigmatization of those over forty has become a particular problem for academics, lawyers, and others in this new century. There is now a glut of lawyers and academics who would be glad to take entry-level jobs despite years of experience.

Because age is so heavily stigmatized in the economic world, Congress passed the Age Discrimination in Employment Act in 1967. Although the purpose of that law was the protection of employees from unfair labor practices based on age, the results have not been as promising as was once anticipated. In fact, a study by industrial psychologists Catherine Jorgensen Snyder and Gerald V. Barrett revealed that 65 percent of cases brought by employees on the grounds of age discrimination were decided by the courts in favor of the employer.[23]

Four areas of economic age discrimination are generally recognized. The first is the practice of refusing work to older workers only because of the age stigma. An example was the erstwhile practice of allowing only young women to work as flight attendants when older women and men could do that job as well. Although the practice of hiring only the most youthful-appearing women as flight attendants has generally ceased, those past age forty are rarely found in flight attendant positions even now.

A second form of economic discrimination based entirely on the age stigma was the practice of discharging employees solely because of their age and without respect to job performance. This practice continues largely today because job performance is a subjective opinion so that it is hard to prove that someone was "fired" only because of age when the employer claims job performance to be the only reason for dismissal. Because the American economy is so exceptionally strong at the end of the twentieth century, the practice of discharging older workers has largely declined as there are few applicants for the most mundane jobs now.

A third method of enforcing the age stigma against employees is to limit promotion to younger workers. This is a very common practice. Beliefs about older people, including older workers, are so entrenched that many an unspoken decision deprives older workers of well-deserved promotions solely because of the stigma attached to being old as defined by someone younger. Psychologists Wanda J. Smith and K. Vernard Harrington have shown that the performance of older workers is generally superior to that of younger workers in terms of productivity but that managers and rating supervisors will attribute poor performance to older workers and rate them lower than younger workers solely because of the age stigma. This means that the age stigma causes many a supervisor to "see" poor performance since their prejudice leads to negative perceptions.[24]

The fourth aspect of economic discrimination based on the age stigma is exclusion. Because of the increase in the life span of Americans many older people now spend three decades of their life in unemployment. Therefore, the aged are stigmatized as nonproductive and hence without social honor. Now it is evident that as longevity has increased, good health in old age has also increased. Therefore we now view the paradox that those who could be most productive are excluded from productivity because of the age stigma, a social definition of old age largely unrelated to the abilities of those excluded.

Exclusion from employment has several consequences in addition to reduction in social honor. Others are higher insurance premiums, difficulties in obtaining credit, and for many poverty. It is of course true that there are more seniors with high incomes today than was ever true in the past. Nevertheless, there are still large numbers of old people in

America today who do not have pensions or insurance plans and, most of all, lack long-term care insurance.

Added to these consequences of the age stigma is territorial segregation of the old. This has now become almost universal in the United States in the so-called Sun-Belt communities which house disproportionately large numbers of the old. Located mostly in Florida, Arizona, and California, these communities are old-age ghettos. It is of course true that these ghettos exist because the old move there voluntarily. Nevertheless, the consequences of such age segregation are quite similar to the consequences of racial and ethnic segregation. Primarily, moving into an old-age ghetto means that the old will know only other old people. It means that friendship between the old and people of younger ages will hardly exist while behavior in such age-segregated communities is rather rigid and uniform since there are no children and no young adults.

THE "LAST SEGREGATION"

If we were to continue the nineteenth-century custom of labeling "old" any American aged sixty-five or more, then one in five Americans will be old in 2030. It is of course unlikely that age sixty-five will for long be maintained as the borderline between middle age and old age. Those who will have reached that age in 2030 will be more affluent in old age than any previous generation, an economic fact already true today. Therefore, the care given the old by their families is and will be less financial but more emotional than was true in earlier years.

The experience of becoming old involves a status change, which is the product of the age stigma as it changes the old from a person to a "nonperson." A nonperson is here defined as someone who is indeed alive but receives no recognition in the most ordinary meaning of that word. Social recognition is of course the very content of life. We are, and perceive ourselves to be, a looking-glass self. This means that our self-image depends largely on how others respond to us. Therefore, those who are ignored, those who are rejected or are treated as if they were not present will not only devalue themselves but will finally regard themselves as having no value and no meaning. In the end, the stigma of old age that promotes this devaluation becomes a life-threatening experience as demonstrated in nursing homes, which are best described as "the last segregation."[25]

An example of the treatment given some patients in this "last segregation" is the recent prosecution of four nurse's aides accused of beating nursing home residents in the Buffalo, New York, area. Included in the charges against these nurse's aides were "assaulting an eighty-year-old female patient in her room," and the charge that two other nurse's aides, "apparently upset with the . . . patient, covered her face with a towel in her room . . . and repeatedly struck her on the head and arms as they swore at her." Yet another nurse's aide was charged with "repeatedly assaulting a ninety-year-old man suffering from dementia, wrapping a bedsheet around his ankles, pulling his legs over his head, and clipping a clothespin to his scrotum."[26] This kind of cruelty perpetrated in nursing homes is by no means unusual, as documented repeatedly in the literature.

Because Americans are becoming older and older we now experience a phenomenon in the United States almost unknown elsewhere: our population is becoming so old that the children of the oldest Americans are now retirement age.

The family was the traditional caregiver in rural America. As the extended, rural family has declined, government and social-service agencies have become more prominent in supporting the old. This development is of course not only true of the family. Business, education, and numerous other needs which were once family responsibilities are now the function of government. This does not mean that the family has nothing more to do for the aged. Now, the family has become mediators between government and the aged individual who needs help. In many instances only the intervention of family secures for the old the benefits to which they are entitled.

Emotional ties between parents and children are of course also still very much in evidence. Because so many parents live so long these ties have also become changes in power relationships. Extreme old age means that many parents cannot take care of themselves and therefore depend on adult children to help them. This may include giving children "power of attorney" over their finances. Therefore, the old feel the stigma of powerlessness not because adult children are less concerned with the welfare of their parents than was true in earlier generations, but because life is so much longer than ever before. This control can also be forced by court order when relatives claim that older persons are unable to take care of their own affairs.

There are unfortunately some among the middle-aged population whose anger and hostility toward the old is so great that they engage in "granny bashing," which is no more than an epithet implying physical violence against the old *because* they are old. Many do not want to see or hear anything about the old even if they live in the same neighborhood or the same family and some of those who want no dealings with the old on occasion beat them.[27]

Because ill will between the old and the young is an ancient reality, religion has attempted to alleviate the stigma that old age brings with it. Nevertheless, beliefs concerning old age influence opinions about the relationship of old age and religion just as such beliefs influence opinions related to anything else in which the aged may be involved. Among these beliefs is the commonly held view that the old are more religious than the young because they are about to face death sooner. Physician David Blazer and gerontologist Erdman Palmore investigated this hypothesis and found that religious behavior as measured by attendance in church or synagogue remains about the same during the lifetime of an American adult and that therefore the view that religiosity increases with age is a myth based on stigma.[28]

A particularly ageist activity in the realm of religion is the use of televangelism as a method of extracting money from the old in the belief that those who are incarcerated in nursing homes, homebound in a house or apartment, or are otherwise unable to continue an active life will more easily succumb to financial appeals than would be true of younger audiences. This effort is based on the age stigma in the belief that the old are incapable of discerning the difference between sincerity and fraud and that the old are an "easy touch" for the delivery of money into the hands of televangelists. The evidence is that among those interested in televangelism are many who were always interested in religion. Likewise, those who rejected such appeals in their youth find no reason to adhere to them now in their old age.[29]

One of the most invasive consequences of the televangelism business is that the televangelist can enter any home and promote a message without consent of the viewers. These viewers are frequently old people who have lost many relationships because of the deaths of their loved ones or because of the rejection which old-age stigma imposes on them. Those who have suffered many such losses need to replace them. If this cannot be done by making new human relationships, then many of the old turn to messianic hopes and "instant pardons for sins," all promised by televangelists in return for contributions. These contributions are frequently donated by housebound old people or others who are alone and in pain. The solicitors usually ask for money for a specific purpose, such as maintaining the present broadcast or building a church, but use the money for something else. This is called the "bait-and-switch" technique. There are also "last-ditch" appeals. These appeals are generally accompanied by selling Bibles, crosses, or such intangibles as "success" or spiritual healing or "God's blessing."[30]

EDUCATION, THE MEDIA, AND THE "OLD MAID"

Education has been the principal elevator of social standing in the United States for the past century. It has also been a means by which we have combated bigotry of all kinds so that there is good reason to believe that education can alleviate the old-age stigma even as it has had some impact on bigotry in other areas such as race, ethnicity, and religion.

To that end the inclusion of courses on the life cycle with particular emphasis on old age have been recommended by psychologists Irene Hulicka and Susan Whitbourne. They recommend that such courses, taught in high schools and colleges, should include such topics as physical functioning, intelligence, and the social psychology of aging. They further suggest that students of aging engage in various activities inside and outside the classroom which can teach more about aging than reading alone can do: for example, visiting an old person in one's neighborhood once a week for an hour or more, visiting day-care centers for the aged, or visiting nursing homes. Shopping with or for the old is of great help as is visiting single occupancy hotels which are almost entirely inhabited by the old who have no family.

Such learning, as promoted by Hulicka and Whitbourne, not only results in decreasing the stigma associated with old age in America but also allows participants, no matter how young, to learn something about their own future. For unlike any other stigma, that of old age will reach everyone later if not sooner and will be directly proportionate to the discrimination against the old as practiced by those once young and now the victims of their own fears and prejudices.[31]

It has been recommended that a curriculum can be developed that will permit students, however young, to identify stereotypes and prejudices against the aged. This is important because even at age three some children already use ageist language and hold negative views concerning the old. It is well known that children's ageist attitudes can hardly be changed after age twelve. All of this is reinforced by children's literature. Such literature either has very few old-age characters or, if the old appear at all, they are portrayed as unimportant, unexciting, dull, inarticulate, unimaginative, and boring, or sinister, crotchety, resentful, ill-tempered, stubborn, and complaining. Other views of old people in children's books show them to be ill, disabled, and ready to die. Children's literature also exhibits the old exclusively as grandparents. Other books show the old as constantly knitting, cooking, fishing, or tinkering with wood in their garage. In such books the old are never shown as workers, leaders, or creative people.[32]

Books are of course not the only source of stigma concerning the old. Traditionally television commercials and magazine advertisements have shown the old almost only as laxative consumers and hearing-aid users. More recently, there has been some change in these portrayals as active seniors have emerged in the media as motorcyclists, parachute jumpers, and hurdle runners. The reason for this gradual change in the stigmatization of old age in the media has been the increase in purchasing power of the over 35 million old people in the United States.[33]

Sociologists Kathy Shepherd Stolley and Archie E. Hill have reviewed twenty-seven textbooks on marriage and the family concerning treatment of the old. They found that the aged receive a limited amount of coverage in such college texts, that they are generally removed from other family issues but are instead associated with specific old-age topics such as retirement, widowhood, and "the graying of America." Stolley and Hill discovered that only 3.6 percent of text space is devoted to the old, that the old are hardly ever mentioned in connection with race and ethnicity, and that, in true puritan tradition, the old are utterly excluded from any discussion of sex or sexuality. Although concerned with grandparents, even that topic occupies only 8 percent of space in such texts and usually shows "grandparents" in pursuit of leisure-time activities such as bowling, playing shuffleboard, or playing cards.[34] These portrayals are also found in popular culture which has been defined as "that which people do when they are not working." Here the old-age stigma has indeed been institutionalized in innumerable jokes, stories, songs, and art.

Palmore has collected numerous jokes concerning the aged including the frequent jokes which reflect the old-age stigma here under discussion. These jokes are a small sample of such stories: "An eighty-nine-year-old man visits a house of ill repute. The madam greets him at the door. 'What can I do for you?' she asks. 'I want the youngest, prettiest blonde you have,' says the old customer. 'Mister, you've had it,' answers the madam. 'How much do I owe you?' says the man, pulling out his wallet."

Likewise there is the story of the old woman who is held up by a robber frisking her for money. After a thorough search of her body he gives up. "Don't stop now," shouts the old woman, "I'll write you a check!" Such jokes are evidently derived from the stigma attached to the view that the old are unable to attract sex partners. Comments concerning "old maids" reflect the same stigma as single old women are labeled "a lemon that has never been squeezed" or "a girl who failed to strike while the iron was hot."[35]

Cartoons and birthday cards also repeat the old-age stigma as they portray aging as negative. Ultraconservatism, wrinkles, lack of sexuality, and gray hair are all standard fare in such publications. Psychologists

Victor Demos and Allan Jache analyzed such cards with reference to old age and found that over half of them portray the aged in a negative light. A similar study found negative stereoytyping in all forms of communication concerning the old but particularly in television programming.[36]

No doubt, much that is seen on television is a myth that nevertheless has real consequences. The sociologist William I. Thomas wrote in 1931 that situations we define as real have real consequences. In light of that insight it is no surprise that the old are stereotyped and are the object of considerable misunderstanding as promoted by television. In addition the responses of the old to televised views concerning them reinforce behavior that corresponds to the myths being offered by the media in which old women are particularly stigmatized.[37]

The number or proportion of old actors shown in television programming is very small. A study by Elliott revealed that only 8 percent of all television characters were old. Of these the bulk were shown as professionals, mostly doctors and lawyers, hardly any of the old characters were retired, and more than 25 percent were shown as belonging to the upper class. Such a portrayal of old age in America does not correspond to reality at all but reveals an effort to avoid the stigma that normally attaches to any view of old age.[38]

Traditionally, the "old maid" among the old is without doubt the most stigmatized status an American can occupy. Before the middle of the twentieth century and the advent of "the women's liberation movement" unmarried women were also called "spinsters." This term literally referred to colonial days when the only occupation available to unmarried adult women was spinning. Such "spinsters" were viewed as asexual characters. Included in that stigmatized category were nuns, social reformers, teachers, and nurses. The media, particularly the movies, portrayed these "old maids" as constantly seeking marriage without success, either because or by reason of their personality, they were unable to relate to men or because their physical appearance made that unlikely.

The two traits that characterize an "old maid" are age and marital status. Hence, an eighteen-year-old would not qualify for the stigma of "old maid" although no specific age for this status role and its connected opprobrium can be established. As portrayed in the media, the "old maid" characters are themselves aware of the stigma attached to their status as their mood of desperation is portrayed in such productions as *Summertime*. In that play the protagonist, Jane, speaks of herself as "middle aged" as she complains that "no one is older than me."

In such films as *Hush, Hush, Sweet Charlotte* (1964) and *Whatever Happened to Baby Jane?* (1962) the "old maid" is portrayed as becoming insane or dying so that her status is never resolved by finding a mate and founding a family. That is also true of such old films as *Arsenic and*

Old Lace (1944) and *Out of the Blue* (1947). There are, however, some other films in which the stigma of "old maid" is finally shed as the protagonist gets married in *The African Queen* (1951), *The Rainmaker* (1956), *Marty* (1955), *The Long Hot Summer* (1957), and *The Music Man* (1962).

Nevertheless it is evident that as the decades progressed, the portrayal of "old maids" changed. This means that until 1950 "old maids" were shown as women in their twenties. Thereafter, and before 1960, "old maids" were shown as women in their thirties and forties. Evidently, this change came about as women delayed marriage in order to seek a career and establish greater independence from men.[39]

Yet, even at the beginning of a new century, the status of single women is still one of opprobrium in America. A stigma attaches to that status which even the feminist movement of the past three decades has not erased. Therefore we shall, in the next chapter, examine the stigma of being a single woman since colonial times.

SUMMARY

The stigma of old age is related to the immigration history of the United States. In the early days of the country the young were able to come here and deal with the physical efforts and dangers that the old could not do. Furthermore, rapid social and technological change put the old at a disadvantage and they were usually unable to learn the latest techniques.

Today, the contempt for the old dating from the days of the frontier represents culture lag because the physical requirements of yesteryear are no longer in evidence. Yet, ageism is a universal American trait. Even our professional literature includes ageist language.

The young view the old as almost a different species despite the fact that the young ageists of today will become the old of tomorrow. This indicates that the stigma of old age is a social construction gradually being alleviated by the ever-increasing wealth of the aged.

The old-age stigma is institutionalized in that it is found in the economy, in religion, in education, and in the media. This stigma is more often applied to old women than to old men at an age when most women are widows. Since single women are the victims of their own unique stigma we shall discuss their plight in the next chapter.

NOTES

1. Robert N. Butler, *Why Survive? Being Old in America* (New York: Harper & Row, 1975), p. 13.

2. Steven G. Kellnian, "As Time Goes By" *Nation* 250, no. 6 (February 12, 1990): 211.

3. U.S. Bureau of the Census, in John W. Wright, ed., *The New York Times Almanac 1998* (New York: Penguin Books, 1998).

4. Life Expectancy Calculator, website: http://www.yahoo.com.

5. Charles W. Purdue and Michael B. Gurtman, "Evidence for the Automaticity of Ageism," *Journal of Experimental Social Psychology* 26 (1999): 199–216.

6. K. Warner Schaie, "Ageist Language in Psychological Research," *American Psychologist* 58, no. 1 (January 1993): 49–51.

7. Susan K. Whitbourne and Irene M. Hulicka, "Ageism in Undergraduate Psychology Texts," *American Psychologist* 45, no. 10 (October 1990): 127–36.

8. William Bytheway, *Ageism* (Buckingham: Open University Press, 1995), pp. 115–19.

9. Simone de Beauvoir, *Old Age* (New York: Penguin, 1970), pp. 11–12.

10. Gerhard Falk, *Hippocrates Assailed: The American Health Delivery System* (New York: University Press of America, 1999), p. 186.

11. Albert Ashburn and Gerald Gordon, "Features of a Simplified Register in Speech to Elderly Conversationalists," *International Journal of Psycholinguistics* 8 (1981): 7–31.

12. S. Healy, "Growing to Be an Old Woman: Aging and Ageism," in Eleanor Stoller and Rose Gibson, *Worlds of Difference: Inequality in the Aging Experience* (Thousand Oaks, Calif.: Pine Forge Press, 1994), p. 82.

13. Naomi Wolf, *The Beauty Myth: How Images of Beauty Are Used Against Women* (New York: Murrow, 1990).

14. Lest Kohlberg and Robert Shulik, *The Aging Person as Philosopher* (Cambridge: Harvard Graduate School of Education, 1981).

15. Paul C. Luken, "Social Identity in Late Life: A Situational Approach to Understanding Old Age Stigma," *International Journal of Aging and Social Development* 25, no. 3 (October 1987): 177–93.

16. Stephen D. Ross, *The Ring of Representation* (Albany: State University of New York Press, 1992).

17. Hugh Aldersey-Williams, "New for Old," *New Statesman* 128 (May 10, 1999): 39.

18. "Persons in the Labor Force," *Time Almanac 1999* (New York: Time, Inc., 1998), p. 842.

19. Daniel Harvey, *The Condition of Postmodernity* (London: Blackwell, 1989).

20. Marilyn Zeitlin, "Too Old for Hollywood," *Progressive* 56, no. 1 (January 1992): 33–34.

21. Wade Lambert, "EEOC Investigates Law Firm Hiring," *Wall Street Journal*, May 26, 1993, p. B5.

22. Ursula Adler Falk and Gerhard Falk, *Ageism, the Aged and Aging in America* (Springfield, Ill.: Charles C. Thomas, 1997), p. 66.

23. Catherine Jorgensen Snyder and Gerald V. Barrett, "The Age Discrimination in Employment Act: A Review of Court Decisions," *Experimental Age Research* 14, no. 1 (spring 1988): 3.

24. Wanda J. Smith and K. Vernard Harrington, "Younger Supervisor-Older

Subordinate Dyads: A Relationship of Cooperation or Resistance," *Psychological Reports* 47, no. 3 (June 1994): 803–12.

25. Ursula Adler, *A Critical Study of the American Nursing Home—The Final Solution* (Lewiston, N.Y.: Edwin Mellen Press, 1991).

26. Matt Gryta, "Four Nurse's Aides Accused of Beating Elderly Patients," *Buffalo News*, October 13, 1999.

27. Theodore Gebhart, *An Inquiry into the Relationship of Caregivers and Receivers of Care in Elder Abuse Situations* (Ph.D., diss., Yeshiva Unversity, 1988).

28. David Blazer and Edward Palmore, "Religion and Aging in a Longitudinal Panel," *Gerontologist* 16 (1976): 82–85.

29. Mark P. Gibney and Jeffrey L. Courtright, "Arguments for the Elimination of Religious Broadcasting from the Public Airways," *Notre Dame Journal of Law* 4, nos. 3–4 (fall–winter 1990).

30. Michael Hueghey, "Internal Contradictions of Televangelism: Ethical Quandaries of 'That Old Time Religion' in a Brave New World," *International Journal of Politics, Culture and Society* 4, no. 1 (fall 1990): 31–47.

31. Irene M. Hulicka and Susan Kraus Whitbourne, "Teaching Courses on the Psychology of Adult Development and Aging," in Iris A. Parham, Leonard W. Poon, and Irene Siegler, *Access: Aging Curriculum Content for Education in the Social-Behavioral Sciences* (New York: Springer Publishing Co., 1990), p. 13.

32. Sandra L. McGuire, "Reduce Ageism in Kids by Screening What They Read," *Childhood Education* 69 (summer 1993): 204–10.

33. *Time Almanac 1999*, p. 797.

34. Kathy Shepherd Stolley and Archie E. Hill, "Presentation of the Elderly in Textbooks on Marriage and the Family," *Teaching Sociology* 24, no. 1 (January 1996), pp. 34–35.

35. Erdman Palmore, "Attitudes Toward Aging as Shown by Humor: A Review," in Lucille Nahemow, Kathleen A. McCluskey-Fawcett, and Paul E. McGhee, *Humor and Aging* (New York: Academic Press, 1986), pp. 101–19.

36. Victor Demos and Allan Jache, "Return to Sender, Please," *Women's Day* (September 22, 1981): 20–21.

37. Elliott S. Schreiber and Douglas A. Boyd, "How the Elderly Perceive Television Commercials," *Journal of Communication* 30, no. 1 (winter 1980): 52.

38. Joyce Elliott, "The Daytime Television Drama Portrayal of Older Adults," *Gerontologist* 24, no. 6 (December 1984): 629–33.

39. Susan J. Ferguson, "The 'Old Maid' Stereotype in American Film, 1938–1965," *Film and History* 21, no. 4 (September 1991): 131–41.

EX MALIS ELIGERE MINIMA 7

CHOOSING THE
SINGLE LIFE*

STIGMATIZING WOMEN

In 1997 only 4.3 percent of American women fifty-five years old or more had never married. This was then also true of men and reflects the popularity of marriage and the overwhelming rejection of the single life in America. In part, this rejection of the single life is visible by inspecting these statistics. However, there are in the United States a good number of women and men who are divorced or widowed and who therefore augment the more than 20 million never-married single women by another 22 to 23 million. In sum, there were nearly 43 million women in an unmarried state in the United States in 1997.[1]

During the two decades preceding 1997 the percentage of American women ages 25 to 29 who had never married more than tripled from 10 percent to 35 percent in twenty years. Among those ages 30 to 34 the never married rose from 6 to 20 percent and among those ages 35 to 39 the never-married population of women rose from 5 to 13 percent.[2]

The stigma that was once attached to unmarried women in the United States and other societies has therefore decreased most precipitously in this country but is most certainly still visible in Moslem society and among many other groups around the world. Nevertheless, even at the beginning of a new century the myths and cautionary tales concerning "spinsters," "old maids," and "maiden aunts" continue to be part of American folklore. That folklore supports a social stigma concerning single women which has by no means abated in small-town America

---

*Choosing the lesser of the evils

151

and is a source of perpetual interest even in large cities as evidenced by such performances as HBO's *Sex and the City* and other forms of entertainment. Also, in a survey of readers of the women's magazine *Glamour* published in April 1997, a majority of women surveyed by that magazine reported that there is still a good deal of bias against them. Many have felt unwelcome in restaurants and hotels and have experienced prejudice and discrimination in the workplace and in the family. Eighty percent of respondents said that they have been victimized because they were single. More than half have felt unwelcome among married friends and 56 percent have been treated like an "oddity" because they were not married at thirty. Among those surveyed 72 percent said that "people can't believe that singlehood is actually a choice."[3]

It is therefore no exaggeration to say that for hundreds of years single women have faced immense pressure to marry and continue to face that pressure today. "In fact," say Carol Anderson and Susan Stewart, "during some time periods single women were viewed as so evil and subversive that they faced not only stigma but overt violence."[4]

The best known and most bizarre form of this violence was the witchcraft craze which gripped Europe and America between 1450 and 1693. While the American version of this seemingly absurd conduct began in the early seventeenth century, the entire Western world was convinced of the existence of witches and undertook the persecution of those accused of such "craft" as early as the middle of the fifteenth century.

These persecutions of single women are best understood as efforts to restrict the rights and freedoms of women generally. Young single women were thus restricted to a minimum life as dictated by their fathers. The behavior of married women was considered the responsibility of their husbands. However, the conduct of adult single women, including widows, provoked a great deal of anxiety among their contemporaries leading then to the witch craze. All over Europe and New England the two centuries beginning in 1450 and ending in 1650 experienced large-scale persecutions of so-called witches. Almost all of those so accused and maltreated were women who lived without men. Among these women, the poor outnumbered the rich, the old outnumbered the young, the widowed outnumbered the single, and only a few wives were accused of "communion with the devil." Accusations, torture, and death at the hands of their neighbors was the usual fate of those so suspected and demonstrates most succinctly the stigma associated with the single status in Europe and America.[5]

The origin of the witch stigma may be found in the beliefs promoted by the Judeo-Christian tradition to the effect that sex is evil, that women are the cause of all the evil that sex contains, and that therefore men must be on constant alert lest the "evil one," i.e., the devil, overwhelm the whole community. This stigmatization of women is the product of the whole Judeo-Christian tradition. Single women were viewed with horror in the world of the eastern European Jews and no provision was made for them. It was believed by the eastern European community that "the dutiful wife sits at her husband's feet and enjoys eternal bliss from him." European Jewish women were given only a minimal education as it was believed that "too much learning is unfeminine and leads women to have a man's head." Eastern European Judaism also taught that woman is by nature sinful so that women must accept the man's view and see themselves in a strictly supporting role. These attitudes were translated into religious action. Hence women were not counted as one of the ten members required among Jews for public worship. Jewish law requires that ten *men* must be present to engage in congregational prayers and the public reading of the Five Books of Moses or any segment thereof. Women were also excluded from reading the Torah or Five Books of Moses, and they could not lead prayer services or perform any other public religious function among Jews.[6]

Since the world of the eastern European Jew was entirely focused on religious observance, the stigma pertaining to being female assailed all Jewish women. Likewise, the Christian community of Europe and America agreed with these Jewish sentiments and added the view that "the head of every man is Christ; the head of the woman is the man; and the head of Christ is God."[7]

These views were repeated in literature and in the popular culture over many centuries. For example, Shakespeare has King Lear say about women that, "the fitchew nor the soiled horse goes to't with a more riotous appetite. Down from the waist they are Centaurs, though women all above . . . beneath is all the fiends'; there's hell, there's darkness, there's the sulphurous pit. . . ."[8]

The expulsion of Ann Hutchinson from the Boston Puritan community in 1630 is yet another example of the stigma that attached to women then. Hutchinson had the temerity to interpret Puritan doctrine to allow women more activity in the religious sphere than had been assigned to them by men. This challenged male authority and raised the specter of Hutchinson being accused of "witchcraft." This illustrates, as does the quotation from Shakespeare, that sex was associated with evil in order to eliminate competition of women for the scarce resources available to the colonists. It is also important to recognize that high social status and power are always scarce in all cultures and that therefore one more function of stigmatizing women is to eliminate competition from one-half of the population. That competition was never forthcoming from the traditional married woman who lived in the restricted world of husband and children. However, competition for power, status, income, and inheritance was potentially possible for single women. In fact, old widows, even in Puritan New England, owned their husbands' estates and therefore were a potential source of influence and power. Witchcraft accusations put an end to any such empowerment of women and secured the male throne as never before.[9]

Indeed, some of the claims made by those who associated seventeenth-century women with witchcraft were utterly preposterous. One such accusation included the power of a witch to "hinder the churning of butter and the brewing of beer." Such tales were taken seriously by the Massachusetts community three hundred years ago just as equally preposterous stories were attributed to so-called child abusers in the 1990s. The infamous McMartin trial in California is only one piece of evidence that witch-hunts still exist.[10] That trial launched similar investigations in many states.

Perhaps the best explanation of these gross accusations and seemingly irrational efforts to stigmatize women, or anyone, is the observation of Émile Durkheim that deviance is indispensable for the existence of any society because deviance affirms cultural values and norms. According to Durkheim, one of the founders of sociology, "even in a society of saints where ordinary crimes are unknown, faults which appear insignificant to the layman will create there the same scandal that the ordinary offense does in ordinary consciousness." Durkheim goes on to show that stigmatizing is a response to deviance; it clarifies moral boundaries and promotes social unity. In addition Durkheim shows that deviance and the stigma associated with it encourage social change because deviance indicates the possibility of alternative values and expectations.[11]

Keeping this in mind we can now understand why the Puritans labeled minor religious differences as crimes since these differences were the only "deviance" they could use to affirm their solidarity and their distinctive values and norms. By banishing Ann Hutchinson from the Bay Colony the Puritans rid themselves of a person who was seriously threatening the privileges of the clergy. She had said that "each individual had a right to interpret the Bible without consulting the clergy." Obviously, Hutchinson was undermining the income, prestige, power, and control that the clergy enjoyed and were not willing to relinquish. Hence, the clergy stuck Hutchinson with the stigma of witchcraft thereby clearly demarking the "in-group" from the "out-group." Erik Erikson, in his extensive study of the Massachusetts Bay Colony, found that the number of stigmatized persons remained always the same because a small number of the stigmatized are always needed to ensure the social functioning of any society. Hence, when witchcraft became unfashionable other "crimes" were found to bring about the same results.[12]

In our own day the use of marijuana was a great crime in the 1970s but is far less of a crime in the 1990s because the middle class and the upper class had begun using this substance themselves. Here is a clear class of stigma change attributable to power.

Lynching of blacks in the South functioned in the same manner during the 1930s and before since it helped to perpetuate the inequalities of the races. Since then, though lynching could no longer be carried out, a variety of racial epithets and deliberate discriminations have served the same function as lynching did years ago.

Stigmatizing women, whether in seventeenth-century New England or here and now, provides a cultural construction of gender in each society. Therefore, 78 percent of all accusations concerning witchcraft were accusations against women with the view in mind that the boundaries between the privileges of men and the submission of women must be kept at all cost.

SINGLE WOMEN, THE "FEMININE MYSTIQUE," AND THE RIGHTS OF WOMEN

Although witchcraft accusations became nearly extinct in eighteenth-century Europe and America, the position of single women continued to be precarious on both continents well into the nineteenth and twentieth centuries. Furthermore, the disapproval visited upon "spinsters" in America was carried to the United States by English novelists of the eighteenth century so that American writers repeated these prejudices in their fiction.

When the British census of 1851 revealed that as many as 30 percent of British women between the ages of twenty and forty were single, a popular writer of that time proposed to forcibly send the single women to "the colonies" so they could mate with the numerous men available there. Such attitudes continued into the twentieth century so that an article appearing in 1911 entitled "The Spinster" described single women as a serious threat to society.[13]

That threat was also seen in America as the proportion of single women increased during the nineteenth century. Thus, 7.3 percent of American women born between 1835 and 1838 were never married as were 11 percent of American women born between 1865 and 1875. In this country, too, writers and commentators on the single-woman threat held that these women should be forcibly shipped to Oregon and California where there was then a distinct shortage of women.[14]

The designation "spinster" originally referred to a woman who spins or makes yarn. Because earlier centuries seldom allowed middle-class single women any other occupation, the term gradually came to mean "single woman." While poor women worked at numerous occupations throughout the history of humankind, "respectable" women did not work outside the home. For Victorian women, whether married or single, this meant that "notions of respectability (prohibited) them from leaving home or engaging in the trades open to working-class women."[15]

Consequently, until after World War I, women who appeared to be too old to ever marry were then saddled with the label "spinster" or "old maid." Both terms constitute a stigma in its most literal form, i.e., a sign of shame, disapproval, and contempt. Furthermore, the "spinster" was enjoined to remain a virgin, utterly self-sacrificing.

After the First World War, during the 1920s the term "spinster" gradually changed to mean only a virgin. Then such women were attacked as "unnatural" by the novelists and sexologists of that time who equated "old maids" with lesbians. The prime purpose of these designations was to emphasize that "old maids" were unwilling to relate to a "significant other," i.e., a man and therefore these "old maids" were seen as a danger to the established social order. Evidently, the hostility to the independent women then emerging was not only related to the possible threat these women posed to married women who feared single women as competitors for their husbands' affections, but were also seen as symbols of defiance against male authority. In an age when it was believed that men alone could support women and children, the "old maid" defied this stereotype and proved that women could satisfy at least their material needs without the help of any man.[16]

Yet, even as single women were gradually gaining some level of self-reliance in the economic sphere, novelists in particular continued to pillory those women who had never married. Novelists until at least 1945, depicted spinsters as objects of pity and ridicule, or old maids as unable to find any satisfaction, respect, or influence even within the few "spinster jobs" available to them. Such "spinster occupations" included teacher, librarian, dressmaker, and the like. In the emotional sphere, spinsters were expected not to talk about themselves or to articulate any desires. These "virtues" are by no means dead but are, even at the end of the century, still expected of single women among many Americans.[17]

As the century progressed the state of single women changed somewhat. Until the middle of the twentieth century the change was quite gradual but discernible nonetheless. An excellent example can be found in the life of an upper-class "spinster" during the last part of the nineteenth century and the early part of the twentieth century. Lillian Wald was born in Cincinnati in 1867 and entered the nursing profession in 1891 after graduating from the two-year nursing program at New York

Hospital. Subsequently this single woman moved into a house on Jefferson Street with a view to helping the poor within their own community. In that effort she was aided by Mary Brewster who was also a graduate of the New York Hospital school of nursing. Both women founded the Henry Street Settlement House in 1895, which they used to bring nursing services to the poor immigrants who were flooding New York City at the time. This activity led to the establishment by Wald of the Visiting Nurse Association as it is called today. Wald called it the Town and Country Nursing Service in 1912. Wald also founded the Women's Trade Union League in order to fight the horrors of the sweatshops in which so many immigrant women worked at the beginning of the twentieth century. In additon, Wald also founded the Vocational Guidance Committee, which led later to the development of the entire vocational guidance profession in this country. In 1919, Wald represented the United States at the International Red Cross Conference in Cannes, France, and in 1924 she founded the National Labor Committee. At the time of her death in 1940, Lillian Wald had become nationally known. She had earned the admiration and cooperation of industrialists and government leaders and today is immortalized by a bronze bust in the Hall of Fame for Great Americans at New York University.[18]

Although Lillian Wald was an upper-class woman and hence could not be compared to the vast majority of poor women who had none of her opportunities, it is nevertheless significant that she and others were able to become professional nurses. Therefore they were able to support themselves during the early years of the century. Consequently she and others were also taken seriously by the American political establishment, the media, and the public. In sum, the life of Lillian Wald represents a break with the traditional strictures placed on all single women before the end of the Victorian age despite the evident fact that this change has not even now led to a total abandonment of the "old maid" image.

That image has survived the twentieth century, albeit with lesser force than before. As late as the mid-1950s the image of marriage and motherhood as the "natural" sphere of women's interests continued. This was true despite the liberation of many women from household chores during the Second World War, when "Rosie the Riveter" became recognized as an authentic American heroine who made it possible for the United States to build "the arsenal of democracy" and allow American men to fight the Japanese and the Germans at the same time.

Shortly after World War II, i.e., beginning in 1946, it appeared that the economic and social gains women had made during the 1940s were lost and that once more marriage and motherhood defined women whose place was to be in the home. Spinsters continued to be pitied as old maids as illustrated by M. B. Smith who wrote in 1951 that "single woman's outstanding questions (are) 'Why am I to be husbandless and childless?' and 'How can I lead this unnatural life with some measure of fulfillment?' and continued that frustration, depressions, restlessness all come from such a disastrous denial of a woman's natural rights to bio-logical and psychological completion."[19]

The decade of the 1950s and the early 1960s revived the nineteenth-century image of the family as an institution involving a sharp delin-eation in sex roles. The ideal 1950s family had a male breadwinner, a female housewife, and three children. Unmarried women were viewed, once more, as stigmatized outsiders (and potential home wreckers) while marriage and motherhood defined women whose place was in the home. Popular culture again relegated spinsters to the status of old maids who were self-supporting out of desperation while decent mar-ried women did not work outside the home. It seemed, therefore, that the nineteenth century had returned. That, however, was a short-term illusion. A truly major revolution was about to engulf the American family and alter the status of the married and the single dramatically.

That revolution became visible in 1963 when feminist activist Betty Friedan published her influential book *The Feminine Mystique* and the Presidential Commission on the Rights of Women issued its first report to President Kennedy. Friedan argued in her book that women were defined exclusively in terms of their relationship to men as mothers, wives, daughters, or girlfriends. She claimed that women suffered from a problem "that has no name" and advised that "the only way for a woman to find herself, to know herself as a person, is by creative work of her own. There is no other way."[20]

The reasons for the liberation of women from the strictures of the 1950s and their redefinition in terms other than their male relationships were to be found in changes within American society as seriously influ-enced by advances in science and technology. First, there was the decline in the birthrate subsequent to the invention of "the pill" and other birth-control devices that dropped the birthrate from 25.3 per 1,000 Americans in 1950 to 14.5 in 1997. This 43 percent reduction in the number of children born to American women allowed numerous women to leave the home and work for money in business and industry.[21]

Even as the number of births declined, average female life ex-pectancy increased to more than seventy-one years by 1950. Since women, and men, lived longer than ever before, more women were able to enter the labor force after their children had left the home. Moreover, there were more labor-saving devices available after 1950 which enabled women to accomplish household chores in far less time than was pos-sible in earlier years. Finally, during the second half of the twentieth century the American labor market required far more office and service work than heavy labor, so the number of jobs women could do increased immensely. The consequences of all these changes were that more and more married women worked at least during school hours and that single women earned more and more money in nonfactory employment. Most important for single women was the change in attitudes toward female independence brought along by the entrance of so many women into the economy. Evidently, single women who worked were no longer the desperate old maids of previous eras since now "respectable" married women also worked outside the home.

Another major change in American family life after 1950 was the ever-rising divorce rate. During the twentieth century the divorce rate had risen steadily. Thus, about 10 percent of marriages begun in 1900 ended in divorce while 50 percent of marriages begun in 1970 have ended in divorce. Therefore, more and more women headed one-parent households after 1965, even as the number of adult women living alone doubled from 7,319,000 in 1970 to 14,592,000 in 1995.[22]

The increase in the divorce rate indicates a greater emphasis on personal success and individualism for American women, together with a lessening of women's dependence on economic support from men and therefore a lessening of the stigma associated with divorce. Numbers alone therefore guarantee at least some relief from the stigma associated with the word "divorcee" which had so negative a connotation at one time that a sociologist who had written his dissertation on divorce in the 1920s found it difficult to maintain his job at the University of Pennsylvania in view of the criticism he received from the board of directors for writing on so "immoral" a subject.[23]

DISCRIMINATION AGAINST THE SINGLE ADULT

The way we analyze the family has evident implications for the status of single women. When it was believed that the only ethical and reasonable lifestyle had to be within the traditional family, then those outside the family were oppressed by reason of their exclusion. This means that being outside the family promotes the marginality of single women even now, but by no means to the same extent as before the advent of the 1990s. Now, single women are not necessarily "old maids" but are often divorced or widowed. Like single women, married women now also seek a career and compete with men for economic advantages. The dichotomy of male breadwinner and female housewife has been greatly weakened at the beginning of the new century so that single women are no longer an anomaly at least in the professional middle class. No longer is it believed that a "nice" girl has to be protected by her father until she is delivered to her husband. No longer is it necessary that girls stay at home "where they belong." No longer is a woman considered "fast" if she moves into an apartment of her own, and it is not shocking to American public opinion that single women engage in sexual encounters. It is true that single women in the working class, even in 2001, still find this a more difficult position to maintain than is true among college graduates. Furthermore, a visible backlash against the emancipation of women has developed in the United States so that everyone is by no means convinced that the single life is as legitimate as the married status. So while the single life is a more acceptable option in America today it is not popular so that the marginalization of single women continues in various forms outside of the economic sphere even now.

Nearly 15 million American women live alone or with children but without the presence of a husband. These single women therefore occupy a number of social statuses. There are over 2 million who are married but whose husband is permanently absent. There are 2.3 million widows and 4.6 million who are divorced. The others are single and were never married. There are also nearly 20 million children who live with one parent. Over 84 percent of these parents were the mothers of the children and of these one half had never married. Therefore, the role of the single woman in America varies. Unmarried mothers occupy a far different status/role than widows and those who have always been single without children. Both lack experiences that are only the province of the divorced.[24]

We repeat that although the status of single American women has greatly improved at the end of the twentieth century, the stigma surrounding that status still abounds and is experienced by many single women every day. The form that rejection of single women now takes differs from the "poor girl" attitudes of previous years. Now, because women do in fact occupy better professional and economic positions than ever before, the single working woman is more often confronted with the stereotype of an "aggressive bitch," a phrase used by Marcelle Clements who interviewed numerous single women for her 1998 book *The Improvised Woman.* A number of complaints by single women are exhibited in that book and they center around several themes. First is the experience of single working women that the stigma of the single life intrudes on their time in that they are constantly asked to entertain and seduce clients, provide an escort for men, serve as a distraction or "an instrument of denial or a buffer."[25]

Single women repeat again and again that the world consists of couples and that they are systematically ostracized and that married people deal with single women "like people who have had some kind of disease" and that "they are afraid." The fear of the single exhibited by the married relates to the possibility of a single woman "stealing" a married woman's husband. Furthermore, there are so many two-income married couples that their financial condition is generally better than a single person's.

Never-married single women face a world that even now abounds with prejudices and the insults and the humiliations which these prejudices provoke. Such comments as "so and so, poor girl, she never married" are quite common and are said in the presence of single women. There is also a great deal of trashing of achievers among single women. All women, whether married or not, are certain to run into a good deal of resentment against achievement as are some male achievers as well. Women who are called "strong" discover that this phrase is a put-down, including the still-surviving belief that weak women must be protected by husbands. That in turn leads to the conclusion that single women, not under the protection of a husband, must be "tough" and can take a load of insults. Single women are also treated to dissertations by married women on how happy the married state is and how the single state is probably "very difficult."

Several "classic lines" are reported to confront single women incessantly. Among these are: "It was never the good old days for single women"; "Why is a pretty girl like you not married?"; or invitations from married men such as "Why don't I come up to your house and bring a bottle?"[26]

Some single women complain that some restaurants seat the single in the rear and the couples in front; that married women "drop in" on singles without announcement on the grounds that they presume singles have nothing to do anyway; and that many a single woman gets married, not for love, but because she can no longer tolerate the discrimination against singles and needs to attain "a position in society."

Prejudice against singles is not limited to women, as was demonstrated when the credibility of Supreme Court Justice David Souter was questioned during the hearings held by the Senate concerning his confirmation. Men who reach forty and have never married are often presumed to be "gay," asexual, or "just plain odd." These attitudes are particularly fostered by Christian fundamentalists whose views were expressed in an article appearing in the *Los Angeles Times*. That article quoted a fundamentalist "reverend" as saying: "Single people aren't providing the same stability to our country, they're not providing offspring, they carry more diseases."[27]

Discrimination against singles, both women and men, is also visible in the economic sphere. Examples include: airlines that offer cut rates to the spouses of frequent flyers; spas and gyms that charge the same dues to a couple as to a single; insurance companies that charge more for singles or even turn them down on the reputed grounds that singles are a greater risk than the married; insurance companies that demand that even a single person name a family member as beneficiary on a life-insurance policy; travel clubs that offer discounts to married people only; landlord discrimination against renting to single women, particularly if they have children; and voluntary organizations that charge higher membership dues to singles than to the married. Hotels usually charge less per person if two occupy a room than if a single rents the room. Most resented of all discrimination against singles is food-store and drugstore packaging which almost always provides large amounts for at least two if not a whole family. And don't forget the restaurant incentives of buy one meal and get the second free. In addition there are still some states which have unenforceable laws against adultery on their books. These laws generally provide that single women, but not men, may be jailed for extramarital sex or "having an affair."

The never-married old woman faces yet another level of hostility, discrimination, and stigma. She is, in the words of sociologist Barbara Simon, "a metaphor for barrenness, ugliness, and death." There is in fact a children's card game called "Old Maid" in which each player tries to avoid coming to the end of the round with the "Old Maid" card in his hand. Evidently, to be stuck with the "Old Maid" card means to lose the game. The phrase "old maid" is also used by many English writers in both fiction and poetry so that William Wordsworth wrote about "maidens withering on the stalk"; William Blake wrote that "prudence is a rich, ugly old maid, courted by Incapacity"; and Alexander Pope talks of his disgust with "old maids" by writing, "My soul abhors the tasteless dry embrace/Of a stale virgin with a winter face." More recent writers have continued the theme of decrying the single woman. William Faulkner wrote that "he was as crotchety about his julep as an old maid" and the novels of Barbara Prym include numerous single women who have all of the negative characteristics associated with the "old maid" stereotype.[28]

Another frequent comment concerning single women is the assertion that single women must all be the same. This assumption is exhibited by saying to a single woman: "You would like my Aunt ——! She never got married either." Such a comment presumes that the master status of the unmarried is their single state and that they have no other attributes. You'll recall that a master status is a characteristic that dominates and even obliterates all others. We could as well assume that anyone who is married must want to befriend anyone else who is married. There are also people who ask Jewish acquaintances whether they know so and so who is Jewish also. Would such a comment be levied at a Christian? The belief that all minorities are the same also affect blacks, Native Americans, and a host of others.[29]

THE SINGLE MOTHER IN AMERICA

Since 1994, no less than a third of all American children have been born to unmarried women. This fact can be interpreted to mean that the American family is in decline and that the absence of fathers from many families will lead to a breakdown of the entire American social order. The high rate of single motherhood can also be interpreted to mean that a new American family is being built and that new types of work and new types of social patterns require this.[30]

Considerable attention has been given to this phenomenon although the focus of that attention has been almost exclusively on the negative aspects of single motherhood. These negative aspects include the disproportionate level of poverty among single mothers, the social consequences of single motherhood, and the relationship of single motherhood to race and class.

The disadvantages for children who live with single mothers are well known. Such children are likely to be poorer than those living in two-parent households. It has been estimated that children experience a 20 percent decline in income when their parents separate. This is largely true because large numbers of fathers fail to support their children after divorce despite the Family Support Act passed by Congress in 1988. This does not deny that collections through wage withholding from the noncustodial parent, almost always fathers, has not increased since that act was passed. Nevertheless, the stigma of receiving welfare payments in the form of Aid to Dependent Children remains with most mothers and children of men who abandoned them.[31]

In view of the stigma generally associated with unmarried motherhood it may be surprising to learn that there are some single mothers who chose to enter that lifestyle which has steadily increased in the United States since 1970. In that year homes maintained by a single mother with children under eighteen made up 12 percent of the U.S. total. Single-mother homes then rose to 19 percent of all homes in 1980 and reached 26 percent in 1996. Meanwhile, nonmarital births increased from 10.7 percent in 1970 to 37.8 percent in 1996 where they have remained the past four years. Consequently there are now 20 million children living in one-parent homes. Of these, 84 percent live with their mother. Many of these mothers are not living alone, however. Around 44 percent have another adult living with them, usually a new husband or male friend who is not the father of her children. This development has been widely criticized both in the academic literature, in the popular media, and by politicians and has led to the stigmatization of both mothers and children particularly if they are dependent on public welfare.[32]

There are now some single mothers who are financially indepen-dent because they work or have other income and who have chosen to become unmarried mothers. Such mothers have challenged the tradi-tional heterosexual, married, two-parent family form. That traditional form of family is still considered the ideal in American life so that all other forms of family are compared to it with the result that single-mother families are generally stigmatized.

The main reason for the development of families in which the mother is single by choice is that some feminists have concluded that women have been oppressed, excluded, devalued, and exploited and that they will therefore defeat this tradition by "running their own show."[33]

The number of single women who have children has increased all over the world in the past three generations. Most of these unmarried mothers are divorced. However, because single motherhood has become more acceptable in many parts of the world this trend has led to debates concerning the rights of fathers and the issues of child support and arti-ficial insemination. Despite this greater acceptance, however, it can be said unequivocally that single motherhood continues to carry a stigma, particularly as political conservatives have succeeded in gaining more and more elected offices in America.

In addition to the stigma experienced by single mothers, and some fathers, these single parents are faced with the need to do a two-person task alone. Included in these tasks are the need to protect and care for children without becoming overprotective and oppressive. This includes dealing with all school problems alone and handling such issues as friends, relatives, and the continued relationship to the "ex" father and husband. The cost of being a parent also usually devolves upon the single mother despite numerous laws seeking to collect child support from errant fathers.

Single mothers almost always face considerable financial problems because the laws concerning single fathers are seldom enforced. This leads to dependency on the state in the form of Aid to Dependent Chil-dren for many unmarried mothers and their children. Such aid carries a great deal of stigma with it as there are always those who hold relief recipients in contempt.

Mothers who seek to support themselves and their children usually find that they are caught in a dilemma. That dilemma is the result of needed child care. A woman who works only part time can hardly earn enough to support herself and family. One who works full time may still not earn enough to hire full-time help.

Single mothers face even more problems. These may be summa-rized as the "overload" problem, including emotional overload and the loss of intimacy and caring which is aggravated by the hostility many single mothers encounter daily. That hostility is largely institutionalized by the manner in which the needs of single mothers are ignored in schools, churches, government agencies, and on the job. Responsibility overload is another aspect of the "overload" problem faced by single mothers. This means that single mothers are generally the only bread-winners for themselves and their children because two-thirds of fathers do not pay the child support assigned to them by the courts. Furthermore there are many other kinds of responsibilities other than finances that single mothers, and fathers, must face alone. This includes dealing with children who are sick and cannot go to school, thereby creating a dilemma for a working mother who must go to her job. This dilemma also occurs in colleges that have a number of unmarried mothers among their students.

SEX AND THE SINGLE WOMAN

Sexual behavior is part of the human condition and like food and drink is an inborn drive. It differs from other drives only in the fact that one can survive without sex. Because that is so there have been many civilizations which have denied sex to the unmarried by stigmatizing it severely through both religious and legal strictures. This meant, conversely, that marriage before the twentieth century was generally thought of as an economic and sexual union because women, more than men, had access neither to economic support nor to sex outside of that institution. However, as contraceptive technology improved and women were no longer dependent on men for financial support sexual activity among unmarried women increased.

That increase became visible in the 1920s so that the sexualization of spinsters became a part of the discussion of the single state in that decade. These were also the years when the study of sexology began, a study which shaped new public attitudes. At first, the psychiatrists and other professionals who described the sexuality of single women stigmatized them to such an extent that they viewed independent single women as hermaphrodites (the word having been taken from the name of the Greek god of male love called Hermes and the goddess of female love called Aphrodite). A good description of what the writers of the early twentieth century thought of independent single women is a paragraph written in 1901 by William L. Howard, an American psychiatrist and novelist: "The female possessed of masculine ideas of independence, the viragint who would sit in the public highways and lift up her pseudo-virile voice, proclaiming her sole right to decide questions of war or religion, or the value of celibacy or the curse of women's impurity, and that disgusting anti-social being, the female sexual pervert, are simply different degrees of the same class-degenerates."[34] Similar complaints against "modern womanhood" were voiced by psychiatrist Wilhelm Stekel who wrote *Frigidity in Women* in which he held that the progress of humanity was being halted because unmarried working women were causing an increase in homosexuality. Stekel actually equated female independence with homosexuality.

Stekel was soon followed by psychotherapist Sigmund Freud and his disciples who wrote that celibacy was caused by some subconscious conflict that leads to a variety of neuroses. Others believed that celibacy gives rise to the "queer" teachers known for their authoritarianism. Even as the single women of the day were stigmatized severely, heterosexuality was praised in men and in women. In fact, heterosexuality in marriage became the model of American conduct in the 1920s with the result that never-married women were viewed as threatening. This attitude damned to self-doubt and rejection and stigma all those women unwilling or unable to marry. They were branded abnormal and pathological. Because the stigma of homosexuality was attached to all single females by popular opinion as fostered by the academics of the day, many who feared the homosexual label married for that reason alone.[35]

According to a massive study by sociologist Edward Lauman et al., the sexual practices of the American public in the 1990s exhibit the following characteristics. First, young people are becoming sexually active earlier than was true before the 1990s. This means that 80 percent of men and 76 percent of women engage in sex by age twenty. Second, the proportion of sexually active women has increased considerably since the 1940s, when only 33 percent of unmarried women had sexual intercourse. In the 1990s that was true of 73 percent of unmarried women. Third, very few Americans have only one sex partner in a lifetime. Fourth, a significant number of Americans have "extramarital affairs" and that is true of about 15 percent of women.[36]

It appears therefore that the stigma associated with premarital sex is greatly weakened by these developments. However, we now see that a new stigma has arisen with reference to premarital sex. That stigma relates to those who do not want to participate or who are sexually less willing than others. Women are generally less anxious to engage in a sexual relationship while single and are therefore stigmatized by some men who believe that they have a right to sexual activity because they spent money on a date or because they view themselves as very attractive.

Sexuality has different meanings to both sexes because male assumptions concerning sexuality differ from female assumptions and representations concerning sexuality. In the traditional male-dominated society, which has by no means been abandoned at the beginning of a new century, the female construction of sexual identity continues to rest on the safeguarding of female sexual morality, however expressed. Single women are faced with the need to avoid the appearance of being sexually available without seeming to be asexual and unfeminine. This means that single women must deal with contradictory trends concerning sex. On the one hand the sexual revolution of the 1960s has had a lasting effect in allowing women to claim the rights of autonomous sexual beings with the same right as men to engage in sexual behavior of their choice. At the same time, however, a moral panic has seized many people in the "conservative right" who preach sexual abstinence, especially for women, and denounce so-called sexual liberalism. Furthermore, women continue to be faced with the age-old threat of pregnancy which all the birth-control devices and abortion techniques available cannot erase. Finally, women, unlike men, are seldom interested in casual sex. Women seek intimacy and relationships as prerequisites for sexual activity without necessarily worrying about prevailing public attitudes concerning sex. Because changes in sexual attitudes and the entrance of women into many heretofore all-male occupations have made single women more accessible to men, single women are seen by many married folks as a threat to family life and stable marriages. In addition, AIDS and other diseases threaten the lives of those who would be promiscuous.[37]

No doubt the "sexual revolution" of the 1960s remains well entrenched. Nevertheless, many of the excesses then practiced have been rejected by the American public at the end of the century even as the stigma of single sexuality has been greatly reduced. That stigma has also been weakened by the growth of pornography in the realm of the Internet, which features an enormous variety of electronic sex experiences without subjecting the participants to scrutiny by others and the stigma associated with numerous sex practices. Moreover, there are women and men who have met in "cyberspace" and conducted sexual liaisons either by means of electronic contacts alone, or by actually visiting each other after first meeting on the computer. Such conduct also escapes the stigma erstwhile and still associated with extramarital sex.[38]

"DIVORCED" AND "WIDOWED"— THE LONELIEST WORDS IN THE WORLD

Divorced women, not remarried, constitute about 9 percent of American women. In one year, 1998 and subsequently, about 2,400,000 Americans were married while 1,200,000 were divorced or annulled. Therefore divorce rates are about 50 percent of all marriages at the beginning of the twenty-first century.

If we view marriage as a contract, then divorce represents the dissolution of that contract. Included in the assumptions about the traditional marriage was the belief that men were responsible for providing money and security and women provided the cooking and the house chores and the child rearing. A number of surveys have shown, however, that working women still do 87 percent of the shopping, 81 percent of the cooking, 78 percent of the cleaning and that those same women pay 63 percent of the bills in many households. This means that the majority of married women who work must work a "second shift" at home because men do not do their share. Therein lies one of the principal causes of divorce.[39]

The majority of divorced women have children and it is in this area that they encounter the stigma associated with being a female head of a household. Women who head their own households have traditionally been refused credit by banks and stores and treated as financially irresponsible. Unlike divorced fathers, divorced women are faced with the support of their families but, by reason of the stigma associated with that position, must deal with beliefs about their sexual availability and the popular assumption that a woman who runs her own household and works full time is "just doing her job." Most important to divorced women with children is that such an arrangement almost always leads to a lesser income for the family without the support of a man. The difference between the median income of men and women in the last decade of the twentieth century was still large. Thus, men earned about $24,000 in median income in 1998 while women earned only $13,000 in median income. The difference is truly astonishing even if those women who hold college-level jobs earn somewhat more in comparison to their male counterparts.[40]

Divorce does not only have financial consequences. Emotional reaction to divorce is a major product of a breakup of a relationship that may have lasted for years and that leads to a great deal of self-accusation and guilt. Moreover, even at a time when divorce is a common experience in America, there are those among family and friends who point a finger at the divorced and sit in judgment on who was at fault. The stigma of having caused the breakup is a severe emotional challenge that can indeed create agony for divorced women. Many women feel diminished by the events leading to the divorce, particularly if they are no longer welcome among friends who were once close to them. There are those who say that even at the hint of a possible divorce they are at once excluded from the social life they once knew as a couple and are almost at once cut off by their married friends.

Similar experiences can be listed for widows although that status differs in some respects from that of the divorced. The word "widow" has been called the loneliest word in the world. The reason for this is that widows are a source of anxiety and discomfort to a society that favors pairs and couples. Unlike the always single, however, widows are neither "old maid" nor married even though widows have the name, the status, and the children of a married woman. In fact, for widows the social issue that arises at once after their husbands' death is "who are you?" Widows find that they have a number of disappearing "friends" who see the widow as a threat to them as the widow is now viewed as an "intriguing" woman alone.

The stigma of widowhood is in part the product of popular myths that nevertheless create a reality for widows with which they must deal. It is common to believe that widows are always depressed and grieving and that they are physically and mentally in poor health. Unmarried older women are also more likely to be impoverished than is true of the married or of single men. Even now many have little experience with financial matters, having relied on their husbands to deal with all that. In addition, widows report a good deal more stress concerning their children because many widows believe that their children and their "in-laws" stigmatize and reject them.[41]

Another source of friction between widows and their adult children and other family members is the assumption that widows are always ready to be unpaid baby-sitters or domestics and that they are not capable of managing their finances, their time, or their responsibilities. This is indeed an entrenched stigma that labels widows as nothing more than utilities to be trotted out when needed and ignored at other times.

This picture of the single woman does indeed support the view that single women are stigmatized in American life. Nevertheless it needs to be said that many married couples believe that single women, and men, are generally reluctant to invite their married friends even as they expect to be invited innumerable times. Many married couples believe that singles consider friendship a one-way street on which they expect hospitality while giving none in return. If that is the case, then the stigmatization of the single may in part at least be alleviated by educating singles to the kind of reciprocity which couples expect from others and from themselves.

SUMMARY

The considerable increase in the number of single women has lessened the stigma associated with that status somewhat. Nevertheless, the long tradition of seeing single women as threats and even witches continues, albeit in altered form.

The origin of the stigma concerning single women may be found in religions of every persuasion, including the Judeo-Christian tradition. That stigma was always a function of the power relations between the genders as men have not only had greater access to material goods but also to social prestige and social honor. Seeking to maintain that power men labeled single women witches because they were not under the supervision of a father or husband and thereby demonstrated that women could live an independent life.

While the belief in witches ceased at the end of the seventeenth century, the "spinster" took her place for many years thereafter. "Spinsters" and "old maids" were once more seen as dangerous and it was suggested they be sent to California and Oregon because those states had an excess of men before the First World War. Nevertheless, a few upper-class "spinsters" succeeded in freeing themselves from the stigma with which other single women had to deal.

As birth control, labor-saving devices, and service work became more frequent than industrial labor, more and more married women went to work, thus freeing single women who had to work from the stigma associated with female employment all through the 1950s. However, resentment of achievement pursued successful single women and perpetuated the stigma against single women in another form. That stigma is felt most severely by single mothers and the divorced although widows are by no means free of the rejection which the single woman has endured for so long.

NOTES

1. John W. Wright, ed., *The New York Times Almanac* (New York: Putnam Books, 1999), p. 280.

2. "Tell Us What You Think? Is Society Biased Against Single Women?" *Glamour* 95, no. 2 (February 1997): 134.

3. "This Is What You Thought: Is Society Biased Against Single Women?" *Glamour* 95, no. 4 (April 1999): 229.

4. Carol M. Anderson and Susan Stewart, *Flying Solo: Single Women in Mid Life* (New York: W. W. Norton & Co., 1994), p. 51.

5. Judith M. Bennett and Ann M. Froide, *Singlewomen in the European Past* (Philadelphia: University of Pennsylvania Press, 1998), pp. 14–15.

6. Mark Zborowski and Elizabeth Herzog, *Life Is with People: The Culture of the Shtetl* (New York: Schocken Books, 1952), pp. 124–41.

7. 1 Cor. 11:3.

8. William Shakespeare, *King Lear* 4.6.123, 126–29, in: *Collected Works of William Shakespeare,* ed. W. G. Clark and Aldis Wright (New York: Greystone Press, n.d.), p. 161.

9. Elizabeth Rice, "The Devil, the Body and the Feminine Soul in Puritan New England," *Journal of American History* 82, no. 1 (June 1995): 16.

10. Margaret O. Thickstun, *Fictions of the Feminine: Puritan Doctrine and the Representation of Women* (Ithaca, N.Y.: Cornell University Press, 1988), p. 6.

11. Émile Durkheim, *The Division of Labor in Society* (New York: Free Press, 1964), pp. 68–69.

12. Kai T. Erikson, *The Wayward Puritans* (New York: John Wiley and Sons, 1966), p. 82.

13. W. R. Gregg, *Literary and Social Judgments* (Boston: James R. Osgood, 1873), p. 277.

14. Lee Chambers-Schiller, *Liberty: A Better Husband* (New Haven: Yale University Press, 1984), pp. 3–9.

15. Sheila Jeffreys, *The Spinster and Her Enemies; Feminism and Sexuality 1880–1930* (London: Pandora Publishing Co., 1985), p. 87.

16. Laura L. Doan, *Old Maids to Radical Spinsters: Unmarried Women in the Twentieth-Century Novel* (Chicago: University of Illinois Press, 1991), p. 7.

17. Dorothy Yost Deegan, *The Stereotype of the Single Woman in American Novels* (New York: Octagon Books, 1969), p. 119.

18. Gerhard Falk, "Lillian D. Wald," in *American Nursing, A Biographical Dictionary,* ed. Vern L. Bullough, Olga M. Church, and Alice P. Stein (New York: Garland Press, 1988), pp. 331–33.

19. M. B. Smith, *The Single Woman Today: Her Problems and Adjustment* (London: Watts Publishing Co., 1951), p. vii.

20. Betty Friedan, *The Feminine Mystique* (New York: W. W. Norton & Co., 1962), p. 344.

21. National Vital Statistics Report, vol. 47, no. 18, 1998.

22. U.S. Bureau of the Census, Web site: www.census.gov.

23. James P. Lichtenberger, *Divorce: A Social Interpretation* (New York: Arno Press, 1931).

24. Terry A. Lugaila, "Marital Status and Living Arrangements: March 1998," *Current Population Reports* (Washington, D.C.: U.S. Department of Commerce, Census Bureau, October 29, 1998).

25. Marcelle Clements, *The Improvised Woman: Single Women Reinventing Single Life* (New York: W. W. Norton, 1998), p. 69.

26. Clements, *The Improvised Woman,* p. 74.

27. Rita Robinson, *When Women Choose to Be Single* (North Hollywood, Calif.: Newcastle Publishing Co., 1991), p. 41.

28. Barbara L. Simon, *Never Married Women* (Philadelphia: Temple University, 1987), p. 3.

29. Everett C. Hughes, "Dilemmas and Contradictions of Status," *American Journal of Sociology* 50 (1945): 353–59.

30. U.S. Bureau of the Census, *Statistical Abstracts of the United States* (Washington, D.C: U.S. Government Printing Office, 1996).

31. Richard K. Caputo, "Receipt of Child Support by Working Single Women," *Journal of Contemporary Human Services* 77, no. 10 (December 1996): 615–25.

32. U.S. Bureau of the Census, *Statistical Abstracts of the U.S.,* 116th ed. (Washington, D.C.: U.S. Government Printing Office, 1996).

33. Valerie S. Mannis, "Single Mothers by Choice," *Family Relations* 48, no. 2 (April 1999): 121–28.

34. Chambers-Schiller, *Liberty*, p. 199.

35. Ibid., 204.

36. Edward O. Lauman et al., *The Social Organization of Sexuality: Sexual Practices in the United States* (Chicago: University of Chicago Press, 1994).

37. Tuula Gordon, *Single Women: On the Margin?* (New York: New York University Press, 1994), p. 117.

38. Gerhard Falk, *Sex, Gender and Social Change: The Great Revolution* (New York: University Press of America, 1998), p. 297.

39. Clements, *The Improvised Woman*, p. 109.

40. Borgna Brunner, ed., *The Time Almanac 1999* (New York: Information Please LLC, 1999), p. 849.

41. D. L. Morgan, "Adjusting to Widowhood: Do Social Networks Really Make It Easier?" *Gerontologist* 29 (1989): 101–107.

THE STIGMA OF RACE 8

NATIVE AMERICANS—
STRANGERS IN THEIR OWN LAND

THE NATIVE AMERICANS: A RACE APART

A race is a biological subdivision of the human species whose members have some physical characteristics in common. This definition of race follows scientific principles and summarizes the findings of biologists and anthropologists in defining racial characteristics as those features of the human constitution which are inherited through the genes.[1]

There is yet another definition of race not relying on biology. That is its social definition. This means that race is also a social construct. Therefore, American and other societies have assigned people to races by public opinion without reference to facts or logic. From a purely scientific point of view only three races can be identified. These are the Caucasoid, Mongoloid, and Negroid races as well as those millions whose ancestry is a mixture of races. Native Americans, also called Indians, are almost always the progeny of two races if not three. This has led various groups of Native Americans to differ among themselves as to the criteria used to determine who is or is not a member of an Indian nation. Among some American Indians one must be able to prove 75 percent Indian ancestry while others are willing to accept members who can prove only 50 percent Indian ancestry. The U.S. government uses a complex number of regulations called the "federal acknowledgment process" to determine who is a Native American. This is important because those defined as Indians by the Bureau of Indian

173

Affairs qualify for educational, housing, and health benefits and are also permitted to manage the natural resources on Indian lands.[2]

This demonstrates that race has a social dimension having nothing to do with biological or anthropological evidence. That social dimension is based on the widespread belief that acquired characteristics are biological attributes and are therefore inherent in the so-called race. In fact, we can define a racist as someone who assumes that learned characteristics are fixed biological features of a group and that these features can be used to rank so-called races as superior or inferior. The most notorious example of such racism is the Nazi ideology which led to the slaughter of millions of European Jews on the grounds that Jews were racially inferior "non-Aryans," a belief long supported by Christian theology before and after Hitler. Specifically, it was an axiom of the Christian worldview for many centuries that Jews are a race, that Jews are evil, and that "an individual's race determines his moral and intellectual qualities."[3]

These beliefs were not confined to Jews. Outsiders, people who dress differently or speak languages other than any observer's native tongue, are viewed as racially inferior in many countries including the United States. Therefore there are many in the United States who attribute racial inferiority to the Native Americans whom Europeans first encountered after invading the native land of the so-called Indians.

That encounter began in 1492 when Christopher Columbus arrived in the New World unexpectedly and unwanted by those already living here. It is therefore reasonable that in 1992 Native Americans found no cause to celebrate the 500th anniversary of Columbus's voyage. From the view of the natives of this continent Columbus and those who followed him were not only explorers but also exploiters and destroyers. Russell Means, a leader in the American Indian community, said that Columbus "makes Hitler look like a Juvenile Delinquent." Likewise, Kirpatrick Sale in his biography of Columbus calls him a "grasping fortune hunter" whose legacy to the Indians was rapine, servitude, and death.[4]

At the 500th anniversary of the voyage of Columbus, a good deal of controversy erupted in the United States and in Latin America as various factions sought to interpret the legacy of Columbus in the light of their own interests. Thus, the Catholic bishops defended the European invasion of the New World despite the "harsh and painful" history of that conquest because it led to the conversion of the "natives" to Christianity. At the same time, Fidel Castro, dictator of Cuba and a man of Spanish heritage, nevertheless denounced the Spanish conquerors as "raping and enslaving our people," thus expropriating the victims of their history for his political propaganda. Whatever side one may want to take in this controversy, there can be no doubt that genocide was practiced on this continent. For example, the island of Hispaniola, where Columbus landed on his second voyage in 1493, had a native population called the Taino, estimated at 8 million at the time of their "discovery." As a result of disease and numerous atrocities inflicted on them their number had declined to 28,000 by 1514 and by 1560 they were extinct.[5]

Evidently, the destruction of Indian lives and culture began almost at once after the arrival of the first European settlers and continued in this country until the middle of the nineteenth century. During that period a true genocide of Native Americans was in progress here. This genocide was justified by stigmatizing American Indians as "savages."[6]

It would be unjust not to recall here that genocide was also practiced by some Indian nations upon other Indian nations. This was surely the case when the Iroquois Confederacy or Five Nations, consisting of the Seneca, Cayuga, Onondaga, Oneida, and Mohawk, totally destroyed the Erie tribe, who had been their neighbors for centuries. While the causes of the Iroquois-Erie war in the 1640s may be in dispute, there can be no doubt that the Onondagas and others "butchered the Erie . . . and wrought such carnage among the women and children that blood was knee-deep in certain places." Not satisfied with that horror, the Iroquois Confederacy used the firearms obtained from the French to slaughter the Erie who did not have that advantage until by 1656 "the extinct Erie slept in unmarked graves." Hence, the Erie language disappeared and all we know of their erstwhile existence are some records the Jesuits preserved concerning verbal, but not written memories of that lost nation.[7]

At the time of the arrival of Europeans on this continent there were about five hundred nations here. The population of North America has been estimated to have been about one million in the sixteenth century. Then the Europeans systematically drove the natives from their lands, destroying their way of life and wrecking their various tribal cultures. This deliberate cruelty was augmented by the diseases Europeans imported into North America so that the native population suffered so great a decline that Europeans believed that the American Indian would soon be extinct. In fact, by the year 1800 the number of Native Americans had been reduced to only six hundred thousand. Fifty years later the wars of extermination against the Indians had reduced that population by another half to three hundred thousand. In 1834 alone four thousand Indians died on a forced march from their homeland in Georgia to reservations in Oklahoma and Arkansas. Likewise the Sioux were forced off their land (in the northern United States and southern Canada) and delivered to a reservation by the discovery of gold in the Black Hills of the Dakotas in 1889. This was followed by the Wounded Knee massacre in 1890 when the Seventh U.S. Cavalry slaughtered two hundred Sioux men, women, and children without provocation. From then until the middle of the twentieth century an effort was made by anthropologists and ethnographers to assure the survival of Indian culture at the end of the twentieth century with a resurgence in Indian self-awareness, cultural differentiation, and self-assertion.[8]

Today about 55 percent of the over two million Native Americans live on reservations while the other 45 percent live in or near urban areas. Those who live on reservations suffer greatly from alcoholism, unemployment, and abject poverty. Thus, the first have become last in their own country.[9]

THE MYTHICAL "INDIAN"

The stigma of racial inferiority is generally supported by an entire literature reflecting the opinions of writers and their readers concerning those held inferior and labeled outsiders. Thus there exists an enormous anti-Jewish literature in the Christian world ranging from the writings of the New Testament and the church fathers through Martin Luther and the Nazi diatribes of the 1930s to current hate publications on the Internet.[10]

Likewise there exists a large literature concerning the American Indian which is mostly the product of the writer's imagination or hearsay unrelated to the facts or the actual history of the natives of the American continent. One of the first to write about Indians without reference to the facts concerning them was Charles Brockton Brown, who wrote a novel called *Edgar Huntley.* This was followed in short order by Washington Irving's *Sketch Book* which includes "Traits of the Indian Character" and which launched the "noble savage" stereotype into American literature by emphasizing the defeat of the Indian but also his "fierce satisfaction in draining the last dregs of bitterness" from that defeat.[11]

James Fenimore Cooper (1789–1851) did more than any other American author to fix stereotypes upon the reputation of the American Indian than anyone before him with publication of several novels between 1823 and 1841. Born in Burlington, New Jersey, he lived his adult life in Cooperstown, New York. His novels include *The Pioneer, The Last of the Mohicans, The Deerslayer, The Prairie,* and *The Pathfinder.* None of these novels had any relationship to the native culture which they claimed to portray. The message of these novels was that the "red man" was being extinguished by the inexorable advance of Western civilization. This, despite the fact that Cooper was undoubtedly an admirer of those whom he thought to be "Indians." This is to say that Cooper did not know Indians but admired traits that his imagination attributed to Indians. Cooper also recognized the cruelties and victimization of the Native Americans by the European invaders of his land.[12]

Not so Samuel Langhorne Clemens who wrote under the pseudonym Mark Twain (1835–1910). An inveterate bigot, Twain attacked Jews, Catholics, blacks, and Indians alike, showing a particular animosity to Indians in his twin novels *Tom Sawyer* and *Huckleberry Finn*. Twain also wrote an essay called "Fenimore Cooper's Literary Offenses" in which he was evidently motivated to savage Cooper because the latter had some admiration for his, albeit fictional, Indians. French authors also participated in creating mythical Indians. The explorer Jacques Cartier wrote that giants were populating the area north of Jamestown in Virginia and dog-headed natives were shown on sixteenth-century maps of North America. Cannibalism was attributed to various Indian tribes but in fact seemed only to be true of some South American Indians (but not of Eskimos, who were included in that practice by European writers).

In 1855, Henry W. Longfellow published *The Song of Hiawatha*, a lengthy poem which ends in the absurd command by the Indian hero to his people instructing them to welcome the Jesuits who had come from Europe to bring the good life to the natives. Longfellow did not hesitate to label "the Jews the tribe accursed" even as he fed his Christian audience the myth that the Indians were "waiting to behold the strangers, waiting to receive the message" of Christian and Western superiority, truth, and the good life.[13]

Numerous other American authors added to the list of nonsense written about the American Indian by John Greenleaf Whittier, Mayne Reed, and Alfred Riggs. In addition to these American authors the German author Karl May added a great deal to the mythological Indian when he published his novel *Winnetou* in 1892. That book and other stories by May predicted the total extinction of the Indian on the grounds that he stood in the way of inevitable progress. May's novel has been so popular in Europe that it has repeatedly been made into various movies in which actors of every European nationality have been featured. May's books contain absurd descriptions of Indians and adventures utterly foreign to Indian experience. In *Winnetou* Germans read about the love of the Indian for his German "white brother." Since May wanted all Indians to become extinct, his hero Winnetou does not marry. May's heroes are of course utterly indifferent to material wealth and have no income whatever. How they survive this lack of funds is never mentioned, even as May deplores Yankees and other greedy business types.

All told, May introduced Europeans to an American Indian who never existed but whom many German visitors still seek to see on coming to this country, one century after May invented him. German-speaking travelers frequently visit American Indian reservations expecting to see the spiritually superior but materially disinterested "pure red men" only to find reality to be quite otherwise.[14]

Today, the mythical Indian continues to exist on the screen. Innumerable "western" movies depict the Indian as he has been drawn by the novelists of the previous century. He is a savage but nevertheless an admirable, always truthful, honest warrior. He is the loser in the battle for control of his land but he is morally superior to the evil white manipulators who never speak the truth. Nevertheless, the depiction of Indians in movies and on television is racist throughout. According to this form of entertainment, Indians are endlessly fighting either for themselves or as allies of one or another white faction. As Ward Churchill has phrased it: ". . . the public perception of the historical existence of Native Americans is of beings who spent their time serving as little other than figurative pop-up targets for non-Indian guns."[15]

The complete story of the Indian then tells of the traumatic experiences of the righteous Indian of North America. In the overwhelming number of stories about Indians written by whites the Indian was conquered "for his own good," to effect "betterment," and to continue "progress." All of these narratives are of course cultural fictions and fabrications which suit the writers and their allies in explaining the past and the present without dealing with the facts concerning Indian stigmatization and genocide on this continent.[16]

THE REAL "INDIAN"

The facts concerning the lives of Native Americans since the coming of the Europeans are the product of culture conflict which was inevitably won by the technologically superior "whites" and their overwhelming numbers. Evidently, then, the stigma suffered by the losers in that conflict were attached to them because they lost. Yet, even after losing their homes, their livelihood, and their culture the North American Indian continued to lose. What the Indian people lost in the end was their independence. That independence was lost because of the stigma commonly believed about Native Americans and it continues to be lost because most of the conditions imposed on Indians by whites create the stigma the oppressors use to justify their acts.

It is an article of faith among activists for Indian rights that the problems experienced by the Native American population is brought about by the unjust treatment accorded Indians by whites and their government. It is further claimed, according to the scripts already discussed, that "Indians" are less materialistic, more spiritual, and more in tune with the earth and the environment than the non-Indian population.

We have already seen that the Spaniards followed a violent course of near genocide in their treatment of the natives they discovered here after Columbus. Nevertheless, the Spanish conquerors did not succeed in exterminating the Indian population of the South American continent. Unlike the European Christians in the twentieth century the Spanish conquerors of the sixteenth and seventeenth centuries were not as systematic and technologically sophisticated as the European Christians, who slaughtered six million "unbelievers" in the 1930s and 1940s.

In North America a modicum of slaughter of Indians was also achieved. However, in the United States the decimation of the Indian population was carried on with far more sophistication than was true in the European experience. In the United States it was stigmatization, branding with shame, and accomplished without bloodshed but by means of depriving Indians of their most basic human rights.

Immediately after the American War for Independence George Washington wrote to a congressional committee to draw a boundary line where the defeated Indians were to live and "beyond which we will endeavor to restrain our people from hunting and settling." Subsequently such boundary lines became ever narrower and the land behind them smaller until finally Indians were forcibly settled on some land generally called "reservations." Evidently, Washington's belief that the Indian "barbarians" should be isolated was also assumed by most other Americans, including later presidents such as Andrew Jackson who demanded that all Indians be removed to an Indian territory.[17]

Consequently the United States made a number of efforts to not only isolate the Indian population but also to cause their disappearance by rejecting the idea of communal ownership of land, which is the very heart of Indian culture and survival. Therefore, despite a number of treaties between the United States and several Indian nations, Congress included in the Appropriations Act of 1871 a rider to the effect that Indians should no longer be "acknowledged or recognized as an independent tribe or power with whom the United States may contract by treaty." Furthermore it was proposed that all Indian landholdings be broken up and given to private individuals so that they could eventually be bought by non-Indians as the Indians assimilated into the Euro-American population and disappeared altogether. This view was further underscored in 1878 when Congress passed the Allotment Act, once more seeking to break up all mutually held Indian lands. In 1895, however, the Supreme Court ruled that the Indian nations were indeed sovereign governments. Finally, in 1934 Congress enacted the Indian Reorganization Act which brought the loss of tribal lands to an end.[18]

Today there are approximately 2,375,000 Indians in the United States including the natives of Alaska. The U.S. Census used that figure as well as the total of 1,878,285 not including Alaskans in 1999. Of these Native Americans about 219,000 live on the ten largest reservations and another 219,000 live on smaller reservations. All others live on privately held land.

Since 1934 Congress has repeatedly dealt with Indian concerns, including the Indian Self-Determination and Education Assistance Act of 1975, and the 1989 U.S. Senate Report of the Select Committee on Indian Affairs. That report seeks a reduction in federal programs supporting Indians living on reservations although tribal leaders have called that report a "blueprint for disaster."[19]

That disaster has been the abject poverty in which most Native Americans have lived for all the centuries since the coming of the Europeans and which continues today. American Indians are the poorest ethnic minority in the United States. Thus, the U.S. Census of 1990 reported that median family income in the United States at that time was $35,225 but that Native American median income was then only $21,750. In 1997 about one-third of all Native Americans lived below the poverty line. In Arizona, Utah, and New Mexico that meant that 70 percent of Native Americans lived in houses without running water, sewage facilities, or electricity—services they very much wanted but which were not available to them.

American Indians have significantly lower life-expectancy and higher infant-mortality rates than other Americans. If ever the stigma directed at Native Americans had real consequences, a shorter life and more childhood death are the most virulent results of that stigma.[20]

Unemployment rates on the reservations reach 50 percent. This is in part due to the lack of higher education among American Indians. The barriers for earning a degree to Indians are great indeed. First among these are conditions on most reservations. These generally include considerable alcoholism and unemployment as well as health problems and isolation. All this militates against the decision of a young American Indian to even consider college as one of his or her options. In addition, the finances needed to go to college are seldom available to a young person from an Indian home. American Indians also suffer from an appallingly high school-dropout rate. The Department of Education has estimated that 40 percent of Indians drop out of high school while only 17 percent of Euro-Americans drop out.[21]

Despite these handicaps, many Indians have continued to retain a sense of significance for their own culture in order to avoid subjugation and remain sovereign nations within their reservations. It is of course important to underscore here that American Indian culture is diverse because there are about five hundred different Indian tribes and other groupings in this country.[22]

American Indians differ from all other minorities in this country since no one else has legal standing and the right to negotiate with the

U.S. government on a government-to-government basis. To insure those rights the American Indian Movement was founded in 1968. This movement augmented the National Congress of American Indians but had far more radical aims than that older organization. The American Indian Movement made a considerable effort to enforce some of the six hundred treaties between the U.S. government and various Indian nations. Furthermore, they sought the return of Indian lands stolen from the native population over many years by demanding the enlargement of reservations now in existence. That demand has been consistently denied and has led to some unfortunate and violent confrontations. The worst example of such a confrontation occurred in June 1975. At that time events took place on the Pine Ridge Reservation in South Dakota which led Democratic senator Frank Church of Idaho to declare that the FBI "engaged in lawless conduct and responded to deep-seated social problems by creating violence and unrest."[23]

There can be no doubt that two FBI agents were killed in a firefight with Native Americans. As a result Leonard Peltier, a leader in the American Indian Movement, was convicted of these murders and sentenced to life in prison. Numerous appeals in the case have demonstrated that the evidence against Peltier was probably manufactured by the FBI and that Peltier's guilt is far from certain. In any event, that encounter and so many other grievances on the part of the Indian nations against the government have made Native Americans suspicious of the Bureau of Indian Affairs and all other government agencies assigned to deal with them.[24]

Because the abject poverty of American Indians continued both on the reservations and in the cities, another demand has been the increase in federal dollars to remedy poverty and unemployment on the reservations. That request has been granted to Native Americans by the introduction of a number of federal programs supporting various benefits. First, there is the U.S. Indian Health Service, which provides health care of every kind without copayment for Indians living on a reservation. The Department of Education also provides Native Americans with a number of "impact aid" programs. This means that school districts with a large number of Indians receive a large amount of aid designed to help with the operating budget of the school or provide Indian-language instruction or support numerous other functions. The Department of Education also supports tribal colleges, which are two-year community programs. "Treaty money" has been given to numerous Indians in lump sums of $10,000 at the age of their maturity.

It should also be noted that Indians who live and work on reservations are exempt from a number of taxes. This pertains particularly to gambling casinos, which have grown in number on Indian reservations and have provided an income for many who live there.

Child care is also federally funded on Indian reservations. Labeled "Head Start," this program does not apply only to Indians. It includes funding of meals, health care, and education for children on reservations and elsewhere. Likewise, welfare regulations in several states exempt Indians from the recent welfare-reform laws, particularly the work requirement. All of this applies to anyone who is one-eighth Indian, so that a good number of people benefit from this program who are not truly associated with Indian culture and heritage.[25]

There are those who view with envy all of these efforts to help the natives of North America. The truth is, however, that these programs create a stigma of helplessness and dependency for those who take advantage of them. These programs have not aided the Indian community as they were designed to do. There are those who have left their jobs and abandoned their ambitions because these programs have crippled their initiative. Worse, these programs have left the impression that all Indians are lazy, dependent, and incompetent, hence stigmatized. The truth is that there are Indian businessmen, ranchers, doctors, scholarship students, farmers, and many others who do not use any of the government programs and who do not exhibit any of the characteristics that dependency and lack of initiative invariably produce.

THE "INDIAN" AS A CARTOON

There can be no doubt that the entertainment industry has contributed greatly to the stigma associated with Indian life in this country. Numerous movies shown in theaters and on television have portrayed Indians as absolutely barbaric. Many of these movies deal only with Indians as living in the past. *Dances with Wolves,* a movie produced in 1990, is at least willing to let the Lakota tribe have normal human emotions even as the Pawnees are portrayed as utter barbarians. The movie does not mention that the Lakota tribe was forced onto reservations in the 1880s. Even more astounding is *The Last of the Mohicans,* inspired by Cooper's nineteenth-century novel which leaves the impression that the Mohicans have died out. This must come as a tremendous surprise to the Mohegans who live in Connecticut to this day. Yet even more unrealistic is the 1995 Disney production of *Pocahontas.* Here children are taught that Indians sing with forest animals, that Indian women wear provocative clothes and have the figure of a Barbie doll. The truth is of course that Pocahontas was only twelve when she met John Smith, never married him, and died in England at the age of twenty-two. Furthermore, the Powhatan Confederacy was nearly slaughtered by English colonists while most others died of disease. None of this is found in the Hollywood versions of events, of course.

Yet more gross and unreal are the many television cartoons about Indians electronically fed to small children every day. These cartoons portray Indians as savages with the result that all over the television world, in Europe, America, and other areas, children play such games as "cowboys and Indians" even though it was the U.S. Army, not cowboys, who fought the Indians. In such portrayals Indians do not speak like normal humans but grunt "ugh" with the result that there are millions of Americans and other television viewers who really believe that Indians, if they speak at all, speak in monosyllabic burps. Then there is the expression "Indian givers" which implies that the Indians took back what they once gave. The truth is of course quite otherwise. It is the U.S. government that has so often violated treaties with numerous Indian nations that the phrase "U.S. government givers" would be far more appropriate.[26]

It is alleged by those who have reviewed American history books concerning Indians that many of these books do not include anything whatever about the natives of this country or that they include a kind of "feel good" history that pretends that all the native people of the Western Hemisphere are content with their fate, namely, subjugation and loss of their culture and civilization. In fact, it is alleged that many historians teach that Indians were just an obstacle to be overcome by Christians who came from Europe to civilize the continent and "rescue" the natives from themselves. Of course, there are also those who teach a different stereotype. That is the old belief that all Indians are "noble savages" who were generous, nature-loving, and pure in heart, only to be seduced into cruelty and savagery by the evils of European civilization. That stereotype always includes the introduction of "firewater" (alcohol) to the Indians, which, according to legend, makes Indians far more violent and bizarre than European drunks.

There are, of course, drunken Indians. There are also large numbers of drunken fraternity brothers in every college. Overall, American adults who are not Indians drink 2.5 gallons of wine, 32 gallons of beer, and 1.8 gallons of liquor a year. This means that alcohol is more popular than either coffee or milk which are consumed at a rate of 21.1 and 24.7 gallons respectively. In view of this popularity of alcoholic beverages in the United States and the large number of known and hidden alcoholics in the Euro-American population, it is evident that the stigma of the "drunken Indian" is the product of prejudice.[27] However, this is unclear because in December of 1997 the Henry Kaiser Family Foundation published a report by Andy Schneider and JoAnn Martinez which claimed that "Native Americans have higher rates of mortality from alcoholism than the U.S. population generally."[28] This does not necessarily mean that Native Americans drink more than other Americans. It may mean that alcohol kills Native Americans sooner and more often than is true of others because Native Americans do not eat as well and are more often ill than other Americans.

One of the reasons for the common belief that alcoholism is more extensive among Indians than the general population is that Indians are more likely to drink in public than is true of Euro-Americans. This makes Indian excesses more visible and therefore more subject to criticism. The public conduct of the poor is in any event the outcome of poor housing, overcrowding, and lack of private facilities. A rich man who gets drunk at his country club or in his own home is invisible. A poor man who does the same in a public bar is dragged into a "paddy wagon" by the police and therefore becomes a public scandal. Poverty, not exceptional alcoholism, is the cause of the stigma concerning Indian addiction.[29]

Addiction to drugs other than alcohol has also been portrayed as an Indian problem with particular reference to the use of peyote among some Native Americans. The Native American Church in Oregon includes peyote in its ceremonies. This is analogous to the use of alcohol in the religious ceremonies of Jews and Catholics. Because peyote is an unpopular drug associated with Native Americans, unlike alcohol, which is used in upper-class American society, the use of peyote is considered "dangerous" by those seeking to suppress the use of such drugs in our society. Consequently the state of Oregon refused to pay unemployment compensation to two Native Americans who had been fired for their use of peyote during religious services at the Native American Church. On appeal from that decision, the U.S. Supreme Court ruled that the state had a right to exclude peyote users from unemployment compensation as long as a "compelling interest" of the state is involved. This ruling was seen as a direct threat to the religious-freedom guarantee of the First Amendment to the U.S. Constitution and led Congress to pass the Religious Freedom Restoration Act in 1993. That act was later found unconstitutional by the Supreme Court. It is significant that even during the failed prohibition policy which was in effect in the United States from 1920 to 1933 the use of alcohol for religious purposes was permitted. Yet, peyote, only used by Indians, was not permitted until President Clinton signed the American Indian Religious Freedom Act in 1994.[30]

Numerous additional stereotypes and stigma attach to American Indians. Included are the belief that Indians had no civilization until Europeans arrived here; that Indians were always fighting and treacherous; that Indians had no religion; that all Indians live on reservations in tipis, wear braids, and ride horses; that Indians are stoics who feel no pain; that Indians are incapable of succeeding in school; and that all American Indians are alike in that there is one Indian nation or community in the United States. Such a belief would be rejected outright were we to claim that all Europeans are alike and have only one culture. In fact, diversity among American Indians is as great as it is among Europeans.

Finally, there is the belief among many that Indians are excessively involved in criminal behavior. The Bureau of Justice Statistics has made an extensive study of this issue and reports that there was approximately one felony conviction for every two hundred American Indians each year during the 1990s. By contrast, whites experienced a felony conviction rate of about one in three hundred and blacks had an adult felony conviction rate of one in fifty-one.

Looking now at violent crimes it is reported by the Bureau of Justice Statistics that the rate of murder among American Indians in 1996 was below the national average for those under age forty and that for those over age forty the murder rates are about the same as the national average.[31]

American Indian murder victims were substantially less likely to be murdered by their own ethnic group than is true among blacks or whites. Among whites 85.6 percent of victims were murdered by other whites; among blacks 94 percent of all black victims are murdered each year by other blacks. Yet, among Indians only 57 percent of all Indian victims were murdered by Indians and the others were murdered almost exclusively by whites.

Although the murder rate experienced by American Indians is the same (i.e., about seven per one hundred thousand in the population as among all Americans), the violence rate among Native Americans is higher than among other Americans. The principal reason for this discrepancy lies in the high assault rate experienced among Native Americans. This means that the aggravated assault rate of 35 per 1,000 is more than three times that of the national rate and twice that for blacks. Normally there is a close relationship between the number of violent assaults and the number of murders in any community because most assaults are committed with a firearm. Whether such an assault then becomes a murder or not depends largely on the speed of the ambulance and the efficiency of the trauma services available in various communities. This means that the greater the use of guns, the greater the number of murders. American Indians, however, are far less likely than blacks or whites to commit murder by means of a gun. In fact, almost 30 percent of Indian murders are committed by knife, compared to less than 20 percent among other racial groups. This indicates that guns are used less often among Indians than others and that therefore the murder rate is less because guns are a far more certain means of killing a victim than is true of other lethal weapons. Sexual assault, another violent crime, led to more than twice the conviction and jailing of American Indians than was true of the general population in 1996. Of all Indians then in jail, 7.1 percent were convicted of sexual assault while only 3.0 percent of others were incarcerated for that offense.[32]

Indians are arrested more often for property crimes than is true of the majority, non-Indian population. For all races in the United States, 1,039 persons per 100,000 are arrested for property crimes. Among Indians 1,369 persons per 100,000 are arrested for property crimes. This 24 percent excess of arrests over the general population concerning property crimes could of course mean that Indians commit more property crimes than do others. However, the attachment of stigma and the negative labeling of minorities is a factor which must not be overlooked. No doubt poor and powerless people are far more often the victims of what sociologists call "secondary deviance." This is distinguished from "primary deviance" in that secondary deviance comes about when allegations of a deviant act, such as a crime, comes to the attention of a social-control agency, usually the police. The primary deviance is the alleged act itself. Secondary deviance produces an amplification effect. Offenders and others who have been labeled outsiders feel isolated from the mainstream of society. They become locked into a deviant role, as they seek others also labeled deviant. This in turn leads to a cycle of deviance, apprehension, more powerful stigmas, and identity transformation. This means that stigma actually transforms the identity of those so affected. Moreover, as sociologist Howard Becker has written, "Social groups create deviance by making the rules whose infraction constitutes deviance so that the deviant is one to whom that label has successfully been applied; deviant behavior is behavior that people so label."[33]

This definition of deviant behavior does not mean that crime, drug addiction, prostitution, and the like are not objective forms of conduct dependent on performance by deviant persons. It does mean, however, that the poor and the powerless are more likely to receive the labels that create stigma in the minds of observers. It is true that the American criminal justice system is formally fair and impartial and that procedural laws are theoretically administered equally to everyone. In practice this is not the case because discretionary decisions control the operation of the criminal justice system at every level. The police decide whom to arrest and whom to only warn or ignore. Prosecutors decide whom to charge and how many and what kinds of charges to bring. The courts decide who will be jailed and who will make bail, and the grand jury together with prosecutors decide who will be indicted, while judges decide the length of a sentence. Finally, parole boards decide who shall be released. In sum, these discretionary decisions work to the detriment of minorities including Native Americans.[34]

The poor and racial minorities are also confronted with the criminal justice establishment practice of refusing to believe the protestations of innocence of minorities even while expensive lawyers for more affluent clients can successfully defend even the most obvious miscreants.[35]

There are of course some very wealthy members of minority groups who can and have defended themselves successfully against most serious accusations. This was the case in the 1995 trial of O. J. Simpson, which was plainly decided by the financial resources of the defendant and the belief by some jurors that they have a right to "jury nullification" as a form of compensation for past injustices. The outcome of these practices within the criminal justice system is that we cannot be certain that those arrested, convicted, and jailed most often are more dangerous than those treated with more leniency.

CULTURE CONFLICT AND THE BUREAU OF INDIAN AFFAIRS

Because Native Americans or Indians have a special history within the American people, those who seek to be of service to the Indian community must deal with a group that has a unique place in American society. Unlike all others who came to North America as immigrants the needs of the original inhabitants of the continent are often overlooked and appear invisible. First, it must be remembered that the federal government and some state governments, and hence the American people, have specific moral and legal obligations concerning Native Americans which differ from the responsibilities of government toward any other group.[36]

The stigma which has for so long been attached to the very phrase "American Indian" can easily prevent those seeking to be of help to that community to approach them with unrecognized biases. It is therefore of utmost importance that anyone seeking to work with the Indian community understand their values, their history, and their norms or expectations. That is of course true with reference to anyone with whom we seek a positive relationship. Obviously, any social situation is shaped by the manner in which it is evaluated by all participants. Therefore, Indians may perceive a problem not recognized by whites because of large gaps between the two cultures and their understanding of the world which both must share. One such example is the issue of Indian burial grounds and their attraction for non-Indian archeologists, curiosity seekers, and tourists. The numerous Indian nations on this continent differ considerably in their cultures. Neverthless we can speak for all Indians when we recognize that their burial sites have frequently been exposed in museums or treated like a sideshow in a circus. One example is the Dickson Mound in Illinois, first discovered by chiropractor Dr. Don Dickson on his family farm in 1927. Unlike previous discoverers of Indian resting places who removed the bones they discovered, Dickson left the bones in place and covered 234 burials with a tent. That tent was later replaced by a building which he operated as a private museum. It attracted professional archeologists as well as forty-nine thousand visitors a year. During the 1940s Dickson sold the site to the State of Illinois which has operated a museum there since 1945. The museum was opened to the public in 1972.

In the 1960s, as all ethnic groups were agitating for their civil rights American Indians also demanded their place in American society. It was then that their objections to the use of their burial sites as museums and tourist attractions became vociferous. In the words of attorney Walter Echo-Hawk, a Pawnee attorney living in Kansas, "If you desecrate a white grave you go to jail—but if you desecrate an Indian grave you get a Ph.D."[37]

For years those who exposed and exhibited the bones of Indians were either oblivious to the significance of human remains to their descendants or cared nothing about this human tradition because of their contempt for Indians. In all human societies the bones of the deceased are honored although not all societies bury their dead. Some cremate them and others find alternative ways of honoring the deceased.

In any case, most museums removed Indian remains from public view in the 1970s and 1980s and in 1988 the federal government passed legislation requiring the return of burial remains to some Indian groups. In the light of these developments Illinois sought to close its Museum at Dickson Mound to public view, only to run into a great legal debate over this move. American Indians generally supported this closure even while others opposed it. Consequently, the museum closed for the installation of new exhibits and reopened in September 1994. Since then the controversy has continued both in Illinois and in other states such as New Mexico, California, Minnesota, and South Dakota. These states have agreed to return their skeletal collections to the Native Americans for reburial.

Nevertheless, the remains of thousands of Native Americans lie in museums such as the Smithsonian in Washington, D.C., which has nineteen thousand skeletons or "specimens." While archeologists have opposed any move to return specimens to their owners, the issue of the skeletons comes down to whether or not Native Americans enjoy the same rights in this country as do other Americans. Would it be permitted for archeologists to dig up Euro-American burial sites without even consulting the communities that own these sites? The fact is that archeologists and others have literally engaged in grave robbing solely because the graves belonged to the stigmatized Indians buried there.

In 1990 the president signed the Native American Grave Protection and Repatriation Act. This law has led to the development of inventories of American Indian artifacts and remains and the repatriation of these items to Native American nations. The law also demands that anyone who discovers any of the items covered by the provisions of the law would have to cease any activity such as logging, construction, and the like; notify the federal land manager responsible and the appropriate tribe; "and make a reasonable effort to protect the items before continuing the activity." Museums, universities, states, and municipalities are required under that law to make inventories of their possessions of Native American human remains and associated funerary objects. It is noteworthy in this respect that federal law makes no provisions for funding these requirements so that the museums and other groups must fund these demands themselves. This is only one more example of how politicians, in their anxiety to exhibit their legislative prowess, are willing to gain public exposure and approval for a measure they have introduced into Congress even while dumping the financial responsibility for its implementation on financially strapped localities.[38]

Another example of the gap between Euro-American views of the world and those of Native Americans lies in the value attached to independence. In the dominant society independence is highly valued, despite the fact that in the age of the big corporation, big government, and big institutions of every kind hardly anyone is indeed independent. In any case, Native American culture does not include the value of independence. Instead, Native American culture prizes connections and close relationships. The group is viewed as more important than the individual. In this connection it needs to be understood that relationships between individuals within the numerous Indian tribes and nations are defined differently within each group so that each nation sets its own requirements for membership. Non-Indians tend to view all Indians as the same and assign to anyone they deem an Indian that designation. Yet, some Indian nations require that ancestry be traced to someone who was on a tribal census in a particular year. Others require a certain percentage of Native American heritage to be considered a member, yet other nations trace descent only through the mother or only through the father. In short, only the nations themselves can set criteria for membership even as non-Indians view all Indians as belonging to the same "race." It is of course an axiom of sociology that out-groups are viewed as all alike by in-groups. Christians are often astonished to discover that Jews differ among each other by denomination as do Christians even as Jews are frequently unable to distinguish a Unitarian from a Catholic. All Moslems are viewed as the same by non-Moslems despite the profound differences between Sunni and Shiite believers even as all blacks are regarded as indistinguishable by whites whose "honky" features seem all the same to some blacks.

All of this bears on the manner in which the federal government has arbitrarily decided who is or is not an Indian by enrolling citizens of American Indian nations on tribal roles. Such enrollment provides access to a variety of social and health benefits through the nation and through the federal government as fulfillment of treaty obligations. There are therefore numerous Indians who are not enrolled either because they do not meet the citizenship requirements of one or another Indian nation or because they have never completed the paperwork needed to be enrolled. Furthermore, the federal government has repeatedly "terminated" Indian nations through legal proceedings to the effect that legally some tribes do not exist. This is an astounding example of contempt and stigmatization on the part of the government. Such "termination" implies that Indian identity is to be treated with contempt and leads to an assault on the self-esteem of those affected. Consider whether an Indian nation could use legal proceedings to "terminate" the United States of America. The purpose of such "termination" is of course to end access to benefits for those so affected. An example of this policy was the "termination" of the Menomenee tribe, an action that was later overturned through the efforts of Ada Deer, a social worker, appointed by President Clinton to head the Bureau of Indian Affairs (BIA). That bureau succeeded the Office of Indian Affairs in the Department of the Interior in 1933. The BIA had begun to establish day schools for Indians as early as 1873 with a view of assimilating Indians into white culture and eventually extinguishing Indian culture altogether. These day schools were followed by boarding schools for Indian children first organized in Pennsylvania in 1879.[39]

The purpose of these schools was first and foremost to "cause them (the Indians) to look with feelings of repugnance on their native state," so wrote one George Wilson in the *Atlantic Monthly* magazine in 1882. Likewise, Commissioner of Indian Affairs John D. C. Atkins said in 1887, "This language (English) which is good enough for a white man, ought to be good enough for a red man." Evidently, those in charge of "Indian Affairs" harbored utter contempt for Indian culture and civilization. Added to this wish to see Indian culture abandoned in favor of English and European culture was the wish to end Indian religions. Only Christianity, it was thought, made "civilization" possible and Indians were viewed as having no culture or civilization whatever. Boarding schools for Indian children were to be schools for civilization and constituted an assault on the cultural identity of the American Indian, derived from a negative view of a culture different from that of the white invaders and hence stigmatized. Without entering into a discussion of the manner in which these schools were organized and run, it is now clear that the case against these off-reservation boarding schools can be made along four lines. First, Indians did not rapidly assimilate; second, these boarding schools were cruel because they led to long separations of parents from their children; third, such schools encouraged long-term government dependency; and finally, Indian lifestyles and culture should not be condemned and destroyed but that the Indian culture should itself be the focus and the basis for Indian education.[40]

In fact, it was G. Stanley Hall, no doubt the most famous psychologist of his generation, who found the prevailing method of Indian education at the beginning of the twentieth century especially cruel. It was Hall who insisted that Indian education be based on the Indian culture and the proclivities of Indians themselves rather than on the view that Indian culture should be obliterated by means of education.[41]

It fell to John Collier, however, to put an end to the effort of the Bureau of Indian Affairs to bring about Indian assimilation by education. Collier founded the American Indian Defense Association, which succeeded in bringing about a detailed study of Indian education by Lewis Meriam of the Brookings Institution. Known as the Meriam Report, that study indicted the entire effort to bring on Indian assimilation by means of education and succeeded in creating a "new deal" for America's Indians after 1927.[42]

At this writing, the Bureau of Indian Affairs has changed considerably. The bureau is now under the jurisdiction of a Pawnee Indian lawyer, Kevin Gover, who serves as Assistant Secretary in charge of Indian Affairs and is a graduate of Princeton University and the University of New Mexico School of Law. Today the Bureau of Indian Affairs sees its mission to "enhance the quality of life, to promote economic opportunity" and to deal with numerous other needs of the Indian population including housing, loan opportunities for businesses, leasing of land, and health services. The BIA now serves about 1.2 million American Indians and Alaska Natives who are members of 557 federally recognized Indian tribes. The bureau administers 43,450,267 acres of tribal land, more than 10 million acres of individually owned land and more than 417 thousand acres of federally owned land held in trust status.

AMERICAN DIVERSITY AND THE PRESERVATION OF NATIVE AMERICAN CULTURE

The stigma attaching to the American Indian has characteristics that can be seen in all stereotypes with reference to any group of humans anywhere. These stereotypes are perpetuated because they offer numerous advantages. The entertainment industry repeats over and over again those opinions of human groups that the public expects and wants to see. Hence all Italians are musical and great lovers, as are the French. Women are portrayed as emotionally unstable, Jews are endlessly persecuted and have no other history or characteristics, Englishmen are bores without any sense of humor, and blacks are permanently engaged in civil rights issues without any other interest. Into this panorama fits the stoic Indian who grunts in monosyllables, is endlessly ready to fight, and lived long ago in the age of the pioneers and the western frontier. Indian images live on in this fantasy world as decorations on T-shirts, posters, jewelry, industrial products, and of course sports paraphernalia associated with such "tribes" as the Cleveland Indians baseball team, the Kansas City Chiefs, or the Washington Redskins.

In addition to the perpetuation of stereotypes by these means there is the public perception that Indian culture, like the culture of other minorities, should be ignored in the great American "melting pot." Sociologists reject this view and prefer to promote the idea that diversity within the American experience can be emphasized without doing harm to American values. More recently this idea has taken hold in the media and among politicians and other opinion leaders. This view holds that an American of Indian descent is as much an American as someone of European or Asian or African descent particularly if he or she displays those traits of culture and personality that have added so much to American success over the years. If this view of American life prevails then there is every reason to believe that the contribution of the Natives of the North American continent to American life will yet be as much appreciated as the contributions of any other group, whatever its origin.

SUMMARY

Race may be defined biologically or socially. In the American past such a distinction was not made with reference to Indians who were generally treated as unworthy of continuing as a culture or civilization. By means of novels and other forms of entertainment Indians have been depicted as savages whose culture should be destroyed. This had been the policy of the Bureau of Indian Affairs and its predecessors for many years both on and off the "reservations." Numerous stereotypes concerning Indians have been fostered to place Indians in a negative light even as Indian remains and artifacts have been used as income-producing curiosities.

In more recent years and today the effort to eradicate Indian culture has ceased. Today the Bureau of Indian Affairs attempts a more positive policy toward Indian needs even as the courts have ruled in favor of Indian demands concerning the return of land and resources assigned to them by treaties. Nevertheless a good deal must yet be done to eradicate the kind of racism and prejudice from which the Natives of this continent have suffered since the coming of the Europeans more than four hundred years ago.

Indians, as well as the mentally ill, homosexuals, the obese, retarded people, the old, and the single, all share a stigma that is not of their making but is imposed on them by others who define their condition negatively and place a stigma on them. That stigma we call an "existential stigma" in contrast with "achieved" stigma which pertains to those who have done something or continue to do something that contributes to the stigma imposed on their conduct. We shall devote the next section of this book to achieved stigma beginning with those who have attained a great deal and are then subject to resentment against their achievements.

NOTES

1. John Marks, "Black, White, Other," *Natural History* (December 1994): 32–35.

2. Erin M. Locklear, *Where Race and Politics Collide: The Federal Acknowledgment Process* (Princeton, N.J.: Princeton University Press, 1999).

3. Daniel J. Goldhagen, *Hitler's Willing Executioners* (New York: Alfred A. Knopf, 1996), p. 28.

4. Cathy Booth and Michael Harrington, "Good Guy or Dirty Word?" *Time* 136, no. 22 (November 26, 1990): 79.

5. Björn Landström, *Columbus: The Story of Don Cristobal Colon* (New York: Macmillan Company, 1967), pp. 132–33.

6. Ward Churchill, *Fantasies of the Master Race* (Monroe, Maine: Common Courage Press, 1992), p. 2.

7. Harry Forest Lupold, *Forgotten People: The Woodland Erie* (Hicksville, N.Y.: Exposition Press, 1975), pp. 44–51.

8. Russell Thornton, "American Indian Fertility Patterns," *American Indian Quarterly* 15 (summer 1991): 359–67.

9. U.S. Bureau of the Census, *Poverty in the United States* (Washington, D.C.: U.S. Department of Commerce, July 24, 1997).

10. Gerhard Falk, *The Jew in Christian Theology* (Jefferson, N.C., and London: McFarland, 1992), p. 3.

11. American Indian Historical Society, *The American Indian Reader: Literature* (San Francisco: American Indian Historical Society, 1973), p. 189.

12. James Fenimore Cooper, *The Best-Known Works of James Fenimore Cooper* (New York: Book League of America, 1942).

13. Henry Wadsworth Longfellow, *The Song of Hiawatha* (New York: Duell, Sloan and Pearce, 1966).

14. Carol Herselle Krinsky, "Karl May's Western Novels and Aspects of Their Continuing Influence," *American Indian Culture and Research* 23, no. 2 (1999): 53–72.

15. Ward Churchill, *Fantasies of the Master Race*, p. 233.

16. James A. Clifton, "Cultural Fictions," *Society* 27, no. 4 (1990): 28.

17. Wilbur R. Jacobs, *Dispossessing the American Indian* (New York: Charles Scribner's Sons, 1972), p. 102.

18. Thomas R. Berger, *A Long and Terrible Shadow* (Seattle: University of Washington Press, 1991), pp. 104–106.

19. Laurence Armand French, *The Winds of Injustice* (New York: Garland Publishing, Inc., 1994), p. 73.

20. Diana Kendall, *Sociology in Our Times* (New York: Wadsworth Publishing Co., 1999), p. 212.

21. Carnegie Foundation for the Advancement of Teaching, "Native Americans and Higher Education: New Mood of Optimism," *Change* (January/February 1990): 29.

22. Richard T. Schaefer, *Racial and Ethnic Groups* (New York: HarperCollins, 1993).

23. French, *The Winds of Injustice,* p. 83.

24. Ibid., p. 90.

25. Hendrik Mills, "American Indians + Welfare Liberalism = A Deadly Mix," *American Enterprise* 9, no. 6 (November–December 1998): 58.

26. Devon A. Mihesuah, *American Indians: Stereotypes and Realities* (Atlanta: Clarity Press, 1996): 10–11.

27. Charles F. Levinthal, *Drugs, Behavior and Modern Society* (Boston: Allyn and Bacon, 1996).

28. Andy Schneider and JoAnn Martinez, "Medicaid and the Uninsured," *Native Americans and Medicaid: Coverage and Financial Issues* (San Francisco, December 1997), p. 16.

29. Levinthal, *Drugs, Behavior and Modern Society,* p. 97.

30. Nat Hentoff, "A Blow to Freedom of Religion," *Progressive* (December 1990): 16.

31. Lawrence A. Greenfield and Steven K. Smith, *American Indians and Crime* (Washington, D.C.: Bureau of Justice Statistics, 1999), p. 19.

32. Ibid., p. 22.

33. Howard S. Becker, *Outsiders: Studies in the Sociology of Deviance* (New York: Glencoe Press, 1963), p. 9.

34. Carl Pope, "Race and Crime Revisited," *Crime and Delinquency* 25 (1979): 347.

35. Leslie Margolis, "Deviance on Record: Techniques for Labeling Child Abusers in Official Documents," *Social Problems* 39 (1992): 58–68.

36. Edward H. Spicer, "The Nations of a State," *Boundary* 19, no. 2 (1992): 26–48.

37. Dean Peerman, "Bare-Bones Imbroglio: Repatriating Indian Remains and Sacred Artifacts," *Christian Century* 107 (October 17, 1990): 935.

38. Francis P. McManamon, "Notice of Inventory Completion for Native American Human Remains," *Federal Register Online GPO Access* 64, no. 216 (November 9, 1999).

39. Arthur C. Bining, *A History of the United States* (New York: Charles Scribner's Sons, 1951), p. 112.

40. David Wallace Adams, *Education for Extinction* (Lawrence: University Press of Kansas, 1995), p. 308.

41. *Proceedings and Addresses of the National Education Association* (1908): 1163.

42. Donald T. Critchlow, "Lewis Meriam, Expertise and Indian Reform," *Historian* 43 (May 1981).

ACHIEVED STIGMA

PART THREE

RESENTMENT AGAINST ACHIEVEMENT

9

STIGMATIZING
SUCCESS

JEWS AS TARGETS OF THE ACHIEVEMENT STIGMA

In 1923 the famous German physicist Phillip Lenard addressed a convention of his colleagues meeting in Leipzig and said: "Relativity is a Jewish fraud which one could have suspected from the first with more racial knowledge than was then disseminated, since its originator Einstein is a Jew. My disappointment was all the greater since quite a predominant number of the representatives of physics more or less conformed to the calculation pretenses [*Rechengetue*] of the Jews."[1] These remarks were made ten years before Hitler became dictator of Germany so that Lenard was under no pressure or obligation to use such language nor was he in any way induced to follow the official "party line" as was the case after the Nazi takeover.

Lenard had won the Nobel Prize in physics in 1905 and was without doubt deserving of it. However, jealousy led him to denounce the work of Einstein, not on the grounds that Einstein's work was flawed but on the grounds that Einstein was a Jew. Here we have a prima facie example of stigma based on ethnic affiliation and related to the long history of such stigmatization now called anti-Semitism. That phrase refers to the belief that all Jews are "Semites" and therefore racially inferior and dangerous foreigners.

Initially the word *Semite* carried no negative connotation. It derived from Genesis which recites the legend of Noah and his three sons, one of whom was named Sem. According to that story, Sem was the ancestor

197

of the people living in the area now called the "Middle East." One of his descendants was reputedly Abraham, the first Jew. Since Abraham was born in Ur in Chaldea or present-day Iraq, linguists chose to call the Hebrew language of the ancient Jews a Semitic tongue. The word *Hebrew* is derived from *Ivri* meaning "to ford." Evidently Abraham forded the rivers Tigris and Euphrates. Languages related to Hebrew such as Arabic and Aramaic are also called Semitic languages.[2]

In 1873, however, the word *Semitic* became a stigma when the German journalist Wilhelm Marr founded the League of Anti-Semites and proclaimed that all Jews were members of the "Semitic race" which the newly founded league sought to oppose. The anti-Semites based their hatred on the age-old Christian disdain for Jews but recognized that such canards as the claim that Jews baked their unleavened bread with the blood of Christian children or poisoned the wells were no longer finding very many adherents in secularized Europe.[3]

By claiming that Jews belong to a separate race, the eliminationist stigma against the Jewish population in Europe became most effective. The label "Semite" served to alter the antagonism of the Germans and other Europeans to Jews from a religious to a secular motive, with the result that the mass murders generally labeled "the Holocaust" became possible. While Christian anti-Judaism sought the conversion of the Jews to the majority religion, anti-Semitism views Jews as having an inherent, biological condition that can only be eradicated by using poison gas in the same sense as one kills vermin. Hence the Nazi doggerel "Die Religion ist Einerlei, in der Rasse liegt die Schweinerei" or "Religion is indifferent—the swinishness lies in the race."[4]

Germany was of course not the only country in which such theories abounded. The stigma of being a Jew as well as its anti-Semitic component was widespread in the United States as well. However, German anti-Semitism was rooted in the writings of Martin Luther (1485–1546) whose book *On the Jews and Their Lies* demanded the expulsion of all Jews from Germany and the burning of all synagogues unless the Jews converted to Luther's brand of Christianity.[5]

The United States has quite different traditions so that religious bigotry has been less secure in this country. This is the consequence of long-established democratic institutions as well as the long-ranging influence of the Founding Fathers. Thus, George Washington, unlike Luther, wrote the following to the Jews of Newport, Rhode Island, in 1791: "The Citizens of the United States of America have a right to applaud themselves for having given to mankind examples of an enlarged and liberal policy: a policy worthy of imitation. All possess alike liberty of conscience and immunities of citizenship. It is now no more that toleration is spoken of as if it was by the indulgence of one class of people, that another enjoyed the exercise of their inherent and natural rights. For happily the Government of the United States, which gives to bigotry no sanction, to persecution no assistance, requires only that those who live under its protection, should demean themselves as good citizens in giving it on all occasions their effectual support."[6]

The effort of those who hold Jews in contempt and are called anti-Semites in this country are therefore a good deal less virulent than was true in Europe. Here anti-Semitism is more often used to stigmatize successful people, although Jews are by no means the only Americans whose success provokes stigmatization. Nevertheless, an excellent example of stigmatizing success including an anti-Semitic undercurrent was the attack on Henry Kissinger, formerly secretary of state in the Nixon–Ford administrations from 1973 to 1976.

Henry Kissinger was born in Germany and came to the United States in 1938 as a refugee from the Nazi terror. A professor of history at Harvard, he was recommended to Richard Nixon by Nelson Rockefeller who had met him in connection with Rockefeller's interest in the "Tri-lateral Commission." Nixon first appointed Kissinger his national security advisor and later to secretary of state. This prominent refugee who had arrived here with literally only "the clothes on his back" received a good deal of admiration from some but also considerable antagonism from others. The very idea of such great success attained by a foreigner angered some commentators immensely. Coupled with traditional anti-Jewish stereotypes, such stigmatization of secretary of state took the form of crude bigotry among some and somewhat more covert attacks by others. One example of a character assassination of Kissinger is the attack on him by Noel E. Parmentel Jr. which appeared in the *Village Voice* on March 11 and March 18, 1972. This was a personal assault ridiculing Kissinger's accent, his nose, his sexual tastes, and his behavior. He is depicted as a crawling sycophant to Nixon, a social climber and evil manipulator, and an unprincipled seeker after power. All this was topped off with the allusion to the novel by Phillip Roth, *Portnoy's Complaint*, concerning the Jewish mafia in American literature.[7]

The sum of Parmentel's description of Kissinger was obvious envy and a need to use the stigma of Jew and immigrant to feed the need to stigmatize anyone who is successful in America. American anti-Semitism is of course a reflection of the stigma that the very word "Jew" has aroused in Western culture for centuries. This stigma is embedded in the religion, philosophy, and literature of the Western world and therefore came to America as well. For example, the popular writer Mark Twain (Samuel Langhorne Clemens, 1835–1910) wrote an article in *Harper's* magazine in 1899 in which he repeated all of the trite anti-Jewish stigma known to him and his readers and innumerable generations preceding them.[8]

Although the same ingredients for targeting Jews were present in America as in Europe, American anti-Semitism never reached European proportions. There are several reasons for this. Among these are, first, that American Jews gained rapid social and economic advancement and were therefore better able to deal with attacks on them. In Europe the opposite was the case. The overwhelming majority of European Jews were the poorest of the poor and had approximately the same status as blacks in Mississippi before the civil rights movement. Therefore, unlike American Jews, European Jews had no resources with which to fight those who attacked them. Another reason for the lesser impact of anti-Semitism upon American Jews than Europeans Jews is the diversity of the American population. Jews are by no means the only minority in America. In fact, almost everyone is a minority in some sense. Hence the attack on minorities was more diffuse here than in Europe and was in fact far more virulent in its hostility to Catholics than to Jews. The celebration of the capitalist way of life also deflects much anti-Jewish sentiment here. Because capitalism favors the accumulation of wealth and power and because popular sentiment admires those who succeed financially, successful Jews are no more targeted for resentment than are others. This does not mean that the successful are not the targets of resentment here. It does mean that Jews are not singled out for such resentment. Finally it can be said that at one time anti-Semitism was a part of a general antiforeign feeling which has, in the main, now dissipated and in any case is no longer applicable to American Jews, who are almost entirely native-born and speak an unaccented English.

Stigmatizing successful people in America is of course not limited to Jewish targets. On the contrary, it appears that almost anyone can become the victim of a media attack if he or she is successful in any manner.

POLITICIANS, ACTORS, AND OTHER ACHIEVERS

Politicians and actors are undoubtedly the most maligned Americans. It is of course necessary for politicians and others who are attacked by the press and the public to first gain some success so as to make themselves targets of the stigma to be attached. Someone who has lost an election or who has failed to receive any attention for his acting talents is hardly a target for stigma of any kind since the public cannot identify the unsuccessful and unknown. Only those who are well known can serve as victims for our never-ending need to tear down today those whom we have built up yesterday. As we shall see, this need to reduce all who are successful to lesser dimensions is related to American egalitarianism and the need for leveling one and all in a country of democrats where all persons are not only created equal but enjoined to remain that way.

Looking over the political landscape during the past several years it becomes blatantly obvious that only someone willing to be treated like fodder for sharks by the media would be willing to risk running for or holding public office at the beginning of this century.

In view of the justified attacks on the character of Richard Nixon (1913–1994), which the Watergate scandal produced, it is seldom remembered that Nixon was himself the target of a media attack which nearly destroyed his chances of becoming vice president in the Eisenhower administration. In 1952, Nixon was accused by the media of having a "secret fund" with which to conduct his political campaigns. The media claimed that Nixon had an eighteen-thousand-dollar fund which, although legal, was kept secret from the media and hence the voters, and this made Nixon suspect in the eyes of the media. Nixon remained on the Eisenhower ticket and was eventually able to catapult himself into the White House. Yet, the rumor about the secret fund nearly cost him his eventual career.

In 1968, George Romney, then governor of Michigan, was a leading contender for the Republican presidential nomination until he told a television anchor that he had been "brainwashed" by some generals to support the Vietnam War. This statement was followed by an immense furor regarding the candidate's support of the then-popular war continuing in Southeast Asia and made it impossible for Romney to gain any support for his candidacy. In short, stigma ruined Romney.

A similar media witch-hunt followed the remark by Nixon's first vice president, Spiro Agnew, that a reporter appeared to him to be a "fat Jap." That happened in 1968. One year later, in 1969, Sen. Ted Kennedy of Massachussetts drove his car off a bridge at Chappaquiddick Island, drowning his campaign worker, Mary Jo Kopechne. It is fair to say that hardly anyone who reported that story believes the explanation put forward by Senator Kennedy. It is also certain that the endless media frenzy concerning the Chappaquiddick incident made in impossible for Ted Kennedy to become president later. Kennedy, like others who are targeted by the media, are not innocent victims. Nevertheless, the media attacks on Kennedy and others demonstrate how someone elected to a high office today may well be maligned most cruelly tomorrow.

In 1972, Edward Muskie entered the New Hampshire primary elections with a view to gaining the Democratic presidential nomination. He won the primary election. However, in the course of a speech denouncing the publisher of the *Manchester Times-Leader* for his personal attacks on Mrs. Muskie, the senator appeared to cry with rage. In any case, it was reported that he had lost his composure, leading to his collapse as a "front-runner" and the loss of any chance at becoming president.

Missouri senator Thomas Eagleton was hospitalized on three occasions for depression and had undergone electroshock therapy on these occasions. That was revealed by the media after Eagleton was chosen vice-presidential running mate of presidential candidate George McGovern in 1972. McGovern promptly lost all chances of winning the election, particularly after columnist Jack Anderson claimed that Eagleton had been repeatedly arrested for drunk driving, a charge which was totally false.

In 1976, Jimmy Carter was elected president of the United States. Carter's election was mainly based on his "clean" image, which contrasted so much with the Nixon-Agnew scandals of the previous administration. He was indeed fortunate to win in view of the media frenzy that ensued when he privately commented to a reporter from *Playboy* that on occasion he "looked on a lot of women with lust" and "had committed adultery in my heart many times." More fuel was added to the flames of criticism when Carter also remarked on a different occasion that he did not care that some people used the word "fuck" (For Unlawful Carnal Knowledge) in his presence.

Despite all this, Carter was elected, in part because the media made an enormous fuss over the error President Ford had made during a debate between him and then-candidate Carter. Ford had said "there is no Soviet domination of Eastern Europe." That was of course not true in 1976. Whatever the reason for this mistake, the media talked only about that error for the rest of the campaign. All other issues were laid aside and Ford was made to look like an ignoramus who "cannot walk and chew gum at the same time." Jimmy Carter had a brother who was undoubtedly crude and insensitive to the public image a president needs to convey. However, Billy Carter was not president. Nevertheless, the media followed him everywhere, reported Billy's drinking habits, foul language, and ethnic bigotry and his acceptance of money from dictator Muammar al-Qaddafi of Libya. There is good reason to believe that Jimmy Carter's failure to be reelected in 1980 was influenced by these reports, however unrelated to the issues at that time.

Certainly it had become evident by 1976 that stigmatizing political leaders at any cost had become far more important in the American political process than discussing the issues.

In 1984, Jesse Jackson became the target of stigma and lost all chance of election to the presidency when it was revealed by the media that he had called New York City "hymietown." The remark had been made to a reporter from a black newspaper in a private conversation. Yet, Milton Coleman, the reporter, printed it and caused an immense uproar which led to labeling Jackson a religious bigot despite his effort to apologize to the Jewish community. All of this was aggravated by the conduct of the anti-Jewish hate monger Louis Farrakhan of the Nation of Islam who threatened violence against Jews on behalf of Jackson.

The dominant issue in the 1984 campaign for president of the United States became the finances of Geraldine Ferraro and her husband, John Zaccaro. Ferraro was the first woman ever to be nominated vice president by a major political party. The nomination seemed at first to be of great help to the Democratic candidate, Sen. Walter Mondale. However, the media made the Ferraro finances the whole issue in the Mondale campaign against Ronald Reagan so that the public hardly heard about anything else. It was even alleged that Zaccaro had Mafia connections which was an utter fabrication, but believable.

As late as 1988, New York Republican congressman Jack Kemp was badgered by reporters concerning his alleged interest in homosexuality. There is no evidence that Kemp had any such inclination at any time. However, in 1967 Kemp had some financial dealings with a man involved with the Reagan campaign. That man owned a lodge in which homosexual parties may have been held. Kemp knew nothing about this and had never visited that lodge. Nevertheless, the allegations of possible homosexuality continued to be a topic of discussion by the media until Kemp left public office and declared that he would not be interested in seeking any office in the future.

In that same year, 1988, Democratic senator Gary Hart (Colo.) had become the front-runner for the Democratic nomination for president. Yet, the media undermined Hart by revealing his "womanizing" in great detail. This was done when the *Miami Herald* staked out Hart's Washington town house and found that a model, Donna Rice, had visited him there overnight, and that he and Rice had been on an overnight cruise to Bimini. Since Hart was a married man he was asked by reporters whether he had ever committed adultery. Instead of answering the question he withdrew from the race in May of 1987. It cannot be known whether Hart would ever have become president or whether he would have been a good president. It is known, however, that media attacks on anyone who has any success seem as certain as the sunrise and apparently are the only criteria by which political candidates are now judged in this country.

The 1988 campaign also included the allegation that the Democratic candidate, Gov. Michael Dukakis of Massachusetts, was emotionally unstable and a psychiatric patient. This rumor had been circulated by the extremist and perennial presidential candidate Lyndon La Rouche whose credibility is highly questionable. Nevertheless, the rumor was repeated and printed by the *Washington Times*.

It was also during the 1988 campaign and thereafter that Dan Quayle became the target of the media when it became known that George Bush had selected him as his candidate for the office of vice president. From that day until he left office four years later Quayle was endlessly portrayed as stupid. His poor academic record was exhumed and he was accused of dodging the draft because he served in the National Guard.

When Quayle went on a golf trip that included Paula Parkinson whom the media portrayed as a seductress, Quayle was smeared as a possible adulterer even though there was no evidence whatever that he had anything to do with Parkinson. George Bush was also accused of having a "mistress," which the *Los Angeles Weekly* repeated endlessly without evidence even as the *Washington Post* printed a demand by Dukakis aide Donna Brazile to "tell the American people who would share that bed with him in the White House."[9]

In view of the foregoing it is no surprise that almost the entire presidency of Bill Clinton became a tremendous source of stigmatization of the president, his wife, and his daughter as well as any associates he had as governor of Arakansas and as president. The immense publicity given to Clinton's adulterous conduct, his and Mrs. Clinton's financial dealings in Arkansas, and his draft-dodging conduct during the Vietnam War were all reported in detail to the American public. Despite these allegations and despite the evidence that Clinton had lied to the American people he was reelected in 1996 to serve another four-year term. Although stigmatized and maligned as never before, Clinton remained in office despite impeachment and unprecedented charges of moral, financial, and sexual irregularities. At the height of the "scandal" *Time* magazine published a cover on its March 21, 1998 issue entitled "Kiss but Don't Tell" which detailed all allegations of a sexual nature then confronting President Clinton.

In 2000 these allegations were once more an issue as Hillary Rodham Clinton became a candidate for the U.S. Senate from New York and the president was serving out his second term, his moral authority gone and his leadership in serious doubt as sex and campaign fundraising, not policy, threatened to become President Clinton's legacy.[10]

Innumerable officeholders from coast to coast were the targets of that well-known stigma "politician." Yet, they were not alone. All achievers, in whatever field, are now viewed as the legitimate carriers of any stigma that the media wish to hang on them. Widely circulated among those who provide the public with a never-ending dose of gossip are the tabloid newspapers.

These "news" papers are in fact a form of American entertainment devoted entirely to stigmatizing anyone whose prominence makes that profitable. An example of the effort to malign well-known Americans is the December 7, 1999, issue of *Globe*. That "paper" features a picture of John F. Kennedy Jr., who died in an airplane disaster on July 17, 1999. Inside this publication is a long story to the effect that Kennedy's wife, Carolyn, had committed adultery with someone and that John intended to divorce her. Since Carolyn Kennedy died in that same disaster there is of course no evidence for these assertions, and the parties so displayed cannot defend themselves. Obviously, the whole intent of this form of "entertainment" is to allow readers an opportunity to reduce an admired person to a lesser stature.

The front page of the *Globe* headlines four additional targets of that day's scandals. Here it is claimed that the actress Kathie Lee (Gifford) "attacks Regis," meaning Regis Philbin who had just succeeded in adding yet another "show" to his long list of money-making endeavors. The *Globe* claimed to know that Kathie Lee was jealous of Philbin's success as host of *Who Wants to Be a Millionaire* and "hates" Philbin with whom she had worked as cohost on another program for years. Such a report is of course without proof but reduces both actors to the status of spiteful children.

Approximately thirty-five additional stories in that tabloid refer to numerous other actors, athletes, and politicians. All of the stories are of a negative nature and range from reports concerning alleged adultery of this one with that one, etc., to unsubstantiated reports concerning illness, drug addiction, and alcoholism and accidents and "sex implant operations." Male targets of these "revelations" are referred to as "tigers in bed," females are invariably labeled "sexy." The reader is also informed that "Hillary will divorce Bill"; that the president's brother, now a success in the music business, was once imprisoned for drug use; and that Demi Moore is involved in a "Love Nest Scandal."

Content analysis of these and other such publications reveal several recurring themes. First, the readers are already acquainted with many of the people included in these gossip sheets. Unknown persons are not mentioned as the entertainment lies obviously in "cutting down to size" anyone who can be easily recognized. A second theme repeated over and over again in these publications is the one-dimensional condition of the people whose lives are analyzed. Evidently all of the achievers depicted are interested only in sex. This is evidently a major interest of the readers of these reports although it is highly unlikely that those who have achieved sufficiently to be included in this array of "sexpots" could have achieved their current prominence if they had only sex in mind. Sexual interest is of course a great leveler so that it becomes obvious at once that the prime purpose of the tabloids is the attainment of egalitarianism in American society. The tabloids are in fact saying to their readers: "See, the 'big shots' are no different than you are. All they do is hop in bed, get drunk, fight, and eat. They aren't such big deals after all." Yet another theme included in the tabloid "papers" is the importance of money. One story in the December 7, 1999, issue of *Globe* discusses that the brother of President Clinton has more money than the president and has bought a large house in California without needing a loan, as opposed to his brother Bill who bought a house in Westchester, New York, by borrowing money guaranteed by friends. The emphasis on money is continued throughout the tabloid, not only by discussing the financial standing of its featured characters but also by advertising numerous "fast buck" moneymaking schemes. Magic is also included in these tabloids. Numerous advertisements refer to astrology and other miraculous means by which the reader may bring upon himself all kinds of sudden success resembling the lifestyle of the characters put down in the present issue of the tabloid. There are appeals to buy "the miraculous water of Lourdes" for only $5, a very cheap price considering that the water is advertised to have "limitless powers." In our success-power-driven society such an advertisement is no doubt profitable since it promises to make the user similar to those whose lives occupy the major amount of space in the publication.

Health and methods of maintaining one's health are also prominent among the advertisements in the tabloids. Every kind of diet is advertised as the reader is told that he need not diet or exercise and yet he/she can still lose weight. Miraculous cures are available in these publications, many provided by "psychics" who promise to introduce the reader to great lovers while predicting the future. Finally, the tabloids have a long list of "Gentlemen" and "Ladies" who seek to meet readers of the same or opposite sex for loving relationships.[11]

The sum of the message in these tabloids is that methods other than the tactics of daily life can bring financial and other advantages to the reader so that she or he can escape the demands of mundane existence and gain without great effort what is normally available only to the fortunate few. Yet, overarching all of these themes is *resentment against achievement,* as described by Robert Sheaffer, a libertarian scholar, in his important study of that phenomenon.

THE NEW "LUDDITES" AND RESENTMENT AGAINST ACHIEVEMENT

According to Robert Sheaffer the achieving society includes a good deal of resentment against achievement on the part of those who, for whatever reason, do not achieve. Sheaffer believes that resentment has become "a profitable strategy" because achievers are so guilt-ridden concerning the failure of others to achieve that government in this country and else-where is supporting all those who "refuse to accept the discipline of work." He objects to the common notion that the poor are forced into crimes of brutality and violence and views such acts as an effort to estab-lish the superiority of the nonachievers over achievers, at least while the criminal has the achieving victim in his power. In this analysis Sheaffer is in accord with recent sociological research indicating that homicide is committed far more often by lower-class persons than those with greater incomes and that those who kill and rape say that they do so in order to enjoy a brief moment of control in a world in which they are ordinarily never in control. In a detailed study of murder the author refers to the sociological term "existential validation" with reference to the need of many violent persons to assert themselves "like a man" in order to show who is dominant in a social situation. For example, one man kills another in the course of an argument over 40 cents. The killer "settles" the argu-ment in his favor by slaughtering his victim, not for the 40 cents, but because he is loaded with resentment concerning his social standing.[12]

Sheaffer shows that religious sentiment to the effect that the world must be a "valley of tears" is grounded in the belief that it is "sinful" to achieve anything and that those who do succeed are to be resented. His principal message is that "our notions of what is good and what is bad should derive from the accomplishments of our finest achievers," not from the resentment of our angriest failures."[13]

The United States can be called an "achieving society." There are of course other achieving societies such as Japan and western Europe. These "achieving societies" are a minority in the world constituting no more than 10 percent of the world's population. Now it is evident that the stigma of being a high achiever could not exist in a society that does not follow an achievement ethos. Therefore it is necessary to briefly trace the history of achievement and its introduction to the Western world.

It is in no sense surprising that individual achievement was embedded in the ancient Greek civilization which has had so much influence on the Western world as it exists today. As early as the sixth century B.C.E. the panhellenic Olympic games fostered individual com-petition so that an athlete, victorious in that or any other panhellenic game, was greeted as a hero because he had enhanced the city's reputa-tion in the world. Later, professional athletes among the Greeks pursued personal careers without representing any city and amassed trophies and prizes for themselves in a purely individualistic fashion. Likewise actors performed before an Athenian audience for glory and prizes. Again, as among athletes, players formed private companies whose members traveled from place to place and won prize money and acclaim for themselves.[14]

Evidently, then, individual achievement entered the Western world from ancient Greece as did so many other features of the Greek mind and Greek civilization. Christianity is another example of this interest in individual distinction. While the Christian message about one man and his messianic message failed to persuade the Jews, it became most successful among the Greeks. The reason for this is that the Jews, then and now, believe that the whole people of Israel were together chosen by their god and therefore were exceptional among the nations as a group. Therefore, the proclamation that one person was now the chosen one or was even the god did not fit the Jewish ethos. Among the Greeks, however, this message was received very well since the Greeks not only glorified the individual achiever but were already celebrating the resurrection of Dionysius who had also been killed by numerous enemies. The Christian story is further enhanced by claiming that the Christian deity was the target of stigma on the part of those who could not tolerate his superiority.[15]

A second example of an achieving society was the Spanish experience between 1492 and 1610 when Spain and Portugal reached the height of their economic and political power. This, too, was the product of individual effort and individual achievement because the power of both countries, and particularly Spain, was gained by the great sixteenth-century navigators who had to be individualists and believers in personal achievement to make their historic journeys. Not only Columbus, but Vasco da Gama, Amerigo Vespucci, Ferdinand Magellan, and a host of others sailed into the unknown and by personal courage and initiative made Spain great. Spain, at the end of the sixteenth century, had become an achieving society as had England, the eventual winner of the contest between the two great European powers. Long voyages, risky business investments, and more and more industrial inventions created the achieving society and therefore the stigmatization of achievers. Where there is no achievement, there is also no stigma or resentment against achievement. This means that in societies dominated by an inherited aristocracy the upper classes are seldom the target of resentment though they may be envied. It is only in achieving societies that achievement is stigmatized because in capitalist democracies in particular, each individual can believe that he, too, should have been or could have been successful. In seventeenth- and eighteenth-century England, individual achievement was also highly prized. This came about not only because so many inventions and discoveries were made in England during that period but also because the English invented capitalism. Individual achievement is in fact the outgrowth of a capitalist economy. Noted German sociologist and economist Max Weber has shown that the Protestant ethic, grounded in the spirit of individual initiative and enterprise, led to the growth of capitalism. His studies revealed that the greatest majority of the most successful capitalists in early America were almost always Protestants. He based this view on the Protestant teaching that each individual must perform good deeds but must also be frugal and abstemious. In *The Protestant Ethic and the Spirit of Capitalism* Weber outlines the means by which much more can be done without any great physical effort. It can hardly be hidden that the achieving American is therefore tied to the capitalist method of earning access to wealth by any means whatever.[16]

Because the early settlers of America were in the main English Protestants it is not surprising that the Protestant ethic of which Weber speaks entered the United States and became one of the principal values in this country. Indeed there are only 95 million Protestants here. No doubt Catholics constitute 60 million and other religions about 25 million in this country. The Protestant ethic, however, is universal in the Western world so that hard work, frugality, and the virtue of anglo-morality is explicitly or implicitly preached everywhere in the United States. Therefore, non-Protestants have become so Protestantized that is can be said that regardless of theology, Americans hold a distinctly Protestant view concerning most events in their lives. Therefore we are justified in viewing our hierarchy of values as Protestant, with the result that the Protestant ethic is very much alive today in America. This then lays the foundation for the argument that personal achievement is of great importance to Americans.

The Protestant ethic and its Western version concerning individualism and self-reliance are not the only values that sustain Americans. There is also in this country a considerable effort to level all persons and to promote egalitarianism. It is the discrepancy between the value of achievement and the belief in egalitarianism that leads to stigmatizing achievers at every level of American society.

When Alexis Clerel, better known as the Count de Tocqueville, published *Democracy in America* in 1835, he included a good deal of discussion concerning the role of egalitarianism he encountered here. Egalitarianism is defined as the belief that all men are not only created equal but should remain equal. This notion is displayed in America, but seldom elsewhere, by ignoring distinctions of rank and privilege even though it does exist. "Despising no one on account of his station, he does not imagine that anyone can despise him for that cause, etc."[17]

Another view of this belief is the assumption by many Americans that no one has the right to display any form of superiority or unusual achievement unless such outstanding characteristics are accompanied by at least a veneer of equality. That veneer consists of the easy use of first names, an almost unheard-of behavior in other societies. Since inherited titles do not exist in the United States such forms of address as doctor or judge or captain are used only briefly with the expectation that those who are so titled will quickly relinquish that privilege and ask to be called by name—first name, of course. In America it is rude to brag about money or social position although there are subtle forms of conversation that nevertheless permit a speaker to point to his own achievements. One definition of egalitarianism seeks to hold everyone responsible for his own well-being. Another definition of egalitarianism calls for equality of outcome, not only for equality of opportunity. In the middle between these extremes is the more common form of egalitarianism which seeks to provide everyone with more opportunities than are presently available, such as a free higher education, yet will not support full welfare for everyone regardless of effort. It is of course possible to favor egalitarianism in some areas, such as infant mortality, while denying equality of resources. Essentially, then, equality of opportunity is the approximate middle ground between those who may be viewed as democrats and those we may view as levelers. The latter will seek to compensate everyone who has less than anyone else with a form of welfare resembling the Marxist dogma that the world can be divided between the corrupt or owners of the means of production and the pure or the romanticized poor. It is in this gross dichotomy that we find the root of the stigma that attaches to achievement even in non-Marxist societies such as the United States.[18]

The American philosopher John Rawls contributed significantly to the stigmatization of achievement in America. In his best-known study titled *A Theory of Justice* Rawls defines justice as fairness and fairness as equality. In Rawls's view this has nothing to do with equality before the law. Instead, Rawls defines equality as equality of "social primary goods." The goods are to be made equal, says Rawls, so that there shall be no inequalities unless to the advantage of the erstwhile disadvantaged. Therefore there shall be no differences among individuals in social position, in education, talent, income, or property unless all this can be demonstrated to be of benefit to others. How such an idea can be enforced is not understood by Rawls or anyone else. In *Political Liberalism*, which Rawls published in 1993, the theory of justice is altered. Significant is this change: instead of the phrase "each person is to have an equal right," Rawls now says "each person is to have an equal claim." This means that Rawls now believes that some rights are more fundamental than others and that equality of social primary goods is not as absolute as his *Theory of Justice* claims. We may ask by what means all musical talent can be held to the same limits or by what means intellectual talent can be leveled. Eighteenth-century French philosopher Jean-Jacques Rousseau already preached such egalitarianism when he called for the abolition of the family, which he correctly identified as one institution that would perpetuate the prejudices of fathers through their association with their children. Evidently, Rousseau and now Rawls sought to stigmatize any achievement whatever in their anxiety to make everyone the same.[19]

Max Weber noted that oppressed people usually insist on their own moral superiority. It is almost as if those who are the victims of all kinds of misfortune know how good they are because bad things keep happening to them. Now it is evident that no one is short unless someone else is tall. No one is fat unless someone else is lean. Therefore, no one is good unless someone else is bad. Therefore, the losers in American society can justly claim that they are pure, decent, good, and honest people and that the winners are crooks, politicians, schemers, and liars. They are evil. They are thus stigmatized and brought down from their pedestals. The world, according to that scenario, is divided between "us" and "them." Those who view themselves as victims generally "hug the status of victim tightly." The poor, the losers, the nonachievers in this country see themselves as unwitting victims of circumstances they did not create and cannot control. Therefore their failure is not their fault. It must then be the fault of the rich, the powerful, and the greedy.[20]

During the second half of the twentieth century, and propelled into prominence by the hostilities engendered by the Vietnam War, there arose in the United States a political movement generally called the New Left. Because the left side of the French Assembly seated the liberal parties and the right side the more conservative parties the word "left" has come to be identified with liberal causes in America. The "New" Left distinguish themselves from the "Old" Left in that the "Old Left" fought for women's suffrage at the end of the nineteenth century while the "New" Left fought for racial equality in the middle of the twentieth century. Both groups were and are identified with "liberal" causes. The word "liberal" has various interpretations. Included among these interpretations is the view that the "oppressed" are the uncontaminated nobility of America who have not been corrupted by wealth and power. This idealized yet unreal picture is used by the New Left to impose on others a worldview generally labeled "politically correct" and consisting of the demand that racial minorities are always right, that Western civilization is a form of oppression, and that all established institutions are the enemies of the "oppressed."

Those who object to many of the established values in American society usually begin by examining old dogmas and to "buy nobody's dogma," in the words of Tom Hayden, a California state senator and a principal leader of the 1960s Students for a Democratic Society (SDS). That organization was undoubtedly instrumental in ending the Vietnam War in the 1970s. However, the rhetoric of the New Left embodied in the

SDS also showed real contempt for the lives of ordinary Americans and their achievements and concerns. Hayden has repeatedly called the lives of the majority of Americans meaningless, as did Mario Savio, also a leader in the 1960s revolt against the unresponsive administration at the University of California. Savio found that the jobs and lives of the overwhelming majority of Americans were "intellectual and moral wastelands" and claimed that "a chosen few will die rather than be standardized, replaceable, and irrelevant."[21]

The most recent developments among the radical opponents of the current system are now focusing on the trashing of Western civilization, which they hold responsible for all the world's ills. Here is a prima facie example of stigmatizing an entire civilization solely on the grounds that it has been successful in comparison to all other civilizations in South America, Asia, and Africa. According to the radical scenario now being preached in many American universities all the problems of the non-Western world are caused by America. In a journal called *Earth First* we are told that the overpopulation of Kenya, where the average woman bears eight children, is the fault of America because one American child uses one hundred times more resources in his lifetime than eight Kenyan children. Famine and hunger in developing countries are also the fault of the West, in particular of America, because the traditional self-supporting agriculture of Third World countries has been ruined by environmental degradation of the Third World caused by Western society and in particular the United States. Even the dictatorial governments of developing countries are blamed on America on the grounds that economic and military aid given to poor countries prop up these dictators.[22]

The message behind all this criticism is of course resentment against achievement by Western industrialized nations and the stigmatization of all success as inherently evil. It was in the light of these attitudes that a large riot led to the failure of the World Trade Organization (WTO) meeting in Seattle, Washington, in December 1999, and again in Washington, D.C., in April of 2000. The purpose of the meetings was to discuss the advantages that free trade would provide all participants but particularly the developing nations. There are of course those who fear that increased world trade will come at the expense of labor rights and environmental rights. Such arguments include the fact that children are exploited in Third World countries as they labor for cheap wages to enrich those who sell the products of child labor for big profits in the United States.

In view of these legitimate criticisms thousands of angry rioters took to the streets of Seattle between November 30 and December 3, 1999, to rally for human rights, labor, the environment, and other issues. The outcome of these riots was first that local merchants lost $17 million in retail sales and that the same merchants suffered $2 million in property damage. These losses are held in contempt by those who organize such riots and indicate yet again the stigmatization of any success whatever by those who seek to blame American business for the failure of the Third World to be the First World. Protests of lesser vehemence accompanied the meeting of the WTO in 2000.[23]

In sum it is evident that like the Luddites the arrogance of the New Left reformers permits them to stigmatize any and all achievement, whether in business or in the arts, in education or in medical care, in literature or in science. Between 1811 and 1816 the British followers of Ned Ludd resisted mechanization of the textile industry by systematically wrecking machinery to which they attributed low wages and unemployment. Unlike the Luddites, the rioters in Seattle were not employed in any of the industries they denounced. Instead, they consisted of activists reflecting numerous disparate causes such as anti-Nike promoters, Zapatistas, butterfly defenders, the Sierra Club, and Ralph Nader. All of these groups demonstrate against capitalism and trade, despite the evidence that capitalism and trade have lifted more people out of poverty than any other method. Yet, all who rioted in Seattle claimed at least that the major problems of the world are related to poverty in the Third World. It appears therefore that according to that "liberal" stance anyone who achieves anything is always wrong and by definition an enemy of the poor.[24]

NIETZSCHE, SEGAL, AND THE FATE OF ROBERT BURNHAM

Stigmatizing achievement is neither new nor limited to an effort to defame the famous in entertainment, sports, and politics. Five examples will show that no one who has achieved is immune and that defamation of the successful is as certain to follow high attainment as the seasons follow one another.

No doubt the German philosopher Friedrich Nietzsche (1844–1900) could not have known that only a few years after his death he would be used and defamed by the most notorious hater of the twentieth century. Yet, through the influence of his sister Elisabeth Nietzsche Förster who lived long enough to meet Hitler and Mussolini, Nietzsche was defamed after his death as a forerunner of fascism and Nazi ideology. It may well be that Hitler, who approved of Nietzsche as an official Nazi philosopher and ideologue, never read *Jenseits von Gut und Böse* (Beyond Good and Evil). In any event, such a reading as well as a brief acquaintance with his several comments on Christianity reveals at once that Nietzsche was a direct opponent of the principal and possibly only purpose of Nazi ideology—the killing of Jews. This is best illustrated by the events of 1942 when the German armies had been driven back over hundreds of miles from the city of Stalingrad and were in disarray and facing even greater military setbacks. At that point the German army desperately needed more supplies at the Russian front. Nevertheless, these were slow in coming because so many trains were in use deporting European Jews to death camps. When the Reichsminister of Transport requested that trains shipping Jews to their deaths be used instead to bring supplies to the front, the Nazi high command decided that the killing of Jews was more important than the needs of the army and continued to use the trains for their murderous purposes.[25]

In view of that attitude it is impossible to look upon Nietzsche as a forerunner of Nazi thought. On the contrary, Nietzsche denounced anti-Semitism repeatedly. He praised Jews as survivors of exceptional ability and strength and wrote in *Beyond Good and Evil* that excessive German nationalism is a "political infection." He set himself in opposition to German culture as expressed in the philosophy of G. W. F. Hegel and composer Richard Wagner, who were undoubtedly forerunners of both fascism and communism. In fact, Nietzsche wrote an anti-Wagner essay "The Case of Wagner" in which he clearly demonstrates his utter disdain for the nineteenth-century ideology that ended in the promotion of Hitler to European dictator. Yet, Hitler was inspired by Wagner and his crude anti-Semitism.[26]

Despite the evidence that Nietzsche was opposed to the nineteenth-century trends which culminated in fascism and nazism, he is denounced, one hundred years after his death, as a Nazi. In numerous academic departments Nietzsche is ignored and those who read little but "hear" much respond at once to the mention of Nietzsche's name to the effect that he was the originator of Nazi ideology. No better example can be found of using stigma to attack achievement than the fate of Nietzsche in the hands of the malicious and the ignorant.

A second example of the wish to stigmatize success was the attack on Erich Segal who rose to prominence in 1970 by publishing his novel *Love Story* which was subsequently made into a movie. At the time Segal wrote that novel he was an associate professor of classics at Yale University. Almost at once Segal's fame brought down on him the force of stigma usually accompanying success. In May of 1971 he had resigned his position at Yale University where he had suddenly been informed that he would not be given tenure as previously promised. Evidently, his department had voted to recommend Segal for a lifetime appointment based on his research in the field of classics. When his novel became popular in the summer of 1970 his department rescinded its recommendation that Segal be given permanent status and did not hesitate to denounce his literary activities in the process. Added to this dilemma, Segal was also the subject of a series of newspaper stories, wholly unsubstantiated, which claimed to know a great deal about his bachelor sex life. In a lengthy interview with Paul Goldberger in the *New York Times* Segal recounted his treatment in the academic world, likening it to that of an untouchable in a Hindu village. Segal left the United States and subsequently moved to England where he became a successful author of novels and movie scripts. Yet, he experienced the abuse which, in Nietzsche's words, asks: "Do I have your permission to be a successful writer?"[27]

On March 20, 1993, an old man who sold paintings of cats in Balboa Park in San Diego, California, died alone at Mercy Hospital of congestive heart failure. He was only sixty-two but the years he spent living in the park had aged him prematurely. In addition to a blood clot in his heart he suffered from gangrene in one foot. He also had pneumonia. He was then buried in a military cemetery where a headstone was attached which misspelled his name. No one at the hospital or the cemetery knew the man and no family member attended his interment.

In October of 1997, the *Phoenix New Times* published a series of articles written by Tony Ortega about the man buried in that military cemetery. Diligent work had uncovered that he was Robert Burnham Jr., the author of *Burnham's Celestial Handbook: An Observer's Guide to the Universe Beyond the Solar System.* A book of 2,138 pages, it has been described as unique. "There is none other like it," wrote Ortega. Burnham was a self-educated astronomer. With only a high school education, he succeeded in finding several comets which made Burnham somewhat of a celebrity in Prescott, Arizona, where he lived with his parents. In 1958 his several successes as an amateur astronomer led to his appointment to a $6,000 job at the Lowell Observatory in Flagstaff. It had been the policy of the Lowell Observatory to hire amateurs to do cheap jobs that professionals would not do. Burnham, however, engaged in making a twenty-year survey of the stars resulting in that eight-volume work.

The work excited the entire astronomical profession. Lowell Observatory, however, fired Burnham in 1979 without anyone on the staff even reviewing the book. It was simply assumed that the book must be full of errors since Burnham had no academic degrees. Since Burnham's lack of academic labels made him unemployable in any college or university he lived on the royalties of his book for a few years. These royalties were meager but did sustain him, a bachelor, until 1985. Thereafter he lived by selling his property and then painting pictures in the park where he spent his last days, the victim of resentment against achievement, stigmatized by those who feared his competence and hated his abilities.[28]

Let us now look at yet another and more recent example of stigmatizing success. This concerns Pete Rose, no doubt one of the most successful baseball players in a generation. Born in Cincinnati, Ohio, in 1942, he was named "Rookie of the Year" in 1963. Thereafter he became National League Batting Champion in his hometown three times in 1968, 1969, and 1973, the year in which the Baseball Writers Association also named him "Most Valuable Player." Pete Rose became manager of the Cincinnati Reds in 1984 and remained in that position until he was banished from baseball in 1989. That banishment resulted from an investigation into allegations that Rose had bet on his own team when he managed a Cincinnati-Montreal game in 1987. Since then Rose has assiduously campaigned for reinstatement as a manager and as a candidate for the Baseball Hall of Fame. In that connection Rose was greatly encouraged when on October 24, 1999, he received a "tumultuous welcome" in Atlanta's Turner Park prior to the 1999 World Series game between Atlanta and New York. Rose had been honored by being elected by the fans to the All-Century Team. Subsequently, Rose was interviewed by Jim Gray of NBC Sports. Instead of permitting Rose his moment of triumph and joy, Gray, seeking to stigmatize Rose, asked him: "Are you willing to show contrition, admit you bet on baseball, and make some sort of apology to that effect?" Rose sought to deflect the discussion and refused to admit wrongdoing as Gray demanded. But Gray would not let up. "With the overwhelming evidence . . . why not make the statement?" pursued Gray. Rose said that the occasion was festive, that he didn't want to discuss the matter, and that he sought to enjoy his present recognition. It seemed to many viewers that Gray had made himself a prosecutor and that Rose is still being persecuted. Whatever one may think of that dispute, the treatment of Pete Rose is without question yet one more example of the stigmatization of success that has hounded so many achievers among us. Yet Einstein, Nietzsche, Segal, Burnham, Rose, and others of great visibility are not the only achievers subject to stigmatization. Even among those not famous the stigma that attaches to achievement operates all the time.

One more example will demonstrate how stigma works in everyday life. Ursula Adler came to America as a ten-year-old immigrant. A Holocaust survivor, she was utterly destitute. Yet, by exceptional intelligence, hard work, and tremendous tenacity she succeeded in improving her situation year after year. On her own, without any help, she earned two college degrees and thereupon succeeded more and more in her chosen profession. Along the way she made many friends and her reputation grew. Then she did the "unforgivable." She earned a doctorate, part time and without fanfare. When she was finally granted the degree her family invited her friends to a party to celebrate this great success. Some came, but others were shocked at this development. They would not attend such a party. They could not celebrate the success of someone who had literally raised herself from destitution to become a true American success. Her boss was equally negative. "What's it for?" he asked when she told him she had earned a doctorate. But the "put-downs" were not yet complete. Adler wrote a book and placed the announcement on the bulletin board where she worked. Each time she did this, the announcement was torn down. Her success angered others so that finally she entered private practice because real competence is hardly employable in a society that continues to hang on to that twin tradition in American life, the Puritan ethic and the legacy of egalitarianism.[29]

SUMMARY

Stigmatizing achievement takes several forms of which religious bigotry is only one. Yet, even Einstein was subject to "anti-Semitism" which seeks to make the very word "Jew" a stigma. While such bigotry has never succeeded in America, the stigmatization of politicians as well as actors and athletes has continued unabated for many years. An entire gossip industry is devoted to the stigma of being a success in America. Using tabloid newspapers, that industry maligns politicians, actors, and anyone else who has achieved anything and seeks to "level" all Americans.

Ours is an achieving society. This is the product of the English as well as the Protestant influence on the United States where hard work, frugality, and capitalism continue to be virtues. Yet, egalitarianism is also a value in America and egalitarianism, mostly preached by the New Left, seeks to eliminate all success and level everyone regardless of individual achievements. Their spokespersons attribute evil motives to all who have succeeded. They trash all Western civilization precisely because it allows an opportunity for the better life that so many immigrants have sought in America for so long. Therefore our next chapter will deal with immigrants, most certainly outsiders par excellence.

NOTES

1. Alan D. Beyerchen, *Scientists under Hitler* (New Haven, Conn.: Yale University Press, 1977), p. 93.

2. Gen. 1:21–31.

3. Solomon Grayzel, *A History of the Jews* (Philadelphia: Jewish Publication Society, 1947), p. 389.

4. Daniel J. Goldhagen, *Hitler's Willing Executioners* (New York: Alfred A. Knopf, 1996), p. 66.

5. Martin Luther, *On the Jews and Their Lies*, in *Luther's Works*, ed. Helmut Lehman and Franklin Sherman (Philadelphia: Fortress Press, 1971).

6. Graysel, *A History of the Jews*, p. 562.

7. Arnold Forster and Benjamin R. Epstein, *The New Anti-Semitism* (New York: McGraw-Hill, 1974), p. 106.

8. Mark Twain, "Concerning the Jews," *Harper's New Monthly Magazine* 99, no. 592 (1899): 527–35.

9. Larry J. Sabato, *Feeding Frenzy: How Attack Journalism Has Transformed American Politics* (New York: Free Press, 1991), p. 8.

10. Eric Pooley, "Kiss But Don't Tell," *Time* 151, no. 11 (March 23, 1998).

11. *Globe* 46, no. 49, December 7, 1999.

12. Gerhard Falk, *Murder: An Analysis of Its Forms, Conditions and Causes* (Jefferson, N.C., and London: McFarland & Co., 1990), p. 49.

13. Robert Sheaffer, *Resentment Against Achievement* (Amherst, N.Y.: Prometheus Books, 1988), pp. 31–93.

14. Nicholas F. Jones, *Ancient Greece: State and Society* (Upper Saddle River, N.J.: Prentice-Hall, 1996), p. 216.

15. Will Durant, *The Life of Greece* (New York: Simon and Schuster, 1939), p. 187.

16. Max Weber, *The Protestant Ethic and the Spirit of Capitalism* (1904; reprint, New York: Scribner's Sons, 1974).

17. Alexis de Tocqueville, *Democracy in America* (New York: Vintage Books, 1961), p. 182.

18. Richard J. Ellis, *Illiberal Egalitarianism in America* (Lawrence: University Press of Kansas, 1998), p. 14.

19. John Rawls, *A Theory of Justice* (Cambridge, Mass.: Harvard University Press, 1971).

20. Reinhard Bendix, *Max Weber: An Intellectual Portrait* (Berkeley: University of California Press, 1962), p. 280.

21. Mario Savio, "An End to History" in Massimo Teodori, *The New Left: A Documentary History* (Indianapolis: Bobbs-Merrill, 1969), pp. 158–61.

22. Todd Shuman, "Misanthropy or No—Where Does It Go?" *Earth First Journal* (May 1, 1999): 9.

23. Associated Press, "Seattle Police Head Quits After WTO" (December 7, 1999).

24. Charles Krauthammer, "The Return of the Luddites," *Time* (December 13, 1999): 37.

25. Martin Gilbert, *The Holocaust: A History of the Jews of Europe During the Second World War* (New York: Henry Holt and Company, 1985), p. 526.

26. Friedrich Nietzsche, *The Case of Wagner*, trans. Walter Kaufman (New York: Vintage Books, 1967), p. 191.

27. Paul Goldberger, "Erich Segal's Identity Crisis," *New York Times*, June 13, 1970, IV, p. 16.

28. Tony Ortega, "Sky Writer," *Phoenix New Times*, September 25–October 1, 1997.

29. Bob Raissman, "NBC's Gray Wrong to Go After Rose," *Daily News*, October 25, 1999.

THE ALIEN AMONG US 10

THE STIGMA OF IMMIGRATION

THE IMMIGRANT AS OUTSIDER

An immigrant is anyone who leaves a country in order to settle permanently in another country. An immigrant is also, by definition, an outsider and hence the target of stigma. The degree to which the stigma of foreigner or alien attaches to an immigrant varies considerably because the experiences and the cultures from whence the immigrant came vary so much. We can therefore construct a range of emotional and cultural distance that an immigrant needs to traverse before he can expect to become an American and be assimilated into the society he has now entered. On one end of that range could be a Canadian and on the other end a Holocaust survivor. The Canadian who moves from Fort Erie, Ontario, to Buffalo, New York, or from Windsor to Detroit will hardly be viewed as a foreigner in America, and he will not feel very foreign in his new country. Such a Canadian immigrant may miss the picture of the English queen hanging on the walls of restaurants or the Canadian dollar coin called a "Loony." Canadians are also sometimes called "Canucks" in the United States and there may well be, here and there, some Americans who seek to distance themselves from Canadian immigrants.

Nevertheless, it is evident that a Canadian who moves from one side of the border to the other side will hardly notice much difference in the culture of the country he has entered from the country he has left. English is spoken with the same intonation in both places, unless the Canadian comes from Quebec. Both countries are democracies, although

Canada has a parliamentary democracy akin to England while the United States is a federal republic. The religions practiced in Canada are in the main Protestant and Catholic Christianity, which is also true in the United States. There are of course differences between the Canadian and American school systems, but not enough to alienate a Canadian from other children in school. Moreover, the entire economic system, industrial capitalism, is the same in both countries.

To top it off, a Canadian who moves to the United States can visit his home at any time. He can see his relatives and friends, communicate with all he knew in "the old country," and, if he moves only from Fort Erie to Buffalo he can drive across a short bridge to his erstwhile home without hindrance or expense.

By contrast we can consider the condition of other immigrants who did not come to America from Canada or Mexico, the country bordering the southern United States. There are also in this country thousands of immigrants who came from England and other English-speaking countries and who are outsiders in America despite their ability to speak English. For neither England, nor Scotland, nor Ireland are the United States. There is a good deal of difference in the culture of Europe and America, which any immigrant needs to learn if he wishes to gain access to American culture by means of assimilation. Assimilation is the process by which two or more cultures merge because the alien learns the culture of the host country, even as the natives of that country adopt some of the cultural features of the newcomers. Now it is obvious that a common language is an indispensable prerequisite for assimilation to be possible at all. Therefore, our Canadian or other English-speaking immigrants suffer far less stigma on arrival in the United States than is true of those who cannot speak English. In fact, failure to speak a common language is an insurmountable barrier to assimilation and is also the primary reason for the attachment of a stigma to the status of immigrant.[1]

It should therefore be easy to agree to the proposition that the greater the difference between the host society and the culture of the immigrant the greater the social distance between them. This also means that those culture traits that are foreign to the host will be evaluated as inferior by the host society and create a stigma that may be insurmountable in one generation.[2]

Excellent examples of this situation are all those immigrants from non-English-speaking countries who arrived in the United States practicing a religion that was either entirely unknown in Protestant Anglo-Saxon America or was hardly represented here. Such immigrants added their minority religion to their lack of English. In recent years, that is, after World War II, the number of immigrants who could not speak English declined considerably because English had become an almost universal language by 1970. For example, the 1990 census showed that of the nearly twenty million immigrants then living in the United States, 21 percent spoke English only, and another 53 percent spoke it very well even though 44 percent had arrived in the United States during the 1980s. The 26 percent who then said they knew no English or knew very little English were among the poorest and least-educated immigrants, who had usually come from Cuba and other Latin American countries.[3]

There were of course large numbers of immigrants in the United States before World War II and even before the First World War who knew no English at all and who had come from southern and eastern Europe. These immigrants seemed utterly alien to the Protestant Anglo-Saxon majority here and are best illustrated by the Italian and Jewish groups who arrived in the main between 1880 and 1920. Both of these large immigrant groups belonged to religions that were, at the time of their arrival, poorly represented here. The Italians were almost all Roman Catholics and the Jews not only belonged to the Orthodox branch of Judaism but also spoke a form of medieval German called Yiddish, which they wrote with Hebrew characters utterly incomprehensible to "real" Americans. It therefore seemed to the Anglo majority that the chances of assimilating people of such utterly different backgrounds would be impossible, particularly because the cultural and acquired behavior of these people appeared inborn to the natives who viewed these foreigners as a race. From the perspective of contemporary society these views would be called racist because racism is defined as the belief that an acquired characteristic is inherited through the genes.

Eighty years have passed since these great eastern European migrations seemed to inundate the United States with these peculiar foreigners. During these years the process of assimilation has proved that anyone can become an American by the use of Anglo-conformity. This means that assimilation takes place on two levels. First, there is behavioral assimilation. This consists of learning to speak the English language, dressing like an American, eating American foods in public, participating in the political process, gaining an American education, etc. This is of course much easier to achieve than structural assimilation, which includes relinquishing the "old language" and giving up bilingualism. Those who have achieved structural assimilation speak English without an accent and, most important, are usually married to someone born in the United States. It was at one time thought that eventually all the immigrants who came here from all over the world would merge in an American "melting pot" and thereby create a new type of human being, utterly American and devoid of foreign traits. This theory was not confirmed over the years. Instead, Anglo-conformity has allowed Americans of all backgrounds to maintain some cultural differences. This now permits numerous groups of various ethnic origins to include their ancestry in their self-identity. Hence we have many so-called hyphenated Americans instead of one uniform, homogenized population. Therefore the stigma of belonging to such groups continues, albeit to a lesser degree into the third generation among Italian-Americans and others.[4]

Between 1881 and 1920, approximately 24 million immigrants, mostly from Europe, arrived in this country. The number of Italian immigrants who came to the United States during those years rose to about 15 percent of the total, or 3.6 million, with more coming in later years. These immigrants were not only outsiders, as all immigrants must be by definition. They were also stigmatized both for their foreign language and culture and for their religion. With few exceptions, Irish and Italian immigrants of the late nineteenth and early twentieth century were Roman Catholics. Members of that religion had already been the object of considerable prejudice since the founding of the country. While the U.S. Constitution did not require any religious test for voting, only three states permitted Catholics the right to vote before the federal Constitution was adopted. These three states were Pennsylvania, Delaware, and Maryland.[5]

Public displeasure with Roman Catholicism was so profound in the early years of the nineteenth century that the great majority of Protestants were willing to believe anything detrimental and negative about Roman Catholics. It was in such an atmosphere of stigma coupled with the belief that the pope meant to rule America and deprive Americans of their freedom that a mob burned a Catholic convent in Charlestown, Massachusetts, in 1834. The hysteria that led to this outrage was coupled with the belief that Roman Catholics were engaged in a conspiracy, directed by the pope, to establish a Catholic dictatorship here. That belief led to numerous "disclosures" by ex-Catholics or others concerning "secret" Catholic practices. Therefore such books as *Six Months in a Convent* by an ex-nun sold hundreds of thousands of copies and were at once imitated by bigots and profit-motivated writers and publishers.

The great inventor Samuel Morse lent his name to anti-Catholic literature and the political party dubbed the Know-Nothings perpetuated such hatred for many years. In St. Louis, Missouri, in 1854 an anti-Catholic riot led to the deaths of ten persons and the wounding of thirty more. These outbursts of anti-Catholic sentiment came at a time when, in the middle of the nineteenth century, there were only 668,000 Catholics in a country whose population stood at twenty-eight million. Catholics were goaded by such organizations as the American Protective Association and other groups devoted to hatred. It was rumored that the pope had ordered the burning of "all heretics, meaning Protestants." Catholics were suspected of disloyalty to the United States on the grounds that they all had to view the pope as head of state and not our president. The Ku Klux Klan and other organizations devoted to ethnic and religious bigotry led the fight against Catholics, Jews, and others so that the Irish, Italian, and Jewish immigrants who arrived here were at once stigmatized by numerous canards against their religion and their culture.[6]

CATHOLICS NEED NOT APPLY

"Catholics need not apply" said many a sign posted above the employment offices of numerous business establishments in New England and elsewhere during the nineteenth and early twentieth centuries. Likewise, newspaper advertisements seeking workers often included that same notice.[7]

The prejudice behind this form of discrimination was first directed against the five million natives of Ireland who entered the United States between 1820 and 1920.[8] The Irish, unlike the British and Germans who preceded them, had become foreigners in their own land since they lost the Battle of the Boyne to the Protestant forces under William III in 1690. In 1691 the British Parliament passed an act debarring from the Irish Parliament all Catholics so that the entire Parliament was thereafter Protestant. That Protestant assembly made Catholic schools and colleges illegal. Catholic priests became subject to deportation, and no Catholic was permitted any arms or to possess a horse worth more than five pounds. Protestant women who married a Catholic were to suffer the forfeiture of their estate even as Catholic land was confiscated until there was no more land to confiscate. Crimes against Catholics were rarely punished in the Irish courts. The English forbade the exportation of wool from Ireland, thereby throwing the population into abject poverty augmented by tremendous tariffs. Thus, after 1696 "famine, beggary, and desperate lawlessness covered the island."[9]

Prior to the American Revolution, the Irish seldom sought to come to America because North America was English. The number of Irish who came to the United States was fairly small before the potato famine of 1845–1850. Nevertheless, Protestant America was not favorably disposed toward any Catholic immigrants in the nineteenth century so that an advertisement such as this one was typical of much of the prevailing sentiment: "Wanted—A Cook or a Chambermaid. They must be American, Scotch, Swiss or African—no Irish."[10]

Because economic discrimination was so common, Irish laborers on the Erie Canal, on the railroads, and in the sweatshops received lower wages than native Americans. It was possible to exploit immigrants in this fashion because in the nineteenth and early twentieth centuries there were so many immigrants willing to work at any wage. Furthermore, labor unions were either nonexistent or impotent. Because the

Irish were powerless they enthusiastically threw themselves into local politics in the hope of alleviating their lot by gaining better control of their lives and future. Precisely that political activity, however, aroused the fears of the Protestant majority so that two new anti-Catholic and anti-Irish parties were organized in the United States between 1830 and 1850—the Know-Nothing Party and the Native American Party. Both political parties fostered the belief that the Roman Catholic Church endangered Protestantism and the democratic institutions of the United States. These parties also published anti-Catholic books and pamphlets and held "no Popery" rallies. Both of these parties also sought to keep aliens from holding public office, to extend the period necessary to attain naturalization, and to keep the Bible in the public schools. While these parties were hardly successful in electing very many candidates to public office, and although both parties disappeared soon because they lacked public support, their ideas flourished just the same.[11]

This is in part illustrated by the political situation in Boston, Massachusetts. Because of the potato famine of 1845 to 1850, large numbers of Irish had come to the United States during those years so that Boston was two-fifths Irish by 1853. Nevertheless, it wasn't until 1870 that the first Irish alderman was elected in that city and it was 1882 before the first Irish congressman was elected there.[12]

The Irish also experienced riots against them in the streets of major American cities. In Boston in 1834 a mob sought to prevent the Irish from voting, leading to a large-scale riot when the Irish fought back. In that same year a mob burned a convent to the ground in Charleston, Massachusetts, directly across the river from Boston. Neither the police nor the fire department of that city made any effort to deal with the mob. The perpetrators were later indicted by a grand jury but found not guilty at their trial. No restitution was ever made by the city.

In 1844 a riot broke out at a convention of the Native American Party. Because Irish militants attempted to break up the Native American meeting a crowd burned eighty-one Irish homes and several churches. In addition an exclusively Irish firehouse and an Irish library were also burned. Forty people were killed during the rioting and sixty were wounded. Two months later a second riot occurred in Philadelphia when a mob attacked a Catholic church, burned it down, and then fought against a militia sent to suppress the riot. There were numerous other incidents of a similar sort all over the United States during those years.[13]

One issue that divided the Irish community from the Protestant Anglo community was abolition of slavery before the Civil War. Fearing that black labor would compete with them if slavery were abolished, and resenting that Protestant leaders in the abolitionist movement were interested in Africans but not in them, the Irish became involved in the antiabolitionist riots in New York in 1834. It is instructive to note that the Irish had no sympathy for blacks and used the same violence in their effort to keep "the Negro in his place" as had been used against them. Mobs, including many Irish, attacked African churches, and burned them and an African schoolhouse.[14]

In the 1840s the use of the Protestant Bible in the public schools of Philadelphia became a source of friction between Protestants and Catholics in that city. Many Protestants became incensed when the Catholic bishop of Philadelphia persuaded the school board to use the Catholic version of the Bible as well. Street speakers used such phrases as "the bloody hand of the pope has stretched itself forth to our destruction" thereby exciting the mob to burn numerous Catholic homes, churches, and other establishments and killing fourteen people.[15]

The 1863 New York draft riots were perhaps the most violent of all the ethnic riots taking place in nineteenth-century America. Many whites believed that the Emancipation Proclamation would allow former slaves to take jobs relinquished by whites drafted into the Civil War fighting. Hence, Irish workers, rather than native Americans, rioted in the streets, leading to the burning of draft headquarters, the tearing up of railroad tracks, the destruction of an African American orphanage, and even an attack on police headquarters in New York City. Evidently the Irish were using the tactics first used against them.[16]

In time, Irish efforts and the processes of invasion and succession permitted the Irish to gain access to the "American Dream" in the same manner as has been traditional in this country for over two hundred years. Nevertheless, many of the prejudices and hatreds of the previous century were continued into the twentieth and were particularly revived in 1928 when the Irish-American governor of New York, Al Smith, won the Democratic nomination for president of the United States. The nomination rekindled nativist fanaticism. The Ku Klux Klan recruited many new members and helped to defeat Smith. It should be understood that the economic boom of 1928 would have elected the Republican Herbert Hoover in any event. However, the Irish in America interpreted the defeat of Smith as a sign that they were still not welcome in America. Subsequently Franklin D. Roosevelt, on assuming the presidency in 1933, appointed many men of Irish descent to political office.

It was the election of John F. Kennedy to the presidency in 1960 that erased any doubts among Irish-Americans that they were finally accepted in the United States. The truth is that Kennedy was a good deal less Irish Catholic than his name would suggest. He did, however, represent the arrival of the Irish as equals to other Americans so that from then on the Irish, in the words of the famous film director John Ford, "felt like a first-class American."[17]

In view of the harmonious relations between Catholics and Protestants in twenty-first-century America it is difficult to understand the hatred that greeted Catholics and the Irish in particular in the America of the two previous centuries. That hate was based on the assumption that all Catholics were more loyal to the Vatican than to the United States; that Catholics were plotting to deprive Americans of their freedom; that the pope and his followers sought to overthrow the U.S. government by force; and that the Irish in particular were all a gang of drunken, superstitious idol worshipers led by immoral priests. These canards then became the substance of the gospel of the Ku Klux Klan, which did not hesitate to assault the next wave of Catholics who came to our shores from Italy.[18]

FROM SACCO AND VANZETTI
TO *THE GODFATHER*

In 1890 there were about twenty-three thousand Italians in New Orleans, Louisiana. Called "dirty, lazy, ignorant, and prone to violence" by the local newspapers, they became the targets of the police department, which attributed every murder or assault to them. In fact, the police went so far in their anti-Italian attitude that they changed the non-Italian names of criminals to Italian ones when reporting crimes. Thus, a John Marti, born in Germany, was called Martini by the police when he was found murdered. It was said that the killing had the "appearance of a Mafia killing" although there was no evidence to support such a theory. In this atmosphere of suspicion, hatred, bigotry, and fear, all fed by the local press, the police chief of New Orleans, David Hennessy, was murdered by unknown assassins on October 15, 1890. Despite the lack of evidence as to his killer, the mayor of New Orleans, Joseph A. Shakespeare, declared this the work of Italians and ordered the police to "arrest every Italian you come across." Subsequently a grand jury indicted nineteen men for this murder of whom nine were put on trial. None of the jury who tried the nine men was of Italian origin. Despite Shakespeare's pronouncements that the nine were guilty and despite the efforts of numerous rabble-rousers including the press, the jury could not find any of the accused guilty. Nevertheless, the nine were not released but continued in jail on other charges. Two days after the acquittal of the nine a crowd listened to a number of speakers who demanded that the jury verdicts be set aside by the citizens. A mob obliged the speakers and stormed the jail and shot to death the nine acquitted men. In addition, two other Italians, not in any manner related to these events, were murdered as well. The *New York Times* headlined its report of this massacre: "Chief Hennessy Avenged: Eleven of His Italian Assassins Lynched by Mob." Evidently the *Times* at a distance of 1,200 miles approved of these murders and blasted all "Sicilians" as "bandits and assassins and cut-throats belonging to secret societies," a sentiment which was shared by large numbers of Americans in all areas of the country. Hence, at least thirty additional lynchings of Italians took place during the remainder of the nineteenth century and during the first part of the twentieth.[19]

The most notorious of these attacks upon Italians driven entirely by stigmatization of an entire ethnic group was the trial and execution of Nicola Sacco and Bartolomeo Vanzetti. In April of 1920 both men were arrested and charged with the murder of Frederick A. Parmenter, a shoe-factory paymaster, and Alessandro Beradelli, a guard, during a robbery in South Braintree, Massachusetts.

Because the Russian revolution had occurred only recently and the Bolsheviks had overthrown and killed the czar and his family, many Americans were terrified that this would happen here. This fear was fostered by the large number of eastern European immigrants arriving daily and by the hysterical writings of A. Mitchell Palmer, Attorney General in the Woodrow Wilson cabinet. Palmer conducted "Palmer Raids" between 1918 and 1921. These raids consisted of smashing union headquarters and the offices of the socialist parties. This was done despite the fact that there were only seventy thousand self-professed Communists in the United States in 1919.[20]

The case was tried before Judge Webster Thayer, a graduate of the Dartmouth class of 1879. Judge Thayer felt threatened by the immigration of so many foreigners whom he called "Reds" and anarchists at every occasion. Thayer made his prejudices most plain as described by William Thompson, the defense attorney for Sacco and Vanzetti. Said Thompson in an appeal to Gov. Alvan T. Fuller: "Thayer is a narrow-minded man . . . he is full of prejudice with his fear of 'reds' which captured about 90 percent of the American people." Together with the prosecutor, Thayer badgered Sacco and Vanzetti during the trial with all the prevailing hatreds and prejudices of the times before a jury which shared these prejudices with a population convinced of the guilt of Sacco and Vanzetti on the grounds of the stigma already attaching to Italian names and origins. Consequently Sacco and Vanzetti were executed on August 22, 1924. In August of 1973 the then-governor of Massachussetts, Michael Dukakis, declared the anniversary of their execution Sacco and Vanzetti Memorial Day.[21]

It was in that same year, 1924, that Congress enacted an immigration law that set a numerical ceiling on the southern and eastern European immigrants allowed to enter this country each year. That law was the culmination of an effort on the part of nativists that had begun in 1911. In 1917 the nativists succeeded when Congress first voted to limit immigration. Finally, the 1924 amendments to that law established the most restrictive "quotas" on immigration yet enacted and reduced immigration to a trickle for a period of forty years.[22] Together with Prohibition, which was also aimed at the great wave of non-Anglo immigrants, these restrictive immigration laws indicate the stigma attached to all immigrants of that period, whether from Ireland, Russia, South America, or Italy. Those who had come from Italy were not only burdened by the stigma that attached to Roman Catholicism and the non-English speakers generally, but in addition they were (and are) stigmatized by the common assumption that anyone with an Italian name must somehow be associated with organized crime.

There is of course no doubt that Italians as well as other ethnic groups participated in criminal activities in this country. There is however no evidence that the amount of crime committed by Italians or persons of Italian descent exceeds in any fashion the amount of crime committed by others. However, criminologists have recognized that there is in this country an "alien conspiracy theory" which features the crimes of persons with Italian names, particularly as it is associated with the Sicilian criminal organization known as the Mafia or, in its American version, La Cosa Nostra. These groups have a membership of about seventeen hundred men and "associates" of about seventeen thousand. Obviously, these numbers are so small that they cannot possibly describe the vast number of Americans of Italian descent living productive lives in this country. Nevertheless, the stigma of having an Italian name was largely associated with the perpetual belief that the name and criminal activity are the same thing. Numerous politicians have over the years benefited by investigating the Mafia or Cosa Nostra. This was particularly true of the Senate Special Investigating Committee headed by Sen. Estes Kefauver (D.-Tenn.) in the 1950s and thereafter by Senator McClelland and Senator Kennedy (Massachusetts). The hearing these committees held were always televised and therefore gave the public the impression that Italians and persons of Italian descent were the only criminals here or were the most dangerous criminal gangs in America. This despite the evidence that the Jews, South Americans, Poles, Irish, and a host of others were equally involved in organized crime as were people of English descent.

Such novels as *The Godfather*, which have been made into movies and television programs, have therefore firmly established the image of Italians as organized criminals despite the indisputable fact that the vast majority of crimes committed in the United States are committed by people who have no connection to Italy, Sicily, or anyone Italian. Even now at the start of the twenty-first century as the majority of organized criminals are of South American descent while others hail from Russia, Vietnam, or China, public perception continues to stigmatize Italians as a group connected to crime and violence of every kind.[23]

During the last century, since a large wave of Italian immigrants came to the United States there has been a considerable assimilation of Italians into our culture. Today Italian-Americans are found in every branch of American life, among politicians and among professionals, among businesspersons, and in the highest ranks of industry and government.

There are many hyphenated Americans who have visited the land of their origins and ancestry and thereby found some connection between themselves and their "roots" which helps a great deal to reduce the anxiety associated with the immigrant experience.

There is in the United States a group of "ethnics" who came at about the same time as the Italians and who have undergone a rather similar Americanization process. There is, however, one large difference between the Italians and the Jews to whom we are here referring. That difference is that the Jews could usually not go home again. Hence only twenty-one thousand of the millions of Jews who entered this country between 1880 and 1924 ever returned to eastern Europe from where they had come. It is this phenomenon among immigrants to America which we will now explore.[24]

THE JEWS IN AMERICA: ESCAPING THE BIGOTS

At the end of the 1870s there were about forty thousand Jews in the United States. Most had come from Germany together with other Germans who settled in the main in St. Louis, Milwaukee, and Cincinnati as well as the East Coast cities. There were also some Russian Jews among them because Czar Nicholas I had issued over six hundred anti-Jewish decrees during his reign between 1825 and 1855.[25]

The Jews of Russia were of course stigmatized outsiders in that Christian land as they had been in all Christian countries for all the centuries since Constantine declared Christianity the state religion of the Roman Empire in 313.[26] Because the Christian religion had the force of public law, Jews became second-class citizens in all Christian countries thereafter. To insure that they remained so, the Fourth Lateran Council of 1215 had ruled, among other indignities, that Jews were henceforth to wear only black clothes as a stigma distinguishing the "Christ Killers," a label which NBC continued to broadcast on its *Saturday Night Live* show on December 4, 1999, and subsequently.[27]

For the Jews of Europe second-class citizenship meant contempt, persecution, and in the Russian Empire "pogroms," a word meaning "like thunder" and referring to sudden violent attacks on the Jewish community resulting in death and destruction. These sporadic "pogroms" had been part of Jewish life in eastern Europe since King Boleslav of Poland invited the German Jews to settle in that country in 1264. The Jews who came to Poland from the West spoke German. Differing in language and religion from their Polish-speaking neighbors, they settled in small towns and villages that were entirely Jewish or in segments of larger towns in which they lived in separate enclaves. As the centuries passed their thirteenth-century German remained as antiquated as it had been on their arrival, because the language became calcified like Pennsylvania Dutch. The German spoken by the eastern European Jews became known as Yiddish or Jewish and distinguished Jews from the Slavic-speaking peoples around them.

When Russia, together with Austria and Prussia, partitioned Poland in 1772 the vast majority of eastern European Jews came under Russian rule and were therefore subject to the anti-Jewish policies of its governments and emperors.[28]

It was 1881 when these policies became most unbearable for the Jews of the vast Russian Empire. In that year Emperor Alexander II was assassinated. His son Alexander III was a malicious anti-Jewish bigot who organized persecutions of Jews throughout his empire, leading to a mass immigration of the Yiddish-speaking Jews to America. It is estimated that 1,600,000 Jews came to the United States between 1881 and 1918. Unlike the Italians and others who came from an independent nation, these Jews came as a whole people who had no nation. While individual Italians or Poles might be in flight, the entire Jewish people were in flight. Italians, Poles, Germans, and others also arrived. However, their nations remained intact. Jews, however, had no nation from which to emigrate. They came as stigmatized people from the old country to which they could hardly return.

As the number of Yiddish-speaking Jews increased in the United States, the Jews, like other immigrants, formed distinct neighborhoods in New York, Boston, Philadelphia, and almost all of the larger American cities. Already the poorest of Europeans, the Jews in America constituted a "proletariat" equal to that of any other immigrant group of the time. Working mostly in the needle trades, the Jews gave native Americans the impression that they were utterly foreign to anything American and probably incapable of ever becoming Americans. Not only were the Jews not Christians, they even used the Hebrew alphabet to write their language. They observed Saturday, not Sunday, as their Sabbath. Housed in the worst tenements, they were so crowded that the space allotted to each person was only 428 cubic feet when the legal limit was 600. The death rate among the Jews of the early twentieth century was 42.4 per 1,000 when the average New York City death rate was 25.7 per 1,000. The *New York Times* repeatedly sent reporters to the Jewish neighborhoods who "recoiled from the clamor and stench of its half-starved inhabitants."[29]

Prior to the mass immigration of the Yiddish-speaking Jews, anti-Jewish conduct was almost unknown in the United States. This was true in part because there were so few Jews in this country. It was also true, however, because the few Jews who were here were almost entirely of German birth. These Jews had already discarded the culture still common to the Yiddish-speaking Jews, a language which the German Jews never used. The German Jews were well educated, were easily capable of Anglo-conformity, and frequently married into non-Jewish families. In short, the German Jews were not very different from other Americans of western European origin.

Beginning however in 1877, anti-Jewish behavior and discrimination against Jews became evident in the United States. This kind of conduct was in part fueled by the same "anti-Semitism" so widespread in Europe. In the main, however, anti-Jewish sentiment was rooted in antiforeign attitudes which affected the Irish, the Poles, and the Italians as much, if not more, than the Jews. Nevertheless, Jews became the objects of stigma derived from both sources. As Jews rose educationally and economically they were shut out of the "best" colleges such as Columbia University and Harvard College. Those Jews who did become college students were shut out of fraternities and certainly were not appointed to any faculty except City College of New York. In urban areas "restrictive covenants" were instituted. These "covenants" were agreements among home owners not to sell to Jews. Jews were therefore unable to live in most suburban neighborhoods. Most important, however, was the economic discrimination. Yet, none of these forms of bigotry were translated into government action. It remained in private hands. This was the great difference between the Jewish experience in America and the Jewish experience in Europe. Jews in America used the commitment of the United States to legal equality as their most powerful weapon in gaining eventual acceptance as Americans. In Europe, private and government-sponsored bigotry finally led to the gas ovens of World War II.[30]

Beginning in 1913, Thomas E. Watson, a successful Georgia lawyer, began a campaign against Jews which, in its vitriol and its eventual outcome, resembled the type of hate Jews had fled in the old country. Watson had already attacked Catholics with the same vehemence in his several publications, including his magazine the *Jeffersonian*, later renamed *Watson's* magazine. Now he used his influence and speaking ability to label Jews as physically filthy and interested only in money and in cheating Christians. Like Shakespeare in *The Merchant of Venice,* Watson repeated every malicious attack ever used against Jews including the accusation that Jews "lusted" for "pure" Christian women. Therefore, when on April 27, 1913, a shop girl, Mary Phelan, was found murdered in the cellar of a pencil factory in Marietta, Georgia, Watson and his followers at once accused the Jewish manager of the factory, Leo Frank, of killing her. It is now known that the murder was committed by Jim Conley, an African American. This appeared to be the case at that time also, however, no effort was made to discover the killer of Mary Phelan. Instead, Leo Frank was arrested, tried, and convicted of this murder on the instigation of Watson and his followers. The jury that convicted Frank was threatened by a mob of Watson's followers outside the courthouse who shouted: "Hang the Jew or we will hang you." Watson exulted in his victory and wrote that Frank was: "A typical young Jewish man of business who lives for pleasure and runs after Gentile girls. Every student of sociology knows that the black man's lust after the white woman is not much fiercer than the lust of the licentious Jew for the Gentile." Watson also accused all Jews of "ritual murder," a charge that had been the mainstay of Christian bigotry over the centuries; it claimed that Jews bake their unleavened bread or matzoh (from the Hebrew *mozo,* "to exit," hence the bread of the Exodus from Egypt) with the blood of murdered Christian children. Hating Catholics with the same venom, Watson also claimed to know that "rich Jews" were supporting the pope and vice versa.[31]

In 1920, Henry Ford, then one of the most prominent Americans, published an English translation of a Russian book called *The Protocols of the Elders of Zion.* Ford owned a newspaper called the *Dearborn Independent* in which he published excerpts from this 1806 French forgery first accusing the Jews of a worldwide conspiracy to overturn civilization and establish Jewish supremacy. *The Protocols* was then later adopted by Russian monks in order to discredit the Russian Jews. Ford claimed to "expose" an international Jewish conspiracy to dominate the world and to undermine "all that Anglo-Saxons mean by civilization." Widely disseminated, many Christian priests and ministers repeated these stories in their Sunday sermons. This kind of calumny was of course not new to the European Jews. However, in America this propaganda could be countered in the press, in the court of public opinion, and in the law. Jews therefore formed the Anti-Defamation League to resist these attacks and were helped in their efforts by numerous Christians and others who were able to invoke the American tradition of equal rights and freedoms for all. It was in the 1920s when Americans succeeded in rejecting Old World hatreds by calling upon these traditions as Jews and others who were under attack used such phrases as the inalienable rights proclaimed in the Declaration of Independence to insure their place in America. The immigrants from eastern Europe fought only to ensure their right to life in America. Their children then secured for themselves political liberty and social equality including the right to work at anything their competence allowed. Finally, the third and fourth generations attained the pursuit of happiness so that at the beginning of 2001 the Jews of America have indeed overcome the stigma of immigration as have others whose forebears came a century ago.[32]

There are in the United States today about 170,000 immigrants who are generally called "Holocaust Survivors." Unlike any other immigrants to this country, these few survivors of the mass murder of European Jews by Europe's Christian population cannot return to their native lands, cannot visit their relatives, cannot hear the language of their youth again, cannot call anyone who knew them in their earlier life, cannot visit their former homes. They are indeed outsiders in the most extreme sense of that word for they carry with them a lifelong stigma inscribed upon their minds and their bodies by a most incredible experience. We have already seen that the Russian Jews who came here in such great numbers in the early years of the twentieth century had little desire to return to the miseries of their previous existence. Nevertheless, they, as well as all other ethnic groups who came here, could write to, visit, or be visited by their families in the Old Country. They could also rejoin those of their families who came here after them. Many, in fact, came with their entire families and settled together in ethnic enclaves where their language was spoken and where they could count on the support of others to help them adjust to their new surroundings.

None of this was true of those who came here as a result of the Holocaust. Those who survived that experience came alone. They had no families or friends or acquaintances because those they knew and cherished in Europe had all been murdered by gas, by starvation, and by mass executions.

The Holocaust (from the Greek *holokaustos*, meaning "burnt whole") refers to the extermination of the European Jews between 1933 and 1945. That extermination was preceded by stigmatizing the Jewish population of Europe in a manner that even the medieval world never attained. Indeed, Martin Luther had called for the expulsion of all Jews from German lands as early as 1542.[33] Nevertheless, this was not carried out until 1939 when the Germans began the systematic transportation of its 503,000 Jews into concentration camps in the conquered lands of Poland, the Baltic countries, and the Balkans. Since the Jewish population of Germany in 1933 constituted only 0.77 percent of all Germans it is evident that many Christians in Germany had never seen a Jew. However, stigma made up for experience. Beginning with the ascension of the Nazi Party to power in that year and ending with the defeat of the German armies in 1945, a total of 431 anti-Jewish decrees were enforced on the European Jewish population from France to Russia and from Norway to Italy as most of Europe had come under Nazi domination. Included in these many decrees was the law of September 1, 1941, which decreed that all Jews had to wear a six-cornered black star on a yellow background including the word JUDE or "Jew" at all times. On March 4, 1942, an additional decree ordered that a Jewish star had to be affixed next to the name of the Jew at all rooms, apartments, or houses in which a Jew lived. Jews were issued special internal identification cards which carried a large "J." On the first of January 1939, all male Jews were forced to use the name Israel and all female Jews were called Sara by German decree. In addition the German government issued a list of about fifty male and fifty female names which Jews were obliged to use because these names were regarded as Jewish and hence stigmatized their users. In addition, in every park there were some yellow benches bearing the logo "for Jews only." Jews were not permitted to sit on any other park benches or to use public transportation or drive a car. These measures made it easy to identify the stigmatized Jews so that they could then be transported to ghettos in the East and finally carted to their deaths in concentration camps such as Sobibor, Auschwitz, Neuengamme, and Buchenwald.[34]

Historian Lucy S. Dawidowicz and others have presented statistics to show the extent of the mass murders carried out in Europe during the years 1933 to 1945. Accordingly, 5,933,900 Jews out of a total of 8,861,800 were slaughtered in those years. The 33 percent who survived consisted mostly of Russian Jews sent to the inner Soviet Union during the Nazi invasion of that country in 1941 so as to escape the killings. Others succeeded in coming to the United States and other countries by a variety of means. In any case, those who survived differed from all other immigrants who had come here in that they had undergone a level of cruelty that they could not forget and that no one else could understand.[35]

Holocaust survivors have internalized the stigma attached to them in their early years. This means that these survivors, like all people, exhibit a personality that reflects their experiences. Therefore many of these survivors display anxieties in situations that do not create problems for native-born Americans. Holocaust survivors display suspicions of others' motives, express the belief that they will be ostracized when that is not intended, feel rejected when no such motive exists, see insults and demeaning situations which others don't see, and generally give the impression that they are defensive and mistrusting. All of these characteristics create additional problems for the survivors whether inside or outside the Jewish community. American Jews are now generally third- and fourth-generation Americans. The immigration of their grandparents or even great-grandparents has become family legend to most Americans. Holocaust survivors, however, carry with them a baggage unknown to anyone else. This produces conduct and psychological projections for survivors frequently leading to their rejection by Americans, whether Jewish or not, so that Holocaust survivors generally are outsiders in American culture. In short, Holocaust survivors do not fit in anywhere and lack the support that ethnic enclaves, relatives, and erstwhile countrymen furnished other immigrants over the years. There is no Holocaust survivor community. There are no Holocaust survivor enclaves. Instead these survivors live in the midst of a large and diverse American community that largely rejects the survivors and finds them peculiar, different, and uncomfortable as indeed they are.

Thus, there exists a range of immigrant experiences from the Canadian who may never feel a stigma of any kind associated with his immigration to the Holocaust survivor who carries that stigma within him and whose experiences affect even the next generation. Holocaust survivors typically exhibit a number tattooed on their inner forearm by their torturers. Like the ancient Greek slaves whose *Stigma* was also etched into their skin, these latter-day slaves of Krupp, Volkswagen, and I. G. Farben remain outsiders for their lifetime. They cannot forget. They can only live with their horrific memories.

THE FAILURE OF THE AMERICAN DREAM

On the West Coast of the United States, in New York, and in a few other communities there were 1.1 million Chinese immigrants in 1999. This may seem surprising to those Americans who recall that in 1882 Congress passed the Chinese Exclusion Act which was repeatedly renewed and extended indefinitely in 1904. This act was finally repealed in 1943 when, during World War II, China had become an American ally in the fight against the Japanese.

The stigma attaching to Chinese immigrants in the 1880s was evidently related to race. Like African Americans, Mongoloid peoples are easily identifiable by physical characteristics that then can be interpreted to indicate inferiority. This is what happened to the Chinese immigrants who had come to this country in the later part of the nineteenth century. At that time these Chinese immigrants, mostly men, were instrumental in building the western railroads. As railroad work was completed, Chinese immigrants sought other work and thereby entered into competition with Americans of European descent. This economic competition led to the widespread assertion that the Chinese were filthy, opium-addicted, and vicious. The *New York Times*, located three thousand miles from the state with at least a fair-sized Chinese population, nevertheless editorialized in 1865 that the increase in Asian, particularly Chinese, immigration would have a negative effect on American civilization, morals, religion, and political institutions.[36]

When in 1882 the Chinese Exclusion Act was passed, the "melting pot" theory was quite popular in the United States. That theory held that immigrants of all European nations would "melt" together into one America as distinct from the Old Country nations as the Italians were from the Germans or from the Russians. It appeared, however, that the Chinese and other Asians would never be able to participate in this great "melting pot" because they differed from the European immigrants physically and culturally far more than was true of Europeans among each other. In short, the Chinese and other Asians did not fit in and carried with them the stigma of their "inferiority" in their Oriental appearance. Speakers and writers on the subject of Oriental immigration talked of the "Yellow menace." Sen. James G. Blaine of Maine, a presidential aspirant, said of the Chinese in 1879: "The Asiatic cannot go on with our population and make a homogeneous element. (They) have no regard to family, do not recognize the relation of husband to wife, do not observe the tie of parent to child, and do not have in the slightest degree the enabling and civilizing influence of the hearthstone and fireside." A more unreal picture of the Chinese family could hardly have been drawn. Yet, stigma convinced many that the senator was right. In California antagonism to Chinese immigrants led to the expulsion of Chinese children from "white" schools in the 1920s, an action upheld by the courts on the grounds that it was necessary to "preserve the purity and integrity of the white race, and prevent amalgamation." These segregated schools were largely abandoned by the 1950s.[37]

Hostility to Japanese immigration to the United States was no less than to Chinese immigration. There had been some immigration of Japanese to the United States in the nineteenth century but that was ended effectively when immigration from most of Asia was banned by Congress in 1917 and when the 1924 Immigration Act established quotas for immigration from various countries. That act included the exclusion of Asian immigrants as of July 1 of that year.

Despite that exclusion, there were about 127,000 Japanese-Americans in the United States in 1940. Of these, 94,000 or 74 percent lived in California. When Japan attacked Pearl Harbor on December 7, 1941, more than 110,000 of our Japanese-American citizens and noncitizens alike were placed in "relocation centers" in Arkansas, California, Colorado,

Idaho, Utah, and Wyoming. Many of those so "relocated" were second- and third-generation Americans. Yet, the stigma associated with Japanese ancestry was so strong that there was hardly any protest against these measures. It was argued at the time that this "relocation" was necessary to insure national security. Yet, this argument has no validity because the Japanese-Americans living in Hawaii were not evacuated. Obviously, the "relocation" was induced by the opposition to Japanese-American ability to produce "a sizable share of the area's agricultural products." This grossly unfair evacuation was nevertheless upheld by the Supreme Court in 1944. Once more stigma became the substitute for reason as the American Dream was tarnished by these events.[38]

THE "NEW" IMMIGRATION

The memories of immigrants, better among some, worse among others, serve to recall the past in a subjective manner. Memories are not history because they are selective. This means that memories of immigration and immigrants revise and interpret the past in the light of remembered experience. Hence there arose some popular myths in American culture that remain with us to this day. These include the belief that in America "all are created equal" and that therefore there is in this country real justice which treats the foreigner and the native as equals. That myth was of course shattered in the days of the "old immigration" from Europe as we have just seen. Now, at the turn of another century, a new immigration had come to the United States. Unlike the European immigration waves that came here until 1924 the immigrants of the past quarter century have come mostly from Latin America and from Asia. As late as the 1980s 26 percent of immigrants knew no English. Today, only 8 percent of immigrants cannot speak English and three-quarters speak English with "high proficiency" within ten years of arrival. The new immigrants differ also in one other important respect from their European predecessors. While the earlier immigrants generally started their American lives in urban slums the "new" immigrants join home owners quickly. In 1996, of all the immigrants who had been in the United States for at least twenty-five years 75 percent owned their own home compared with 70 percent of native-born Americans.

Unlike the Europeans who usually never saw their home countries again and like the Canadian immigrants at the northern border of the United States, the large contingent of Mexican immigrants can get off a bus in downtown Los Angeles, watch Mexican television, keep in contact with their relatives, and return home for several weeks each year.[39]

Once more the arrival of so large a contingent of foreign-sounding and foreign-looking immigrants has made immigration a contentious issue in America. Again, such nativists as the perpetual presidential candidate Pat Buchanan worry that the newcomers are not willing to undergo assimilation and that most of them are here illegally. The facts are of course otherwise. Of the nearly 20 million immigrants who were counted by the 1990 census only 15 percent were here illegally. In addition, one-third of the immigrants had asked for naturalization and had sworn allegiance to the United States. Twenty million is of course a large number. Yet, that represents only 8 percent of the total American population, a share of the population much lower than it was during the 1870 to 1920 period when 15 percent of all American residents were foreign born.

Another great difference between the "new" immigrants and those who had come in earlier years is their level of education. Today about one-third of legal immigrants over age twenty-five have college degrees and only one-quarter have less than a high-school education. As a consequence legal immigrants now in the United States have incomes that fall short by only 7 percent of those of natives. All this is true of legal immigrants but not of illegal immigrants and of refugees who also arrive here in considerable numbers each day.

As in earlier years, immigration is once more an urban phenomenon that affects some states considerably and other states very little if at all. Today California receives 40 percent of all immigrants and New York, New Jersey, Illinois, Texas, and Florida most of the others. More than 93 percent of immigrants now settle in cities as was true in earlier years.[40]

There is now a considerable debate in the United States concerning the one million immigrants who come here each year. That debate centers not only on the issue of cost but also on the issue of culture. Because immigrants, particularly those at the Mexican border, draw a great deal from American health and education resources it has been estimated that immigrants cost the taxpayer $40 billion annually. In addition to this expense, it is the cultural issue that has many Americans worried about the new immigration. Because so many of the new immigrants are from South America they can now easily communicate with their relatives and friends in the country of origin. Fax machines, long-distance telephones, and foreign-language TV broadcasts all seem to perpetuate an "enclave" mentality among the newcomers. Unlike the Europeans of earlier years the present migrants need not disconnect from their home countries but can in fact establish their home countries here. There were of course always "little Italys" and "little Polands," and Chinatowns in American cities. However, as the generations changed these enclaves disappeared. The children and the grandchildren of the European immigrants seldom knew the language of their forebears and generally married someone equally assimilated. Not so the recent immigrants from Spanish-speaking countries. They receive a constant influx of yet more natives from Mexico and South American countries so that they appear to have no need to learn English or to assimilate the American culture.[41]

The face of the American nation is changing. As the proportion of European immigrants declines there are those who feel threatened by the great wave of South American and Asian immigrants. The fact is, however, that even now only 11 percent of U.S. residents are Hispanic and only 4 percent are Asian. Evidently the stigma of foreign speech, foreign features, and an "outsider" culture distorts the danger to American institutions as coming from foreigners.

Essentially, emigration and immigration are centered on existential validation, a phrase derived from the Latin word *vale*, meaning "strong." That concept refers to the experience of many twentieth-century people who learned in the course of two world wars and other forms of mass destruction that life may be meaningless in the restless anonymity of Western life. Among those who have generally been subject to the feeling that their existence is no longer valid or incontestable are some immigrants who need to reestablish themselves in a new culture and in new surroundings. Immigrants, however, are not the only people whose existence is in jeopardy. The homeless in America surely live on the edge of an abyss that denies the validity of their existence. Their condition as stigmatized outsiders is indisputable and is the subject of our next chapter.

SUMMARY

Immigrants are by definition outsiders and therefore are subject to stigma in proportion to their social and spatial distance from the host culture. Hence, Canadians are least stigmatized and Holocaust survivors the most. This is true because Canadian immigrants speak an unaccented English while others speak no English whatever or do so poorly. Language is the most important means of gaining assimilation that may be behavioral or structural.

In the past, Irish, Italian, and Jewish immigrants seemed most foreign to Americans although the Irish spoke English at arrival. However, all three groups differed in religion and many other customs from the great majority of Protestant, Anglo-Saxon Americans and were therefore the target of numerous forms of stigma as expressed in riots, social and economic discrimination, and political rejection. As these "old" immigrants assimilated and/or died their descendants became native-born Americans even as the "new" immigration from South America and Asia came into ascendancy. These immigrants are far better educated than was true of the nineteenth- and early twentieth-century immigrants and they frequently speak English. Nevertheless, the cultural differences that they exhibit once more lead to fears that the country will be inundated by people who cannot ever be Americans and whose background is both inferior and frightening.

Fear of those who are different is of course behind the stigma that attaches to outsiders including Americans who are homeless and therefore physically and socially on the outside. The next chapter will be concerned with those who live "on the streets."

NOTES

1. Robert E. Park and Ernest W. Burgess, *Introduction to the Science of Sociology* (Chicago: University of Chicago Press, 1924), p. 739.

2. W. Lloyd Warner and Leo Srole, *The Social Systems of American Ethnic Groups* (New Haven, Conn.: Yale University Press, 1945), p. 285.

3. Rubén J. Rumbault, "Origins and Destinies: Immigration to the United States since World War II," *Sociological Forum* 9, no. 4 (1994): 583–621.

4. Milton M. Gordon, *Assimilation in American Life: The Role of Race, Religion and National Origins* (New York: Oxford University Press, 1964).

5. Gustavus Myers, *History of Bigotry in the United States* (New York: Capricorn Books, 1960), p. 55.

6. Ibid., p. 16.

7. Gerhard Falk, *A Study in Social Change* (Lewiston, N.Y.: Edwin Mellen Press, 1993), p. 104.

8. Lawrence J. McCaffrey, *Textures of Irish America* (Syracuse, N.Y.: Syracuse University Press, 1992), p. 10.

9. Will and Ariel Durant, *The Age of Louis XIV* (New York: Simon and Schuster, 1963), p. 303.

10. George Potter, *To the Golden Door: The Story of the Irish in Ireland and America* (Boston: Little Brown & Co., 1960), p. 168.

11. Carl Wittke, *The Irish in America* (Baton Rouge: Louisiana State Unversity Press, 1950).

12. Potter, *To the Golden Door*, p. 281.

13. Ibid., pp. 421–26.

14. Richard Hofstadter and Michael Wallace, *American Violence* (New York: Random House, 1970), pp. 341–42.

15. Ibid., 305.

16. Ibid., 212.

17. McCaffrey, *Textures of Irish America*, p. 42.

18. Wittke, *The Irish in America*, p. 117.

19. Jerre Mangione and Ben Morreale, *La Storia: Five Centuries of the Italian-American Experience* (New York: HarperCollins Publishers, 1992), p. 203.

20. Burl Noggle, *Into the Twenties* (Urbana: University of Illinois Press, 1974), p. 106.

21. Ibid., p. 301.

22. Roy Beck, *The Case Against Immigration* (New York: W. W. Norton, 1996), p. 45.

23. Larry J. Siegel, *Criminology* (Belmont, Calif.: Wadsworth/Thompson Learning, 1999), p. 416.

24. Irving Howe, *World of Our Fathers* (New York: Simon and Schuster, 1976), p. 326.

25. Ibid., p. 6.

26. Gerhard Falk, *The Jew in Christian Theology* (Jefferson, N.C., and London: McFarland & Co., 1992), p. 11.

27. Steve Gorman, "NBC Reneges on Promise to Jewish Group, Says It Will Repeat Spoof that Stirred Protest," *Buffalo News,* December 21, 1999.

28. Abraham Leon Sachar, *A History of the Jews* (New York: Alfred A. Knopf, 1970), p. 224.

29. Howe, *World of Our Fathers,* p. 87.

30. Ibid., p. 410.

31. Myers, *History of Bigotry,* p. 208.

32. Abraham J. Karp, *Golden Door to America* (New York: Penguin Books, 1977), p. 16.

33. Martin Brecht, *Martin Luther: Die Erhaltung der Kirche* (Stuttgart: Calwer Verlag, 1987), p. 336.

34. Bruno Blau, *Das Ausnahmerecht für die Juden in Deutschland 1933–1945* (Extraordinary Laws Concerning the German Jews 1933–1945) (Düsseldorf: Kalima Druck, 1965).

35. Lucy S. Dawidowicz, *The War Against the Jews 1933–1945* (New York: Holt, Rinehart and Winston, 1975), p. 403.

36. Vincent N. Parillo, *Strangers to These Shores* (New York: Macmillan Publishing Co., 1990), p. 272.

37. Ibid., p. 277.

38. Yuji Ichioka, *The Isse* (New York: Free Press, 1988), p. 245.

39. "The Melting Pot Survives," *Economist* 352 (July 3, 1999): 24.

40. Jeffrey S. Passel and Michael Fix, "Myths About Immigrants," *Foreign Policy* 95 (summer 1994): 151.

41. James C. Clad, "Slowing the Wave," *Foreign Policy* 95 (summer 1994): 139.

"ON THE STREETS" 11

THE STIGMA OF HOMELESSNESS

NO HOME AND NO IDENTITY

Existential validation refers to the inclusion of almost everyone in a web of relationships that support our existence. Included in that concept is the view that life has meaning and that the meaning of life is derived from families, work relationships, friendships, and associations.[1] Existential validation is connected to some physical symbols and manifestations which define who we are. Our names, our families, our occupations, our associations, and certainly our addresses are parts of that definition. Therefore the 700,000 Americans who are homeless on any one night are by that very condition invisible nonpersons among their fellow citizens. This is also in part true of the 2 million Americans who are homeless at least one night in the course of one year. A survey undertaken in 1999 revealed that twelve million adult residents of the United States have been homeless at some time in their lives and that 470,000 people were homeless on an average night in February 1999.[2]

In 1987, Pres. Ronald Reagan signed into law the Stewart B. McKinney Homeless Assistance Act. That act was named after its Republican sponsor who had been a representative from Connecticut. The McKinney Act is the only legislation Congress has passed to help the homeless. Title I of that act defines a homeless person as "someone who lacks a fixed, regular and adequate nighttime residence." The McKinney Act contains eight additional titles that authorize the emergency food and shelter program, the emergency shelter and transitional housing program, the use of federal facilities in assisting the homeless population, healthcare services to the homeless, education for the homeless, the food-stamp program, and the Veterans Job Training Act. Congress has amended the McKinney Act several times since its passage in 1987. This has been done because of the continuing existence of homelessness in this country, which shows no sign of abating. The act seeks to deal with the immediate needs of the homeless. However, as the then Sen. Albert Gore remarked on March 23, 1987: "McKinney is an essential first step toward establishing a national agenda for action to eradicate homelessness in America. No one in this body should believe that the legislation we begin considering today is anything more than a first step toward reversing the record increase in homelessness."[3]

In 1998 the U.S. Conference of Mayors' survey of homelessness in thirty cities found that children under the age of eighteen accounted for 25 percent of the urban homeless population. In addition, 3 percent of the urban homeless were "unaccompanied minors," i.e., children who are living alone on the streets. Hence, 72 percent of the homeless are adults, including the old. According to that survey, men are three times more likely to be homeless than women. The single were also disproportionately involved. Forty-five percent of the homeless were single men and 14 percent were single women. The others were homeless families of whom the majority lived in cities.

The mayors' survey also discovered that 49 percent of all the homeless were of African descent. This is a far greater number than should be expected from a population comprising only 12 percent of all Americans. Hispanics, Native Americans, and Asians were also overrepresented in that survey. One-third of the homeless surveyed in the 1998 report were Caucasian. Evidently, whites were underrepresented among the homeless yet whites constitute 83 percent of the American population.[4]

Homelessness is not equally distributed among the American population. It clusters around single men and minorities. The failure to have a home is therefore related to the status/role differences encountered by the genders and by different ethnic groups in America. Psychiatrist Ellen Bassuk has argued that "homelessness is often the final stage in a lifelong series of crises and missed opportunities, the culmination of a gradual disengagement from supportive relationships and institutions."[5]

This academic definition hides some stark facts, including the fate of Yetta Adams. Adams went to sleep on a bus bench in Washington, D.C., on the night of November 29, 1993. The next morning this mother of three grown children was found dead on that bench, surrounded by shopping bags and covered only by a thin blanket. Yetta Adams, unlike many others who die under similar circumstances each winter, died right across the street from the U.S. Department of Housing and Urban Development. She received a good deal of nationwide attention in the media *after* she died. Many others who die on the streets each winter are of course ignored. In fact, they are frequently not identified and therefore buried in unmarked graves.[6]

The stigma of homelessness is such that the homeless are indeed "invisible" in that hardly anyone even wants to know that the homeless exist. Like the old, the homeless are shunned and their presence ignored. Homelessness, therefore, is not only a painful experience, because living in the streets has so many dangers and physical horrors, but because the stigma associated with homelessness does not even allow the victims the status of a member of American society. The homeless are indeed "nonpersons" to whom the old adage "Out of sight-out of mind" all too readily applies.[7]

In our science-driven society it is common to seek causes of any difficulty with which we are confronted with a view of "curing" the problem once the cause has been found. The search for causation is always far more difficult than appears on the surface. We are always tempted to assume that an antecedent event must be the cause of a subsequent event. This is a fallacy which can be easily exposed. Sociologist Robert MacIver, in his famous discussion of social causation, makes this distinction: "The light of mid-day is followed by the darkness of night; it is a sequence more invariable than any other, but we do not think of the light as the cause of the darkness." Likewise the noise of a train is heard before the train appears but we do not think of the noise as the cause of the train approaching. However, if we throw a stone into water and the water splashes we are justified in labeling the stone as the cause of the splash. It is important to make this distinction here lest we be tempted to assume that homelessness or any other social phenomenon is always caused by events preceding it.[8]

There is of course no lack of assertion concerning the causes of homelessness. Leading all other beliefs concerning the causes of homelessness is poverty, including lack of affordable health care. Also included in that list are mental illness, single motherhood, and addiction disorders. No doubt all of these claims are based on some evidence. It is necessary to remember, however, that all these "causes" of homelessness also occur among people who have a home so that neither the entire list, nor any one of its components, can be safely considered "the cause" of homelessness.

There are two tests of the validity of any social cause. One is statistical in that we correlate the phenomenon under consideration with any other phenomenon. The other method is sociopsychological in that we seek to find causes by reconstructing events in a synthetic history that must of course be interpreted in the light of the time in which it is written and under the circumstances in which it is read. Therefore, complete certitude eludes us because absolute unanimity concerning any social phenomenon cannot be obtained. There are those who will say that homelessness is caused by "factors" that others deny. Then there are those who like to make a list of such social "factors" and rank the list in order of importance. Yet, here again, agreement is hardly possible. Keeping these cautions in mind we begin by looking at poverty and its contribution to homelessness.[9]

Poverty may be understood in two categories. First, there is relative poverty which must be universal because it refers to the deprivation of some people relative to others who have more. Since everyone is rich or poor compared to someone else, relative deprivation cannot be avoided and may even be found among millionaires who are less wealthy than billionaires.

There is also absolute poverty, which is life-threatening, and it is this kind of poverty that affects the homeless. From a purely statistical point of view poverty consists of any income which is below the poverty threshold as defined by the Census Bureau. According to the Department of Health and Human Services that threshold was $16,700 for a family of four in 1999 with the proviso that the threshold should increase by $2,820 for each additional person.[10] For a single person the poverty threshold was $8,240.

In view of rent requirements in America's large cities an income of $16,700 for four people is evidently unrealistic. In Los Angeles a two-bedroom apartment rents for $1,000 a month or $12,000 a year. In New York City a one-bedroom apartment costs at least $900 a month and in Boston the costs are even higher. A look around the country reveals rental costs of approximately the same level compared to income.[11]

There are in this country today numerous homeless people who are working but cannot afford to pay rent. The truth is that the working homeless are a growing reality. For example, in Washington, D.C., "The nightclub doorman stands in the long line, waiting for a bed at the Central Union Mission, his arthritis aching in the chill December mist. In line, too, is Michael Turner, 36, . . . a day laborer. Behind him is a young man . . . wearing a spotless white technician's uniform."[12]

According to the Department of Housing and Urban Development, 44 percent of homeless people nationwide were working in December of 1999. In addition, 67 percent of adults who requested emergency food aid in twenty-six major American cities during 1999 were employed.[13]

Michael Turner, interviewed by a reporter of the *Miami Herald*, said that on a Monday night he was shut out of a shelter because he worked too late to get in line for a bed at 4:30 P.M. So he slept in a park in soaking rain. The next day he was lucky as he stood in the day-laborers line. He was picked and earned $33. That night he got one of the 110 beds at the shelter.

Another example of a working homeless man is "Jim," whose experiences mirror those of many others now in homeless shelters. After his divorce he worked for fourteen years in low-paying jobs which made it barely possible for him to earn enough to pay the rent. In the course of all those years, however, a number of unexpected events forced him to give up his apartment and live in the street. Once he was laid off. Then he became ill and then his brother needed financial help. Invariably all of these emergencies made "Jim" homeless again and again because he never had any resources other than his low-paying jobs.[14]

Another example of a working homeless man is Kenneth Lindo, who works as a messenger on Wall Street earning only $5.50 an hour. Unable to afford a weekly rent of $140 for his Harlem room he was forced to move to the Thirtieth Street Men's Shelter in Manhattan. His situation illustrates how the booming economy during the Clinton administration has simultaneously increased the number of low-paying jobs and the cost of housing. Kenneth Lindo is one of the fortunates who sleeps in one of the "assessment beds" in his shelter. Derek Wall-Carty is not so lucky. Like many other homeless, Carty must wait each night at any shelter he can find to see if he can get in. He walks the "overnight circuit" each night until he finds a place to sleep or until he must return to work as a cook without sleeping at all. For example, on one night Carty found a bed at the Wards Island shelter. This forced him to ride two and one half hours by bus, subway, and Long Island Railroad to reach his 9 A.M. shift after waiting for a bed the whole night.[15]

Many of the homeless who work in these circumstances have families they cannot support and from whom they have consequently become estranged.[16]

Believing that the least-paid workers should be helped, forty-two American cities adopted a "Living Wage Law" since Baltimore first inaugurated that requirement in 1994. These laws generally cover security guards, janitors, construction workers, clerical, and service workers. Those who favored these laws did so because Congress has not raised the minimum wage from $5.15 an hour since September 1, 1997. Now, in Baltimore, construction and service businesses under contract with the city must pay employees at least $8.03 an hour. In Chicago the minimum pay in these same categories is $7.60 an hour. In Los Angeles the minimum pay for similar employees is $7.51 an hour. There are those who believe they have helped the working poor by these laws. Many business people contradict that view. They claim that these higher wages actually deprive the working poor of jobs because the higher-paid jobs go to college graduates or second- and third-income workers and not the poor.

In Chicago more than six hundred thousand people live at or below the poverty level. Of these only five thousand are covered by the living-wage law. In Los Angeles about 2.2 million people live at or below the poverty level although the living-wage law guarantees the working poor about $25,000 a year.[17]

In an effort to alleviate the homelessness of these working poor, President Clinton announced on December 29, 1999, that he will propose to Congress that 120,000 new families be added to the federal housing subsidy program in the 2001 budget. That budget begins on October 1, 2000. This housing program consists of housing vouchers which permit the recipient a choice as to where to live compared to government-run housing projects. The average monthly federal housing subsidy is $400 with renters contributing another $223.

Amidst charges that his announcement was politically motivated, President Clinton also announced that the federal government would spend $900 million to help the homeless across the nation get off the streets and pursue productive lives. About $750 million of that money will be spent on programs including drug treatment, job training, and other social services. The other $150 million is to be spent on short-term aid to provide shelter and food to the needy.[18]

These programs are necessary in view of the number of Americans living in extreme poverty now. The U.S. Bureau of the Census estimated that 13.3 percent of the U.S. population lives in poverty and that 41 percent or 14.6 million of the 35.6 million poor in this country have incomes of less than half the poverty level.[19] Poverty and the stigma associated with poverty is then the first reason for homelessness in America.

THE INVISIBLE HOMELESS

In 1901, Winston Churchill, a future prime minister of England, reviewed a book by Seebohm Rowntree called *Poverty*. That review included this: "It is pleasurable to dwell on the extremes of wealth. We do not wish to contemplate the extremes of poverty."[20] Churchill's meaning was clear. The stigma of poverty and in particular the stigma of homelessness makes the poor invisible. The truth is, of course, that physically the poor can be seen by those who wish to look. However, social visibility is the product of social distance and the social distance between the homeless and everyone else in American society is considerable.

The concept of "social distance" was first used by sociologist Emory Bogardus to describe the avoidance patterns of Americans toward those whose ethnic group seemed unacceptable to them. In 1959 when Bogardus began social-distance studies his work was confined to studies of interaction between white and black Americans and was later expanded to include social distance between other ethnic groups. This concept may be applied to the condition of the homeless who are socially as distant from the preponderance of Americans as the blacks of Mississippi were from the white population before the civil rights movement. Indeed, the homeless may be seen on the streets of America's cities, but even today they are treated with indifference by nearly all who pass them by.[21]

The homeless wander the streets of America with their possessions in shopping bags, searching through garbage cans in pursuit of food and asking for handouts. These urban wanderers became far more numerous than ever before when, in the 1980s, America suffered its worst recession in half a century. At that time many people believed that homelessness would be only a temporary problem and would disappear as economic conditions improved. This has not happened at the end of this decade despite the immense improvement in the American economy.

Instead, the spread of homelessness has made most everyone aware that something has gone wrong with our institutions even as well-to-do Americans prefer not to face the despair and misery that homelessness depicts.

Homelessness has political implications. It is for that reason that the number of the homeless has been in dispute for some time since it is in the interest of the homeless and their advocates to talk of a greater number of the homeless and in the interests of government to minimize the problem. Big numbers are politically much more useful than small numbers. For that reason some activists for the homeless have inflated the number of the homeless in the interests of "lying for justice."

In 1989, sociologist Peter Rossi published his sensational book *Down and Out in America.* This study was based on Rossi's 1985 effort to count all the homeless in Chicago by visiting public places such as doorways, parks, or free shelters. His subsequent estimates were that then about 1,400 people were sleeping in the public streets, bus stations, all-night movie theaters, airports, and restaurants. Rossi also found another 1,400 homeless were sleeping in shelters. Rossi repeated his study in 1986 and found the same number of homeless in similar places. He therefore concluded that about 0.1 percent of Chicago's three million people were then homeless.

It is reasonable to assume that Rossi missed a good number of the homeless despite his efforts because many homeless sleep indoors in such places as basements and hallways which the owners will make available at night in return for daytime work.[22]

Between 1990 and 1991, Jennifer Toth, a reporter for the *New York Times*, investigated the homeless in New York City. New York differs from Chicago with respect to shelter for the homeless because New York has numerous tunnels that were built in the nineteenth century for railroads and subways. Many of these tunnels have now been abandoned although they can be reached from the streets. In *The Mole People*, Toth describes the people who now live in these tunnels. According to her estimates and those made by others, around 5,500 people live underground in New York City. In addition, about 11,000 people sleep in the city's shelters every night.[23]

Despite the low temperatures which the homeless suffer on the streets there are many who avoid these shelters for fear of theft and assault and the noise that does not cease all night. There are also families with children who sleep in the offices of the New York City Emergency Assistance Unit. They sleep on the floor and on chairs in that intake unit while waiting for city investigators to verify their claims of homelessness.[24]

The Urban Institute made a comprehensive survey of homelessness in March of 1987 in a representative sample of American cities of more than 100,000 population. Interviewers talked with randomly selected homeless adults in shelters, soup kitchens, bus stations, and street corners. This revealed that only one-third of adults had slept in a homeless shelter the night before they were interviewed while 96 percent of homeless families with children had used a shelter the night before.

As the number of the homeless grew in the 1980s, more and more reporters, police, and other observers concluded that the homeless must be the products of the mental hospitals which had recently released so many former patients. This belief was based in part on observation because so many of the homeless seemed so bizarre to all observers. In 1988 and several previous years, there were many releases from mental hospitals. Yet, Martha Burt and Barbara Cohen, researchers at the Urban Institute, in their detailed study of the homeless in that year found that only 24 percent of the homeless said that they had ever spent time in a mental hospital. This does not mean that only a quarter of the homeless are or were mentally ill. No doubt, many who were at one time mental patients will not admit this to interviewers. Furthermore, there are many mentally ill people who were never in a psychiatric facility. Clinicians and the homeless themselves estimate that about a third of the homeless have had severe mental problems. These estimates are based on positive responses to such questions asked by Burt and Cohen as these: "Do you hear voices that others cannot hear? Do you see things others cannot see? Do you have special powers that others do not have? Has your mind been taken over by forces you cannot control?"[25] In addition to those who hear voices and cannot control their own feelings there are those who suffer from manic-depression, also known as bipolar disorder. That condition can make patients delusional resembling schizophrenia and leads as well to a condition of fatigue so that the manic-depressive cannot work. Although manic-depression can be treated by a combination of mood stabilizers and antidepressants, such psychiatric intervention is seldom available to the poor. Instead, excessive absenteeism, poor performance, and a loss of concern about one's appearance that lead to a loss of work and homelessness is its final outcome.[26]

A good number of the mentally ill who are roaming the streets of America today are the victims of the Supplemental Security Income (SSI) policy established by Congress in 1972. That policy provided that anyone judged by the Social Security Administration as being incapable of holding a job could receive a monthly check from Social Security. Because this money was not available to mental hospital patients, state hospitals discharged a number of patients who then became eligible to receive this money when they moved into a "board-and-care" facility. These board-and-care facilities collected the SSI checks and then did very little if anything to help the former mental patients. Hence, many of these mentally ill people, along with drug users and alcoholics, walked out of their board-and-care facilities and became cut-off from their families. Unable to manage their affairs, including paying their rent, they became homeless and dependent on day labor to maintain themselves. They no longer received SSI benefits after leaving the board-and-care facility in which they had lived. Now depending on themselves alone, many of these day laborers faced competition from new immigrants from Asian countries who were, in any event, considered more reliable by employers than were the homeless.[27]

Thus, poverty and mental illness both contribute to homelessness in America particularly because poverty and mental illness are heavily stigmatized in this country. We concur with Christopher Jencks, professor of social policy at Harvard University, who in 1994 wrote that "no other affluent country has abandoned its (homeless) mentally ill to this extent."

Addiction to a number of drugs is another cause of homelessness. Traditionally, alcohol had always been associated with about a third of the homeless. This is in part due to the existence of an "alcohol culture" in America best illustrated by the following 1997 U.S. Census statistics. According to the bureau, on average, adults consume 3 gallons of wine, 1.9 gallons of liquor, and 33.9 gallons of beer each year. Milk consumption is only 24 gallons per year. Therefore milk is consumed less than beer. Coffee consumption on average is only 23.5 gallons each year. Some Americans do not drink alcohol. Therefore, the total consumption of alcoholic beverages is imbibed by fewer adults and adolescents than are present in the population. More important is to recognize that one-half of all the alcohol consumed is taken in by only 10 percent of all the drinkers in this country.[28] Among these drinkers have always been the traditional "skid-row" alcoholics. Therefore the current increase in homelessness can hardly be attributed to alcoholism. This does not mean that alcohol is not involved in homelessness. It does mean, however, that it is not involved in the *increase* in homelessness during the past decade. That increase is much more associated with the easy availability of crack cocaine. Because crack cocaine costs only $3 a "hit" its use has become widespread among the poor and is so common among the homeless that a survey in New York City showed that 66 percent of those in public shelters exhibited traces of cocaine in their urine during a voluntary test conducted there. Similar findings were recorded in Dallas, Detroit, San Diego, Philadelphia, Houston, Chicago, and Los Angeles.[29]

A fourth reason for homelessness in America is unmarried motherhood. This became evident in the 1980s and continued throughout the 1990s despite the ever-increasing work opportunities women have enjoyed during the last twenty years. Even as female income has increased from about 65 percent of male income in 1980 to 79 percent of male income in 1999, the number of the female homeless increased as well because the minority of women who did not work often did not have a husband and were mainly unskilled, but did have children.

Thirty percent of the illegitimate births in this country occur among females less than twenty years of age. At least 71 percent of teen mothers are unmarried, of whom one-half go on welfare within one year of the birth of their child. By the time an illegitimate child is five years old 72 percent of white children and 84 percent of black children receive Aid to Dependent Children from the federal government.

Today one out of every three American children is born to a single mother. In 1970 only one child in ten was born to a single mother. If this trend continues it is probable that in 2015 one-half of all American children will be born to single mothers. Seven million children are now living with a single parent. Among black children the illegitimacy rate is now 68 percent, among Hispanic women it is 41 percent, and among white children it is 22 percent, a tenfold increase since 1960. Women with college degrees contribute only 4 percent of white illegitimate babies, while white women with a high-school education or less contribute 82 percent of the single mothers in America today. The other 14 percent are either African American or are of Oriental heritage. Income reflects these educational levels. Hence, women with family incomes of $75,000 or more contributed only 1 percent of white illegitimate babies in 1999 while women with family incomes less than $20,000 contributed 69 percent. Among white women living below the poverty line, 44 percent of births have been illegitimate, while 6 percent of births among those white women above the poverty line were illegitimate. Within two years of having a first child, more than 31 percent of unwed mothers have a second child.[30]

Among those women who have these children but cannot support them are those who can hardly sustain themselves on their Aid to Dependent Children money, particularly if they cannot exercise the utmost frugality such dependency requires. Some of these women and children become homeless. There are others, however, who never qualified for such aid because they live with parents who support them and their children. Those who cannot sustain such a close relationship with their parents will then move onto the street rather than stay at home and listen to constant complaints about their child's illegitimacy. An example of the kind of family that became homeless while the mother was alone in charge of her children is this: "Mrs. Lukless with two female children aged 18 months and 3 years lived in 'Baghdad Inn,' a shelter in Arid Acropolis. She referred to the father of the children as Mr. Lukless and called herself 'Mrs.' although she was never married. The father of the children abandoned his family as soon as the younger child was born. Unable to pay rent, Mrs. Lukless moved into a homeless shelter. From there she was again placed into an apartment but was evicted when she could not pay the rent. Then, Mrs. Lukless moved into a homeless shelter where she was allowed to stay for ninety days. At the end of that time Mrs. Lukless had not found an apartment for her family but was evicted from the shelter and then became homeless as did her children."[31]

HOMELESS CHILDREN AND FAILED ADULTS

The National Coalition for the Homeless reports that in 1999 at any one time 1.1 million children lived in emergency shelters somewhere in this country. Forty-three percent of these children were male. Of the 57 percent of female children who live homeless on America's streets 2 to 5 percent have children of their own. In 1989 there were only 500,000 homeless children in this country. Since the population of the United States did not even approach doubling in ten years it is evident that this 100 percent increase in homeless children is not merely demographic[32] but a result of changes in attitudes toward homelessness and drug use.

These numbers include only children seventeen years old or less. Those over seventeen are not considered children by those who count the homeless. Sixty-five percent of runaway children in shelters are female and 38 percent of both sexes are younger than fourteen. About 6 percent of children served by the Children's Defense Fund are homosexual. Every ethnic group in America is represented among homeless children although minorities are very much overrepresented.[33]

Homeless children who belong to homeless families represent mostly the poorest of the poor Americans. Homeless children living with homeless families are even more often from a one-parent family than is true in the general population, whose rate of illegitimacy is 33 percent. Unaccompanied children who are also called "runaways" represent a wider range of socioeconomic background than is true of homeless families.

The stigma of being a "runaway" or "throwaway" is considerable. Blaming the victim is a widespread attitude concerning homeless children who are viewed as "bad" by Americans who do not understand why any child would abandon his or her family and live on the streets. Few "normal" people can imagine how a child can take care of himself in a homeless situation. Therefore, such children are frequently stigmatized, alone because they don't go to school, have no curfews, and all together don't behave like "good" kids. Because homeless children have no visible means of support it is also frequently assumed that such children must be thieves and shoplifters and must be making their living by some dishonest means.[34]

It is commonly believed that homeless children could go home if they wished. But this is not true. A large number of homeless children have been turned away by their parents. They have been locked out of their houses. They have been sent to nonexistent relatives or abandoned on the road. Others come from families so abusive and cruel that the street seems like a haven to them.

Looking at the experiences of children who are homeless it becomes obvious that such children have generally been victimized by adults. Sexual abuse is high on the list of such victimization. Studies have shown that up to 90 percent of children who live on the streets were sexually or physically abused before they became homeless. Such sexual abuse is mainly related to the 50 percent divorce rate in this country because so many of the divorced remarry and thereby introduce stepparents to their families.

A good number of runaway children become homeless because they have no idea of what faces them if they leave their home. Adopted children run away to find their physical mothers, others run away because they want to escape parental authority, and yet others imagine they can support themselves by working as waitresses in any restaurant. The consequences of leaving home are not foreseen by many a young person. Consider Sarah, who could not tolerate the long hours and hard work in a greasy diner where she found work as a waitress after leaving home. She was forced to take that job because no one else was willing to hire someone without proof of age. In the diner she met some "street-smart" children whom she joined after only two days on the job. The group she joined lived in a "crash pad." A crash pad is any place in which one may sleep without payment or ownership. There she was required to engage in sex with others in the group and to earn money by having sex with strangers. She also stole food, dealt drugs, and lived in filth and misery. Any money she earned was kept by the group so that she could not even make a telephone call to ask for help. Finally she succeeded when she saw the 800 number of Covenant House which helped her.[35]

Covenant House is only one of a number of agencies designed to help homeless children. These shelters and other emergency programs proliferated in the United States after Congress passed the Runaway and Homeless Youth Act in 1971. These agencies are, for the most part, refitted orphanages or relatively new operations. They are small. The average homeless runaway youth program has from six to fifteen residential places, time limits of two weeks to a month, and two employees and some volunteers.[36]

Homeless children have no rights. Teens generally get no help from child-protection agencies but are too young to receive legal standing. Homeless children do not qualify for welfare because parents, not children, receive Aid to Dependent Children's payments.

In view of the ever-increasing importance of education as a means of living a self-supporting life in America, life on the streets deprives children who live there of the most essential means of ever leading a normal life in the new century.

Included in the Stewart B. McKinney Homeless Assistance Act or Public Law 100-77 is a provision that funnels federal money to states for the education of homeless children. The policy of Congress under that act was to give homeless children access to the same education given other children. An example of the manner in which this mandate was carried out is the Pennsylvania plan. This plan seeks to first eliminate the residency and guardianship requirements that many school districts use and which would keep homeless children out of school. Transportation to and from school is another barrier a homeless child must overcome. The homeless have no address. They need to have an agreement with a school regarding a place of departure for school and return after school. In addition, homeless children seldom have school records. Yet, schools require such records before enrolling anyone. School districts therefore have to take children who have no such records as was also the case among immigrants who had survived the Holocaust and whose entire life records had been burnt by the German government.

Homeless children also add to classroom size and to the emotional situation in classrooms everywhere. This increases the pressure on teachers to deal with children whose problems are unimaginable to those who come from secure homes. Therefore, the federal budget for 2000 included $28.8 million for Education for Homeless Children and Youth Programs, a sum which is exactly the same as it was in 1999.[37]

In addition to the major problems faced by school systems in attempting to educate homeless children, the children themselves face a number of obstacles relative to attaining even a minimum education.

Homelessness is associated with developmental delays, emotional problems, poor school attendance, and low academic performance. Several studies have confirmed that half the homeless and runaway youths were dropouts, severely truant, or expelled. Evidently then, these children are also at high risk of school failure. Furthermore, in achievement tests homeless children score far below averages for other children in both mathematics and reading.[38]

All of this is easily understood if we consider the differences between the manner in which homeless children must face the world each day. At once it is evident that homework and other requirements normally associated with American school experiences cannot be fulfilled by a homeless child. There is no place to do the homework. There is no parent to help with the homework. No one visits the teacher on behalf of a homeless child and there is no one around to admire the child's success or to support her when she fails. Homelessness therefore leads to emotional stress, which interferes with school success. The stress of survival alone keeps homeless children from concentrating on schoolwork and paying attention to classroom procedures.

Normally, schoolchildren are given school supplies and clothes by their parents. Homeless children have no means of buying such supplies and are unlikely to wear acceptable clothes. Many homeless children are rejected and segregated in school because they seldom have good clothes. Even those homeless children who live with their families cannot expect any financial support from them. In fact, many homeless families include alcoholic and other drug-abusing parents and frequently include both physical and emotional abuse. The consequences are that homeless children, already frightened and insecure, are alienated from other children in school and can hardly be expected to succeed.[39]

More than six hundred children in the Hartford, Connecticut, schools are homeless. These children generally live in one of Hartford's eleven shelters after having been abandoned by one or both parents. While the youngest abandoned children are normally placed in foster homes by the Connecticut Department of Children and Families, children as young as twelve live alone in these shelters. Many of the female children already have babies yet must make an effort to do their homework in these shelters and stay in school. These children get free breakfast in school if the school bus is on time. Otherwise they must wait until they receive a free lunch in school. Cynthia Winer, coordinator for homeless education in the Hartford schools, believes that the problem of homeless children will increase in the near future because welfare reform seeks to curtail the help given the homeless, including children.[40] These children rarely succeed in finishing school so they in turn become the homeless adults of the next generation. These children have never seen academic success and are often incapable of staying in school because they suffer from blind rage and other disruptive feelings which make it extremely difficult for teachers to reach them or to teach them anything. Schools are organized to permit middle-class and upper-class children to succeed in the economic and social sphere of adult life. The homeless who do not fit into the school situation also find that they are therefore ill prepared to deal with the economic and social requirements of adult life in America, so that homelessness tends to perpetuate itself over the generations.[41]

THE HOMELESS ORGANIZE

Although the median age of the homeless in America is now thirty-four, about 6 percent of the homeless are old, i.e., aged sixty-five or more. Their age alone, therefore, makes them particularly vulnerable and their options of ever returning to the dominant economic and social structure of American society are negligible. In addition, the physical capacity of the old to withstand living on the street or in shelters is limited. Because of their age the old homeless are more likely to have a steady source of income than is true of younger people. For men, these sources of income are Social Security benefits, veteran's benefits, and other pensions. Women are seldom entitled to veteran's benefits and have less access to pensions as well. Homeless old women are therefore much more likely to depend on government-sponsored programs than is true of old homeless men.

Old women and men who are homeless exhibit a high incidence of mental-health problems. These problems are generally related to excessive use of alcohol but are also the product of the lifestyle of someone existing on the street. It may be debatable whether mental illness is the cause of homelessness in the first place or whether homelessness leads to mental illness. Whatever the cause or effect, a study conducted in a well-known shelter in Boston discovered that 90 percent of women and 40 percent of men using that shelter exhibit psychiatric illness.[42]

The old, whether homeless or not, also suffer more physical illness than younger people. Arthritis, diabetes, fractures, and pneumonia are the most frequent physical problems of the old and homeless. Added difficulties are vision and hearing losses. Yet, very little if anything is ever done to treat these problems since the homeless are unlikely to have insurance or any other means of paying for medical services.

About a third of homeless men and some women fit the stereotype of the homeless usually portrayed by the followers of former president Ronald Reagan who claimed that the homeless are so situated by choice.

Those who agree with Reagan claim that the behavior of the homeless themselves creates their condition. "Many of the homeless have willingly chosen to be homeless and chosen to steal, take drugs, and abandon their families for a life free of ties and responsibilities," wrote the news reporter Theodore Papas in 1994.[43]

This view is in part supported by a New York City study which revealed that "fully half of all homeless families placed in permanent housing returned to the shelter system." That study and others also show that many of the families placed into clean and often new housing by the city then destroy the houses they are assigned. In numerous cases it was discovered that kitchen and bathroom plumbing is ripped out, that furniture has been sold, that there is trash all over the house and graffiti on the walls. In many such homes the children are neglected and abused and are "out of control."[44]

A California study of four hundred homeless families found that they were often not as poor as families with homes and that poverty was not always the cause of a lack of shelter. Personal problems including family conflicts were cited as major causes of homelessness. Here it was found that many of the homeless have never worked and will not work no matter how many jobs are available. It is argued by those who view homelessness as the result of lack of will that the size of the homeless population remains always the same, in prosperity and in depression, in good times and in bad.

Those who hold the homeless themselves responsible point out that the homeless create problems for themselves but also for everyone else. They object that "decent" people have to climb over alcoholics in the streets, that sandboxes in parks become urinals, that park benches become the permanent home of dozing alcoholics, that swings for children are broken, and that ordinary citizens cannot use these "dead" parks because they are the headquarters of homeless drug pushers.[45]

Many citizens are afraid of the homeless. These "street people" are seldom clean. They often smell from alcohol and dirt since they have no means of maintaining personal hygiene. A good number of the homeless sit for hours in public libraries, train stations, bus stations, and other enclosed places. Fearing they will be mugged or otherwise molested, a good number of citizens are particularly afraid for their children in the presence of a seemingly irrational homeless person.

Those who hold the view that the homeless are themselves responsible for their misfortune also believe that welfare payments should be reduced and "workfare" substituted. They believe that those receiving benefits from the taxpayer should work for their money by doing public service such as street cleaning and various kinds of community service.[46]

There are also some homeless people who engage in scams. These homeless people make the rounds of private and government agencies and collect handouts and/or vouchers, some of which they then sell to other homeless for cash, liquor, or drugs. These are the homeless who are seen as not down on their luck but as cunning manipulators of the welfare system. It is claimed by those who see the homeless as responsible for their own situation that their advocates have made them into romantic rebels who need not be civil, are utterly autonomous, and should not have to work. Adherents to that view also believe that the prime reason for poverty is illegitimacy and that poverty is not an economic but a moral issue. Those who hold these "conservative" views also claim that a whole welfare industry has developed in the United States which has an interest in keeping the poor and the homeless in that condition in order to continue collecting federal and state aid. It is claimed that shelters compete for clients, as for example the recent marketing campaign by the Grand Central Neighborhood Social Service Corp. which sought to engage new clients by offering them a free breakfast and $5.

The most stringent complaint by those holding the homeless themselves responsible for their situation is the insistence that the homeless should have to work for their shelter and their food. That opinion has been adopted by New York City, where the homeless are employed cleaning Central Park, leading to a reduction of the welfare rolls by 30 percent.[47] In view of all this there are those who insist that the homeless are themselves responsible for their situation and should not be "coddled" by people willing to work.

The sight of the homeless on the streets evokes a good deal of hostility among some people and leads not only to the stigmatization of the homeless but even to name-calling and assault.

An excellent example of the treatment the homeless can expect are the experiences of those who live in Camp LaGuardia, a 365-acre camp for the homeless owned by New York City. That camp is located near Chester, New York. The camp employs a van to drive the homeless to the Chester Mall each day. There the homeless buy crackers, soup, and soda and other items and then wait until the van returns them to camp. While waiting, the homeless become subject to hostile remarks and even efforts to run them down in the street. Some of the homeless walk the three miles between the camp and the town. This permits truck drivers to swerve at homeless men and to abuse them verbally as well.

Local residents claim that the homeless are criminals and that their behavior is offensive, leading to a county lawsuit against the City of New York despite the fact that the local police could recall no serious crime against a local resident by anyone from the LaGuardia camp. In fact, one murder and one armed robbery in Chester in recent years were committed by local residents. Of the men living in the camp about one-third stay all winter because they are sick, disabled, or frail. The level of hostility to the homeless in Chester is illustrated by the arrest of a man under the "open-container law" for drinking a soft drink. Because this law is enforced only against camp residents the man sued and won a $30,000 settlement.[48]

The tension between the camp residents and the surrounding small towns is not only related to the stigma attached to homelessness generally but is also aggravated by the racial differences between the mostly black and Hispanic camp residents and the middle-class whites who own homes in that area.[49]

The rejection of the homeless in Chester and elsewhere is of course largely based on the belief that the homeless are themselves responsible for their condition. Yet, those who see homelessness as caused by society itself argue that social organization as it is now arranged causes homelessness. It is lack of affordable housing, say the proponents of the "Society Is Responsible" view of homelessness.

The National Coalition for the Homeless has calculated that during the twenty years ending in 1993 over 2.2 million low-rent housing units disappeared from the market even as "the number of low-income renters increased by 4.7 million."

Further, the National Coalition for the Homeless found that the number of housing units that rent for less than $300 declined from 6.8 million in 1996 to 5.5 million in 1998, a 19 percent drop of 1.3 million units. This came about because of condominium conversions, rising operating costs, the abandonment and demolition of deteriorated units, and the shrinking of housing in the private market. Additionally it needs to be recognized that nearly 30 percent of the American workforce is earning below the factory level.

Therefore, argues the National Coalition, high rent, overcrowding, and substandard housing has forced many people to become homeless. As the housing shortage increased, the waiting time to enter affordable housing provided by the U.S. Department of Housing and Urban Development also increased from an average of twenty-two months to thirty-three months between 1996 and 1998. Therefore, people must remain in shelters and inadequate housing arrangements longer than before. These facts are evidently the reason for the inclusion of a proposal for additional housing in President Clinton's budget message to Congress for 2001.

In the year 2000 there was a minimal effort to reverse the reduction of low-rent housing which has now been continuing for five decades. In New York City, both public and private funds are now being used to construct "efficiency units" for at least a few hundred of the thousands of homeless there. These "efficiency units" are the successors to the Single-Room Occupancy apartments that have housed so many over the years who could not afford the lowest rents. At one time New York City had two hundred thousand Single-Room Occupancy apartments. Today, there are only sixty-four thousand of these units left. This came about because many of these Single-Room Occupancy hotels have been renovated recently to serve the thousands of tourists who come to New York at all times. These tourists pay much more for these renovated rooms than was possible for those whose rent was paid previously by welfare allocations.

New York City began construction of thirteen efficiency-apartment buildings in 1998. Nevertheless, it is expected that even after these apartment buildings are ready for use there will still be 7,200 single adults living in shelters throughout the city.

New York City also has a program called the "Doe Fund Ready, Willing, and Able Program." This program provides housing in exchange for work, usually on a street-cleaning crew. Those who work there earn $5.50 an hour and pay $50 per week in rent to live in transitional housing. The city also has a "Supportive Housing Program" funded by the Department of Mental Health and accessible by only the mentally ill.[50]

Lack of job opportunities is considered yet another reason for homelessness by those who believe that the homeless themselves are not at fault. Lacking the necessary education and job skills to maintain a steady income, they are offered only "dead-end" jobs in America's technological economy. Therefore, say advocates, the homeless must panhandle, pick crops at low wages, or prostitute themselves. Many of the homeless, we are told, cannot even look for work because they are unshaven, unclean, use poor clothes, are unable to list a steady telephone number where a potential employer might reach them, and are shifted from shelter to shelter so that they have no permanent address at which to receive mail. Homeless mothers lack cooking facilities so that their children have to eat almost exclusively in fast-food restaurants. In addition, homeless families wait for hours at medical clinics to get prescriptions; visit numerous government offices to get food stamps, healthcare vouchers, and welfare checks. Single mothers are even worse off. They must endlessly defend against sex molesters, thieves, batterers, drugs, and the violence associated with drugs In fact, one reason for the increase in homeless women and children during the past twenty years has been an increase in domestic violence. Stacey Chambers, assistant editor at Public Affairs Information Service, writing in the *Humanist,* claims that 92 percent of homeless mothers and 82 percent of low-income mothers have experienced an assault at least once in their lives. One-half of such women have suffered major depression stemming at least in part from the extremely small support network of friends, family, and coworkers who are so much more available to those who have a home.[51]

There are those who were once homeless but have regained a home. Among these is Lars Eighner, who was interviewed about his three years on the streets of Austin, Texas. That interview revealed some differences between home ownership and homelessness that cannot be recognized by someone who always had a home. "Your house is someplace that you can exclude people from," says Eighner. He explained that in the streets the homeless have no right to be where they are and cannot exclude anyone from their living space. Yet, living in his own apartment, Eighner feels isolated and distant from his neighbors. He also worries that he may end up in a homeless situation again. Most striking is his analysis of reality as the homeless see it. To them, reality is the constant worry about finding a place to sleep that night or finding food in dumpsters even as those who have all these things worry about such media events as the latest sex scandal or conditions in Yugoslavia. Eighner shows that the homeless lifestyle is emotionally draining and physically exhausting and offers little opportunity to escape the endless cycle of poverty, failure, and social exclusion. That exclusion is particularly strong relative to those who live on the street and practice prostitution, an occupation which is undoubtedly the most stigmatized means of earning a livelihood anywhere.[52]

SUMMARY

The homeless are treated as nonpersons. This means that no one will look at the homeless except as objects lying in the street. The homeless receive no response, no recognition, and have no security. The stigma of homelessness is also comparative in that the homeless know that they have no address, receive no mail, and belong to no neighborhood like "normal" people do.

The stigma is internalized in that the homeless feel they have no purpose and no meaning in this world. The homeless have no real identity because they do not belong to any group of people and have no relatives willing to acknowledge them.

Identity in American life depends largely on occupation. Therefore the homeless lack the most essential aspect of social acceptance in America—a job or a profession. Without a family, friends, or a means of earning a livelihood, who are we?

There are about two million Americans who are homeless one night every year and seven hundred thousand who are homeless for long periods of time. In 1987 Congress attempted to deal with this problem by passing the McKinney Act. Additional attention has been given to this problem in 1998 by the Conference of Mayors. The conference found that most homeless are single men, that there are some single homeless women, and that there are a considerable number of homeless families. Minorities are overrepresented among the homeless.

Many homeless people work but earn so little they cannot pay rent. This situation has led to the "Living Wage Laws" in some cities and to President Clinton's proposal to spend $900 million to improve the lot of the homeless.

There are also a good number of homeless who suffer from drug addiction, alcoholism, and mental illness. Furthermore, unmarried mothers often become homeless because they have no support from the fathers of their children. These children need special help to attend school but generally cannot overcome the handicaps they face in trying to meet school requirements.

There are those who claim that the homeless want to be homeless. Others view the homeless as victims of the organization of American society per se and seek to remedy homelessness by providing more low-cost housing and more occupational training so that those who have no skills at all need not resort to extreme measures to survive. Prostitution is one such extreme approach and is the subject of our next chapter.

NOTES

1. Viktor E. Frankl, *Man's Search for Meaning*, trans. Ilse Lasch (New York: Washington Square Press, 1963).

2. National Law Center on Homelessness and Poverty, *Out of Sight—Out of Mind? A Report on Anti-Homeless Laws, Litigation and Alternatives in Fifty United States Cities, 1999* (Washington, D.C.: National Law Center on Homelessness and Poverty, 1999).

3. Albert Gore, "The McKinney Act," *Congressional Record* (March 23, 1987): S3683.

4. *A Status Report on Hunger and Homelessness in American Cities* (Washington, D.C.: U.S. Conference of Mayors, 1999).

5. Ellen Bassuk, "The Homeless Problem," *Scientific American* 25, no. 1 (1984): 40.

6. Mimi Hall, "Painful Path of Homelessness," *USA Today*, December 9, 1993: 8A.

7. Yvonne M. Vissing, *Out of Sight—Out of Mind* (Lexington: University of Kentucky Press, 1996).

8. Robert M. MacIver, *Social Causation* (New York: Harper Torchbooks, 1964), p. 5.

9. Ibid., p. 391.

10. "1999 HHS Poverty Guidelines," *Federal Register* 64, no. 52 (March 18, 1999): 13428.

11. Citidigs, The Internet Guide to Apartment Hunting, Yahoo, December 30, 1999.

12. Mary Otto, "The Working Homeless Is a Growing Reality," *Miami Herald,* March 26, 1999, p. A40.

13. Conference of Mayors.

14. Skip Barry, "Homeless at Fifty," *Commonweal* 126, no. 8 (1999): 12.

15. Nina Bernstein, "With a Job, Without a Home," *New York Times,* March 4, 1999, pp. B1–2.

16. Mary Otto, "The Working Homeless."

17. Abe Estimada, "Living Wage Is Guarantee for Only a Few," *USA Today,* December 28, 1999, p. A3.

18. "Clinton Proposes Expanding Housing Aid Program," *Daily News,* December 29, 1999.

19. National Coalition for the Homeless, "Why Are People Homeless?" *NCH Fact Sheet No.1* (December 29, 1999), p. 1.

20. Martin Gilbert, *Churchill: A Life* (New York: Henry Holt and Company, 1991), p. 146.

21. Emory S. Bogardus, "Comparing Racial Distance in Ethiopia, South Africa and the United States," *Sociology and Social Research* 52, no. 2 (January 1958): 140–60.

22. Peter H. Rossi, *Down and Out in America* (Chicago: University of Chicago Press, 1989).

23. Jennifer Toth, *The Mole People; Life in the Tunnels beneath New York City* (Chicago: Chicago Review Press, 1993).

24. Somini Sengupta, "Despite Cold, Some Homeless Devise Strategies to Avoid Shelters," *New York Times,* January 4, 1999, p. B5.

25. Martha R. Burt, *Over the Edge: The Growth of Homelessness in the 1980s* (New York: Russell Sage Foundation, 1992).

26. Lynette Holloway, "Seeing a Link Between Depression and Homelessness," *New York Times,* February 7, 1999, secs. 4–3.

27. Christopher Jencks, *The Homeless* (Cambridge, Mass.: Harvard University Press, 1994).

28. U.S. Bureau of the Census, "Alcohol Consumption," *Statistical Abstract of the United States* (Washington, D.C.: U.S. Department of Commerce, 1996).

29. Christopher Jencks, *The Homeless,* p. 104.

30. Family Research Council, "A Few Facts About Illegitimacy," *In Focus* (January 2000): 1.

31. Ione Y. DeOllos, *On Becoming Homeless* (Lanham, Md., and New York: University Press of America, 1997), p. 160.

32. Paul G. Shane, *The State of America's Children* (Washington, D.C.: Children's Defense Fund, 1992), p. 109.

33. Paul G. Shane, *What About America's Homeless Children?* (Thousand Oaks, Calif.: Sage Publications, 1996), p. 15.

34. Ibid., p. 18.

35. Margaret O. Hyde, *Missing and Murdered Children* (New York: Franklin Watts, 1998), p. 35.

36. Shane, *What About America's Homeless Children?* p. 183.

37. Commonwealth of Pennsylvania, *Pennsylvania Homeless Student Initiative* (Harrisburg: Pennsylvania Department of Education, 1989).

38. P. David Kurtz, Sara V. Jarvis, and Gail L. Kurtz, "Problems of Homeless Youths: Empirical Findings and Human Services Issues," *Social Work* 36, no. 4 (1991): 309–14.

39. Robert Gewirtzman and Isidore Fodor, "The Homeless Child at School: From Welfare Hotel to Classroom," *Child Welfare* 66 (1987): 237.

40. Nancy Polk, "Homeless Children Find an Advocate," *New York Times*, May 9, 1999, p. C1.

41. Crystal Mills and Hiro Ota, "Homeless Women with Minor Children in the Detroit Metropolitan Area," *Social Work* 34, no. 6 (1989): 485.

42. Elizabeth A. Kutza and Sharon M. Keigher, "The Elderly 'New Homeless': An Emerging Population at Risk," *Social Work* 36, no. 4 (1991): 288.

43. Katie de Koster, *Poverty: Opposing Viewpoints* (San Diego: Greenhaven Press, 1994), p. 65.

44. Ted Gottfried, *Homelessness: Whose Problem Is It?* (Brookfield, Conn.: Millbrook Press, 1999), p. 51.

45. John Leo, "Homeless Rights, Community Wrongs," *U.S. News and World Report* (July 24, 1989): 56.

46. Gottfried, *Homelessness*, p. 58.

47. Dyan Machan, "Free Lunch—No Dishes to Wash," *Forbes* 16, no. 3 (1998): 64.

48. Nina Bernstein, "An Uneasy Coexistence: Tensions between Town and Shelter Flow Both Ways," *New York Times*, May 4, 1999, pp. B1–2.

49. Nina Bernstein, "Mayor Acts on Complaints Over City's Upstate Men's Shelter," *New York Times*, April 14, 1999, pp. B1–2.

50. Dennis Hevesy, "Building Homes for the Single Homeless," *New York Times*, April 25, 1999, sec. 11, p. 4.

51. Stacey Chambers, "How Any Person on the Street Can Help a Street Person," *Humanist* 59, no. 1 (1999): 21–26.

52. Melanie Rehak, "A Roof of One's Own," *New York Times*, March 7, 1999, sec. 7, p. 23:1.

PROSTITUTES 12

STIGMA, EXPLOITATION, AND CONTEMPT

SEX, REJECTION, AND CONTEMPT

"Sordidness and ugliness are the concomitants of prostitutes' commonplace, everyday routines of living. Here are people narcotized to accept hurts, humiliations, and abasements as their daily portions. Here are people who know nothing of hope of joy or uplift." So say Judge John Murtagh and social worker Sara Harris in their classic book on prostitution, *Cast the First Stone.* For surely, if there is any occupation that is stigmatized it is that of prostitution.[1]

It was not always so, however. According to Sir James G. Frazer, the great British student of religion, no doubt the foremost authority on ancient rituals, magic, and religion "the practice (prostitution) was clearly regarded not as an orgy of lust, but as a solemn religious duty performed in the service of that great Mother Goddess of Western Asia, etc." Frazer lists Babylon, Baalbec in Syria, the Phoenician temples, the city of Byblos in Egypt, Armenia, and numerous other places where "sacred prostitution" was practiced. Frazer writes: "their commerce [sexual union] being deemed essential to the propagation of animals and plants at the sanctuary of the goddess for the sake of thereby ensuring the fruitfulness of the ground and the increase of man and beast."[2]

The Greco-Roman goddess Aphrodite was the goddess of love and the ancient Greek city of Corinth was dedicated to her. Here a great temple was erected in honor of the goddess whose devotees established there a "paradise of sacred sex." The sacred prostitutes who serviced men in the confines of that temple prayed there for the salvation of the

Greeks from the invading Persians in the early fifth century B.C.E. "so that all of Greece took seriously the temple-prostitutes of Corinth."[3]

Likewise in India some "servants of the gods" were in fact prostitutes who were also called "sacred women" and whose duties included entertaining Brahmans, or the priestly class. This behavior was by no means viewed as immoral, as respectable women now and then dedicated a daughter to the role of temple prostitute in a manner resembling the dedication of a son to the priesthood today.[4]

Because the very word "prostitution" is stigmatized and arouses contempt and rejection, a great deal of dispute has arisen over the years concerning the ancient practice of sacred prostitution as practiced in most parts of western Asia, in India, and elsewhere. The dispute arose chiefly in the nineteenth century when British and other students of ancient civilizations first discovered descriptions of sacred or temple prostitution. A good number of those who made these discoveries were clergy who had an interest in classical scholarship and were unwilling to admit or recognize that prostitution was not always and everywhere the target of stigma and rejection. These "Victorian divines" kept silent about this subject or denied the evidence for fear of offending those who delighted in upholding everything Greek and ancient.[5]

In ancient Greek society, those whom others would later refer to contemptuously as whores achieved a level of autonomy leading to education and high status. With the rise of Christianity, however, whores lost that standing and were contrasted with the ideal of the good wife and mother. That contrast led to the stigmatization of whores as bad girls and sinners, particularly in Protestantism. In the Victorian era in England and America ideals of social purity and morality contrasted even more strongly with these ancient ways so that the clergy in particular found prostitution despicable.[6] That is still true in current American thinking despite the evidence that prostitution is widespread and by no means abating at the end of the twentieth century. In fact, sociologists estimate that despite the threat of AIDS there are about 336,000 prostitutes in the United States today. The number of prostitutes appears to be increasing in America. In New York City, also called the Prostitution Capital of the United States, escort services have increased their supplies of prostitutes to hotel guests by 400 percent during the decade ending in 1998.[7]

There are several explanations for the continuing existence of prostitution. First among these is the functionalist argument that prostitution serves the strengthening of "morality." According to proponents of that view, prostitution serves an important function for society because it helps to "protect the family and keeps the wives and daughters of the respectable citizenry morally pure." This belief is based on the assumption that men who visit prostitutes will therefore avoid driving "respectable" girls into premarital sex, extramarital sex, or "immoral" sex as defined in the law or in the broader social mores.[8]

The functional view of prostitution was undoubtedly supported by nineteenth-century and early twentieth-century sexual conduct in America. However, ever since the "sexual revolution" of the 1960s and 1970s functionalism is very much in doubt. This is so because sex among single women and men has become commonplace, extramarital sex is practiced by a large minority of both sexes, homosexuality is much more accepted than ever before in American experience, and "cybersex" has taken the opprobrium out of pornography because it is hidden and private despite its appearance on the Internet.[9]

Nevertheless, the functional point of view is frequently supported by the customers of prostitutes generally called "johns." Men who visit prostitutes have rarely been studied by sociologists although they are the vast majority in the economic exchange that prostitution implies.

Normally, sexual relations between women and men occur in a close relationship which may be called a "gift exchange." Therefore, both participants in the exchange give of themselves freely with a view of establishing and reaffirming a reciprocal connection. Therefore, relational sex carries no stigma because the actors are "in a state of reciprocal independence." Such exchanges occur between actors in an established social relationship such as marriage or friendship and therefore support a community's social fabric. Social life is more secure and a community more stable as reciprocal sexual relationships increase because each party to such a relationship affirms willingness to be held accountable and responsible for the welfare of the "other."[10]

This view can of course be criticized as hypocritical because there are undoubtedly those who withdraw any emotional support from casual sex partners. Nevertheless, even the most casual sexual interchange, not based on money payments, retains a sentimental function and lacks the economic contract conditions pertaining to prostitution. Prostitution does not pretend to have any sentimental content. Unlike sex between committed partners and unlike even casual sex partners, prostitution is free of even the appearance of love, honor, or generosity.

This lack of sentiment is a necessity for the prostitute. This excerpt from an interview with a "john" reveals the business of prostitution as it was experienced by a first-time customer: "She kept talking me out of more money, and I didn't understand what was going on. It was like she was offering me more stuff if I would pay her more money before we did anything. So I kept pulling out more money . . . and then it was over real quick and she hustled me out of there. Until the point when the act was completed she seemed interested in me . . . and then it was like get this guy out on the street and do the next one."[11]

In part, then, the stigma of prostitution arises from the fear that prostitution might compete successfully with marriage and/or other stable social relations and that it could therefore threaten that stability. Stated in its most extreme form we could ask: "Could a society survive for long if all marriage and all sentimental alliances between the sexes were replaced by prostitution?" No matter how that question is answered, it transforms prostitution into a threat and a danger and drives its practitioners into the role of outsiders.

Prostitution is a commodity exchange. In a capitalist economy such an exchange resembles the purchase of other services such as medical care; legal advice; and the payment of psychologists, accountants, and other providers. There is, however, a limit to what may be provided even in a capitalist economy that tends to affirm the right of citizens to turn any service into a profit-making venture. For example, selling babies, body organs, or political favors are all prohibited, as is prostitution, even in capitalist economies. There are some things that, although done, are stigmatized because they violate the moral order and reach the limits of what money can buy. Plainly then, the opponents of prostitution who stigmatize this kind of work are also opponents of extreme capitalism. The customers of prostitutes and the prostitutes themselves, however, are supporters of pure capitalism and say that they have every right to buy and sell whatever they please, including sex.[12]

This belief, that sex may be sold for money, is embodied in the "freedom of contract" doctrine that drives the capitalist world. Therefore, prostitution, like any other commodity, depends on the ready availability of the goods or objects to be sold and the willingness of buyers to pay. This is evidently true of prostitution since willing women and even men are available at all levels of the market for anyone who can afford one. The contract between a prostitute and the client is regarded as a private transaction as are all capitalist contracts not involving government. Approximately 1.5 million Americans, almost all of them men, avail themselves of the services of a prostitute every week.[13]

There was a time, prior to the effort of women to liberate themselves from economic dependence on men, when some writers argued that marriage and prostitution were at bottom the same thing. Emma Goldman, Simone de Beauvoire, and Cicely Hamilton, all writers active in women's causes, agreed with the sentiment that "it is merely a question of degree whether a woman sells herself to one man, in or out of marriage, or to many men." De Beauvoire wrote that a wife is "hired for life by one man; the prostitute has several clients who pay her by the piece. The one is protected by one male against all the others; the other is defended by all against the exclusive tyranny of each."[14]

In 1909, Cicely Hamilton wrote that women were prevented from bargaining freely in the only trade open to them, marriage, but that they could exercise this freedom in their illegitimate trade, prostitution. Since those words were written, a radical change has occurred in the status of American women, so that Hamilton's view of marriage is utterly antiquated in contemporary society.[15]

Now, when almost all adult women work and have access to any occupation of their choosing, prostitution is seen by some feminists as just another form of work. This argument holds that prostitutes, like all workers, are paid for their efforts and ability. That effort and ability is called labor power and is therefore to be rewarded with money like all work. The erstwhile view was that a prostitute sells herself or her sexual parts. The present argument is that a prostitute sells her services, just like the doctor or the dentist or the lawyer. Just as these servers of man's needs sell not themselves but their services, so the prostitute sells her services. She is therefore to be called a "sex worker" argue these feminists who view prostitution as an industry which includes a trade fit for the entrance of anyone wishing to do so. The defenders of these views call prostitutes "therapists" and liken them to psychologists, social workers, and nurses.[16]

It needs to be noted here that some prostitutes are men and that therefore the view of prostitutes as "sex workers" must be extended to men as well. Most male prostitutes service other men, although male prostitutes who service women are increasing as the needs of unattached, working, and traveling females also increase. Nevertheless, as always, women are the major suppliers of prostitution and men almost the exclusive buyers. However, because prostitution is traditionally criticized as a woman's problem, or as a problem caused by women, the male participants, either as providers or as consumers, are generally ignored.

Because the male role in the transaction between prostitute and "john" is usually ignored, the principal question that arises in this connection is seldom answered. That question is: "Why do so many men believe that satisfaction of a natural drive must take the form of public access to women's bodies in exchange for money?" Evidently, the day when "decent" women did not deal sexually with men outside of marriage is over in the United States and Europe. Therefore, sex outside of marriage is readily available, and it is reasonable to assume that prostitution flourishes even now because the men who rent the services of a prostitute do so to gain power and ascendancy over a woman or several women by means of the sex act. We argue here that prostitution from the male point of view resembles rape, which is also an effort to gain ascendancy and power over women. Both prostitution and rape are indeed sexual in nature. Yet, the motive for both actions is power and the male need to dominate. The evidence for this view is found in the observation that "nearly all men . . . complain(ed) about the emotional coldness and mercenary approach of many prostitutes they had contact with," so that the wish to dominate is defeated by the attitudes of prostitutes generally.[17]

The complaint by male patrons concerning prostitutes is voiced by many men who want to pay not only for the sexual service rendered by prostitutes but also for some sentimental attachment. That, however, is impossible since the very nature of prostitution negates any sentiment on the part of the prostitute in favor of the money paid for her services. Furthermore, men who employ prostitutes in a society that allows considerable access to sexual expression in and out of marriage are announcing their wish to divorce sex from emotional attachments of any kind. Almost every study of the male customers of prostitutes concludes that men who buy the services of a prostitute do want to engage in sex without having to express any commitment to their sex partners. This means that men can buy and use women as objects.[18]

Therefore, proponents of conflict theory hold that prostitution is the very epitome of exploitation and that prostitution reinforces the old patriarchal system of male dominance over women. The patriarchal system of social organization from which the United States is only now emerging encourages prostitution by socializing boys to be dominant over girls and men to dominate women. Simultaneously, girls are socialized in any patriarchal society to be submissive to boys and men at play, at work, and in sex. In fact, women are relegated to many low-status jobs in any patriarchal society so that as late as 1999 the average income of American women was only 75 percent of the average income of American men. Prostitution therefore fits into this arrangement since it is a low-status job. In traditional male-dominated societies prostitution reflects the entire gender arrangement prevailing there. This assumes of course that in a traditional patriarchal society, marked by great gender inequality, there is no free choice for women who become prostitutes.[19]

While this analysis of prostitution in a traditional patriarchal society may fit many areas of the world today, it does not reflect the current reality of gender relations in the United States. In 2000, American women who enter prostitution do have a choice to refrain from that occupation. There are, however, some women who see prostitution as the best job they can get. Viewing sexual relations with strange men as a commercial transaction and not an emotional experience, these women enter prostitution in interaction with friends already associated with prostitution or because of the offer of money from men or because of the protection offered by pimps. Because a majority of prostitutes have been abused by their fathers, that majority has learned to detach themselves emotionally from sex with strange men. Parental abuse teaches children not to feel affectionate toward the abusive parent and to be emotionally detached in almost any relationship. It is that emotional detachment that makes prostitution possible for many engaged in that occupation.[20]

Sexologists Vern L. Bullough and Bonnie Bullough, following Stein, report that a study involving 1,230 men who had encountered "call girls" found that all wanted their sex needs met conveniently, professionally, and " without obligation but the momentary one. . . ."[21] Emotional detachment has always been a mark of occupational relationships. Millions of Americans work every day in numerous occupations without becoming emotionally attached to those with whom they work. In fact, it is an underlying assumption of work in capitalist societies. Work is a means of satisfying needs. Many kinds of employment are also tedious and lead to alienation. Author Studs Terkel in his well-known book *Working* illustrates by means of workers' words how dull and alienating work is for millions of Americans. Terkel shows that because the product of work belongs to the capitalist and not the worker, workers do not invest themselves in their work. Human companionship and positive relations with other workers are therefore limited or nonexistent. Factory work in particular is a dehumanizing experience, although many professions, particularly the academic profession, are equally alienating and devoid of emotional attachments.[22]

Prostitution may therefore be seen as just another form of work in a capitalist market. In light of that insight, prostitutes have recently organized and formed a number of unions devoted to insuring their rights as workers. Most prominent among these organizations is COYOTE, which uses an acronym for "Call Off Your Old Tired Ethics." There is also PONY or "Prostitutes of New York," HUM or "Hookers Union of Maryland," NTFP or "National Task Force on Prostitution," PUMA or "Prostitutes Union of Massachussetts Association," and many others around the country. Those who organize prostitutes in this manner seek to remove the stigma of prostitution by legitimizing the sex trade and even "celebrating it." Demanding the rights enjoyed by workers in other industries, organized prostitutes engage in public debates on television programs. There they have demanded the end of discriminatory law enforcement such as entrapment and quarantining. *Entrapment* refers to the instigation of a crime by law-enforcement officers in order to find grounds for criminal prosecution. *Quarantining* refers to the isolation of prostitutes in jails for the purpose of a physical examination to detect sexually transmitted diseases. Further, they demand the passage of the Equal Rights Amendment to the United States Constitution, the suppression of pornography, the end to the unjustified belief that they are the cause of the AIDS epidemic, and an end to violence against women.[23]

COYOTE leaders have also insisted that most prostitutes chose their occupation and were not coerced into that line of work as is popularly believed. Sociologists estimate that only 15 percent of American prostitutes are coerced into their work either by force or by the need to survive. Hence, prostitute organizations have made that occupation into a civil rights issue. These organizations argue that prostitutes have the right to work as freelance workers just as nurses, typists, doctors, lawyers, or anyone else. Those who defend this position also hold that "sex is a commodity just like anything else and, like any other commodity, operates on the law of supply and demand."[24] In addition, organized prostitutes demand that they be given paid vacations, health insurance, workers' compensation, and Social Security. Above all other demands is the demand that prostitution be legalized.[25]

Legalization has had many defenders who think that when sex work is clean, safe, and less publicly visible it is preferable to street prostitution that has none of these characteristics. Many sex workers, however, and in particular the International Committee for Prostitutes' Rights, do not support legalization of prostitution. To them, legalization represents a yet more blatant male method of control of female sexuality than is true under existing laws. Moreover, they point out that in countries such as Germany where prostitution is legal it has not proved successful. There, and elsewhere, many women refuse to provide sex for taxed pay in a state brothel and work illegally and privately instead. In addition, women who are barred from the legal brothels in Germany because of diseases or other sickness continue to work outside the law. Therefore, the International Committee for Prostitutes' Rights includes in their "World Charter" the total abolition of all laws limiting or prohibiting prostitution in favor of the granting of a benefits system to sex workers. These benefits are to include support for women seeking to leave that occupation, enforcement of existing legislation concerning coercion of sex workers, rape, fraud, and child abuse.[26]

Child abuse is also the principal focus of the United Nations Children's Fund Convention of the Rights of the Child. According to Article 34 of that convention: States Parties undertake to protect the child from all forms of sexual abuse. For these purposes, States Parties shall in particular take all appropriate national, bilateral, and multilateral measures to prevent (a) the inducement or coercion of a child to engage in any unlawful sexual activity; (b) the exploitative use of children in prostitution or other unlawful sexual practice; (c) the exploitative use of children in pornographic performances and materials. That convention also includes the findings of the Congress Against the Commercial Sexual Exploitation of Children. This congress represents 133 nations each of which has declared that there is a child-prostitution problem in their country. Despite the considerable participation of so many nations in the congress unanimity concerning child prostitution has not developed among them. This is true because there are different interpretations of the word "child." In the United States a child is generally someone not yet eighteen years old or, at the most, someone under the age of sixteen. In primarily rural societies, however, the word "child" refers to those much younger than eighteen and sexual maturity is often attributed to children as young as thirteen. Hence the definition of "child" is a combination of emotional, physical, mental, and sexual attributes in which the family and the social environment also play a role. Therefore, the ages at which various nations confer the status of adulthood range from ten to twenty-four, including the assumption that a young person can consent to sex at such an age.[27]

Therefore, in order to accommodate these differing views and also avoid making government-supervised brothels legal employers of prostitutes, there are those who suggest that the prostitutes themselves be licensed. The advantage of such a move would be that the prostitute would not depend for her livelihood on a madam or a pimp but only on herself. Such licensing would also serve to decriminalize prostitutes. Feminists have long argued that criminalizing prostitutes intensifies female inequality and discriminates against women. In addition to all the other difficulties associated with prostitution, the policy of criminalization forces prostitutes to bear the additional burden of being identified as criminals. This is particularly true for the street prostitutes who are victimized daily by police, judges, prosecutors, and pimps. Feminists therefore argue that sexual behavior should be the choice of each adult woman or man and that prostitutes should have the right to protection without such demands as mandatory physical examinations, which are seen by feminists as efforts to "increase male control over women's bodies."[28]

We have already seen that there are those who seek the decriminalizing of prostitution and the issuing of a state license to all prostitutes. Such a licensed prostitute could then work for herself almost anywhere. Those who favor licensing prostitutes want to establish state boards of prostitution similar to the boards that now regulate medicine, law, and social work. Those prostitutes who feel vulnerable vis-à-vis men could be encouraged to form a cooperative that could help in defending them from violence by providing security. Such a license would also give prostitutes near-professional status thereby giving them the right to protest the lack of sex workers' rights. A license would make sex workers less dependent on large, commercial interests and would render prostitutes less vulnerable to pimps, customers, and the police. Finally, a license would give customers reassurance that some standards concerning the health of the prostitute have been observed.[29]

There are those feminists who argue that prostitution should not be legal. They defend their position on the grounds that prostitution is mainly caused by poverty and that poverty deprives those who enter prostitution of free choice. Opponents of legalizing prostitution also argue that women's bodies should not be for sale any more than there should be an open market for babies or human organs. It is further argued by opponents of legalizing prostitution that such legalization would reduce the number of work opportunities for women in other occupations and that legalizing prostitution would insure the subordination of women by law.[30]

SOCIAL STRATIFICATION IN THE "OLDEST PROFESSION"

All occupations are stratified subcultures. This means that every occupation has practitioners who have high prestige within the occupation and some whose prestige is ranked lower. A subculture is a variation on a mainstream culture and consists of a group whose values and norms or expectations set them apart from the broader culture. In addition, all subcultures use language not in general use by those who do not belong to the subculture. That is true of lawyers, accountants, physicians, and prostitutes.[31]

Examples of such language are these: A "john" or a "mark" is a customer of a prostitute, a "trick" is a sexual performance, a "pimp" is an agent for prostitutes, a "madam" owns a brothel, a "hooker" is a female prostitute, a "jane" is a lesbian customer of a prostitute, a "stable" is a group of prostitutes controlled by one pimp, to "get burned" is to give service without getting paid, and a "quota" is the number of johns a prostitute must see each day.[32]

Among those who practice this occupation are prostitutes who manage to collect a large fee for their services because they wear expensive clothes and have a veneer of education permitting them to converse with or listen to the customer. Such prostitutes generally make a glamorous appearance and can serve as escorts for men with large wallets and expensive tastes.

In 1984 the police closed a house of prostitution run by Sydney Biddle Barrows, whom the media labeled "The Mayflower Madam." Her "escort service" in New York City earned $1 million per year renting twenty women to her clients at rents from $125 per hour to $400 an hour. Barrows kept 60 percent of their take. Because Barrows is the descendant of a socially prominent family who did indeed arrive with the ship *Mayflower* her conduct became a media sensation. Not only was

Barrows from an establishment family but, according to police, her appointment book read like a social register.

As is true with so many prostitutes, Barrows learned about the opportunity to earn a good deal of money from a coworker. Since Barrows earned no more than a department store salesclerk's wage the large fee collected by a prostitute for one night's work attracted her. She says that she had no moral problem in entering the prostitution business because she believed that prostitution "filled a human and age-old need." She believes that her male clients were gentlemen who were paying for an "elegant escort." Therefore she opened an escort service that employed only women who looked good and knew how to dress well. Barrows and her employees were of course only interested in the money to be earned. Unlike lower-ranking prostitutes, Barrows taught her girls to be most polite and to use a variety of speech patterns that would make the "client" feel important and that would produce a maximum of income.

Prostitutes at all levels of occupational prestige learn their trade from those already involved. This is not surprising, since all occupational skills and the values associated with such skills must be learned in association with those already holding these skills. First, prostitution novices learn "The Hustling Rap." This "rap" concerns the initial conversation between the client and the prostitute and deals with the wishes of the client and the money demanded by the prostitute for rendering a service. "The hustler must maintain a steady patter of verbal coaxing, during which her tone of voice may be more important than her actual words."

Madams and other teachers of prostitutes also instruct the needed physical skills and the values associated with the profession. Lectures and discussions are used to teach these skills. The lessons often include guest speakers who have a good deal of experience. Evidently, then, escort services are good businesses.[33]

Many of the women who worked for the escort service also held daytime jobs in business and industry or were college students. Yet others were actresses; Barrows says that she liked to hire actresses because they were more capable of pretending an interest in the client. These actresses also faked enjoyment where there was only money and were also capable of portraying a whole scene demanded by the client. The prostitutes hired by Barrows sold not only sex but also companionship and intimacy. This means that many male customers of the prostitutes spent a good deal of time discussing their professional and family problems with the paid prostitutes they were now engaging. Many of the men who used prostitutes to discuss their life situation claimed that they had no one else willing to listen to them, not even their wives.

Others, however, were indeed close to their wives but used prostitutes to talk to them and be intimate with them whenever they were out of town and had no opportunity to see their wives. Barrows claims that a good number of such men were getting along fine at home but were lonely when in New York on business and in need of companionship.

For centuries prostitutes have been used to initiate young men into sexual experiences. This was also true of the Mayflower Madam and her employees, who were sometimes paid by the father of a young boy in order to teach him all about sex.

In sum, Biddle describes the so-called high-class whore who costs more because she appears closer to the American ideal of womanhood than those with lesser prestige. Nevertheless there can be no doubt that even the Mayflower Madam and those associated with her were and are held in contempt by large numbers of Americans and that all of these women were and are stigmatized for who they are and what they do.[34]

"Call girls" have been labeled the "aristocrats of prostitution." They charge customers $1,500 per night and can earn over $100,000 a year. Some gain clients through employment in escort services or by other means that permit them to develop independent customer lists. Many call girls come from middle-class families and service upper-class customers. To dispel the notion that they merely provide sex for money, they give the clients the impression that they are fascinated by the clients' importance, intelligence, and competence. "Call girls," as the term implies, make dates on the telephone with men whose names they obtain from bellhops, cab drivers, waiters, and other employees working in various service industries. These girls either entertain clients in their own apartments or visit the client at his home or hotel. Evidently, this occupation is very risky since the call girl is not protected against violence and other forms of abuse.[35]

Although violence occurs only on occasion and is by no means the rule, all prostitutes have at some time been the subject of violence and are always aware that violence may occur at any time. The reason for much of the violence experienced by call girls and other prostitutes is that for some johns prostitution is not about sex but about power. In present-day American society a good deal of power and authority is still vested in men. Despite "women's liberation," which has affected mostly the educated segment of the American population during the last twenty-five years of the twentieth century, large numbers of Americans, even now, expect that the relationships between men and women continue to be structured along the lines of male superiority and male dominance.

Although rapists are hardly an example of the average American man, it is nonetheless instructive to note that the justification rapists use for their action has traditionally been that their female victims are at fault. Such justification for so brutal an act includes the belief that women who were raped brought it on themselves by dressing in a provocative fashion, or by ingesting too much drugs or alcohol. Rapists and their apologists believe that a woman who engages in such behavior has waived her right to be treated with respect. Men who rape evidently seek to assert their dominance over women, and in particular women who are "forward." Because prostitutes are sexually available it is believed by many Americans that rape is less of a crime when a prostitute is victimized than when so-called good women are so treated. In fact, sexual solicitation is viewed by some to invite violence so that there are even those who argue that prostitutes cannot be raped because of the work they do. The belief that prostitutes are subject to violence because of their work is supported by the evidence that violence against prostitutes is hardly ever reported to the police and is generally ignored by the police when it is reported. Even judges have been heard to say that a prostitute who has been raped is less damaged emotionally by such an experience than other women because of their line of work. All of this indicates more forcefully than anything else that prostitution is severely stigmatized, so that the stigma alone removes normal protection against violence from prostitutes.

Because protection against violence is so hard for call girls and street prostitutes to achieve, another method of delivering the services of prostitutes to men willing to pay is the so-called brothel, bordello, house of ill repute, sporting house, or cat house. Such establishments were most common in the nineteenth century but are still available today. Generally, these houses are run by "madams" who employ the prostitutes, supervise their behavior, protect them from violence, and receive the fees for the "working girls" in their establishments. Out of these fees the madam usually pays the prostitutes between 40 percent and 60 percent of their earnings. Usually the madam in such an establishment is a retired prostitute who makes arrangements for bringing in customers, hiring prostitutes, bribing the police, and dealing with neighbors.[36]

Ranking a good deal lower in the hierarchy of prostitution are "circuit travelers." These are women who move around in groups of two or three to lumber camps, labor camps, and agricultural camps. With permission of the foreman, these "circuit travelers" will service all the men in a camp on one night and then travel on. Some "circuit travelers" seek clients at truck stops and rest areas. There are "circuit travelers" who have been forced into prostitution by brutal pimps who lure young Mexican women into Florida and other southern states with promises of employment in restaurants, nursing homes, and with other healthcare providers. Raped, beaten, and forced to have abortions, these foreign women, unable to speak English, are helpless victims of so-called ticketeros who charge the customer $20 for each sex act and give the prostitute $3.

On the bottom of the prostitution hierarchy are "skeezers." These are women who barter sex for drugs. An investigation in Chicago and New York revealed that more than half of all prostitutes are drug users who support their habit with prostitution. Psychologist Paul Goldstein and his associates have studied this behavior in some detail and found that contrary to popular opinion, skeezers are not exploited but view themselves as engaged in an economic transaction in which they come out ahead. The skeezers believe that gaining drugs for a few minutes of sex is a transaction that favors them.[37] These skeezers and other street-walkers are of course the most visible of the prostitutes working in American cities. The street prostitutes, more than any others, are subject to a whole spectrum of behavior by the communities they enter. Street prostitutes are exposed to name-calling, physical assault, and occasionally rape and murder. There are people who "cruise" in areas where street prostitutes wait and shout insults and obscenities at them. An example of such violence is recorded by Neil McKeganey, professor at the University of Glasgow:

> Marina and I were approached by a woman whom we have chatted to on many nights. She had a black eye and a heavily swollen cheekbone. She explained that she had been set upon by a punter earlier that week. [A "punter" is the British term for a prostitute's client.] He had stopped and had asked her for business. Although she had been a bit weary he had used her name. Once in the car she had given him her usual directions to the place she normally used but he had turned unto the motorway. She had protested but he turned off near the fruit market, pulled the car up near some darkened factories, ordered her to strip and then tied her hands with bin liners. He then punched her in the face and pushed her out of the car. She thought for sure he intended running her over but she managed to scramble over a fence and into a nearby field.[38]

This and numerous other examples, including the use of guns and knives, are the constant companions of prostitutes' lives.

Assaults from customers is not the only source of violence suffered by prostitutes. Pimps, men who control prostitutes and furnish them with some protection, are notorious for beating and even knifing these women. Many pimps have violent tempers and make it a practice to savagely beat the girls working for them. Yet, few prostitutes ever complain about such beatings because they have incorporated into their own self-evaluation the belief that they deserve nothing better. It is very common for all who are rejected and stigmatized to finally accept the view of others as their own and to reject themselves and to view themselves in the same ugly light that their persecutors have imposed on them. That is certainly as true of prostitutes as it is of racial and ethnic minorities, homeless people, and obese people.

MALE PROSTITUTES AND JOHNS

The participation of men in prostitution is generally overlooked as male prostitutes call themselves "hustlers" rather than prostitutes. These "hustlers" frequent gay bars and homosexual baths or walk the streets looking for business. Some "hustlers" are "kept boys" by one wealthy man while yet others are "call boys" or work in a "massage parlor" which is in fact a homosexual brothel. There are also "gigolos," a word derived from the French *giguer* meaning "to dance." "Gigolos" are male prostitutes who service women. They operate out of escort agencies or dance studios and offer companionship and sex for money. Some are "kept" by wealthy women.[39]

Male prostitution is practiced unevenly in the United States. While there are undoubtedly some male prostitutes in all parts of the country, San Francisco has been the capital of male homosexual activity for some time and therefore houses a larger contingent of male prostitutes than any other American city. Unlike female prostitutes who chiefly service men, most male prostitutes service homosexuals and not women. Hence the customers of male prostitutes are ordinarily men, so that both sexes service men more than women.

It is claimed that San Francisco's involvement with male prostitution began during the "gold rush" when boy brothels operated there from 1840 until 1910. It was not only the entrance of so many men into California in search of gold which led San Francisco to become the American headquarters of homosexual prostitution. A second reason for this development was the diversity of the California population, which led to a far greater tolerance in that state for deviant lifestyles than is true in other parts of the country.

During the 1960s "hippie" era male prostitution received more attention than ever before. At that time a good number of drug-addicted young men moved into San Francisco. These young men were usually heterosexual but permitted homosexuals to use them for the money they needed to feed their drug habits. Such heterosexual youths may be called "situational hustlers" as they prostituted only on some occasions. These "situational hustlers" are distinguished from "habitual hustlers" consisting of homosexual males who prostituted regularly. There are also "vocational" male prostitutes who consider themselves professionals.[40]

While there is a massive amount of research describing the background of female prostitutes there are very few studies of male prostitutes. D. Kelly Weisberg, professor of law at Hastings College in San Francisco, did make such a study including research in the metropolitan areas of Boston, Houston, Los Angeles, Minneapolis, New York, San

Francisco, and Seattle. Because Weisberg's study is national in scope it is reliable as a source of knowledge concerning American male prostitution generally.

It is surely not unexpected that the Weisberg study found family background to have a major influence on prostitution. Evidently, many prostitutes, both male and female, come from homes involving parental alcoholism and frequent fighting among parents. Long absences of the father or his permanent desertion of the family are common experiences of such boys (and girls). Many prostitutes, both male and female, come from homes dissolved by death or divorce. In fact, the Weisberg study showed that only one-third of all the boys Weisberg studied came from intact families. A large number of prostitutes are raised by a single parent, usually the mother.

Another study of male prostitutes shows that only eighteen of ninety-eight youths in that study had an intact family, but even in these families poor relationships were the rule. Physical and emotional abuse were also common in the families of prostitutes, both male and female. Such abuse often included severe beatings and constant humiliation. Neglect and abandonment are also common experiences of prostitutes. There are children who are kicked out of the house at very young ages so that they have no choice but to become street people. "I lived on the streets since I was nine," says one boy interviewed by psychologist Robert W. Deischer in his study of male prostitutes in San Francisco, while another boy told an interviewer: "My mom moved. She told me I am on my own."[41]

Although the sexual exploitation of children is known in the United States it is far more common in Asian countries such as the Philippines which for years hosted a number of American naval and military bases. There "thousands of children were under the control of pimps and performed any service for anyone who could pay." Australian news commentator Cameron Forbes claimed that "thousands of boys and girls were for sale (in the Philippines). The youngest was five years old." Forbes then describes prostitution in the Philippine town of Pagsanjan. "Pedophiles flocked to the lodges along the river and took their pick of the boys in the swimming pools. And they all fed on the poverty of Pagsanjan."[42]

Sexual abuse is a common characteristic of the family background of male and female prostitutes. The abusers include fathers, mothers, siblings, and other relatives. Others report that they were sexually abused by nonfamily members at very young ages. Even those who do not report sexual abuse generally recount sexual experiences at ages as young as five or six. Most male prostitutes were paid for sexual acts before they were eleven years old. Weisberg concluded that 74 percent of her respondents began prostitution on a regular basis within the year in which they were paid for their first encounter. Regular prostitution was defined by Weisberg as participating in prostitution several times a month. The interest in engaging in "regular prostitution" is of course aroused by the realization that prostitution is a source of money or other rewards. While money is the principal reason for engaging in male prostitution, drugs, sex, and adventure are also mentioned as motivations. Whatever the motivation, prostitution, like all occupations, involves certain norms or expectations that must be learned if one is to be successful. Generally, these norms are learned from a friend already engaged in the occupation and involve instructions as to how to "pick up" a customer, how to charge for the service, and how to perform.[43]

Male prostitutes have paid and unpaid sex with multiple partners. Many engage in risky sexual behavior involving illicit drugs. Their partners may be homosexuals, heterosexuals, or bisexual men and women. Sociologists Jacqueline Boles and Kirk W. Elifson report that their study of male prostitutes revealed that one-half of the men in their sample consider themselves heterosexuals.

"SEX WORK": ORGANIZED PROSTITUTION

As I have already stated, prostitution has most recently been relabeled "sex work." The reason for this change is of course to escape the stigma associated with that kind of barter. The phrase "sex work" also serves to ally prostitutes with other working people so that prostitution may appear as "normal" work. The effort to normalize prostitution has been challenged by those who agree with the stigmatization of prostitution and whose objections may be summarized in the following seven propositions. First, that "sex work" or prostitution is inherently immoral. Those who disagree with that view claim that the very designation "immoral" precludes any rational discussion and that therefore such a designation is ipso facto useless. The second objection against prostitution is that sex between a "sex worker" and her client is cold, unemotional, and impersonal. The counterclaim here is that even in marriage sex can have those characteristics. It is further argued that sex without love is not necessarily "bad" sex. Third, those opposed to prostitution argue that sex workers are defenseless against physical violence and that many sex workers are themselves prone to physical and mental illness. The counterclaim is that there are many hazardous occupations and that the difficulties sex workers encounter are the outcome of the stigma that attaches to their work. Absent the stigma, sex work would no longer be dangerous. Therefore, those who are opposed to sex work and want to rehabilitate the prostitutes are confronted with the argument that we need to minimize the risk of doing sex work rather than creating difficulties for these workers. Yet another argument against prostitution is a reflection of the old Marxist idea that prostitution represents exploitation of all workers. Marx had argued that prostitution exists only in capitalist societies and is an example of how all labor is exploited. Yet today prostitution exists in all countries, many of which are not capitalist. Then there is the feminist argument contending that the prostitute has the status/role of an object while the customer is the subject. This is best expressed by the claim that the prostitute is "merchandise." The counterclaim here is that prostitutes do not sell themselves but only their services. It is argued that if the prostitute is only "merchandise" then that would also have to be true of all professionals who render a service. Furthermore, those who find the "merchandise" argument spurious say that sex is as important as food and drink and that nourishment as well as sex can be bought. The sixth objection against prostitution is commercialization. Those who counter this objection claim that the sex industry is a symptom and not a cause of capitalist commercialization of everything. Finally, it is argued that prostitutes are subject to a disturbed emotional life caused by the exploitation they suffer. That argument is countered with the insistence that it is not "sex work" per se, but the stigma associated with that kind of work which leads to emotional problems on the part of the worker.[44]

Whatever the arguments for or against prostitution, it is evident at the beginning of a new century that prostitution in the United States is faced with competition from a number of sources. First and foremost among these sources is the ever-increasing willingness of young unmarried women to engage in sexual activity. Today the rate of premarital sex relations for women is approaching that of men so that prostitutes are by no means the only sexual outlets available to unmarried men. Furthermore, women no longer believe that they are not sexual beings and must merely endure male sexual advances. The "sexual revolution" of the 1960s led to the assumption that women are equally interested in sex and hence more accessible than before. In addition, effective contraception such as "the pill" and the cervical cap have allowed men greater and more frequent access to their spouses without fear of unwanted pregnancy, thereby making visits to prostitutes less necessary. Divorce is more frequent than ever before so that couples who are sexually incompatible need not stay together which might have steered the husband toward the services of a prostitute. There are also singles bars, swing parties, and a good deal of premarital cohabitation, all of which compete effectively with prostitution.[45]

In view of these developments there are those who believe that prostitution will soon come to an end as the "market" arrangement between customers and "workers" will have too much competition. This view overlooks the fact that many of the customers of prostitutes are men who do not want to enter into any close relationship with any woman and even shy away from the temporary obligations which a sexual liaison implies. These men want to pay and "get it over with."

There is yet another reason for the perpetuation of prostitution despite the "amateur" competition to which it is subject. That is the recent introduction of the drug culture into the sphere of the American prostitute. Drug addiction has led girls as young as eleven to be used by gang members to make money. These gangs were at one time engaged in robbery and assault but later found that they can use girls, including children, as a means to attract customers to their drug business. According to the Federal Office of Juvenile Justice and Delinquency Prevention, women and girls constitute 11 percent of the estimated 816,000 gang members in the United States. In some cities female gang members account for 20 percent of all members. In October of 1998 more than one hundred members of seven gangs operating in Manhattan were arrested on charges of using prostitutes to sell drugs. Richard J. Estes, professor of social work at the University of Pennsylvania, claims that "all across the United States young women (are) joining gangs where their major contribution is sex."[46]

There are some areas of large cities where gangs have high social standing and where girls join such gangs in order to share in that status arrangement. The need to belong, the need for the money and the protection such gangs afford these girls leads them to independence from parental supervision and consequently to prostitution and drug addiction. It is drug addiction and the stigma of drug use which shall therefore be the topic of our next chapter.

SUMMARY

Although Western civilization generally stigmatizes prostitution today, this sex activity was at one time considered a sacred occupation since it was believed that demonstration of human sexuality would induce the gods to permit agricultural growth. Until the rise of Christianity, prostitutes were held in high esteem in ancient Greece and Rome. Later, prostitution was seen as functional and a method of preserving the chastity of "good" women. Yet, prostitution resembles a capitalist commodity exchange because it lacks all sentiment.

We have seen that "sacred" prostitution was acceptable and in fact commendable in the ancient Near East. This was true because the idea that women were more than male appendages never occurred to these ancient people. It is unlikely that the concept of social disease was known to the ancients, as the germ theory did not exist. Furthermore, biological reproduction was not understood. It is unlikely that the concept of social disease was known to the ancients, as the germ theory did not exist. Furthermore, biological reproduction was not understood. Therefore, prostitution served the purpose of illustrating the wishes of the population for the reproduction of food. This had to be conveyed to gods that were in fact dumb statues.

Once Judaism and its daughter, Christianity, became influential in the Greco-Roman world, these customs changed. Foremost, Judeo-Christian scriptures denounce prostitution vigorously. That was possible because it came to be believed that an invisible god could be approached through sacrifice and prayer so that demonstrations of what was wanted were no longer needed. Furthermore, Judaism and thereafter Christianity viewed sexual intercourse as a sacred institution to be practiced inside marriage only. The reason for this was the need to insure that offspring could be identified as being certainly from only one father. The ancient peoples did not understand the relationship between coitus and birth because these events do not necessarily follow one another. However, later developments led to that recognition and to the patrilineal requirements just outlined.

With the rise of Christianity women were given a somewhat better status than was true in the ancient world. Married women could object to the practice of husbands visiting prostitutes. As Christianity progressed, prostitutes came to be seen as rivals of married women. Since Judaism and Christianity did not include prostitutes in religious rites, their function changed. Prostitutes now serviced men in a manner that "moral" married women would not. As centuries of prudery taught that women did not really like sex but were mere passive objects of men's lust, some men sought the company of prostitutes who were not included in these female prohibitions and who did all those things the in-group married woman was enjoined not to do. This served the function of securing marriages which would otherwise have been dissolved or held together miserably because of the sexual frustration of husbands. In short, prostitution served the function of maintaining the group as out-groups always do. The married woman was told that if she did not behave as she should, then she would be as despised and as miserable as the prostitute. This meant that prostitutes were needed to keep women "in line." In this sense, prostitutes served the same function as Jews. Christians were told that they would be as miserable as the Jews if they did not believe what the clergy taught them.

All this continued into the first half of the twentieth century in

Western civilization and is still true in much of the world. However, the advance of science and education has liberated women and given them greater economic opportunities than were available before the 1960s. Prostitution then became even more stigmatized than before, because many people now believe that those who prostitute themselves could do something else to earn a livelihood. That may not be true because almost all prostitutes are involved in the use of drugs and are therefore dependent on not only these illegal substances but also on male "pimps." In American society occupation is the most important criterion of social prestige. Not only money but also the means by which money is earned are decisive in determining prestige or social standing in the twenty-first century. Those occupations which require the most education, have the greatest autonomy, supply the public with important services, and allow practitioners a great deal of "conspicuous consumption" have the highest rank among the occupations. Therefore it is not surprising that physicians have consistently outranked all occupations in all public opinion surveys concerning occupational prestige.

Evidently, then, prostitution ranks the lowest among occupations because it is believed that it requires no skill or education, it appears to be socially harmful, and its practitioners are viewed as utter dependents. This is not entirely true, but it is the perception of an occupation, and not its actual condition, that creates prestige.

In addition to all these negative evaluations, prostitution is also seen as a health hazard even for those who never visit a prostitute. AIDS and the fear of AIDS have led to a real concern for those who may become infected by men or women who have had contacts with prostitutes and then seek out other sex partners. The threat to marriage is obvious.

In view of all of these negative evaluations, the prostitution business continues to exist. This is true despite the "sexual revolution" of the 1960s and beyond which has made sexual intercourse available to unmarried women and men to a greater degree than ever before. It is therefore not the lack of sexual opportunity that leads "johns" to visit prostitutes but the belief that prostitutes will somehow satisfy men more than "decent" women. That belief is fostered by the entertainment industry and therefore contributes to the stigma associated with prostitution.

Prior to the "sexual revolution" of the 1960s there were some who equated marriage with prostitution, an argument that can no longer be supported at the end of the twentieth century. Instead, there are those who now seek to label prostitution "sex work" and hope to unionize "sex workers" with a view of giving them the same benefits other unionized workers already have. Likewise, sex workers seek the decriminalization of prostitution.

Prostitution is learned by association with those already in the "profession." There is a hierarchy of prostitutes ranging from "call girls" to drug-dependent street prostitutes. There are also male prostitutes who service both homosexuals and heterosexuals of both sexes.

In the main, prostitutes, both male and female, are the children of dysfunctional families. Abandoned and "thrown away," many become involved in drug and alcohol dependency, creating a close link between addiction and prostitution. Therefore, the stigma of addiction shall be the topic of our next chapter.

NOTES

1. John M. Murtagh and Sara Harris, *Cast the First Stone* (New York: McGraw-Hill, 1957), p. vii.

2. James G. Frazer, *The Golden Bough: A Study in Magic and Religion* (London: Macmillan, 1924), p. 385.

3. Mary Beard and John Henderson, "With This Body I Thee Worship: Sacred Prostitution in Antiquity," *Gender and History* 9, no. 3 (November 1997): 480.

4. Will Durant, *Our Oriental Heritage* (New York: Simon and Schuster, 1954), p. 491.

5. Beard and Henderson, "With This Body," p. 480.

6. Nicki Roberts, *Whores in History: Prostitution in Western Society* (London: HarperCollins, 1992).

7. Alex Thio, *Sociology* (New York: Longman, 1998), p. 214.

8. Kingley Davis, "Sexual Behavior," in *Contemporary Social Problems,* ed. Robert Merton and Robert Nisbet (New York: Harcourt Brace Jovanovitch, 1971).

9. Gerhard Falk, *Sex, Gender and Social Change: The Great Revolution* (Lanham, Md., and New York: University Press of America, 1998), chap. 10.

10. Monica Prasad, "The Morality of Market Exchange: Love Money and Contractual Justice," *Sociological Perspective,* 42, no. 2 (summer 1999): 183.

11. Ibid., p. 194.

12. Ibid., p. 203.

13. Carole Pateman, "What's Wrong with Prostitution?" *Women's Studies Quarterly* 27 (spring/summer 1999): 53.

14. Simone de Beauvoir, *The Second Sex* (New York:Vintage Books, 1974), p. 619.

15. Cicely Hamilton, *Marriage as a Trade* (London: Women's Press, 1981), p. 37.

16. M. MacIntosh, "Who Needs Prostitutes? The Ideology of Male Sexual Needs," in C. Smart and B. Smart, *Women, Sexuality and Social Control* (London: Routledge and Kegan Paul, 1978), p. 54.

17. Eileen McLeod, *Women Working: Prostitution Now* (London: Croom Helm, 1982), p. 84.

18. Jody Miller, "Feminist Theory," in Alex Thio and Thomas Calhoun, *Readings in Deviant Behavior* (New York: HarperCollins, 1995).

19. Kathleen Barry, *The Prostitution of Sexuality* (New York: New York University Press, 1995).

20. Alex Thio, *Sociology,* p. 215.

21. Vern L. Bullough and Bonnie Bullough, *Women and Prostitution; A Social History* (Amherst, N.Y.: Prometheus Books, 1987), p. 299.

22. Studs Terkel, *Working* (New York: Pantheon Books, 1974), p. 57.

23. Valerie Jenness, *Making It Work: The Prostitutes' Rights Movement in Perspective* (New York: Aldine De Gruyter, 1993), p. 1.

24. Sydney Biddle Barrows, *Mayflower Madam* (New York: Ivy Books, 1986), p. 171.

25. Ibid., p. 72.

26. Gail Pheterson, *A Vindication of the Rights of Whores* (Seattle: Free Press, 1989).

27. Philip Alston, *The Best Interests of the Child* (Oxford: Clarendon Press, 1994), p. 1.

28. Barbara Meil-Hobson, *Uneasy Virtue* (New York: BasicBooks, 1987), p. 217.

29. Graham Scambler and Annette Scambler, *Rethinking Prostitution: Purchasing Sex in the 1990* (London and New York: Routledge, 1997), p. 188.

30. Diane Post, "Legalizing Prostitution: A Systematic Rebuttal," *Off Our Backs* 24 (July 1999): 8.

31. Linda L. Lindsey and Stephen Beach, *Sociology: Social Life and Social Issue* (Upper Saddle River, N.J.: Prentice-Hall, 2000), p. 75.

32. David Knox, *Human Sexuality: The Search for Understanding* (New York: West Publishing Co., 1984), p. 460.

33. Barbara Serman Heyl, *The Madam as Entrepreneur: Career Management in House Prostitution* (New York: Transaction Publishers, 1979), chap. 5.

34. Barrows, *Mayflower Madam*, p. 367.

35. Paul Goldstein, "Occupational Mobility in the World of Prostitution: Becoming a Madam," *Deviant Behavior* 4 (1983): 267.

36. Nils Christie, "Conflict as Property," *British Journal of Criminology* 17 (1977): 1–15.

37. Lisa Maher and Kathleen Daly, "Women in the Street-Level Drug Economy," *Criminology* 34 (1996): 465–91.

38. Neil McKeganey and Marina Bernard, *Sex Work on the Streets* (Philadelphia: Open University Press, 1996), p. 72.

39. Knox, *Human Sexuality: The Search for Understanding*, p. 463.

40. D. Kelly Weisberg, *Children of the Night: A Study of Adolescent Prostitution* (Lexington, Mass.: Lexington Books, 1985), p. 22.

41. Donald M. Allen, "Young Male Prostitutes: A Psychosocial Study," *Archives of Sexual Behavior* 9, no. 5 (1980): 400.

42. Cameron Forbes, "Child Exploitation in the Philippines," in Caroline Moorehead, *A Report on Violence Toward Children in Today's World* (New York: Doubleday, 1990), p. 236.

43. Weisberg, *Children of the Night*, p. 56.

44. Scambler, *Rethinking Prostitution*, p. 181.

45. Bullough and Bullough, *Women and Prostitution*, p. 291.

46. Kit Roane, "Gangs Turn to New Trade," *New York Times*, July 11, 1999, p. I23.

ALCOHOLICS AND OTHER ADDICTS 13

THE DRUG CULTURE
REJECTS ITS OWN

DRUNKEN IRISHMEN AND OTHER "TRASH"

Addiction to drugs is severely stigmatized in America, although sociologists have called the United States an "alcohol culture." This may seem to be a contradiction. However, sociologist Émile Durkheim taught that every group needs to designate someone as an outsider in order to promote social cohesion among the "insiders."[1] Therefore, those who participate in the use of alcohol are motivated to call all those who use other drugs "drug addicts." In fact, the very word "drugs" means, in common parlance, any and all drugs other than alcohol. This despite the fact that in 1997 there were 19,576 alcohol-induced deaths in the United States, a number far greater than deaths from all other drugs combined.[2]

The overwhelming popularity of alcohol in comparison to the use of other drugs is best understood if we consider that approximately 66 percent of Americans used alcohol in 1998. And in that same year 32 percent of children ages 12 to 17 also used alcohol. All other illicit drugs were used by an estimated 13.6 million Americans during that year. This represents only 6.2 percent of the population twelve years of age or older. Sixty percent of those using "illicit" drugs chose only marijuana. Evidently then, alcohol is ten times more popular than all other drugs combined. Furthermore it is significant that 60 percent of those who use illicit drugs used marijuana and only 40 percent used such drugs as hashish, cocaine, hallucinogens, inhalants, or psychotherapeutics.[3]

Drugs other than alcohol carry with them the stigma that originates in the foreign, mainly Spanish-sounding, names which stigmatize such drugs in American society. It is well known that many nonalcoholic drugs are imported to this country from South America. Included in such imports is marijuana, which has so distinct a Spanish name that its use carries the stigma of its alien origin. Cocaine is likewise an import from Columbia and other South American areas. Alcohol, however, despite its Arabic name, carries no stigma per se unless used to excess.[4] This may be attributed to the widespread use of alcohol among the wealthy and the most prestigious members of American society. Alcohol is distributed in bottles carrying fancy labels. Merchants who deal in alcoholic beverages pride themselves on the extent of their stock, the variety of their offerings, their knowledge of wines, the prestige of their customers, and a host of other signals of their acceptance in their communities. Before the 1920s the position of the users and distributors of other drugs was not much different from the users and distributors of alcohol. In fact, during the nineteenth century there was no effective regulation of narcotics in the United States. Various derivatives of opium were freely available and were widely used. There were then some municipalities that prohibited the use of opium and its derivatives such as morphine and heroin, but these laws were hardly enforced. Anyone could gain access to alcohol or opium or any drug whatever at little cost. During the nineteenth century, pharmacists sent messenger boys to deliver vials of morphine to private homes and to "houses of ill repute." Narcotics were usually included in "patent medicines" and doctors prescribed opiates to their patients at a time when medicine had no cure for most ailments while opiates alleviated the symptoms and insured the doctors the continued patronage of their chronically ill patients. These practices resulted in the opium addiction of about three hundred thousand Americans and an equal number of users of other drugs excluding alcohol in 1900. At that time the country had a population of only seventy-six million.[5] Today there are about five hundred thousand heroin addicts in the United States. In addition, there are slightly more than five million Americans who regularly use illicit drugs other than marijuana so that the proportion of such users is about the same as it was one hundred years ago.

Yet, today the use of the "illicit" drugs is greatly rejected and subject to stigma as well as law enforcement while alcohol is freely used despite its obvious deleterious consequences for some 40 percent of the American population. This means that four in ten Americans are now exposed to alcoholism in their families and that ten million American women, men, and children suffer from alcoholism. In addition, another fourteen to eighteen million Americans are problem drinkers. A "problem drinker" is someone who drinks or is drunk while driving or whose drinking affects his job performance. In addition, problem drinkers create difficulties for their families, including the use of physical violence. Nevertheless, nonalcoholic drug users are most rejected in this country. This rejection has been achieved by the alcohol industry whose money and political "clout" has driven all other drugs "underground."

It has been estimated that one in ten Americans has attended an Alcoholics Anonymous (AA) meeting and that one in eight has attended the twelve-step program of that organization. These steps are: Step 1. We admit we are powerless over alcohol—that our lives have become unmanageable. Step 2. We came to believe that a Power greater than ourselves could restore us to sanity. Step 3. We made a decision to turn our will and our lives over to the care of God as we understand Him. Step 4. We made a searching and moral inventory of ourselves. Step 5. We admit to God, to ourselves, and to another human being the exact nature of our wrongs. Step 6. We are entirely ready to have God remove all these defects of our character. Step 7. We humbly ask Him to remove our shortcomings. Step 8. We made a list of all persons we have harmed and are willing to make amends to them all. Step 9. We will make direct amends to such people whenever possible, except when to do so would injure them and others. Step 10. We continue to take personal inventory and when we are wrong will admit it. Step 11. We seek through prayer and meditation to improve our conscious contact with God, as we understand Him, praying only for knowledge of His will for us and the power to carry that out. Step 12. Having had a spiritual awakening as a result of these steps, we try to carry this message to others and to practice these principles in all our affairs.

This list of twelve steps indicates that Alcoholics Anonymous views alcohol addiction as a thinking disorder which can be cured by participation in the AA program and professional treatment working together.[6] Alcoholics Anonymous believes that alcoholism is caused by first thinking one needs alcohol and then carrying out what one thinks.

Because the AA program relies so heavily on belief in a supernatural being, it is questionable whether that program can help the millions of Americans who are not believers. The reason for this reliance on religious belief is that the AA program reflects the concerns of nineteenth-century middle-class Protestants who associated alcoholism with Catholic immigrants, urban blacks, criminals, tramps, casual laborers, and others of low social standing.

The consequences of these beliefs were that native Protestants organized reform movements that were not only seeking to uplift drunkards but who were also hoping to control the conduct of those involved in wife abuse, child abandonment, sexual incontinence, insanity, early death, and eternal damnation. Finally, this wish to control these "low" elements led to the constitutional prohibition of all alcohol and all the consequences that resulted from that prohibition.

There can be no doubt that the stigma of using alcohol after the nineteenth century was mainly related to the immigration into this country of millions of eastern and southern Europeans. During the fifty years between 1870 and 1920 that immigration had begun to rival the number of immigrants from traditional western European sources of immigration. Thus, between 1870 and 1900 only 23.5 percent of all immigrants had come from southern and eastern Europe. Then, during the fifteen years ending in 1915 approximately 47 percent of all immigrants had come from eastern and southern Europe.[7] Moreover, the urban population of the United States grew greatly at the same time. Again we look at 1870 when 79 percent of all Americans were living in rural areas. Thirty years later that proportion had declined to 61 percent even as more than 1.25 million immigrants arrived in this country every year between 1900 and 1907.[8]

Anti-Catholic and anti-Jewish groups sought to limit immigration from eastern and southern Europe. By relating the evils of alcohol to these recent immigrant groups and to the evils of the big cities, often described as hotbeds of all sins, nativists hoped to keep the foreigners out. The temperance movement in the United States had of course originated much earlier than the era of large-scale immigration from the "wrong places" in Europe. Thus, the Women's Christian Temperance Union was established in 1874 and the American Anti-Saloon League in 1895. In those years, however, these groups were concerned with the use of alcohol because alcohol had such visible and scandalous consequences. Heroin and other drugs could of course be used without creating any scandal. For that reason nineteenth-century opium addiction was widely accepted among upper-class and middle-class women so that two-thirds of those addicted to opiates in the nineteenth century were female. These female addicts were of course peaceful, quiet, and docile, unlike the male drinkers who "raised hell" regularly.[9]

Therefore, greater visibility of drinking and prejudice against non-western Europeans combined to promote prohibition in 1919–1920. This culminated in the passage of the Eighteenth Amendment to the Constitution of the United States in 1918 and the passage of the Volstead Act in 1919. That legislation prohibited the manufacture, transportation, and sale of alcoholic beverages. Before the Eighteenth Amendment passed there were a number of "dry" states (states which prohibited the sale or use of alcohol) already, so that Prohibition was not a new idea at its first federal adoption.[10]

These historical experiences with alcohol and other drugs indicate therefore that there is a social construction of addiction that depends a good deal on the prejudices of the day. This can be seen if we consider the various efforts by lawmakers to oppose the use of drugs. For example, in 1875 the city of San Francisco passed an ordinance against the Chinese opium "dens." An opium den was a public place where Chinese laborers smoked opium. This aroused a great deal of antagonism among the American public. In practice, these laws were anti-Chinese laws. Therefore opium, which had been highly regarded when used by Euro-Americans, became dangerous when used by Chinese. The stigma attaching to opium was indeed a stigma attaching to Chinese immigrants.[11]

Likewise, around 1900, laws prohibiting the use of cocaine were really anti-black laws as it was believed that the use of cocaine would cause blacks to attack whites physically. In 1937 Congress passed the Marijuana Tax Act which was in effect an anti-Hispanic law. Anglo-Americans in the Southwest claimed that Hispanics would, under the influence of marijuana, kill, rape, and assault "whites." It was believed that the tax would make the drug too expensive for Hispanics and therefore reduce its use.

Then, in the 1950s during Sen. Joseph McCarthy's hysterical attacks on Communists, this Cold War adversary was blamed for "pushing" heroin. That belief led to the passage by Congress of the Narcotics Drug Control Act of 1956 which promised the death penalty to heroin peddlers.

When, in the 1960s, many college students refused to be drafted to fight in Vietnam and when these and other students rioted against oppressive government generally, new federal and state laws were enacted that increased the penalties for using "illicit" drugs. The real reason for these laws was to punish youths who had rejected old, established values and scorned the "establishment." In sum, we see in these drug laws an effort to war against various minorities, be they the foreign born, racial minorities, or people with the " wrong" politics.[12]

Today, alcohol is no longer stigmatized because of its erstwhile association with the foreign born. This is in part the case because of the failure of Prohibition and the repeal of the Eighteenth Amendment. To a much larger extent, however, alcohol use is not always stigmatized. This is so because alcoholism has been medicalized in America. Therefore, it has become difficult to reject out of hand those who suffer from the illness of alcoholism and who are seen by some as no more responsible for their alcohol problem than anyone with any other disease.

THE DRUNK AS PATIENT: ALCOHOLISM BECOMES A DISEASE

The process of the medicalization of alcoholism began in the 1970s when the American Medical Association began to define alcoholism as a disease. This definition of alcoholism has been in use for twenty-five years without convincing everyone. While the medical definition of alcoholism is used among professionals there are still many Americans who hold the alcoholic responsible for his or her drinking and for the consequences of that drinking.

In 1992 the Joint Committee of the National Council on Alcoholism and the American Society of Addiction Medicine defined alcoholism as "a primary chronic disease with genetic, psychosocial, and environmental factors influencing its development and manifestations."[13] If this definition of alcoholism had been universally accepted then those who drink too much for any reason would all have benefited from the cultural definition of illness that is attributed to the sick in American society. That cultural definition deals with the appropriate behavior of and response to people labeled as sick. Sick roles are of course not determined by universal standards but by cultural understandings. For example, as we have seen in chapter 2, in some societies mentally ill people are seen as possessing unique spiritual qualities; in others they are seen as being possessed by the devil and in yet others as having a character deficiency. Likewise, alcohol abusers have been seen as sinners, malicious offenders, or moral weaklings. This is still true for many Americans who will not allow the medicalization of alcoholism to affect their judgment. For those who do see alcoholism as a disease the role of sick persons relieves the alcohol abuser of the stigma associated with that behavior as long as the alcoholic meets the requirements demanded of the sick. These requirements include the right to be excused from social responsibilities and other normal social roles. The sick person is not held responsible for the illness even if the illness, as in the case of alcohol abuse, results from a lifestyle that produced it. It is however the obligation of the sick person to seek medical help in order to get well. Failure to do so relieves significant others of the obligation to treat the person who is sick accordingly. It is this requirement that most alcoholics cannot and will not meet because denial is so common a characteristic of alcohol abuse and because there is really no medical cure for this condition.

Because in today's society alcoholism is seen as an illness, alcoholics expect and often receive the sympathy of family, friends, and employers for their illness. In fact, many employers have special programs designed to keep alcohol abusers on the job. In addition, governments and private foundations spend a great deal of money on research aimed at finding a cure for this illness. This contrasts sharply with those who use cocaine and heroin. Such users are defined as criminals (possessors of a controlled substance) and are sent to prison. This illustrates that stigma is not related to the danger of a drug but rather to the cultural label to which it is subject.[14]

Because the word "alcoholic" carries a stigma and because the word can hardly be erased from the American vocabulary, the World Health Organization recommended in 1979 that the phrase "alcohol dependence" be substituted for the word "alcoholic." In 1980 the American Psychiatric Association followed that recommendation and adopted the "alcohol dependence" label. This measure was taken because it was believed that the frequent denial of alcoholism by alcoholics is not a denial of their drinking but a denial designed to avoid the diagnosis "alcoholic." No doubt, the adoption of the disease concept concerning alcohol dependency is widely known. It was therefore hoped that the disease concept would also decrease the stigma associated with the word "alcoholic." This, however, has not happened. Despite every effort by the medical profession and educators "alcoholic" continues to be a "dirty word" and those to whom it is applied continue to have good reason to feel the weight of stigma upon them.[15]

A study conducted by Dr. Raul Caetano of the Medical Research Institute in San Francisco concerning public opinion about alcoholism and its treatment discovered that Americans are highly ambivalent concerning the condition. Even as a large majority of Caetano's respondents agreed that alcoholism is a disease, 70 percent of the same people also agreed that "being an alcoholic destroys a person's reputation." Further, it was agreed by that group that "I wouldn't want a place where people with alcohol problems get treated to be near where I live." Evidently, the nineteenth-century temperance movement is not entirely forgotten in this country. Furthermore, the public sees alcoholism as a condition involving some personal responsibility despite the disease concept, particularly since all the money and time already spent on seeking a cure has so far not succeeded.[16]

The evidence that alcoholism is still seen as a matter of personal responsibility and that the disease concept has not succeeded in convincing the public that alcohol abusers are sick is that in 1996 Congress amended the Social Security Disability Supplemental Income provisions to exclude from that program any disabled person for whom drug addiction and/or alcoholism are material to his disability. This was signed by President Clinton and became law in 1997.

Alcoholics and others who are stigmatized are not seen as an undifferentiated mass of abnormal people. Sociological research has shown that the stigmatized are viewed as demonstrating various grades of offensive behavior. This distinction can be seen by examining the different degrees of social distance that Americans take from the stigmatized. For example, the physically disabled are subject to less social distance from "normal" people than is true of alcoholics because alcoholics seem more threatening than the disabled and because they are still viewed as people who bring their "disability," i.e., their alcoholism, upon themselves. People will require a good deal of social distance between themselves and those who are suspected of disrupting normal social interaction. Many people do not know how to deal with an alcoholic, and others believe that their own character will be in doubt if they are found to associate with a "drunk."

Evidently, as the perceived cost of interacting with a stigmatized person increases, social distance also increases. In addition, visibility of a stigma escalates the social distance to which an obvious drunkard will become subject. It is of course one of the features of alcoholism that it becomes evident in public and cannot be well hidden, as is the case with other drug addictions. Alcoholics are further burdened with the moral stigma that their habit evokes. As we shall see, the moral stigma attaches even more to ex-convicts who nevertheless have the opportunity to hide their past, an opportunity a binge-drinking alcoholic does not enjoy. Because drinking is a chronic condition, alcoholics who appear sober at the moment will nevertheless experience social distance by others because their condition is so unstable and may, and generally will, return.[17]

Social distance as a product of stigma is particularly employed against alcoholic women. The view that "ladies don't get drunk" is by no means dead at the beginning of the twenty-first century. Professor of psychology Edith Gomberg of the University of Michigan reports that alcoholic women themselves have a more negative attitude toward their own drinking than is true of alcoholic men. Younger women who drink are also more frequently confronted with family and social rejection than is true of older women who drink. This may well be attributed to the more public drinking by younger women who do not have a home, and of older married women who do have a home. Older women are more likely to drink at home, alone, than is true of younger women of dating age. Furthermore, even now, younger unmarried women are more likely to be employed than older women so that their drinking will interfere with job performance more often than is true of older women. The sight of a young woman drinking also arouses more social hostility than the sight of an older woman or man drinking because younger women are of childbearing age so that drinking on their part suggests the possibility that their drinking interferes with their reproductive function.[18]

It is generally argued that men abuse alcohol in order to feel aggressively powerful. No doubt some men drink for that reason. There are however a host of other reasons for drinking which have been recited in a vast body of literature without coming to agreement between researchers and students of this addiction. Nevertheless, most observers agree that women do not abuse alcohol for the same reasons as men. Instead, women are more likely to abuse alcohol because of a conflict within their social role. The traditional feminine role consisted of passivity, dependence, and submission. That role has been severely challenged during the past twenty years. Women are now told that they should be assertive, preserve their personal autonomy, and reject the traditional female role of alma mater, the nourishing mother. This leads to a forfeit of expressiveness and warmth as is usually expected of women. In turn, conflicting expectations create a good deal of self-doubt and confusion for many women, resulting in many cases in drinking behavior designed to ease the pain derived from these anomic requirements. This situation is called "sex-role conflict" by sociologists.

Many alcoholic women share emotionally brutal childhoods. This often includes divorced parents, desertion, or death while they were children. Alcoholic women are likely to have seen alcoholism in their family, as reported in some studies showing that up to one-half of all alcoholic women have alcoholic fathers. Many alcoholic women and men have also been the victims of physical violence and/or sexual abuse in their childhood.[19]

A study by Dr. Caroline Easton, professor of psychiatry at Yale University, discovered that 37 percent of all patients entering an outpatients substance abuse clinic had a history of physical violence from a family member. A similar finding was reported by Bennett and Lawson, whose study concluded that 46 percent of substance-abusing men were batterers who abused their families and 42 percent of women receiving domestic violence treatment were substance abusers.[20]

Research with populations of alcohol abusers has found high rates of psychopathology among the sexually abused. The Alcohol Problems Questionnaire has been used to discover that the sexually abused start drinking earlier than other drinkers and that the sexually abused are more likely to take psychotropic drugs than those not so treated. Sexual abuse is also related to major depression which in turn is related to alcohol abuse. While studies concerning alcoholism among sexually abused men are inconclusive, it appears that sexual abuse and alcohol abuse among women go "hand in glove."[21]

In fact, the literature on alcoholism indicates a high correlation between antisocial behavior and alcohol abuse, so that the erstwhile victims of such mistreatment in turn become the abusers of their own families thereafter. Among such alcoholics are those who may be called high antisocial drinkers and those who are known to professionals as low antisocial drinkers. The high antisocials exhibit overt, disturbed interaction patterns. Such drinkers are very impulsive, which leads to considerable family dissent and disturbed relationships. In many families that have an alcoholic member, usually the father and husband, the wife and any children will avoid aggressive and angry exchanges by leaving the household temporarily until the alcoholic has become sober.

When mothers are involved in the excessive use of alcohol the problems for her family become severe. Mothers are primary socializers and caregivers of their children. Therefore, children direct more of all their communication to mothers rather than fathers. Hence, alcoholism of mothers is even more likely to produce alcoholic children than is true of alcoholic fathers although children of alcoholics of both sexes are at an elevated risk for various mental-health outcomes including substance abuse.[22]

CHILDREN OF ALCOHOLICS

One of the consequences of parental alcoholism for children is the decreased academic performance of these children. Such poor school performance in turn leads to the stigmatization of these children of alcoholics. Difficulties in school lead to peer rejection as well as criticism by teachers and others. Some teachers publicly criticize poor students. In addition, parents and relatives criticize such children. Furthermore, those who feel they are academic failures tend to feel stigmatized. That in turn can translate into peer rejection which then leads to a decrease in self-esteem and association with others who are linked to antisocial behavior and substance abuse.

Several studies of children of alcohol abusers indicate that such children tend to have disturbed academic histories and lower academic achievement than other children. They are also more likely to repeat a grade in school than other children and they are more often than others referred to a school psychologist. A study by Sher revealed that college student children of alcohol abusers achieved a lower rank and performed more poorly on college entrance exams than did a control group, despite the fact that both groups performed equally on intelligence tests.[23]

Claire E. McGrath, professor of psychology at Arizona State University, tested the relation between parents' alcoholism and adolescents' academic performance. Results of that study indicated that parental alcoholism had a significant negative effect on both English and math grades. Similar findings were reported by other researchers. Parental alcohol dependency was associated with poor test scores on the Wide

Range Achievement Test (which measures nonverbal-reasoning and problem-solving skills independent of educational curricula and student cultural background) and the Peabody Individual Achievement Test (which tests language development in grade-school students). The evidence further indicates that children of alcoholic parents are more easily distracted than other children. Youngsters who have alcoholic parents experience difficulty maintaining a normal level of attention and commitment to academic work. Therefore, these children have difficulty orienting toward a task and carrying it out. There is also a possibility that the poorer ability of children of alcoholic parents to do academic work is the product of fundamental cognitive defects in children whose mothers drank alcohol during pregnancy.[24]

Among college students there is also a significant number who are the children of alcoholic parents. Estimates vary from 17 percent to 33 percent of all college students. These studies conclude that adult children of alcoholic parents have low self-esteem, excessive anxiety, and stress.[25]

"UNDER THE INFLUENCE"

Substance abusers, but particularly alcoholics, have employment difficulties. The link between unemployment and substance abuse can easily be documented and is most severe in connection with alcoholism. In fact, 70 percent of those admitted to facilities for substance-abuse treatment are unemployed. This high number of the unemployed among substance abusers is to be expected in all parts of the country and has been substantiated by the findings of the New Hope Foundation, whose intake records have at some times shown that 81 percent of those seeking treatment for substance abuse are unemployed. Furthermore the U.S. Department of Health and Human Services has collected significant national data to confirm these findings.[26]

It is not certain whether substance abuse is the cause of unemployment among those who cannot work for that reason, or whether unemployment and the inability to establish a successful career leads to substance abuse. If we consider that unemployment carries a severe stigma in our work-oriented society, then it is reasonable to expect that at least some of the chronically unemployed became involved in substance abuse for that reason. That unemployment carries a severe stigma in American society is easily confirmed by the numerous prestige rankings of various occupations. The unemployed are always at the bottom of such rankings.[27]

There is also a connection between work stress and substance abuse, particularly because the employed have the money to buy drugs or have greater access to drugs than the unemployed. The stresses to which the employed may be subject include sexual harassment, discriminatory treatment, psychological humiliation, time pressures, and work overloads. There are also workers who have to deal with physical difficulties in their jobs and with job insecurity. Substance abuse may seem to those who face these problems every day as a method of coping with these stressors. Furthermore, there are some forms of employment that include a subculture of substance abuse.[28]

Nursing, medicine, dentistry, and pharmacy are undoubtedly in the forefront of those professions that include numerous practitioners at risk of becoming involved with drugs. Those who practice these professions and then become addicted to drugs project an image of dangerous incompetence, failure to assume responsibility for their job performance, and risking the health and lives of their patients. Although a great effort has been made to view those professionals who use controlled substances as sick or the victims of an illness, the moralistic view of substance abuse by health professionals prevails to this day. This is particularly true with reference to health professionals since the public believes it should be able to rely on the sober judgment of these professionals and not be placed at risk by them.[29]

There are of course numerous health professionals and others who daily face all those difficulties which employment inevitably brings with it and who nevertheless do not feel great stress or use drugs to deal with their situation. Therefore, it is perceived stress which has more to do with addiction than stress itself. The concept of perceived stress is more valid because it reflects not life events themselves, but "a relationship between the person and the environment that is appraised by the person as taxing or exceeding his/her resources and endangering his/her well-being."[30]

One fashion in which alcoholics and their children indicate the stress that alcoholism produces is the high level of aggression among alcohol abusers. Psychologists Thomas Kelly and Don Cherek found in an extensive study of the correlation between alcohol consumption and aggression that whenever the relation between the two is measured it comes out positive. Kelly and Cherek claim that there is a positive correlation between the quantity of alcohol consumed and the frequency and intensity of child abuse, sexual abuse, domestic aggression, aggressive crimes such as assault and homicide, and interpersonal aggression. This relationship holds both for perpetrators of violent acts and their victims. Nevertheless it can plainly be shown that there are many who consume alcohol who never show any aggression thereafter and that there are some very aggressive persons who consume no alcohol at all.[31]

The most dangerous form of aggression involving alcohol is the pattern of drinking and driving, which is so common in America and has caused so much pain, suffering, and death. Since about one-half of all traffic accidents are related to the use of alcohol the Centers for Disease Control has estimated that about thirty thousand unintentional injury deaths each year are directly attributable to alcohol. There are also fifteen thousand to twenty thousand suicides and homicides each year that can be attributed to alcohol abuse.

Those who drive under the influence of alcohol are deemed to be impaired if their blood alcohol concentration reaches 0.05 percent. This means that the amount of alcohol in the bloodstream makes it difficult for a driver to concentrate on driving tasks. Visual functions, perceptions, psychomotor performance, all are impaired. There are of course also encounters with alcohol abusers behind the wheels of cars who only injure but do not kill their victims. In any event, nothing so fuels public resentment against alcoholics as the unintentional killing of children by drunk drivers. It is therefore far from an exaggeration to say that drunk driving is stigmatized.

In order to know whether or not someone is driving under the influence of alcohol, police use a Breathalyzer test, which measures the amount of alcohol in the bloodstream. For example, someone with a blood alcohol concentration of 0.10 percent has one part of alcohol per 1,000 parts of blood in his body. Evidently, those who drink and drive are the subject of stigma on the part of the public in general and in particular on the part of the survivors of someone killed needlessly.[32]

According to the U.S. Department of Education, 31.5 percent of children enrolled in the seventh through twelfth grades in American schools experience "binge" drinking—consuming five or more drinks in a row and that more than 40 percent drink alcohol each week. A survey of fourth-, fifth-, and sixth-graders revealed that 21 percent of these children have used alcohol and that they believe wine coolers are not a drug, while only one-half of children in these grades believe that beer, wine, and liquor are drugs. There are of course a large number of adults who also ignore that alcohol is a drug and who are convinced that they cannot be alcoholics if they drink only beer, no matter how much.[33]

In all states the minimum age to buy alcohol is twenty-one. Nevertheless, almost anyone younger than twenty-one has easy access to alcohol because it is in their homes, because friends twenty-one years old or older buy it for them, because some stores sell to minors, or because the youngsters solicit a stranger to buy alcohol for them.[34]

The consequences of alcohol use most criticized in the United States are alcohol-related traffic fatalities. There are about forty-one thousand traffic fatalities in the United States each year of which 38.4 percent or 15,935 are alcohol-related. This means that in 1998 there were two alcohol-related deaths per hour, forty-five such deaths per day, and 315 alcohol-related deaths per week. In 1997, intoxicated young drivers were involved in 1,037 of these. In addition to the fatalities caused by drunk driving there are a large number of drunk-driving episodes that do not cause death or injury. The most frequently committed crime in the United States is drunk driving, which resulted in 1.4 million arrests each year during the 1990s.

It is instructive to note that more than half of all traffic fatalities occurring on holidays are alcohol-related. On New Year's Day 1998, figures show that 68.4 percent of the traffic fatalities involved alcohol. Likewise, 52 percent of fatalities occurring on Memorial Day involved alcohol, as did 53 percent on Labor Day, 57 percent on Halloween, and 48 percent on Christmas. This leaves no doubt that holidays or holy days are viewed as drinking occasions by large numbers of Americans.[35]

There are about 3.8 million sixteen-year-olds in the United States, constituting 1.8 percent of the American population old enough to drive. Since everyone who has attained the legal age needed to hold a driver's license does not drive, sixteen- to twenty-four-year-olds are 20 percent of those who have a driver's license. Yet, sixteen-year-olds alone are involved in 40 percent of all single-car, alcohol-related crashes in this country and sixteen- to twenty-four-year-olds are involved in 42 percent of all *fatal* crashes.

The high rate of death and trauma resulting from all of these accidents illustrates a severe culture conflict within American society. While young men in particular, and some young women, view excessive drinking as "macho" behavior and pressure each other to drink and drive, other Americans condemn drinking and driving in particular or condemn drinking alcohol in any situation in general. The conflict concerning alcohol use is an example of anomie as Durkheim understood it. Because drinking alcohol is so widely approved it turns out that an estimated six million American children between the ages of fourteen and seventeen have problems with alcohol.[36]

THE DRUG CULTURE

Alcohol abuse is of course not the only drug abuse that is stigmatized and yet widely used in America. According to the National Household Survey of Drug Abuse conducted by the Department of Health Education and Welfare there are fourteen million current users of "illicit" drugs in the United States. This survey also found that drug use increased substantially between 1991 and 1996 and has stabilized since then. Sixty percent of those who use illicit drugs use marijuana, 20 percent use marijuana and some additional drug, and 20 percent use drugs other than marijuana or alcohol.[37]

Large numbers of young people are involved in using "illicit" drugs. A study by the University of Michigan indicates that 29 percent of eighth-graders regularly use illicit drugs, that this is also true of 45 percent of tenth-graders, and that over 54 percent of twelfth-graders are involved in illicit drugs.[38]

There are a number of explanations for involvement in the use of "illicit" drugs in the United States. Some of these explanations are rooted in psychiatric research while others have a sociological origin. Psychoanalysts speak of ego-constricting drugs by which they mean that heroin addicts are people with a weak "ego" or self-image, which causes them to seek quiet and lonely lives aided by narcotics. Psychoanalysts also distinguish ego-expanding drugs which, like cocaine and amphetamines, permit users to gain a strong and "expanding," competitive personality.[39]

Followers of behaviorism as first taught by Harvard University psychologist B. F. Skinner seek to understand the abuse of stimulants and depressants in the light of the rewards that such use gives the user. For example, cocaine elevates the mood of the user and provides him with a sense of well-being, strength, and energy. A cocaine user who stops using that drug suffers the "coke blues" or depression and will soon want to alleviate that feeling by using more cocaine. Likewise heroin addicts find that physical and psychological pain is greatly reduced, that heroin provides the user with a sense of euphoria. In the words of sociologist Alfred Lindesmith, "persons become addicts when they recognize or perceive the significance of withdrawal distress which they are experiencing."[40]

The National Institute of Drug Abuse has outlined some of the sociological factors that contribute to adolescent substance abuse. Included are families whose members have a history of alcohol and/or drug abuse and/or a history of antisocial behavior and criminality. Inconsistent parental supervision is also regarded as a contributor to drug abuse as is parental approval of drug use. Then, the institute cites friends who use drugs as a contributing cause of addiction and adds that children who show no interest in school, either in the grades or in adolescence, are also at risk of becoming addicts. Finally, the institute holds that alienated, rebellious, and aggressive children are possible drug abusers.[41]

Drug abusers view their ability to obtain illegal drugs as an achievement as explained by Betram Sackman in this fashion: "(The typical heroin addict) exhibits as much pride in his heroin-getting skills as does the licit craftsman. He thinks about hustling and heroin, he talks about his exploits to other addicts, and his righteousness about heroin is rewarded by his women in the admiration and respect they accord him and his skills."[42]

Initiation into drug use appears to be dependent on peer association. "The first source of contact with the drug (heroin) was usually through a friend. Usually, a new user receives his first taste of a drug from another new user who is not yet addicted and is willing to share his drug supply free. Observers of the drug 'scene' say that initiation into drug use is therefore mostly fortuitous rather than deliberate. This first use can occur at the home of a friend or at a dance or at a party. If such a first user then becomes 'hooked' he is then connected to a lifestyle which leaves little room for any other activities unless such activities lead to 'scoring' and fixing heroin."[43]

Drug subcultures are also responsible for much addiction. A subculture is a group who have had significantly different experiences from those of most members of any society. Such a definition certainly fits drug addicts. It is further a mark of any subculture that those who belong share values, rituals, and traditions that are foreign to the majority and that are usually rejected by the majority. That, too, is true of those addicted to drugs.[44]

All of these conditions finally lead to a damaged self-image derived from the stigma conferred upon drug addicts and excessive users by almost everyone with whom they come in contact. A damaged self-image finally becomes a self-fulfilling prophecy in that those branded as "addicts" will find it extremely difficult to alter their identity and be anything else. This is exactly what happened after the passage of the Harrison Act by Congress in 1914, which restricted the importation, manufacture, sale, and dispensing of narcotics.

PROHIBITION AGAIN: THE "WAR ON DRUGS"

The extensive use of "illicit" drugs demonstrates once more that prohibition is as much a failure in 2001 as it was in the1920s and that the so-called war on drugs cannot be won. The war on drugs was officially declared by Pres. George Bush and Congress when the latter passed the Anti-Drug Abuse Act of 1988, which even includes the death penalty for drug-related killings.[45] When chemists succeeded in evading the restrictions included in that law by inventing "designer drugs," altering the molecular structure of controlled substances, Congress amended the law to include these analogs among the controlled substances.[46]

The war on drugs other than alcohol had actually begun much earlier with the Harrison Narcotics Act of 1914. That law was amended in 1937, and in 1956 the Narcotic Control Act increased penalties for drug offenders. In 1965, the Drug Abuse Control Act defined legal use of barbiturates, amphetamines, LSD, and any other "dangerous" drugs, again exempting alcohol. In 1970, the Comprehensive Drug Prevention and

Control Act listed whole categories of prohibited drugs and associated penalties for their use and distribution. Although numerous agencies were at one time responsible for enforcing these drug laws all of these agencies were welded into the Drug Enforcement Administration or DEA in 1973. Since then the war on drugs has continued to escalate. In the 1980s President Reagan and later President Bush appointed a "drug czar," conservative political writer William Bennett, who sought the death penalty for those convicted of selling drugs. The Bush administration also increased the budget for the war on drugs to $10.4 billion, which was a 62 percent increase over the 1989 budget and a tenfold increase over the 1985 budget. Seventy-five percent of the money was to be spent on law enforcement.[47]

The Clinton administration had increased the budget for the war on drugs by another 25 percent so that during the first Clinton term the number of marijuana-related arrests increased by 43 percent and more Americans were in prison for such offenses than ever before. The Clinton administration had also proposed conditioning teenage driver's licenses, parole, and welfare payments on mandatory drug testing. Furthermore the director of the Office of National Drug Control Policy sought to nullify the "medical marijuana" initiatives passed by the voters in California and Arizona by threatening to revoke the DEA registration of any physician who recommends or prescribes medicinal marijuana for pain relief. Doctors were also threatened with exclusion from Medicare and Medicaid programs if they prescribed marijuana for cancer patients needing help to alleviate the side-effects of chemotherapy.[48]

The consequences of this war on drugs has been the expenditure of $15 billion in federal tax money and an additional $33 billion in state and local funds. Furthermore, the United States now imprisons more of its citizens than any other country on earth. Of the eight million prisoners incarcerated the world over, more than two million are in American prisons although the United States has only 4.5 percent of the world's population. Only seven hundred thousand of these two million prisoners have been convicted of violent crimes. The other 1.3 million are almost all drug offenders or are innocent of any crime. The cost of this massive incarceration is $26 billion annually, a cost that is more than the government's entire expenditure for welfare and social security programs.[49]

Although the war on drugs is a massive failure, these policies continue because they benefit the criminal justice industry in several ways. First, there is the increase in the budget for the Drug Enforcement Administration, which rose from a mere $770 million in 1990 to $1.47 billion in 2000. This budget permits the employment of over nine thousand DEA personnel who are of course interested in continuing the war on drugs to secure their own jobs. Additional benefits of the war on drugs is the assets-forfeiture provision of the Comprehensive Drug Prevention and Control Act. That provision allows law-enforcement agencies to keep and use the proceeds from asset forfeitures. This provision benefits local and state police, who receive 80 percent of property forfeited while the federal government receives 20 percent of property thus forfeited. This forfeiture law raises a great deal of money for police departments all over the nation, particularly because those whose assets have been taken by the police and who are found not guilty of the accusations against them cannot retrieve their assets any more than those who are found guilty of drug violations. At present Congress is debating an amendment to the Comprehensive Drug Prevention and Control Act that would make the government justify seizure of property with "clear and convincing evidence." [50]

This policy also encourages police to raid the homes of innocent citizens with a view to seizing their property. A particularly outrageous incident of this kind was the murder of Donald Scott by the Los Angeles Police Department in 1992. Scott's estate was raided on October 2, 1992, on the basis of a false warrant. No marijuana was found on Scott's property but Scott was shot to death by the police raiders without any provocation.[51]

The war on drugs has also benefited the prison industry. This is so because during the two decades ending in 1999 roughly a thousand prisons have been built in the United States even as the rate of violent crime in this country has dramatically decreased. That decrease is the result of a reduction in the birthrate after 1970, producing fewer young men in the age range sixteen to thirty. That age range generally includes most violent offenders. Nevertheless, the war on drugs has led to an increase in the inmate population in this country of about seventy-five thousand persons a year. Hence, the rate of incarceration in America, 445 inmates per one hundred thousand of population is now the highest in the world and tops any earlier rates of incarceration in the United States. Before the drug war in the 1970s that rate was a steady 110 persons per one hundred thousand but has now risen to four times that number.[52]

It has been estimated that in California, which has one hundred forty thousand prisoners, one hundred thirty thousand are substance abusers. Only three thousand of these prisoners receive drug treatment behind bars. Approximately eighty thousand of California prisoners are parole violators who have committed a technical violation such as failing a drug test. This demonstrates that the huge prison system built in California and in other states at great expense is nothing more than a revolving door for poor, dysfunctional, and illiterate drug abusers who cannot possibly rid themselves of their addiction by being sent to prison again and again. Evidently, then, drug addiction is a source of income to prison officials, prosecutors, judges, and politicians and is therefore not attacked by treating the addicts with a view of freeing them of their addiction.[53]

Although the war on drugs focuses primarily on law-enforcement strategies, drug education and prevention receives some attention as well. These efforts are aimed at convincing children not to get involved with tobacco, drugs, or alcohol. The program most widely known in this respect is Drug Abuse Resistance Education (DARE), which employs uniformed police officers as speakers in elementary schools. These speakers provide accurate information about tobacco, alcohol, and drugs; teach students techniques to resist peer pressure to use such substances; try to instill respect for the law and law enforcers; encourage some alternatives to drug use; and attempt to promote self-esteem among students. DARE is based on the assumption that children need specific social and analytic skills to resist peer pressure and refuse drugs. It is estimated that more than forty million children attend DARE seminars each year at a cost of $90,000 for each police officer-trainer. In 1997, President Clinton announced that drug education was the major focus of his drug-control policy. To date that policy has not been very successful although it also includes an antidrug advertising campaign conducted in the media.[54]

Yet another strategy included in the war on drugs is the government's drug-testing program. That program has been extended to private employment and criminal offenders as well as government employees and is believed to enhance on-the-job safety. In some industries, such as mining and among the forty million transportation workers, drug testing is mandatory because drug use is viewed as a threat to others. In more than 40 percent of large American industries mandatory drug testing is commonly used. Criminal defendants are routinely tested at all stages of the criminal justice procedure from arrest to parole. The evidence is that such monitoring of defendants' and convicts' behavior does not reduce drug use. However, it does increase the stigmatization of those who are processed through the criminal justice system and increases the difficulties faced by those generally labeled ex-convicts. The stigma attaching to that status shall be the subject of our next chapter.[55]

SUMMARY

Alcohol is the most popular and the most deadly drug used in America. It is common to omit alcohol from the usage of the word "drug" which, in common parlance, refers to all drugs other than alcohol. The reason for this is that alcohol use is prestigious in this country while drugs such as marijuana imported from Spanish-speaking countries are viewed with contempt.

Before 1920 there was no antidrug campaign in the United States.

Then, doctors prescribed opium routinely. Today, there are five million "illicit" drug users in the United States, a ratio to the total American population that is the same as it was one hundred years ago. At that time, the use of alcohol was viewed with alarm because alcohol abuse was attributed to immigrants from eastern and southern Europe. The alarm concerning foreign drunks finally led to the restrictions on immigration and the prohibition of alcohol use altogether during the 1920s. This illustrates the social construction of addiction that follows the prejudices of the day.

In the 1970s alcoholism became medicalized as alcoholics were labeled "sick" by the medical profession. Despite this, large numbers of Americans still view alcoholism as a moral stigma as evidenced by the elimination of alcoholics from Social Security Supplemental Insurance benefits in 1997. These benefits were denied all drug addicts at that time.

Many people seek to place a social distance between themselves and those who in their opinion are stigmatized. This is as true of those who are stigmatized by reason of alcoholism as it is of those who carry a stigma for other reasons. There are several reasons for stigmatizing drug users and alcoholics. First among these is the ambiguity in social interaction that results from excessive drinking and the use of illegal drugs. People who are not alcoholics and do not use drugs feel uncomfortable around those who drink too much or use drugs because they don't understand the behavior of such people and don't know how to interact with them. This can easily be observed at parties at which someone becomes loud and boisterous after drinking excessively. Excessive drinkers and particularly drug addicts become a threat to the social well-being of others. This means that many people fear that association with drunks and addicts will taint their reputation. Some people also fear violence and bodily harm from drunks and addicts and therefore reject them.

There are also a number of people who stigmatize drunks and addicts because they are physically repelled by the smell and sight of such conduct. Others consider the drunk and the addict as "morally weak" and stigmatize such behavior for that reason alone. Addicts and drunks are not in control in our puritanical society. Since Americans generally favor those who are self-controlled and hardworking, addicts and drunks are viewed by many people as out-of-control failures and weaklings.

Although the American Medical Association labeled alcoholism a disease in 1956, this view has not made much of an impression on the vast majority of Americans. Generally, the image of the alcoholic remains highly stigmatized. It is for this reason that some have proposed the abandonment of the word "alcoholism" and sought to substitute the phrase "alcohol dependence." It is unlikely, however, that such a change in the label will do much to minimize the stigma associated with excessive drinking.

Alcoholics are the targets of social distance, a treatment accorded to female alcoholics even more than to male alcoholics. Female alcoholism is viewed as even more egregious than male addiction.

Children of alcoholic parents have more difficulty in academic performance in school than do other children, even as adult drinkers have more difficulty dealing with their employment than sober employees. Those who consume large amounts of alcohol are also responsible for many traffic accidents leading to serious injury and death.

Sixty percent of those who use "illicit" drugs in this country use only marijuana. This includes children. Because drugs other than alcohol are viewed with so much disdain, a "war on drugs" has been declared by the U.S. government leading to huge expenditures by an entire army of enforcers. Consequently, 1.4 million of the over two million Americans now in prison are there because of drug abuse. This leads to the stigmatization of all those who are returned to society without any treatment but who nevertheless carry the label of "convict," which will be the topic of our next chapter.

NOTES

1. Émile Durkheim, *The Rules of the Sociological Method* (1895; reprint, New York: Free Press, 1964), p. 68.

2. Faststats, *Statistical Rolodex*, http://www.cdc.gov./nchs/FASTATS/alcohol.htm.

3. Ibid.

4. Will Durant, *The Age of Faith* (New York: MJF Books, 1950), p. 244.

5. David T. Courtwright, *Dark Paradise: Opium Addiction in America Before 1940* (Cambridge, Mass.: Harvard University Press, 1982), chap. 1.

6. Fran Steigerwald and David Stone, "Cognitive Restructuring and the 12-Step Program of Alcoholics Anonymous," *Journal of Substance Abuse Treatment* 16, no. 4 (1999): 321.

7. Adna Ferrin Weber, *The Growth of Cities in the Nineteenth Century* (Ithaca, N.Y.: Cornell University Press, 1963), p. 21.

8. Thomas A. Bailey, *The American Pageant* (Boston: D.C. Heath & Co., 1961), p. 781.

9. David Courtwright, Herman Joseph, and Don Des Jarlais, *Addicts Who Survived: An Oral History of Narcotics Use in America, 1923–1965* (Knoxville: University of Tennessee Press, 1989), p. 3.

10. Jennings B. Sanders, *History of the United States* (Evanston, Ill.: Row, Peterson and Co., 1962), p. 208.

11. John Helmer, *Drugs and Minority Oppression* (New York: Seabury Publishing Co., 1975).

12. Gordon Witkin, "Why This Country Is Losing the Drug War," *U.S. News & World Report* (September 16, 1996): 60.

13. Karen Belliner, ed., *Substance Abuse Source Book* (Detroit: Omnigraphics, Inc., 1996), p. 99.

14. Jeffrey A. Schaler, "Drugs and Free Will," *Society* 28 (September 1991): 42.

15. James C. Dean and Gregoray A. Poremba, "The Alcholic Stigma and the Disease Concept," *International Journal of the Addictions* 18, no. 5 (July 1983): 750.

16. Raul Caetano, "Public Opinion about Alcoholism and Its Treatment," *Journal of Studies on Alcohol* 48, no. 2 (March 1987): 157.

17. Gary L. Albrecht, Vivian G. Walker, and Judith J. Levy, "Social Distance from the Stigmatized," *Social Science and Medicine* 16, no. 14 (July 1982): 1319.

18. Edith S. Lisansky Gomberg, "Alcoholic Women in Treatment: The Question of Stigma and Age," *Alcohol and Alcoholics* 23, no. 6 (1988): 507.

19. Marian Sandmaier, *The Invisible Alcoholics: Women and Alcohol Abuse in America* (New York: McGraw-Hill Book Co., 1980), p. 92.

20. Caroline J. Easton, Suzanne Swan, and Rajita Sinha, "Prevalence of Family Violence in Clients Entering Substance Abuse Treatment," *Journal of Substance Abuse Treatment* 18 (2000): 26.

21. John Moncrieff and D. C. Drummond, "Sexual Abuse in People with Alcohol Problems," *British Journal of Psychiatry* 169 (1996): 355–60.

22. Theodore Jacob et al., "Home Interactions of High and Low Anti-Social Male Alcoholics and Their Families," *Journal of Studies on Alcohol* 61 (2000): 72.

23. Kenneth J. Sher et al., "Characteristics of Children of Alcoholics," *Journal of Abnormal Psychology* 100 (1991): 427–48.

24. Claire E. McGrath et al., "Academic Achievement in Adolescent Children of Alcoholics," *Journal of Studies on Alcoholism* 60, no. 1 (January 1999): 24.

25. Kathy E. Fischer et al., "The Relationship of Parental Alcoholism and Family Dysfunction to Stress Among College Students," *Journal of American College Health* 48, no. 4 (January 2000): 151.

26. Anthony W. Comerford, *Substance Abuse and Cost Savings to Business, Fact Sheet #6* (Rockville, Md.: Center for Substance Abuse Treatment, 1997).

27. Linda L. Lindsey and Stephen Beach, *Sociology; Social Life and Social Issues* (Upper Saddle River, N.J.: Prentice-Hall Inc., 2000), p. 261.

28. John Howland et al.,"Work Site Variation in Managerial Drinking," *Addiction* 91 (1996): 1007–17.

29. Mary R. Haack and Tonda L. Hughes, *Addiction in the Nursing Profession* (New York: Springer Publishing Co., 1989), p. 25.

30. Richard Lazarus and Susan Folkman, *Stress, Appraisal and Coping* (New York: Springer Publishing Co., 1984), p. 21.

31. Thomas H. Kelly and Don R. Cherek, "The Effects of Alcohol on Free-Operant Aggressive Behavior," *Journal of Studies on Alcholism,* Supplement #1 (September 1993): 40.

32. Belliner, *Substance Abuse,* p. 147.

33. U.S. Department of Education, National Center for Education Statistics, *Ten Critical Threats to America's Children* (Washington, D.C.: U.S. Goverment Printing Office, 1999), p. 25.

34. Belliner, *Substance Abuse,* p. 200.

35. MADD Statistics at http://www. Madd. org/stats/repeat.SHTMI.

36. Jean McBee Knox, *Drinking, Driving and Drugs* (New York: Chelsea House Publishers, 1998), p. 19.

37. U.S. Department of Health and Human Services, *The Household Survey of Drug Abuse* (Washington, D.C.: U.S. Government Printing Office, 1998).

38. Lloyd Johnston, Jerald Bachman, and Patrick O'Malley, *Monitoring the Future* (Ann Arbor, Mich.: University of Michigan, 1998).

39. Henry Krystal and Herbert A. Raskin, *Drug Dependence: Aspects of Ego Function* (Detroit: Wayne State Unversity Press, 1970), p. 65.

40. Alfred C. Lindesmith, *Addiction and Opiate* (Chicago: Aldine Publishing Co., 1968), p. 8.

41. National Institute on Drug Abuse, *Drug Abuse and Drug Abuse Research* (Rockville, Md.: National Institute on Drug Abuse, 1987).

42. Howard Abadinsky, *Drug Abuse: An Introduction* (Chicago: Nelson-Hall, 1989), p. 129.

43. Richard P. Rettig, Manuel J. Torres, and Gerald R. Garrett, *Manny: A Criminal Addict's Story* (New York: Houghton Mifflin, 1977), p. 210.

44. William Kornblum and Carolyn D. Smith, *Sociology in a Changing World* (New York: Harcourt College Publishers, 2000), p. 80.

45. U.S. Congress, 101st Session, *Anti-Drug Abuse Act of 1988, Public Law No. 100-690;* Sub-Title A-Death Penalty, Sec. 7001 (June 1, 1989).

46. Abadinsky, *Drug Abuse,* p. 106.

47. Phillip Shenon, "Administration Offers a Tough New Drug Bill," *New York Times,* May 17, 1990, p. A21.

48. Joshuah Shenck, "Doctors Given Federal Threat on Marijuana," *New York Times,* December 31, 1996, p. A1.

49. BBC News, "Anger Grows at U.S. Jail Population," February 15, 2000.

50. Editorial, "A Matter of Basic Justice," *Buffalo News,* February 28, 2000, p. B2.

51. Brenda Grantland, "L.A. Forfeiture Squads Kill California Millionaire," *F.E.A.R. Chronicles* 1, no. 5 (November 1992).

52. Eric Schlosser, "The Prison-Industrial Complex," *Atlantic Monthly* (December 1998).

53. Ibid., p. 12.

54. Robert Jackson, "Clinton Targets Youth in New Drug Plan," *Boston Globe,* February 26, 1997, p. A3.

55. Ernst Drucker, "Drug Prohibition and Public Health: Twenty-five Years of Evidence," *Public Health Reports* 114 (1999): 14–15.

THE MARK OF CAIN 14

CRIMINALS, CONVICTS, AND OFFENDERS

THE STIGMA OF ARREST IS NO DETERRENT

The legend of Cain and Abel demonstrates the horror all peoples derive from the ultimate crime, murder. The stigma associated with taking the life of another human being has not only extended to those who were regarded as murderers because they killed someone in their own group. That stigma has also devolved upon those who killed outsiders, even enemies. This is illustrated by "Manslayer Taboos" which have existed in many human cultures and exist today. Those who have killed are considered "impure" and are isolated from ordinary society until their purity can be restored by a variety of rituals. For example, on the island of Timor, which has been part of Indonesia since 1976, the leader of a victorious warrior expedition was forbidden to return at once to his home. Instead he had to spend two months in a special hut undergoing bodily and spiritual purification lest the ghosts of those he killed in war came to haunt the entire community.

In other communities among the South Pacific islanders special sacrifices were offered to the gods after a victorious head-hunting expedition so as to appease the soul of the dead whose heads had been taken. There are also those who hold a special dance accompanied by a song that laments the death of the slain man and his forgiveness is entreated.

Similar ceremonies existed among the natives of North America, of Africa, and of South America as well as the ancient Greeks. The Greeks demanded that someone who had committed involuntary homicide had to depart from his country for a year so that the anger of the dead man's spirit could cool off. The killer also had to offer sacrifices and undergo ceremonies of purification.[1]

We have seen those who kill others in war or by accident were nevertheless obliged to participate in some ritual that would allow them to return to the group. It is therefore easily understood that those who are held guilty of a crime carry a stigma with them from which they may never be able to escape. That stigma may be called "The Stigma of Conviction." Those who carry such a stigma find that their social and economic opportunities are limited in American life. Their status and role are forcibly changed so that it becomes necessary for those so labeled to seek the company of others who are also regarded as criminals. This permits each of the stigmatized outsiders to draw on the support of others in the same situation until the erstwhile stigma becomes a status symbol. William I. Thomas, one of the founders of American sociology, in pronouncing his famous dictum wrote this: "If men define situations as real, they are real in their consequences." This summarizes that being labeled a criminal has serious social consequences including the difficulty of ever removing a deviant label.[2] This indicates that unofficially we do not like to accept former convicts as rehabilitated and equal.

It is important to recognize that the stigma of criminal, offender, or convict need not always attach to someone who has actually committed a crime. An innocent person, convicted in a court or even by public opinion or in the media, also carries a stigma about him. In addition, people whose conduct is unknown except to themselves may well have done numerous deeds that would be stigmatized as crimes were they to come to the attention of the criminal justice system. Absent such recognition, many offenders are not so stigmatized because they do not carry a criminal label.

Those with the power to stigmatize, such as police, court officials, teachers, "experts," and other officials, have great power in determining who is an offender. In addition, bureaucrats "process" human beings according to certain rules that apply indiscriminately to those so handled, even if there is no basis for handling everyone in the same fashion.

This is illustrated by the numerous false convictions that are included in criminal justice procedures in this country every day. Great publicity is generally given those who are thought to have "beaten the system," and hardly any effort has been made until recently to publicize the degree of malfeasance in our law-enforcement community. In the past few years however, DNA tests have brought to light a number of cases of innocent people wrongly convicted. One of the few who escaped execution was Randall Dale Adams who had spent twelve years on death row but was finally released when new evidence proved his innocence. After spending all the years from 1976 to 1989 on death row, an appeals court finally admitted that the guilty verdict against Adams came after prosecutors suppressed evidence and used perjured testimony.[3] Likewise, Kevin Bird was released after serving twelve years in a Texas prison for a rape conviction that DNA tests later showed he could not have committed.[4]

Such false convictions are by no means rare. On the contrary, it can be reasonably estimated that at least 1 percent of the two million Americans now in prison are the victims of false convictions. That would mean that twenty thousand Americans are unjustly imprisoned, killed, or stigmatized by the officials of the criminal justice establishment every year. The *Chicago Tribune* discovered in a special report that since 1963 homicide convictions numbering 381 were overturned by appeals courts because of serious misconduct of prosecutors, including using false evidence or concealing evidence that suggested innocence.[5] Consequently the American Bar Association's House of Delegates resolved in 1997 that the death penalty be abolished in this country as it is administered in a "haphazard mass of unfair practices." [6]

These wrongful convictions serve to demonstrate that a stigma may attach to someone only because a label has been delivered to that person by the bureaucracy empowered to do so. The consequences of being so labeled are called "secondary deviance" by sociologists. "Secondary deviance" is distinguished from "primary deviance" in that the former consists of behavior that results from being so labeled. "Tertiary deviance" occurs when the stigmatized person accepts the role assigned him or her by a bureaucracy but rejects the stigma that is associated with that role because the subject of the label did not engage in the presumed behavior in the first place. This is exactly what happens to people who are falsely imprisoned, for they think and act very much like those who are justly imprisoned.[7]

Stigma leads to deviant identity. This means that the stigmatized will define himself as a deviant, i.e., a criminal or junkie or drunk. The process of acquiring a deviant identity consists of a social transformation in which the new self-image and new public definition of a person emerge. We have already seen how this is true of numerous people who have contributed nothing to their deviant identity except a physical or mental condition not under their control. Examples include people seen as overweight and those considered "crazy" which may or may not indicate mental illness.

That is of course not true of actual criminals, convicts, and delinquents. These are people who do indeed contribute to the stigma associated with them particularly if they engage in a criminal career. A criminal career refers to the sequence of crimes committed by some people who are socialized into a criminal social role. In that role they are encouraged to commit crimes again and again by others also engaged in crime and by the material advantages the criminal career has for them. For those committed to a criminal career it becomes important that they act according to the demands of their reference group so that a gang will expect each member to commit some or many crimes in order to prove membership and career orientation.[8]

The community also contributes to criminal careers because those who are arrested and run through the criminal justice system are thereby encouraged to continue along a criminal path. For example, an arrest on weapons charges can be viewed as a rite of passage in the same fashion as graduation from high school or the attainment of a driver's license. Such an arrest brings increased prestige to the convicted person among his peers in delinquency and promotes his social standing among them. One of the great errors made by the enforcers of the criminal justice system is the belief that the stigma of arrest is a deterrent. That is no doubt true for those holding middle-class values. It is not true for the deviant community. There, arrest and incarceration increases the social standing of the persons punished by authorities. Such punishments become a badge of honor among some young people and among adults committed to the criminal lifestyle.[9]

Therefore, criminal justice faces a dilemma as incarceration increases in this country so that now over two million Americans are imprisoned. Even as prison is used to deter some from committing crimes, others are actually encouraged by the criminal justice system to continue a criminal lifestyle. A number of studies have shown that institutionalized youths maintain close associations with other delinquent youths and persisted in delinquent behavior because of peer support.[10]

THE "STREET CULTURE"

The importance of the foregoing is that criminal or deviant behavior is not just the behavior of some maladjusted individuals but that it often takes place within a group so that there are some groups in American life who are actually organized around social deviance. These communities maintain their own values, their own norms or expectations, their own rewards and their own conduct. Joining such a deviant or criminal community cuts one off from conventional society. That removal from conventional society leads to accepting rewards from within the deviant group that has its own symbols of success and membership. Therefore gangs wear "colors" and have their own music and their own insignia.

There is in the United States a "street culture" of offenders who lack social stability and have no conventional sources of support or income. Included among such "street persons" are those who have only a minimal concern for obligations or commitments to others and whose interests and choices are mainly gambling, hard drug use, and heavy drinking. Sociologists Neil Shover and David Honaker present this interview as an example of the attitude of robbers who see their criminal activity as a right derived from a determination to access instant gratification. "I have a gambling problem and I . . . lose so much so I have to do something to get the cash to win my money back. So I go out and I rob someone." [11]

Those who commit such crimes again and again generally see the future as gloomy, depressing, and harsh. They see no point in long-range planning. Many are urban nomads who sleep in a different place every day. Even those who have a home spend most of their time on the streets. Included in the "cult of the streets" is the display of the latest status symbol, clothing and accessories. Such a display is designed to proclaim that the wearer has the money to equal the local drug dealer or other street aristocrat. The central motive of street criminals is self-aggrandizement driven by a desperation that dominates almost all of the offenders' lives. In this desire street offenders resemble many middle- and upper-class citizens who also seek to show off clothes and cars and otherwise participate in conspicuous consumption. The difference between street offenders and other citizens is, however, that street offenders will not spend money on mundane financial concerns, such as paying the rent. This suggests that unchecked spending by street criminals creates the very condition that drives them back to more street crime. Under constant pressure to generate more money and without any skills or without motivation to work in legitimate occupations, street criminals live in a cycle of criminal behavior and high spending. That cycle goes on and on until they are incapacitated by arrest and conviction or are too old to take the risks which theft, robbery, and burglary include. [12]

Almost all street criminals are unskilled and lack the education to get jobs that pay more than the minimum wage. Needing money for their lifestyle they see no alternative than to commit robbery or other street crimes that pay more and pay it faster than any employment available to an unskilled worker. Furthermore, normal employment requires that the employee accept authority and restrictions of all kinds. Normal work requires conformity to schedules and limits visiting and moving about. Normal work also requires that the employee come to work sober and alert. Yet, street culture rests on the conspicuous display of independence. Those who do what they please are seen as "cool," an attitude which conflicts directly with gaining an education or holding a legitimate job. One of the most persistent complaints by street criminals is that they cannot get a "good-paying job" that allows them "to be somebody." That complaint overlooks, of course, that many who hold such jobs underwent years of deprivation and hard work to achieve such a status. Street criminals want the rewards such employment provides but they do not want to postpone gratification to the future. In this new century there is hardly any employment for the unskilled as the electronic economy has made advanced education even more necessary than it has ever been. In fact, there is now a considerable lack of legal income options for those whose skills are limited. Furthermore, recent reductions in government-sponsored programs have marginalized precisely those who are at greatest risk of committing street crimes. Many persistent offenders know this and resign themselves to never finding a job. Crude manners, poor schooling, and an attitude not considered "nice" by employers prevent street people from ever finding employment. Yet, precisely the "not-nice" attitude is needed to survive on the streets.[13]

In sum, street culture includes the pursuit of drugs, a disdain for conventional living, a lack of future orientation, and an utter rejection of responsibility. That disdain goes together with an immense need to project an image of affluence by which street offenders are judged and which they and their cohorts believe proves that they have "made it." The function of that charade is to avoid staring failure in the face.[14]

Street crime, like almost all crime, is learned. The commission of crimes depends on knowing how to do the crime and how to live with being a criminal. Therefore, interaction with others who are already involved in crime is an important aspect of doing street robbery, burglary, auto theft, drug dealing, and a host of other offenses, including "white-collar" crime. Therefore, a low IQ, family problems, or personality characteristics do not ipso facto propel anyone into a life of crime. Edwin H. Sutherland, who may be regarded as the founding father of American criminology, has shown that to become a criminal it is necessary to interact with people already involved in that behavior. That is of course also true of all other occupations. Surely we cannot become professionals or business people without learning the techniques of doing this kind of work. Exactly that is true of criminal activities as well. Young criminals learn from others how to pick a lock, how to shoplift, how to obtain and use narcotics, how to steal and then sell a car, and how to rationalize and justify such actions.[15]

The stigma that results from delinquent and criminal activities is of course not unknown to those who engage in such conduct. It is impossible to live in America, or anywhere else, and not know that murder, rape, assault, larceny, burglary, and arson are condemned and in fact major felonies. Therefore, those who do these things must have some means of rationalizing their conduct. We are entitled to ask: "How do those who regularly persist in crime justify their mode of living?" Sociologists Gresham M. Sykes and David Matza explained in 1957 the techniques used by outsiders, by stigmatized people, and particularly by criminals in living with the stigma resulting from their deviant behavior and actions. Evidently stigma is much easier to bear when some method can be found permitting the stigmatized to live with the rejection that stigma implies. This means that many criminals ignore conventional expectations or norms because they view the law as a flexible suggestion or guideline but not an absolute command. Therefore, said Sykes and Matza, delinquents and criminals often deny responsibility for their actions and argue that their conduct was beyond their control. They blame slum conditions, poor opportunities, poverty, and other social factors for their failure to conform. Criminals also like to deny that any injury occurred. This argument claims that no harm was done. This argument is often used by female shoplifters who say that the department store can well afford some theft because prices are too high in the first place. There is also denial of the victim. If responsibility cannot be denied and harm did plainly occur, then the aggressor will often argue that the victim deserved to get hurt. This argument was used by the German people after World War II when it was widely claimed that the Jewish victims of mass murder brought this on themselves by numerous characteristics the perpetrators chose to attribute to their victims and all Jews. Many offenders also condemn the condemners. This technique of neutralization consists of claiming that those who condemn criminal behavior are even worse than the offender. This method of neutralization holds that all police are corrupt, that judges are low-down politicians, that probation officers are "on the take," and that prison officials are themselves criminals. Finally, Sykes and Matza discuss appeal to higher loyalties as a technique of neutralization. Here the offender argues that he committed his crimes for the good of the group to whom he is loyal. Many a heinous crime has been committed in the name of patriotism. In Northern Ireland numerous murders have been committed in the name of religion. In this country, gang members and racial bigots will use the most horrendous violence against a perceived out-group or enemies as good cause for any cruelty, including murder.[16]

An example of such violence is the murder rate among Mexican and Cuban Americans. Sociologist Ramiro Martinez has shown that homicide is the third most frequent cause of death among both of these groups precisely because their stigmatized, out-group experience leads them to aggression against each other. Martinez found that as the income gap within the Latino community increases, homicide increases as well. The reason for this is relative deprivation. Relative deprivation occurs when we become convinced that we have been deprived of something that should be ours because those who possess it are like us. *Relative deprivation* refers to the comparison people make between themselves and their reference groups. A *reference group* is a group of persons whose expectations or norms are meaningful to their members. Hence, the achievements of people within a group lead to a great deal more anxiety among nonachievers than the achievements of people one does not know or include in any reference group. It is not Bill Gates and his billions that worry a Latino immigrant. It is the success of another Latino who thereby makes the poor feel even poorer and even more rejected and stigmatized. This in turn leads to more violence by Latinos against one another.[17]

Homicide is always more frequent among the poor than among other economic groups because the stigma of poverty permits the poor to blame others for their situation so that aggression among the poor is other-directed. The reverse is true among members of the middle and upper classes. Suicide is more common among those with more income and more social prestige because those who have benefited from the social arrangements in which they live are more inclined to blame themselves rather than others for frustrations in their lives. Therefore, middle- and upper-class Americans are more likely to kill themselves rather than others.[18]

WOMEN IN PRISON

The stigma of being an outsider can lead to a great deal of violence and is responsible for a large share of the over twenty-three thousand killings in America every year. These killings are committed almost entirely by men. Not only murder but male crime rates generally are much higher than female crime rates. That is true in the United States and in all other countries. The reason for this may lie in part in biological differences but is also influenced by the social roles each gender must play. Uniform Crime Reports (UCR), the statistical summary of American crime published each year by the FBI, shows in detail how 80 percent of all complaints concerning criminal behavior concern men and only 20 percent involve women. The UCR arrest statistics also indicate that the overall male-female arrest ratio is about 3.5 male to 1 female offender and that for violent crimes the ratio is closer to 5 males to 1 female.[19]

Although the discrepancy between female and male crime rates remains large, there has been a considerable increase in the female arrest rate during the ten years ending in 1998. During that time, the male arrest rate increased 11 percent while that for females increased 40 percent. More recently, between 1993 and 1997 male arrests increased 6 percent while female arrests increased 19 percent. The arrest rate for teenage girls between 1993 and 1998 increased 25 percent while the arrest rate for teenage boys during the same period grew by only 11 percent.[20]

There has been some controversy among criminologists concerning the role the women's liberation movement has played in the increase of female crime. There is some support for the theory that women today are more often engaged in crime because they are now more assertive. Evidently, women are more willing to respond to provocation with violence than with the anxiety and depression so prevalent among their numbers prior to the women's liberation movement. There are others who deny that women are more violent than in prior years and claim that there is no association between economic development and female crime rates.[21]

One of the most popular beliefs concerning criminality is that strain in the form of frustration and anger is the cause of much aggression. A good case can be made for the assertion that females are more subject to strain and stress than is true of males. That argument is usually related to the observation that women must not only deal with the vagaries of employment but are also responsible for supplying the daily needs of their families. This means that many women must carry a "double burden." Nevertheless, women commit far fewer crimes than men despite their greater stress.[22]

There is a good deal of difference between the socialization of women and men. Men generally respond to criticism and frustration with aggression. Women usually internalize such stress and are more likely than men to blame themselves for difficulties in their lives. Hence women strike out only under extreme provocation so that at least one-half of all female violence is the product of victim-precipitated crimes.[23]

Women who are in prison for violent offenses generally grew up in violent homes and married in order to escape the violence of fathers who frequently were alcohol abusers. Those who then find that their husband is also violent feel utterly trapped and feel that they cannot escape the constant beatings and furious outbursts of their husband or live-ins. Such women have come from a parental home that was a prison, married into another violent prison, and finally are condemned to a state prison for killing their tormentor. Few of these women have ever been arrested before or have ever known any freedom. In the words of criminologist Carol Burke: "(Their) crime was the cataclysmic act in their lives, the first and perhaps last independent action they would ever take."[24]

Because expectations concerning female behavior differs from those concerning male behavior it is common for judges to punish women not only for their crimes but also for conduct contrary to the judge's belief concerning the role of women. The stigma that results from such punishments, i.e., incarceration, also stigmatizes the children of imprisoned women. This cannot be avoided because one in four adult women entering prison either are pregnant or gave birth to an infant within the previous twelve months. Therefore, some children are born in prison. These children are then either aborted, placed with relatives, placed into foster care, or put up for adoption. All of these "solutions" are of course extremely painful to the incarcerated mother and to her children, whom she may not see for years and who may then become utterly alienated from their mother.[25]

It has been estimated that 80 percent of incarcerated women are mothers. The frequency with which children are discussed by imprisoned mothers and the numerous pictures of children incarcerated women keep in their cells indicate the immense emotional meaning that separation has for these mothers. Many women feel that their families and their friends have abandoned them when they are sent to prison. This occurs just when these women are at the lowest point in their lives. Prisoners, and particularly female prisoners, are ashamed, lonely, depressed, and guilt-ridden because of their children. Their self-esteem is also severely affected by imprisonment. Family members can of course visit, send money, write, call, and guard the property of the imprisoned mothers. Therefore, visits from family are of the greatest importance to these women. There are, however, numerous institutional barriers to such visits, which even the most determined of relatives may not wish to confront. Many institutions are located in faraway rural areas that are hard to reach by relatives, particularly those who need to use public transportation. For example, the village of Attica, New York, where a large male prison is located is 400 miles from New York City, the home of most of the inmates there.

Other discouraging factors that create barriers to visits in prisons are the need to submit to searchers upon entering, being too poor to afford hotel expenses, or having work schedules that do not permit long absences. There are also "visitor unfriendly" situations in many prisons. There may be only one large room where all families gather at once and no privacy is afforded. Lack of children's toys or playgrounds creates real difficulties for those who must or want to bring children with them. Some prisons do not allow children to visit at all while many will not allow the visit of a child under eighteen. There are of course some prisons that allow conjugal visits, permit mothers to cook for their children, and include a policy of furloughs and halfway-house placements.[26]

One additional problem which affects both women and men in prison is homosexuality. There is very little reliable literature concerning female homosexuality in prison. It is fairly certain that homosexuality is even more prevalent in female prisons than in male prisons because so many of the women in the prisons have been so badly abused by men before their incarceration.

On entering prison, female prisoners find that the abuse that dominated their lives continues. The use of handcuffs, strip-down searches for contraband, and distinctive prison clothing are all designed to increase the sense of humiliation and stigma that all prisons provide. There are also medical examinations to discover venereal disease and psychiatric evaluations to determine the possibility of mental illness.

Extensive rules and regulations govern every prison. These serve to infantilize prisoners and make them entirely dependent on the staff. Prisoners generally understand that the purpose of all these rules and regulations is to diminish the maturity of the prisoner. An example of such rules is the requirement to recite the Lord's Prayer at bedtime. Most important in this connection is the lesson taught by the prison: incarcerated women have failed to meet their adult responsibilities. Inevitably, a contradiction appears in the treatment programs designed to educate women to meet these responsibilities. That contradiction is that prisoners are denied choice. Even the smallest detail of a prisoner's life is regulated. Prisoners are told when to get out of bed; what time they will eat; when they may read or write a letter; when they may watch television; and when they will go to bed. The rules continue to undermine self-esteem when prisoners are addressed as "girls" regardless of age, yet they are forced to address staff members as "Miss."

Finally, the arbitrary and capricious nature of parole boards wears down inmates' ability to become self-reliant and to plan for their release. This is true for both women and men and serves to defeat the rehabilitation of former prisoners in advance.[27]

VIOLENCE IN PRISON

The overwhelming number of inmates in American jails and prisons are men. It is therefore appropriate to ask whether the prisons as now constituted achieve the purpose of reducing crime and making life safer for the large, noncriminal majority. In view of the high incarceration rate in the United States, involving more than two million prisoners in 2000, it appears to some that the U.S. crime rate is down precisely because so many offenders are in prison. There is good reason to believe that this is in part true. It must not be overlooked, however, that the birthrate in the United States has declined significantly since 1964 when the nation experienced over twenty live births per one thousand population. In 2000 only fifteen children were born per every one thousand population, constituting a decline of 25 percent. Therein lies a major cause for the decline in the rate of violent crime since there are fewer sixteen- to twenty-six-year-old males in the population. It is of course this age group that commits most of the violent crimes.[28]

Abortion has also increased during the years since *Roe* v. *Wade* made this legal in 1972. At that time the number of legal induced abortions per one thousand women aged fifteen to forty-four was only thirteen. That number rose to twenty-four by 1990 and has remained at this level since then. Therefore, abortion has contributed to the falling violent crime rate.[29]

In any case, the violent crime rate in the United States was as low in 1999 as it had been in 1985 before the emergence of crack cocaine and its violent consequences. In fact, the national violent crime rate dropped 12 percent between 1998 and 1999 and had dropped 5 percent the previous year. Even as this drop in violent crime occurred, the rate of incarceration in the United States rose from a stable 110 per one hundred thousand in the mid-1970s and before to 445 per one hundred thousand persons, including women and juveniles. Among adult men it is now 1,100 per one hundred thousand. This huge increase in the prison population was achieved by criminalizing the use of drugs and numerous other forms of human conduct so that roughly a thousand new prisons and jails have been built in the United States during the past two decades.

The "raw material" of this prison-industrial complex are the poor, the homeless, the mentally ill, drug addicts and alcoholics. Nearly 70 percent of those in prison are illiterate and two hundred thousand suffer from some serious mental illness. Eighty percent of those in prison have a history of substance-abuse. One-half of all prisoners are of African descent, nearly one-half are of European descent, and a few are Asian.

The beneficiaries of all this are first the politicians who use the "tough on crime" issue to get elected. In addition, the prison-construction industry has made billions on the prison boom of the last few years. Then there are those areas of the country, such as the Adirondack area of New York, whose economy has been in decline for years and whose income depends now almost entirely on prison employment. There are also private prison corporations, such as the Corrections Corporation of America, that run prisons for profit and whose executives earn upward of $400,000 a year even as they trade their stock on Wall Street and their investors take home large dividends.[30]

Those who are locked into our prisons are expected to have learned from that experience. Politicians of all stripes claim that imprisonment solves the crime problem, particularly if the experience is harsh and painful. To that end several states have adopted "three strikes and you are out" laws. These laws force judges to hand three-time felons mandatory life sentences. Some states have eliminated "good time" laws* so that prisoners cannot be released before they have served their entire

---

*Laws designed to provide for early release on parole for those inmates who have demonstrated good behavior.

sentence. Even weight rooms and other physical exercises have been taken away from prisoners in some states while others have gone so far as to eliminate all educational opportunities. These changes in the treatment of prisoners are believed to influence prisoners to mend their ways and refrain from offensive behavior in the future. These alterations in punishments have received a great deal of media attention and seem to have vote-getting appeal. However, since legislators do not ask prisoners or prison officials whether their ideas work, a study by Patricia Van Voorhis, Sandra Lee Browning, and Marilynn Simon, professors at the University of Cincinnati, concerning the meaning of punishment for inmates illustrates the outcome of these recent measures.

This research discovered that the meaning of the prison experience is the same for maximum- and minimum-security inmates. The reason for this similarity is that minimum-security prisons house prisoners who lack much prison experience while maximum-security facilities have the most experienced prisoners. Therefore, the minimum-security prison includes as much deterrence for the inexperienced as the maximum-security prison holds for those who have been behind bars before. In both groups there are those who doubt that prison is a deterrent. Older inmates are less likely than younger inmates to see prison as a deterrent. Younger inmates with less of a prison record than older inmates view prison more often as a deterrent, or at least that is what they said to interviewers. Young, uneducated, and minority prisoners differ from other inmates in that they are more likely to believe they can get something out of the prison experience. Those who believe in the benefits of prison are generally illiterate but seek to learn to read in prison; many had no employment prior to arrest; and a good number are nonwhite and therefore forced to accept the most menial of jobs. These young, uneducated, minority members have very little work experience and usually no prior prison experience.[31]

All prisoners, and particularly young men, become the targets of homosexual rape and other forms of violence in American prisons. While public entertainment, in particular television movies, attribute prison violence to brutal guards, the principal and overwhelming amount of violence in prisons is inmate to inmate. Lee Bowker found that there are about ten attacks on inmates per year for every one hundred inmates in a Virginia prison. In another study, Matthew Silberman, professor of sociology at Bucknell University, reported a rate of thirty-three attacks per one thousand inmates, and Charles Couch and James Marquart, professors of sociology at Mississippi State University, found a similar rate of assault in eight Texas prisons. Large numbers of inmates are injured by assaults. Hans Toch, professor of criminology at the University at Albany and no doubt one of the foremost of American prison experts, wrote this in 1976: "Inmates are terrorized by other inmates, and spend years in fear of harm. Some inmates request segregation, others lock themselves in, and some are hermits by choice." [32]

Much of the violence in prison is produced by racial and ethnic gangs. Many of these gangs originated on the streets of American cities and continue their feuds inside the prisons. These gangs control the prison drugs, gambling, loan sharking, prostitution, extortion, and debt collection. These gangs also protect members from other gangs and furnish the membership with friends and associates. [33]

There is of course also prisoner-to-guard violence. This violence becomes very visible when there are riots; guards and other employees are taken hostage and some are injured and killed. Because riots can break out at any time, correctional officers do not carry weapons inside the prison since weapons could be seized by inmates. Riots often break out because an officer breaks up a fight or moves a prisoner to segregation. The possibility of an unexpected attack exists in the mind of all officers and employees in prison. The threat of violence is reinforced by verbal threats, thrown objects, and "accidents" such as the sudden fall of an officer down the stairs. [34]

There is yet one more form of violence in prison: guard-to-inmate violence. There are some guards who routinely use violence on prisoners and there are also "goon squads" in many prisons. Such squads consist of physically powerful officers who keep the prisoners "in line" and maintain order in the prison. Because prisoners routinely complain about officers' brutality, these complaints are seldom believed. Yet, there are numerous instances of guard brutality in every prison. [35]

JUVENILE DELINQUENCY

On March 7, 2000, California voters approved Proposition 21 which will send young offenders to adult courts and prisons and will also institute the death penalty for juveniles. Labeled a "war against children and youth" by its opponents, the California initiative reflects a widespread attitude among many Americans concerning the treatment of juvenile offenders in this country. That attitude displays a rejection of the special treatment given young offenders for the past one hundred years on the grounds that the juvenile-justice system appears to have failed and that therefore more extreme measures must be used to prevent and punish juvenile crime.

In light of these frequently held beliefs, the U.S. House of Representatives recently passed legislation that would give federal prosecutors nonreviewable discretion to try youths as young as fourteen in adult courts for both violent and nonviolent offenses. This practice already exists in Florida and has led prosecutors in that state to send as many juveniles to adult court as to juvenile court. Despite this practice Florida has a violent juvenile crime rate of 764 per 100,000 among youths aged ten to seventeen, a number that far exceeds the U.S. State Average Violent Crime Rate for children of the same age. That average is only 517 per 100,000.[36]

Nationwide 9,700 youths were tried in adult courts in 1998. Approximately 8 percent of prisoners in adult prisons are younger than twenty-one. Some of these prisoners are younger than seventeen. The risks youngsters face in adult prisons are a good deal greater than is true for adults. That includes the risks faced by young people in jails during pretrial detentions for offenses from which many are later exonerated. Youths are five times more likely to becoming a victim of rape when held in an adult facility than when held in juvenile detention. Youngsters in adult jails are also twice as likely to be beaten by staff and 50 percent more likely to be attacked with a weapon. The suicide rate of children in adult jails and prisons is more than seven times greater than it is for children held in juvenile facilities.[37]

Approximately 2.9 million persons under age eighteen are arrested in this country every year. Of these arrests 123,000 involve accusations of violent crimes, nearly 702,000 are arrests for property offenses, and all others are for "non-index" crimes ranging from forgery to disorderly conduct. An *index crime* is a crime included by the FBI in constructing an annual crime index from statistics related to murder, rape, assault, robbery, burglary, larceny, auto-theft, and arson. All other crimes are *non-index* crimes.

Juveniles who are arrested and tried in either children's facilities or adult courts often exhibit one or more of six characteristics that contribute to delinquent behavior and that are visible before delinquency actually occurs. These characteristics consist of persistent behavior problems during elementary school, the onset of aggression and/or drug use between the ages of six and eleven, antisocial parents, weak social ties between the ages of twelve and fourteen, membership in delinquent gangs, and drug dealing.[38]

In any one year about 1.7 million children are referred to juvenile court of whom about one-third are placed in a reform school, training school, or some other institution. These institutions allow the residents very little freedom because usually the school is on the campus of the institution and each resident must also contribute to the maintenance of the institution. This means that these reform schools are the equivalent of adult prisons and therefore have some of the same problems that adult prisons have. Violence, sexual assault, staff-resident conflict, and disciplinary difficulties of all kinds occur every day. In fact, fights and aggression are even more common in juvenile institutions than among adult institutions because younger people are emotionally more volatile than adults.

This volatility refers to lack of emotional control, which in turn has been related to offending behavior. Fear, anxiety, and embarrassment lead many young people into violence. Children who are institutionalized because of violent conduct are evidently more amenable to change than those who are incarcerated because of theft or burglary. Those who have committed violent acts are more likely to exhibit remorse for their actions and can be taught more self-control and to think before acting. Burglars and other property offenders show little remorse and come to see prison as an occupational hazard. This is true of young people as well as adults. Using the Gibbs Sociomoral Reflection Measure* researchers have found that the moral development of burglars was the lowest of all offenders. In fact, the link between delinquency and lower levels of moral reasoning has been supported by various studies because low moral reasoning is a prime crimogenic factor.[39]

Numerous studies since 1972 have demonstrated that about 6 percent of all delinquents are morally so deficient that they commit over 70 percent of the homicides, rapes, robberies, and aggravated assaults committed by all delinquents. This means, conversely, that 94 percent of all delinquents share 29 percent of all these violent crimes and that therefore the vast majority of delinquents are not violent. It is the chronic offender, then, who contributes most to delinquency statistics. It is therefore far more important and expedient for district attorneys and judges to focus on chronic offenders than on all offenders. It is the realization that a few commit most crimes while most folks commit few if any crimes that has led the criminal justice system to introduce the "three strikes and you are out" policies that result in life sentences for some repeat offenders.

In view of the eagerness shared by many citizens and by many employees in the criminal justice system to do something substantial concerning juvenile crime there are those who have suggested eliminating the juvenile courts altogether. These courts were first introduced into the criminal justice system when Cook County, Illinois, opened the doors of the first American juvenile court in 1899.[40] Since then American life has changed a great deal so that the juvenile courts have come under a great deal of criticism from those who see these courts as too lenient and those who claim that the courts do not adequately protect

---

*Developed by John Gibbs, professor of psychology at Ohio State University, this is a "personality profile" and general behavior inventory.

the rights of children. There are yet others who suggest that the juvenile courts and the adult courts should merge with a view toward having the juvenile-court model extend to the adult courts. This is suggested on the grounds that many adult crimes are neither more or less serious than juvenile crimes. Travis Hirschi and Michael R. Gottfredson claim that both juvenile and adult crime are the result of poor self-control and that therefore adults are as amenable to reform as are juveniles. Such a system, it is argued, would be more cost-effective and would also focus more resources on the prevention of criminal behavior.[41]

Another suggestion is that juvenile justice be "reinvented" by using four steps. These suggested "steps" are first that a public-health approach be used. This concerns placing greater emphasis on environmental factors that contribute to delinquent behavior. Second, knowledge about child development would be included in juvenile-court process. Third, the juvenile-court procedures would be changed to protect the legal rights of children in the same constitutional fashion as now applies only to adults. Fourth, the "whole child" would be treated by means of a comprehensive approach to youth problems.[42]

This brief outline of the position of women, men, and children involved in the criminal justice system demonstrates that those caught up in that system are indeed outsiders who must face the severe stigma of criminality, however labeled. It is significant that the stigma of criminality does not normally end when an offender has finished incarceration or probation or other punishments. The fact is that those who have once been tainted by the label of criminal or delinquent or convict continue to be viewed with a good deal of suspicion. When that suspicion is converted into a stigma it makes the readjustment of those once convicted very difficult.

Those who have been in prison are of course aware that their status as ex-prisoners gives them an identity in the eyes of others over which they have little control. Moreover, that identity dominates all other aspects of the ex-prisoner's biography once it becomes public. Sociologists call such an exceptionally powerful feature of a person's identity his "master status." It is precisely this kind of a negative master status that is called a "stigma." [43]

It is because of this stigma that juvenile courts were established because the proceedings of the courts do not allow the publication of the child-defendant's name thereby protecting him from the broader social effects of stigmatization. Of course, those who frequently come in contact with the juvenile courts will gradually acquire a reputation for delinquent behavior despite the secrecy surrounding these contacts. It is therefore the policy of some courts to remove frequent offenders from the jurisdiction of the court and to remand these offenders to social-work agencies. "Status offenders" are children who violate a law pertaining only to those under sixteen years of age. Examples are truancy or drinking alcohol.[44]

REHABILITATING THE STIGMATIZED

Adults, much more than children, face several problems after release from prison. These may be categorized as feeling estranged on reentry, unmet personal needs, and barriers to success.

Strangeness at reentry refers to the letdown many parolees and ex-convicts experience after several years of incarceration. The people they knew, and they themselves, have changed. Many have moved away, taken different jobs, or grown up. Many relatives and friends have become strangers and relationships have weakened or disappeared altogether. Furthermore, the ex-prisoner must now make his own decisions after years of doing only what he was told.

Unmet personal needs refers to such basic needs as housing, education, and most of all a job. It is in the area of employment that the ex-prisoner meets his greatest challenge. Many employers hesitate to hire a parolee or ex-convict for fear he will not be trustworthy. In addition, parolees cannot take any employment that requires a license. Licenses are denied ex-convicts. A good number of jobs require that the applicant give evidence of "good" moral character. All states restrict the right of former offenders to work as barbers, beauticians, or nurses. Civil service statutes also bar former offenders. Well-paying jobs will usually go only to people with no criminal record. Criminal justice occupations will not even accept someone with a juvenile delinquency record. Although these records are supposed to be sealed, such employers know because those who work in the criminal justice professions have friends among court personnel. In addition many juveniles are sent to adult courts. In view of all this, former prisoners need to decide whether they should lie on any job application or whether they should be satisfied with the most menial jobs available.

In view of all these difficulties, Ohio has instituted an Offender Job Linkage program which connects ex-offenders with Ohio businesses. This is facilitated by inviting business people to job fairs in prisons. These job fairs have made it possible for about 26 percent of inmates to find jobs upon release. All of this is made possible because Ohio has a prison work program that teaches prisoners a variety of skills useful on the outside. Ohio also has a strong educational program for inmates which ranges from accounting to auto-body workshops.

The federal government also runs a job-finding program administered by the Federal Prison Industry. This has resulted in the listing of job openings for ex-prisoners by some of America's most successful corporations. No doubt these efforts will continue and alleviate the difficulties of reintegrating an ex-prisoner into the community.[45]

There is yet another disability with which ex-offenders must contend. That is the loss of civil rights, i.e., the right to hold public office and the right to vote. In ten states anyone convicted of a felony loses these rights for life. In fifteen states civil rights are restored after an offender serves his full sentence and in the other states civil rights are returned after various requirements have been met.[46]

In sum, all of these difficulties constitute a severe stigma for the ex-offender so that many return to prison because they cannot surmount the barriers to a normal life that their conduct has provoked and that an unforgiving world imposes on them.

SUMMARY

In primitive societies and in technological societies, crime is stigmatized. Many a criminal never arrested is not stigmatized. Yet, innocent persons, convicted of a crime, are labeled criminals. Recent DNA testing has shown that numerous prisoners are in fact innocent. Nevertheless, the great majority of convicts contributed to their condition themselves.

There are professional criminals who live on the street and who cannot accept the routine of holding a job. Some of these people resort to constant criminal behavior such as robbery for their entire income. These chronic offenders use techniques of neutralization to defend their behavior.

There are considerable differences between women and men as to the amount and kind of crime each sex commits. There are also differences between the criminal conduct of adults and adolescents.

With two million Americans now in prison, politicians and others benefit from the employment and money that imprisonment provides outsiders. Currently a "get tough" attitude prevails in the American public, so that California, Florida and other states allow prosecutors and judges to send children to adult court where they are subject to adult punishments and adult prisons.

Labeling creates stigma. Therefore, those who are labeled criminals, convicts, ex-convicts, or juvenile delinquents become social outcasts who may then be prevented from gaining education, work, income, and other social benefits.

Conviction in a court of law and even accusations not proven lead to public condemnation. This is no doubt the most important part of the stigmatization process. Included in this process are status-reduction ceremonies such as a "hearing," a "trial," and the establishment of a public record of such a procedure. Sociologists refer to these transactions as "degradation ceremonies." These place the individual affected outside the legitimate order and outside the world of citizens of good standing.

The stigma of "ex-con" or prisoner or criminal redefines the whole person. People who carry the stigma of "criminal" are expected to be tough, mean, sneaky, dangerous, aggressive, and untrustworthy. It is of course quite possible that those so defined have none of the characteristics attributed to them by the stigma. Nevertheless, the attributes associated with the stigma are attached to them. Therefore, people react to the content of the label and not the person carrying the stigma. The significance of the stigma takes precedence over the behavior of the person affected. Sociologists use the term "retrospective reading" to refer to the process by which the stigmatized person's life is reviewed in light of the new label given to him. The new outcast status is then used to reinterpret his earlier life. Suddenly it is "found" that the newly labeled criminal was suspicious, withdrawn, unfriendly, and belligerent in his youth. Such reviews are used to insure the accuracy of the stigma now imposed on the subject.

Stigma also becomes a personal identity. The negative feedback of law-enforcement agencies will lead the stigmatized person to believe that he is as evil as the authorities say he is. Sociologists call this the "dramatization of evil." This means that the person becomes that which the traits that are associated with the stigma predict. It is for this reason that it is so difficult for former prisoners to reestablish a normal identity.

NOTES

1. James G. Frazer, *The Golden Bough: A Study in Magic and Religion* (New York: Macmillan Company, 1960), p. 249.

2. William I. Thomas, *The Child in America* (New York: Alfred Knopf & Co., 1928), p. 572.

3. Mark S. Warnick, "Feeling Free, Wrongly Jailed for Twelve Years, Randall Adams Is Having His Say," *Chicago Tribune,* June 28, 1991.

4. *New York Times,*(October 9, 1997), p. A18.

5. "Concealed Evidence Led to Wrongful Convictions," *Chicago Tribune,* January 15, 1999.

6. Richard P. Koch, "1997 Conference of Delegates—Approved Resolutions" (Chicago: American Bar Association, 1997), p. 1.

7. Edwin M. Lemert, *Human Deviance: Social Problems and Social Control* (Englewood Cliffs, N.J.: Prentice-Hall, 1972).

8. Thomas Scheff, *Being Mentally Ill: A Sociological Theory* (Chicago: Aldine Publishing Co., 1987), p. 87.

9. LaMar T. Empey, Mark C. Stafford, and Carter H. Hay, *American Delinquency: Its Meaning and Construction* (Belmont, Calif.: Wadsworth Publishing Co., 1999), p. 305.

10. Daniel Mears, Matthew Ploeger, and Mark Warr, "Explaining the Gender Gap in Delinquency: Peer Influence and Moral Evaluations of Behavior," *Journal of Research on Crime and Delinquency* 35 (1998): 251–66.

11. Neal Shover and David Honaker, "The Socially-Bounded Decision Making of Persistent Property Offenders," *Howard Journal of Criminal Justice* 31 (1992): 283.

12. Jack Katz, *Seductions of Crime: Moral and Sensual Attractions in Doing Evil* (New York: BasicBooks, 1988).

13. Shover and Honaker, "The Socially-Bound Decision Making," p. 290.

14. Richard T. Wright and Scott H. Decker, *Armed Robbers in Action* (Boston: Northeastern University Press, 1997), p. 44.

15. Edwin H. Sutherland and Donald R. Cressey, *Criminology*, 10th ed. (Philadelphia: J. B. Lippincott & Co., 1978), p. 80.

16. Gresham M. Sykes and David Matza, "Techniques of Neutralization: A Theory of Delinquency," *American Sociological Review* 22 (December 1957): 664–70.

17. Ramiro Martinez Jr., "Latinos and Lethal Violence: The Impact of Poverty and Inequality," *Social Problems* 43 (May 1996): 131–46.

18. Gerhard Falk, *Murder: An Analysis of Its Forms, Conditions and Causes* (Jefferson, N.C.: McFarland & Co., 1990), p. 90.

19. Federal Bureau of Investigation, *Crime in the United States* (Washington, D.C.: United States Government Printing Office, 1998).

20. Ibid., p. 219.

21. Roy Austin, "Recent Trends in the Male and Female Crime Rate: The Convergence Controversy," *Journal of Criminal Justice* 21 (1993): 447–66.

22. Gerhard Falk, *Sex, Gender and Social Change: The Great Revolution* (Lanham, Md., and New York: University Press of America, 1999), p. 250.

23. Lisa Broidy and Robert Agnew, "Gender and Crime: A General Strain Theory Perspective," *Journal of Research in Crime and Delinquency* 34 (1997): 275–306.

24. Carol Burke, *Vision Narratives of Women in Prison* (Knoxville: University of Tennessee Press, 1992), p. 8.

25. Lance Coutourier, "Inmates Benefit from Family Service Programs," *Corrections Today* 57, no. 5 (1995): 100–107.

26. Peter Breen, "Bridging the Barriers," *Corrections Today* 57, no. 7 (1995): 98–99.

27. Barbara H. Zaitzow, "Treatment Needs of Women in Prison," in *Turnstile Justice: Issues in American Corrections*, ed. Ted Alleman and Rosemary Gido (Upper Saddle River, N.J.: Prentice-Hall, 1998), p. 148.

28. Bureau of the Census, *Statistical Abstract of the United States* (Washington, D.C.: United States Government Printing Office, 1996), p. 9.

29. Borgna Brunner, ed., *Time Almanac 1999* (Boston: Time, Inc., 1999), p. 809.

30. Erich Schlosser, "The Prison-Industrial Complex," *Atlantic Monthly* (December 1998): 1.

31. Patricia Van Voorhis, Sandra Lee Browning, and Marilyn Simon, "The Meaning of Punishment: Inmates Orientation to the Prison Experience," *Prison Journal* 77 (1997): 73.

32. Hans Toch, *Peacekeeping: Police, Prisons and Violence* (Lexington, Mass.: Lexington Books, 1976), p. 47.

33. C. Ronald Huff and Matthew Meyer, "Managing Prison Gangs and Other Security Threat Groups," *Corrections Management Quarterly* 1 (fall 1997): 11.

34. Stephen C. Light, "Assault on Prison Officers: Interactional Themes," *Justice Quarterly* 8 (June 1991): 343.

35. Todd R. Clear and George F. Cole, *American Corrections*, 5th ed. (New York: West/Wadsworth, 2000), p. 262.

36. Jeffrey A. Butts and Adele V. Harrell, *Delinquents or Criminals: Policy Options for Young Offenders* (Washington, D.C.: Urban Institute, 1998), p. 6.

37. Kathleen Maguire and Ann L. Pastore, eds., *Sourcebook of Criminal Justice Statistics 1998* (Washington, D.C.: Bureau of Justice Statistics, 1998).

38. U.S. Department of Justice, Office of Juvenile Justice and Delinquency Prevention, *Juvenile Offenders and Victims: 1997 Update on Violence* (Washington, D.C.: U.S. Government Printing Office, 1998), p. 25.

39. Allison Dalkin and Sarah Skett, "The Young Offender Program," *Corrections Today* (February 1999): 64.

40. Dean Champion, *The Juvenile Justice System: Delinquency, Processing and the Law* (Upper Saddle River, N.J.: Prentice-Hall, 1998), p. 241.

41. Travis Hirschi and Michael R. Gottfredson, "Rethinking the Juvenile Justice System," *Crime and Delinquency* 39 (1993): 262–71.

42. Barry Krisberg, Ira M. Schwartz, and Edmund F. McGarrell, "Reinventing Juvenile Justice: Research Directions," *Crime and Delinquency* 39 (1993): 3.

43. Linda L. Lindsey and Stephen Beach, *Sociology: Social Life and Social Issues* (Upper Saddle River, N.J.: Prentice-Hall, 2000), p. 88.

44. Champion, *The Juvenile Justice System*, p. 42.

45. Timothy Mann, "Pride in the Name of Jobs," *Corrections Today* (October 1999): 114–16.

46. *New York Times*, October 23, 1998, p. A12.

"LOGOS," THE MEANING OF STIGMA AND STIGMATIZATION 15

THE PROTESTANT ETHIC AS A BASIS FOR STIGMATIZATION IN AMERICA

It has now been nearly a century since the great German scholar Max Weber published his famous and definitive study, *The Protestant Ethic and the Spirit of Capitalism*, in which he demonstrated that the Protestant ethic and its concomitant, individualism, are the core values of American society. This means that in these beginning days of 2001, behavior in the United States is judged by assuming that we are all responsible for our own actions, social standing, and achievements, or lack thereof. Consequently the root of stigmatization in America lies in the perceived or assumed discrepancy between that core value and the perceived or assumed deviation from that norm (expected behavior).[1] For example, it is expected in this country and at this time that we maintain a socially determined minimum level of bodily cleanliness, that we eat with implements and not our hands, that we conduct our bodily functions in private, and that we display at least a minimum of courtesy toward others. Failure to remain within these norms leads to criticism if not ostracism and major deviations from expected behavior can lead to imprisonment and even death.

We have therefore learned in this volume that both ascribed and achieved stigma in twenty-first-century America are produced by the inability of many of us to live in conformity with the publicly proclaimed norms taught in our schools, through our media, and in informal communication (i.e., gossip and innuendo). Conformity here means adherence to the teachings of the sixteenth-century theologian John Calvin (1509–1564) whose doctrines were the very foundation of the ethics imposed on all citizens in the original Massachusetts Bay Colony founded by the Puritan English immigrants who came here on the *Mayflower* in 1620.

Some may believe that the ethics of those who lived and flourished nearly four hundred years ago could not possibly have any influence on us now. Yet, that is precisely the case. Religion and philosophy leave lasting impressions on innumerable generations. The evidence for this is not only the history of Christianity and its mother, Judaism, but the yet older religions of the East such as Hinduism. Moreover, the philosophical contributions of Plato (427–347 B.C.E.) and so many other Greek thinkers before and after him are even now very much part of the American school curriculum. Sociologist Gerhard Lenski has shown in his excellent study *The Religious Factor* that the Protestant ethic is very much alive, not only among American Protestants but among Catholics and Jews as well.[2]

That ethic is an ideology that includes the belief that individual hard work leads to success and that lack of success is caused by moral failings, self-indulgence, and a lack of self-discipline. Those who believe these doctrines will therefore also believe that any success they may have is attributable to them and that they have a great deal of control over their own lives. Therefore, Americans are likely to take credit for any outcomes in their lives which can be viewed as successful and generally approved. Consequently it is evident that those among us who deviate from the Protestant ethic will be stigmatized and that the subscribers to that ethic, i.e., most Americans, will severely reject those who deviate from these norms the most. Hence, members of stigmatized groups are seen as violating traditional American values.[3] It is therefore reasonable to hold that stigmatized Americans will blame themselves even as they are blamed by others for their shortcomings, be they real or imagined.

Although in this book we have distinguished ascribed and achieved status, those who judge others and stigmatize them know not of such differences. Those who are stigmatized by their own families by reason of sexual orientation, overweight, or mental retardation will experience stigma as well as those who "brought it on themselves" such as high achievers, the homeless, or immigrants.

Now it is evident that "high achievers" differ radically from homosexuals as designated targets for rejection and stigma. It is of course possible, and even commonplace that a "high achiever" is also a homosexual and can therefore be stigmatized twice. However, the reasons for the rejection of the homosexual are not the same as the reasons for the rejection of the "high achiever." Let us consider the situation of the homosexual first.

Surely, the Protestant Ethic which we have just discussed is based upon the Bible and its teachings. In fact, the Puritans and other Protestants sought to anchor their religious beliefs in the ancient Hebraic tradition in an effort to "skip over" Roman Catholicism to the extent possible. This led the early Protestants to have a considerable interest in the Hebrew language, a language which Luther learned so that he could thereafter translate the Five Books of Moses, the Prophets, and the Writings into German.[4]

Included in that Bible are a number of references to homosexuality. These references are not merely negative but condemnatory. Strong language, such as "abomination," is used in the Judeo-Christian scriptures concerning homosexual practices. For example, in Leviticus 20, which deals in the main with sexual practices, verse 13 is translated: "And if a man lie with mankind, as with womankind, both of them have committed an abomination : they shall surely be put to death. . . ."[5]

In other words, those who take the Pentateuch literally believe that homosexual conduct deserves the death penalty. This may be appalling to us, but it was assumed as right and true among the Puritans of New England in the 1600s. Therefore, the stigmatization of homosexuals is the product of the Judeo-Christian tradition even if that tradition has been greatly altered and weakened in present-day, secular America.

Indeed there are innumerable Americans who have never read the book of Leviticus. However, beliefs remain long after their source has become obscure because these beliefs are also incorporated in the popular literature, media entertainment, novels, jokes, and hence, common assumptions. Since there are cultures, such as ancient Greece, where homosexuality carried no stigma it is evident that the rejection of homosexuals is learned and culturally induced.

The same may be said of people who are overweight or who are retarded. Both can become the targets of the Puritan mind as the first is seen as overindulgent and a glutton, and the second is seen as useless albeit not because of his own doing. In all our examples, whether the mentally ill or the homeless, whether the immigrant or the alcoholic, stigma is attached to them because the Puritan or Protestant ethic demands it and produces it.

STIGMATIZATION AND THE WESTERN TRADITION

The Protestant, Puritan ethic is not the only source of values in America. The other source is the Western Tradition. That tradition began in ancient Greece and was kept alive throughout the ages until it reached America with Thomas Jefferson and Thomas Paine. It is that tradition which explains how high achievers are stigmatized along with prostitutes and criminals.

The answer to such a seeming riddle lies in the contradictory message that this ethic projects. Even as it demands conformity to a set of theological dictums, the Protestant ethic also promotes the individual as the final arbiter of his own fate. In accord with Luther who denied *ex cathedra non sallus est* (outside the church there is no salvation), who insisted that salvation comes from personal Bible reading and not from the church, the Puritans demanded both conformity and individual responsibility. One of the true differences between Roman Catholicism and Protestantism is the willingness of the Roman church to be the agent for "salvation" for its followers. The church of Luther would not allow such an agency. Therefore, individualism, self-reliance, and secularism derived from Luther despite his denunciation of all of these beliefs. It is well known that Luther opposed the peasant revolt that occurred in his own lifetime because he supported monarchy despite his religious message.

The Western tradition as applied to America gave that tradition a unique opportunity to test itself. It was in the United States and Canada that those who were dissatisfied with the Puritan east went west "with a rifle in one hand and a plow in the other." A good description of these pioneers may be found in Robert Caro's biography of Lyndon Johnson who was born in Texas in 1908, the son of migrants from Tennessee who literally fought Native Americans while farming in the virgin land of their adopted state.[6] The experiences of the Johnson family and millions of others with similar histories led to a belief, still common in America today, that exceptional ability is somehow suspect and undemocratic. Many Americans are at heart "levelers," a term used in sixteenth-century England for the followers of John Lilburne who would not recognize any lawful authority and declared that no government had more authority than he had himself.[7]

Therefore, high achievers appear to a good many Americans as arrogant, undemocratic, and un-American. If "all men are created equal" then Pete Rose is suspect because he is not equal. He is better at baseball than most anyone else. If all men are in fact equal then "eggheads" are suspect because they read too much, use foreign-sounding words, title themselves "editor" or "professor," and seem to want to "lord it over us." That is why we call everyone by his first name at second meeting. The Western tradition demands it. This then leaves us with a conflict which runs through all of our history. We are both repressive Puritans who know that "there ought to be a law against that" and liberty-loving followers of Thomas Jefferson who denounced the clergy of all denominations at every turn and viewed himself a deist as was his contemporary Benjamin Franklin.[8]

DIVERSITY AND IMMIGRATION—
THE WEAKENING OF THE
PROTESTANT ETHIC

The Protestant ethic is a western European tradition. Therefore, the Protestant, white, western European population which constituted the vast majority of Americans during the seventeenth, eighteenth, and nineteenth centuries laid the foundations of the American value system. This means that religion, literature, folklore, and all aspects of popular culture have supported the Protestant ethic and continue to do so even now.

Nevertheless, and despite what is learned in every American grade school, a weakening of that ethic has occurred during the twentieth century. That reduced influence on American thinking which has so long dominated the American psyche came about as the diversity of the American population increased, particularly after 1890.

Immigration historians call the western European immigration, which predominated before the end of the nineteenth century, the "old" immigration. More than 60 percent of these western Europeans came from England, 14 percent came from Scotland, and the others were Dutch or Scandinavian or German. After 1890, however, eastern European immigrants predominated. In fact, in 1896 the Catholic and Jewish immigrants from Poland, Russia, and Italy increased so much that they outnumbered the immigrants who came that year from western Europe. As a consequence of this immigration, in 1980 only 22 percent of Americans were of English descent. Others who were almost entirely of Protestant origin were and are the Scottish and Scandinavian segments of American society. Indeed, 21 percent of Americans are of German origin but one-half of the German population in Germany now is Catholic as are their descendants in the United States. People of Irish descent, almost all Catholics, constituted 17 percent of all Americans in 1980. More Catholics had come from Italy and Poland in the early part of the century so that they and our Mexican population at that time together accounted for another 11 percent of people with a Catholic heritage. Evidently then, Americans of Protestant conviction were being challenged by a large number of non-Protestants. These non-Protestants also included some five million Jews.[9]

It has been observed that the Catholic population of the United States, which now numbers about sixty million, has accepted Protestant values in the sense that Catholics, and also Jews, have adopted the Protestant ethic for themselves. To the extent that behavioral assimilation is necessary in order to succeed in American public life, that may be the case. However, structural assimilation, which included the core beliefs of a person or family, is not so easily attained by people of different origins so that the Protestant ethic is by no means supported as much by our large non-Protestant population as it once was practiced by the nearly total WASP group who dominated American life until the middle of the twentieth century.

There are in the United States about thirty-three million people of African descent. In 1980 there were twenty-one million people of African descent in this country constituting 9 percent of the population at that time. While African Americans are almost all Protestants, they do not share in the Protestant ethic to any large extent, not only because the slavery experience tore their families apart, but also because many view the conduct and the beliefs of the white majority with disdain in view of the oppression they have experienced for so many years.

Since 1980 there has been yet another shift in the U.S. immigration pattern. In the past twenty years almost five million people have come to America from Asia (Japan, China, Korea, India, Pakistan, and the Middle East). Very few of these people are Christians so that the Protestant ethic is unknown to them.

In sum, these developments are a major cause for the weakening of the Protestant ethic in the United States so that the acceptance of deviance from that fundamental system of values is related to attitudes and beliefs which were not Protestant in the first place. Add to this the fact that so many Americans are now members of minorities of every kind, whether religious, ethnic, or racial, it is therefore in the self-interest of all of these people to accept other minorities, including homosexuals, Native Americans, overweight people, or those who are homeless.

Diversity rules. Uniformity is questioned and stigmatization of the "outsider" is more difficult to attain as almost anyone may be an outsider in American society at the beginning of the twenty-first century.

THE RISE OF TECHNOLOGY AND THE WEAKENING OF THE PROTESTANT ETHIC

Our argument is that stigma is attached to those who digress from the core values of any society and that the American core values were and are determined by the Protestant ethic of the seventeenth century. However, as diversity of the American population has increased, that core value has weakened and a greater acceptance of those stigmatized is now occurring. This new acceptance is not only related to the diversity of the American population but also to the immense increase in technology and science as experienced during the last quarter of the twentieth century.

A belief in science and its benefits is so common in America today that those few fundamentalists who still deny evolution are viewed as "freaks" and "crazies" by the overwhelming majority of Americans. While the Scopes "monkey trial" of 1925 represented the strength of the Protestant ethic of that time, such a trial is truly impossible today despite the effort of some citizens of Kentucky to include "creation science" in the curriculum of their schools. Science, not fundamentalism, rules the thought processes of America today. Therefore, stigmas as we have known them are being questioned by scientifically minded Americans who subscribe to the dictum of noted French philosopher René Descartes, "*De omnibus dubitandum*" or "doubt everything."

Science does not easily lend itself to the unquestioned acceptance of stigma or anything else. The reason for this lies in the nature of science. That nature consists first of *universalism* which holds that the truth of any proposition must be determined by the impartial criteria of the scientific method and not by some unsubstantiated belief or dictum of this or that theologian. A second aspect of the nature of science is its *common ownership*. This means that scientific findings are published and available to everyone. Therefore, stigmatizing others has become more difficult than ever before. It is almost impossible now to disregard scientific facts concerning those who are obese or homosexual or retarded when that information is public property and is widely disseminated. A third aspect of scientific thinking is disinterestedness. This means that scientific observations are unbiased and not influenced by the prejudices of the day. Therefore, on these grounds alone, it is hard to hang on to prejudices which stigmatize some people when unequivocal evidence contradicts the prejudice. It is for this reason that the science of sociology has been the most effective enemy of stigmatization because sociology will not succumb to mere beliefs or finger-pointing but insists on relying only on social facts.

THE FUNCTION OF STIGMA

We have seen in the first chapter that despite the weakening of stigma in American society because of diversity and technology, it is here to stay. Stigmatization is a social fact and will always be with us. To speak of "good" or "bad" stigma is as fruitful as speaking of "good" or "bad" gravity. The latter is a physical fact that has no moral attributes and the former is a social fact that is equally impervious to any evaluation in terms of ethics or morals.

Stigmatization serves the function, i.e., anticipated consequence, of furnishing every human group with the social solidarity needed to insure the group's survival. As Émile Durkheim has shown and we have already discussed, "the establishment of a sense of community is facilitated by a class of actors who carry a stigma *and are termed deviant.*"[10]

It is therefore certain that someone will always be stigmatized in any and all human groups. Stigmatization permits the division of any group into insiders and outsiders. Hence, "insiders" depend on the existence of "outsiders" who create a boundary that permits the insider to know who belongs, who does not belong, and what is right or legitimate and what is not. This means that stigmas have function for every society and will therefore always be with us.

Because social solidarity is so important for the survival of any society, we can anticipate that some groups of Americans will always carry a stigma. No doubt there are groups of stigmatized persons who will not carry a stigma in the future. It is most likely that homosexuals, racial minorities, the single, and the old will be relieved of the prejudices now affecting them. Others, however, such as the retarded, mentally ill, prostitutes, and the homeless will continue to be viewed as outsiders in American culture because their stigma is as important to social solidarity in this century as the stigmatization of European Jews was in Christian society for nineteen centuries.

NOTES

1. Max Weber, *The Protestant Ethic and the Spirit of Capitalism* (1904; reprint, New York: Scribner Publishing Co., 1958).

2. Gerhard Lenski, *The Religious Factor* (Garden City, N.Y.: Doubleday and Co., 1961).

3. M. Biernat, T. K. Vescio, and S. A. Theno, "Violating American Values: A 'Value Congruence Approach,' to Understanding Original Attitudes," *Journal of Experimental Social Psychology* 32 (1996): 387–410.

4. Gerhard Falk, *The Jew in Christian Theology* (Jefferson, N.C., and London: McFarland & Co., 1992), p. 62.

5. Lev. 20:13.

6. Robert Caro, *The Years of Lyndon Johnson* (New York: Alfred Knopf, 1983).

7. André Morois, *A History of England* (New York: Grove Press, Inc., 1958), p. 312.

8. John M. Robertson, *A Short History of Free Thought* (New York: Russell and Russell, 1957), p. 376.

9. U.S. Bureau of the Census, *Ancestry of the Population by State, 1980* (Washington, D.C.: U.S. Government Printing Office, 1983), p. 2.

10. Émile Durkheim, *The Rules of the Sociological Method* (New York: Free Press, 1964), p. 68.

BIBLIOGRAPHY

Abadinsky, Howard. *Drug Abuse: An Introduction.* Chicago: Nelson-Hall, 1989.

Adams, David Wallace. *Education for Extinction.* Lawrence: University Press of Kansas, 1995.

Adler, Selig. *The Isolationist Impulse.* New York: Collier Books, 1996.

Adler, Ursula. *A Critical Study of the American Nursing Home: The Final Solution.* Lewiston, N.Y.: Edwin Mellen Press, 1991.

Albrecht, Gary L., Vivian G. Walker, and Judith J. Levy. "Social Distance from the Stigmatized." *Social Science and Medicine* 6, no. 4 (July 1982): 39.

Aldersey-Williams, Hugh. "New for Old." *New Statesman* 28 (May 10, 1999): 39.

Allen, Donald M. "Young Male Prostitutes: A Psychosocial Study." *Archives of Sexual Behavior* 9, no. 5 (1980): 400.

Allport, Gordon W. *ABC's of Scapegoating.* New York: Anti-Defamation League of B'nai B'rith, 1969.

Alston, Philip. *The Best Interests of the Child.* Oxford: Clarendon Press, 1994.

American Broadcasting Co. *Turning Point* (television program). November 6, 1996.

American Indian Historical Society. *The American Indian Reader: Literature.* San Francisco: American Indian Historical Society, 1973.

Anderson, Carol M., and Susan Stewart. *Flying Solo: Single Women in Mid Life.* New York: W. W. Norton & Co., 1994.

Angermeyer, N. C. "Normal Deviance—Changing Norms under Abnormal Circumstances." In P. Pichot et al., *Psychiatry, The State of the Art.* vol. 7. *Epidemiology and Community Psychiatry,* 473–79. New York: Plenum Press, 1983.

Asch, Samuel E. "Forming Impressions of Personality." *Journal of Abnormal and Social Psychology* 4 (1946): 258–90.

Ashburn, Albert, and Gerald Gordon. "Features of a Simplified Register in Speech to Elderly Conversationalists." *International Journal of Psycholinguistics* 8, no. 3 (1981): 7–31.

Associated Press. "Seattle Police Head Quits After WTO." December 7, 1999.

Atkins, Robert. *Dr. Atkins' New Diet Revolution.* New York: Avon Books, 1997.

Austin, Roy. "Recent Trends in the Male and Female Crime Rate: The Convergence Controversy." *Journal of Criminal Justice* 2 (1993): 447–66.

Averett, S., and S. Korenman. "Black-White Differences in Social and Economic Consequences of Obesity." *International Journal of Obesity* 23 (February 1999): 73.

Bagley, Sharon, and Andrew Murr. "The First Americans." *Newsweek* (April 26, 1999): 56.

Bailey, Thomas A. *The American Pageant.* Boston: D.C. Heath & Co., 1961.

Barker-Benfield, G. C. *The Horrors of the Half-Known Life.* New York: Harper and Row, 1976.

Baroff, George S. *Mental Retardation.* New York: Harper & Row, 1986.

Barrows, Sydney Biddle. *Mayflower Madam.* New York: Ivy Books, 1986.

Barry, Kathleen. *The Prostitution of Sexuality.* New York: New York University Press, 1995.

Barry, Skip. "Homeless at Fifty." *Commonweal* 26, no. 8 (1999): 2.

Bassuk, Ellen. "The Homeless Problem." *Scientific American* 251 (July 1984): 40–45.

Baym, Nina. "At Home with History: History Books and Women's Sphere before the Civil War." *Proceedings of the American Antiquarian Society* 101, no. 2 (October 1991): 275–95.

BBC News. "Anger Grows at U.S. Jail Population." February 5, 2000.

Beard, Mary, and John Henderson. "With This Body I Thee Worship: Sacred Prostitution in Antiquity." *Gender and History* 9, no. 3 (November 1997): 480.

Beck, Roy. *The Case Against Immigration.* New York: W. W. Norton & Co., 1996.

Becker, Howard S. *Outsiders: Studies in the Sociology of Deviance.* New York: Glencoe Press, 1963.

——. *The Other Side.* New York: Free Press, 1964.

Behrendt, Patricia F. *Oscar Wilde: Eros and Aesthetic.* New York: St. Martin's Press, 1998.

Bellavia, Charles W., and Paul A. Toro. "Mental Disorder Among Homeless and Poor People: A Comparison of Assessment Methods." *Community Mental Health Journal* 35, no. 1 (February 1999): 57–67.

Belliner, Karen, ed. *Substance Abuse Source Book.* Detroit: Omnigraphics, Inc., 1996.

Bendix, Reinhard. *Max Weber: An Intellectual Portrait.* Berkeley: University of California Press, 1962.

Bennett, Judith M., and Ann M. Froide. *Singlewomen in the European Past.* Philadelphia: University of Pennsylvania Press, 1999.

Berger, Thomas R. *A Long and Terrible Shadow.* Seattle: University of Washington Press, 1997.

Berkman, Cathy S., and Gail Zinberg. "Homophobia and Heterosexism in Social Workers." *Social Work* 42, no. 4 (July 1997): 319–32.

Bernstein, Nina. "An Uneasy Coexistence: Tensions between Town and Shelter Flow Both Ways." *New York Times,* May 4, 1999, p. B2.

———. "Mayor Acts on Complaints Over City's Upstate Men's Shelter." *New York Times,* April 4, 1999, p. B2.

———. "With a Job, Without a Home." *New York Times,* March 4, 1999, p. B2.

Beyerchen, Alan D. *Scientists under Hitler.* New Haven, Conn.: Yale University Press, 1977.

Biddle, Stuart. "Exercise and Psychosocial Health." *Research Quarterly for Exercise and Health* 66, no. 4 (1995): 292–97.

Bining, Arthur C. *A History of the United States.* New York: Charles Scribner's Sons, 1950.

Birenbaum, Arnold. "The Recognition of Acceptance of Stigma." *Sociological Symposium* 7 (1997): 5–22.

Blau, Bruno. *Das Ausnahmerecht für die Juden in Deutschland 1933–1945.* Düsseldorf: Kalima Druck, 1965.

Blazer, David, and Edward Palmore. "Religion and Aging in a Longitudinal Panel." *Gerontologist* 6 (1976): 82–85.

Bogardus, Emory S. "Comparing Racial Distance in Ethiopia, South Africa and the United States." *Sociology and Social Research* 52, no. 2 (January 1958): 40–60.

———. "Measuring Social Distance." *Journal of Applied Sociology* 9 (1925): 2199–2308.

Booth, Cathy, and Michael Harrington. "Good Guy or Dirty Word?" *Time* 36, no. 22 (November 26, 1990): 79.

Boswell, John. *The Marriage of Likeness: Same-Sex Unions in Pre-modern Europe.* London: HarperCollins, 1995.

Brecht, Martin. *Martin Luther: Die Erhaltung der Kirche.* Stuttgart: Calwer Verlag, 1987.

Breen, Peter. "Bridging the Barriers." *Corrections Today* 57, no. 7 (1995): 98–99.

Broidy, Lisa, and Robert Agnew. Gender and Crime: A General Strain Theory Perspective." *Journal of Research in Crime and Delinquency* 34 (1997): 275–306.

Brooke, James. "Gay Man Dies From Attack, Fanning Outrage and Debate." *Washington Post,* March 5, 1999.

Brunner, Borgna, ed. *The Time Almanac 1999.* New York: Information Please, 1999.

Bullough, Vern, and Bonnie Bullough. *Women and Prostitution; A Social History.* Amherst, N.Y.: Prometheus Books, 1987.

Bullough, Vern, Bonnie Bullough, and R. Smith. "Masculinity and Femininity in Transvestite, Transsexual and Gay Males." *Western Journal of Nursing Research* 7, no. 3 (1985): 37–332.

Bullough, Vern L., Olga M. Church, and Alice P. Stein. *American Nursing: A Biographical Dictionary.* New York: Garland Press, 1988.

Bunzel, Joseph H. "Concept, Meaning and Treatment of Gerontophobia." *Zeitschrift für Alternsforschung* 25, no. 1 (January 25, 1997): 5–9.

Bureau of the Census. *1990 Census of Population: Social and Economic Characteristics.* Washington, D.C.: U.S. Government Printing Office, 1990.

———. *Statistical Abstract of the United States.* Washington, D.C.: United States Government Printing Office, 1996.

Burke, Carol. *Vision Narratives of Women in Prison.* Knoxville: University of Tennessee Press, 1992.

Burt, Martha R. *Over the Edge: The Growth of Homelessness in the 1980s.* New York: Russell Sage Foundation, 1992.

Butler, Robert N. *Why Survive? Being Old in America.* New York: Harper & Row, 1975.

Butts, Jeffrey A., and Adele V. Harrell. *Delinquents or Criminals: Policy Options for Young Offenders.* Washington, D.C.: Urban Institute, 1998.

Bytheway, William. *Ageism.* Buckingham: Open University Press, 1995.

Caetano, Raul. "Public Opinion about Alcoholism and Its Treatment." *Journal of Studies on Alcohol* 48, no. 2 (March 1987): 57.

Cahill, Joseph B. "Credit Cards Invade a New Market Niche: The Mentally Disabled." *Wall Street Journal,* November 10, 1998, p. 1.

Cameron, Paul, and Kirk Cameron. "What Proportion of Newspaper Stories about Child Molestation Involves Homosexuals?" *Psychological Reports* 82 (June 1998): 863–97.

Cancian, Francesca M. *Love in America: Gender and Self-Development.* New York: Cambridge University Press, 1987.

Caputo, Richard K. "Receipt of Child Support by Working Single Women." *Journal of Contemporary Human Services* 77, no. 10 (December 1996): 615–25.

Carnegie Foundation for the Advancement of Teaching. "Native Americans and Higher Education: New Mood of Optimism." *Change* (January/February 1990): 29.

Cash, T. F., and Ted Pruzinsky. *Body Images: Development, Deviance and Change.* New York: Guilford Press, 1990.

Chadsey-Rusch, Janis, and Patricia Gonzalez. "Analysis of Directions, Responses, and Consequences Involving Persons with Mental Retardation in Employment and Vocational Settings." *American Journal of Mental Retardation* 100, no. 5 (March 1996): 481–592.

Chambers, Stacey. "How Any Person on the Street Can Help a Street Person." *Humanist* 59, no. 1 (1999): 2–26.

Chambers-Schiller, Lee. *Liberty: A Better Husband.* New Haven, Conn.: Yale University Press, 1984.

Champion, Dean. *The Juvenile Justice System: Delinquency, Processing and the Law.* Upper Saddle River, N.J.: Prentice-Hall, 1998.

Christie, Nils. "Conflict as Property." *British Journal of Criminology* 17 (1977): 1.

Churchill, Ward. *Fantasies of the Master Race.* Monroe, Maine: Common Courage Press, 1992.

Clad, James C. "Slowing the Wave." *Foreign Policy* 95 (summer 1994): 139.

Clear, Todd R., and George F. Cole. *American Corrections.* 5th ed. New York: West/Wadsworth, 2000.

Clements, Marcelle. *The Improvised Woman: Single Women Reinventing Single Life.* New York: W. W. Norton & Co., 1998.

Clifton, James A. "Cultural Fictions." *Society* 27, no. 4 (1990): 19.

Collins, M. E. "Body Figure Perceptions and Preferences among Pre-adolescent Children." *International Journal of Eating Disorders* 10 (1991): 199–208.

Comerford, Anthony W. *Substance Abuse and Cost Savings to Business, Fact Sheet #6.* Rockville, Md.: Center for Substance Abuse Treatment, 1997.

Commonwealth of Pennsylvania. *Pennsylvania Homeless Student Initiative.* Harrisburg: Pennsylvania Department of Education, 1989.

"Concealed Evidence Led to Wrongful Convictions." *Chicago Tribune,* January 5, 1999.

Congregation for the Doctrine of the Faith. *Letter to the Bishops of the Catholic Church on the Pastoral Care of Homosexual Persons.* London: Catholic Truth Society, 1986.

Cooley, Charles H. *Human Nature and the Social Order.* New York: Schocken Books, 1964.

Cooper, Charlotte. *Fat and Proud: The Politics of Size.* London: Women's Press, 1998.

Cooper, James Fenimore. *The Best-Known Works of James Fenimore Cooper.* New York: Book League of America, 1942.

Cormack, Stephanie, and Adrian Furnham. "Psychiatric Labelling, Sex Role Stereotypes and Beliefs About the Mentally Ill." *International Journal of Social Psychiatry* 44, no. 4 (1998): 235–47.

Courtwright, David T. *Dark Paradise: Opium Addiction in America Before 1940.* Cambridge, Mass.: Harvard University Press, 1982.

Courtwright, David, Herman Joseph, and Don Des Jarlais. *Addicts Who Survived: An Oral History of Narcotics Use in America, 1923–1965.* Knoxville: University of Tennessee Press, 1989.

Coutourier, Lance. "Inmates Benefit from Family Service Programs." *Corrections Today* 57, no. 5 (1995): 100.

Crandall, Charles, and Robert Martinez. "Culture, Ideology and Anti-fat Attitudes." *Personality and Social-Psychology Bulletin* 22 (1996): 227–43.

Critchlow, Donald T. "Lewis Meriam, Expertise and Indian Reform." *Historian* 43 (May 1998).

Cunningham, Michael, et al. "Consistency and Variability in the Cross-cultural Perception of Female Physical Attractiveness." *Journal of Personality and Social Psychology* 68 (1995): 26–79.

Dalkin, Allison, and Sarah Skett. "The Young Offender Treatment Program." *Corrections Today* 61 (February 1999): 64.

Darling, Rosalyn. "Parental Entrepreneurship: A Consumerist Response to Professional Dominance." *Journal of Social Issues* 44 (1988): 141–58.

Davis, Kingsley. "Sexual Behavior." In *Contemporary Social Problems,* edited by Robert Merton and Robert Nisbet. New York: Harcourt Brace Jovanovitch, 1997.

Dawidowicz, Lucy S. *The War Against the Jews 1933–1945.* New York: Holt, Rinehart and Winston, 1975.

Dawson, Daniel A. "Ethnic Differences in Female Overweight: Data from the National Health Interview Survey." *American Journal of Public Health* 78 (1988): 326–29.

de Beauvoir, Simone. *Old Age.* New York: Penguin, 1970.

———. *The Second Sex.* New York: Vintage Books, 1974.

de Koster, Katie. *Poverty: Opposing Viewpoints.* San Diego: Greenhaven Press, 1994.

de Tocqueville, Alexis. *Democracy in America.* New York: Vintage Books, 1996.

Dean, James C., and Gregory A. Poremba. "The Alcoholic Stigma and the Disease Concept." *International Journal of the Addictions* 8, no. 5 (July 1983): 750.

Deegan, Dorothy Yost. *The Stereotype of the Single Woman in American Novels.* New York: Octagon Books, 1969.

Demos, Victor, and Allan Jache. "Return to Sender, Please." *Women's Day* (September 22, 1998): 20–22.

DeOllos, Ione Y. *On Becoming Homeless.* Lanham, Md., and New York: University Press of America, 1997.

Disease, Condition and General Health Topic: Down Syndrome. Yahoo Health on Internet.

Doan, Laura L. *Old Maids to Radical Spinsters: Unmarried Women in the Twentieth-Century Novel.* Chicago: University of Illinois Press, 1997.

Docherty, John P. *Inpatient Psychiatry in the 1990s.* San Francisco: Jossey-Bass, 1994.

Dodds, E. R. *Pagan and Christian in an Age of Anxiety.* New York: Cambridge University Press, 1990.

Drucker, Ernst. "Drug Prohibition and Public Health: Twenty-five Years of Evidence." *Public Health Reports* 4 (1999): 4–5.

Duberman, Martin B., Martha Vicinius, and George Chauncey Jr. *Hidden from History: Reclaiming the Gay and Lesbian Past.* New York: Meridian/Penguin Books, 1990.

Dudley, James R. *Confronting the Stigma in Their Lives: Helping People with a Mental Retardation Label.* Springfield, Ill.: Charles C. Thomas, 1997.

Durant, Will. *Our Oriental Heritage.* New York: Simon and Schuster, 1954.

——. *The Age of Faith.* New York: MJF Books, 1950.

——. *The Life of Greece.* New York: Simon and Schuster, 1939.

Durant, Will, and Ariel Durant. *The Age of Louis XIV.* New York: Simon and Schuster, 1963.

Durkheim, Émile. *The Rules of the Sociological Method.* New York: Free Press, 1964.

——. *The Division of Labor in Society.* New York: Free Press, 1964.

Eagleton, Frank. *The Columbia Encyclopedia.* 5th ed. New York: Columbia University Press, 1993.

Easton, Caroline J., Suzanne Swan, and Rajita Sinha. "Prevalence of Family Violence in Clients Entering Substance Abuse Treatment." *Journal of Substance Abuse Treatment* 18 (January 2000): 23–28.

Eberle, Paul, and Shirley Eberle. *The Abuse of Innocence: The McMartin Preschool Trial.* Amherst, N.Y.: Prometheus Books, 1993.

Elliott, Joyce. "The Daytime Television Drama Portrayal of Older Adults." *Gerontologist* 24, no. 6 (December 1984): 629–33.

Ellis, Richard J. *Illiberal Egalitarianism in America.* Lawrence: University Press of Kansas, 1998.

Empey, LaMar T., Mark C. Stafford, and Carter H. Hay. *American Delinquency: Its Meaning and Construction.* Belmont, Calif.: Wadsworth Publishing Co., 1999.

Erikson, Kai T. *The Wayward Puritans.* New York: John Wiley and Sons, 1966.

Estimada, Abe. "Living Wage Is Guarantee for Only a Few." *USA Today*, December 28, 1999.

Evans, Elizabeth. "Why Should Obesity Be Managed?" *International Journal of Obesity* 23, no. 4 (May 1999): 53–55.

Falk, Gerhard. *Hippocrates Assailed: The American Health Delivery System.* Lanham, Md., and New York: University Press of America, 1999.

———. *Sex, Gender and Social Change.* Lanham, Md., and New York: University Press of America, 1998.

———. *A Study in Social Change.* Lewiston, N.Y.: Edwin Mellen Press, 1993.

———. *The Jew in Christian Theology.* Jefferson, N.C., and London: McFarland, Inc., 1992.

———. *Murder: An Analysis of Its Forms, Conditions and Causes.* Jefferson, N.C., and London: McFarland & Co., 1990.

Falk, Ursula A., and Gerhard Falk. *Ageism, the Aged and Aging in America.* Springfield, Ill.: Charles C. Thomas, 1997.

Family Research Council. "A Few Facts About Illegitimacy." *Focus* (January 2000): 13.

Farina, A., and K. Ring. "The Influence of Perceived Mental Illness on Relationships." *Journal of Abnormal and Social Psychology* 70 (1965): 47.

Faststats. Statistical Rolodex, http://www.cdc.gov/nchs/FASTATS/alcohol.htm.

Federal Bureau of Investigation. *Crime in the United States.* Washington, D.C.: Government Printing Office, 1998.

Ferguson, Susan J. "The 'Old Maid' Stereotype in American Film, 1938–1965." *Film and History* 21, no. 4 (September 1999): 3–4.

Fischer, Kathy E., et al. "The Relationship of Parental Alcoholism and Family Dysfunction to Stress Among College Students." *Journal of American College Health* 48, no. 4 (January 2000): 5.

Flynn, Kristin, and Marian Fitzgibbon. "Body Image Ideals of Low-Income African-American Mothers and Their Preadolescent Daughters." *Journal of Youth and Adolescence* 25, no. 5 (October 1996): 65.

Forbes, Cameron. "Child Exploitation in the Philippines." In Caroline Moorehead, *A Report on Violence Toward Children in Today's World.* New York: Doubleday, 1990.

Forssmann, Werner. *Experiments on Myself: Memories of a Surgeon in Germany.* New York: St. Martin's Press, 1964.

Forster, Arnold, and Benjamin R. Epstein. *The New Anti-Semitism.* New York: McGraw-Hill, 1974.

Frable, Deborah E. S., Camille Wortman, and Jill Joseph. "Predicting Self-Esteem, Well-Being, and Distress in a Cohort of Gay Men: The Importance of Cultural Stigma, Personal Visibility, Community Networks, and Positive Identity." *Journal of Personality* 65, no. 3 (September 1997): 599–624.

Frankl, Viktor E. *Man's Search for Meaning.* Translated by Ilse Lasch. New York: Washington Square Press, 1963.

Frazer, James G. *The Golden Bough: A Study in Magic and Religion.* London: Macmillan, 1924.

French, Laurence Armand. *The Winds of Injustice.* New York: Garland Publishing, 1994.

Friedan, Betty. *The Feminine Mystique.* New York: W. W. Norton & Co., 1962.

Frisancho, Albert, William Leonard, and L. Bollenteno. "Blood Pressure in Blacks and Whites and Its Relationship to Dietary Sodium and Potassium Intake." *Journal of Chronic Diseases* 37 (1984): 55.

Galanis, Clifford M. B., and Edward E. Jones. "When Stigma Confront Stigma: Some Conditions Enhancing a Victim's Tolerance of Other Victims." *Personality and Social Psychology Bulletin* 2, no. 2 (June 1986): 69.

Garfinkel, Harold. "The Encounters Where Individuals Are Conferred the Stigmatized Status Have Been Called 'Degradation Ceremonies.' " *American Journal of Sociology* 6 (1956): 420–24.

Gebhart, Theodore. *An Inquiry into the Relationship of Caregivers and Receivers of Care in Elder Abuse Situations.* New York: Yeshiva University, 1988.

Gerald, L. B., et al. "Social Class, Social Support and Obesity Risk in Children." *Child Care, Health and Development* 20, no. 3 (May–June 1993): 45–63.

Gewirtzman, Robert, and Isidore Fodor. "The Homeless Child at School: From Welfare Hotel to Classroom." *Child Welfare* 66 (May–June 1987): 237–45.

Gibbons, Frederick X. "Stigma Perception: Social Comparison Among Mentally Retarded Persons." *American Journal of Mental Deficiency* 90, no. 1 (July 1985): 98–106.

Gibney, Mark P., and Jeffrey L. Courtright. "Arguments for the Elimination of Religious Broadcasting from the Public Airways." *Notre Dame Journal of Law* 4, nos. 3–4 (fall–winter 1990).

Gilbert, Martin. *Churchill: A Life.* New York: Henry Holt and Company, 1996.

———. *The Holocaust: A History of the Jews of Europe During the Second World War.* New York: Henry Holt and Company, 1985.

Gilliam, David T. "Oophorectomy for the Insanity and Epilepsy of the Female: A Plea for Its More General Adoption." *Transactions of the American Association of Obstetricians and Gynecologists* 9 (1896): 320.

Gilmore, David D. *Manhood in the Making.* New Haven, Conn.: Yale University Press, 1990.

Globe 46, no. 49 (December 7, 1999).

Goffman, Erving. *Stigma and Stigmatization: Notes on the Management of Spoiled Identity.* Englewood Cliffs, N.J.: Prentice-Hall, 1963.

Goldberg, Carey. "Hawaii Judge Ends Gay-Marriage Ban." *New York Times,* December 4, 1996.

Goldberg, Vicki. "Looking Straight Into the Eyes of the Dying." *New York Times,* March 3, 1996, sec. 2, pp. 34, 37.

Goldhagen, Daniel J. *Hitler's Willing Executioners.* New York: Alfred A. Knopf, 1996.

Goldstein, Morris J. *New Developments in Interventions with Families of Schizophrenics.* San Francisco: Jossey-Bass, 1998.

Goldstein, Paul. "Occupational Mobility in the World of Prostitution: Becoming a Madam." *Deviant Behavior* 4 (1983): 267.

Gollay, Edward, et al. *Coming Back: The Community Experiences of Deinstitutionalized Mentally Retarded People.* Cambridge, Mass.: Abt Books, 1978.

Gomberg, Edith S. Lisansky. "Women in Treatment: The Question of Stigma and Age." *Alcohol and Alcoholics* 23, no. 6 (1988): 507.

Goodell, William. "Clinical Notes on the Extirpation of the Ovaries for Insanity." *American Journal of Insanity* 38 (January–April 1882): 295.

Goodman, Neil, S. M. Dornbusch, and Samuel A. Richardson. "Variant Reactions to Physical Disabilities." *American Sociological Review* 28 (1963): 429.

Goodstein, Laurie. "The Architect of the 'Gay Conversion' Campaign." *New York Times*, August 3, 1998, p. A10.

Gordon, Milton M. *Assimilation in American Life: The Role of Race, Religion and National Origins.* New York: Oxford University Press, 1964.

Gordon, Tuula. *Single Women: On the Margin?* New York: New York University Press, 1994.

Gore, Albert. "The McKinney Act." *Congressional Record* (March 23, 1987): S3683.

Gorman, Steve. "NBC Reneges on Promise to Jewish Group, Says It Will Repeat Spoof that Stirred Protest." *Buffalo News*, December 2, 1999, p. 10.

Gottfried, Ted. *Homelessness: Whose Problem Is It?* Brookfield, Conn.: Milbrook Press, 1999.

Grantland, Brenda. "L.A. Forfeiture Squads Kill California Millionaire." *F.E.A.R. Chronicles* 1, no. 5 (November 1992).

Grayzel, Solomon. *A History of the Jews.* Philadelphia: Jewish Publication Society, 1947.

Greenfield, Lawrence A., and Steven K. Smith. *American Indians and Crime.* Washington, D.C.: Bureau of Justice Statistics, 1999.

Greg, W. R. *Literary and Social Judgments.* Boston: James R. Osgood, 1873.

Gryta, Matt. "Four Nurse's Aides Accused of Beating Elderly Patients." *Buffalo News*, October 3, 1999.

Haack, Mary R., and Tonda L. Hughes. *Addiction in the Nursing Profession.* New York: Springer Publishing Co., 1989.

Hacker, Helen M. *The Feminine Protest of the Working Wife.* Garden City, N.Y.: Adelphi University, Department of Sociology, 1968.

Hall, Mimi. "Painful Path of Homelessness." *USA Today*, December 9, 1993, p. 8A.

Hamilton, Cicely. *Marriage as a Trade.* London: Women's Press, 1998.

Hannah, Mary E., and Elizabeth Midlarsky. "Competence and Adjustment of Siblings with Mental Retardation." *American Journal on Mental Retardation* 104, no. 1 (January 1999): 33.

Harkness, Georgia. *The Modern Rival of the Christian Faith.* New York: Abbington-Cokesbury, 1952.

Harvey, Daniel. *The Condition of Postmodernity.* London: Blackwell, 1989.

Hatfield, A., ed. *Families of the Mentally Ill: Meeting the Challenges.* San Francisco: Jossey-Bass, 1987.

Healy, S. "Growing to Be an Old Woman: Aging and Ageism." In Eleanor Stoller and Rose Gibson, *Worlds of Difference: Inequality in the Aging Experience.* Thousand Oaks, Calif.: Pine Forge Press, 1994.

Helmer, John. *Drugs and Minority Oppression.* New York: Seabury Publishing Co., 1975.

Hentoff, Nat. "A Blow to Freedom of Religion." *Progressive* (December 1990): 6.

Herek, G. M., and E. K. Glunt, "Interpersonal Contact and Heterosexuals' Attitudes toward Gay Men: Results from a National Survey." *Journal of Sex Research* 30 (1993): 239–44.

Hevesy, Dennis. "Building Homes for the Single Homeless." *New York Times*, April 25, 1999, XI–4.

Heyl, Barbara Serman. *The Madam as Entrepreneur: Career Management in House Prostitution.* New York: Transaction Publishers, 1979.

Hirschi, Travis, and Michael R. Gottfredson. "Rethinking the Juvenile Justice System." *Crime and Delinquency* 39 (1993): 262–71.

Hofstadter, Richard, and Michael Wallace. *American Violence.* New York: Random House, 1970.

Holloway, Lynette. "Seeing a Link Between Depression and Homelessness." *New York Times*, February 7, 1999, IV–3.

Horner, Matina. *The Challenge of Change; Perspectives on Family, Work and Education.* New York: Plenum Press, 1983.

House of Representatives. *Congressional Record* 42 (1996): 2905–47.

Howe, Irving. *World of Our Fathers.* New York: Simon and Schuster, 1976.

Howland, John, et al. "Work Site Variation in Managerial Drinking." *Addiction* 9 (1996): 1007–17.

Hueghey, Michael. "Internal Contradictions of Televangelism: Ethical Quandaries of 'That Old Time Religion' in a Brave New World." *International Journal of Politics, Culture and Society* 4, no. 1 (fall 1990): 3–47.

Huff, C. Ronald, and Matthew Meyer. "Managing Prison Gangs and Other Security Threat Groups." *Corrections Management Quarterly* (fall 1997): 11.

Hughes, Everett C. "Dilemmas and Contradictions of Status." *American Journal of Sociology* 50 (1945): 353–59.

Hyde, Margaret O. *Missing and Murdered Children.* New York: Franklin Watts, 1998.

Ichioka, Yuji. *The Isse.* New York: Free Press, 1988.

International Gay and Lesbian Association. "Being Gay and Lesbian: The Legal and Social Situation of Gay Men—Country by Country Survey." *Los Angeles Times*, December 9, 1992, p. H6.

Jackson, Robert. "Clinton Targets Youth in New Drug Plan." *Boston Globe*, February 26, 1997, p. A3.

Jacob, Theodore, et al. "Home Interactions of High and Low Anti-social Male Alcoholics and Their Families." *Journal of Studies on Alcohol* 6 (2000): 72.

Jacobs, Wilbur R. *Dispossessing the American Indian.* New York: Charles Scribner's Sons, 1972.

Jeffreys, Sheila. *The Spinster and Her Enemies; Feminism and Sexuality 1880–1930.* London: Pandora Publishing Co., 1985.

Jencks, Christopher. *The Homeless.* Cambridge, Mass.: Harvard University Press, 1994.

Jenness, Valerie. *Making It Work: The Prostitutes' Rights Movement in Perspective.* New York: Aldine De Gruyter, 1993.

Jimenes, Mary Ann. "Madness in Early American History: Insanity in Massachussetts from 1700 to 1830." *Journal of Social History* 20, no. 1 (1986): 25–26.

Johnson, Ray W. "APA, Science and the Defense of Marriage Act." *Psychological Reports* 8, no. 3, pt. 1 (December 1997): 1010.

Johnston, Lloyd, Jerald Bachman, and Patrick O'Malley. *Monitoring the Future.* Ann Arbor, Mich.: University of Michigan, 1998.

Jones, Nicholas F. *Ancient Greece: State and Society.* Upper Saddle River, N.J.: Prentice-Hall, 1996.

Kaplan, H. J. "The Psychosomatic Concept of Obesity." *Journal of Mental Disorders* 25 (1957): 8.

Kardiner, Abram. *The Individual and His Society: The Psychodynamics of Primitive Social Organization.* New York: Columbia University Press, 1939.

Karp, Abraham J. *Golden Door to America.* New York: Penguin Books, 1977.

Katz, Jack. *Seductions of Crime: Moral and Sensual Attractions in* Doing Evil. New York: BasicBooks, 1988.

Kellnian, Steven G. "As Time Goes By." *Nation* 250, no. 6 (February 12, 1990): 211.

Kendall, Diana. *Sociology in Our Times.* New York: Wadsworth Publishing Co., 1999.

Kenworthy, Tom. "Gay Student's Attacker Pleads Guilty, Gets Two Life Terms." *Washington Post*, April 6, 1999, p. A2.

King, Beverly R., and Kathryn R. Black. "Extent of Relational Stigmatization of Lesbians and Their Children by Heterosexual College Students." *Journal of Homosexuality* 7, no. 2 (1999): 65–81.

Klamen, Debra L., Linda S. Grossman, and David R. Kopacs. "Medical Student Homophobia." *Journal of Homosexuality* 37, no. 1 (1999): 54–63.

Knox, David. *Human Sexuality: The Search for Understanding.* New York: West Publishing Co., 1984.

Knox, Jean McBee. *Drinking, Driving and Drugs.* New York: Chelsea House Publishers, 1998.

Knox, John. *The Works.* Edited by David Lang. 1854. Reprint, New York: AMS, 1966.

Koch, Richard P. *1997 Conference of Delegates-Approved Resolutions.* Chicago: American Bar Association, 1997.

Kohlberg, Lest, and Robert Shulik. *The Aging Person as Philosopher.* Cambridge, Mass.: Harvard Graduate School of Education, 1998.

Kornblum, William, and Carolyn D. Smith. *Sociology in a Changing World.* New York: Harcourt College Publishers, 2000.

Krauthammer, Charles. "The Return of the Luddites." *Time* (December 3, 1999): 37.

Kravetz, Daniel. "Consciousness Raising and Self Help." In *Women and Psychotherapy: An Assessment of Research and Knowledge.* Edited by A. M. Brodsky and R. T. Hare-Mustin, pp. 267–83. New York: Guilford Press, 1998.

Krinsky, Carol Herselle. "Karl May's Western Novels and Aspects of Their Continuing Influence." *American Indian Culture and Research* 23, no. 2 (1999): 53–72.

Krisberg, Barry, Ira M. Schwartz, and Edmund F. McGarrell. "Reinventing Juvenile Justice: Research Directions." *Crime and Delinquency* 39 (1993): 3.

Kroll, Jerome. "A Reappraisal of Psychiatry in the Middle Ages." *Archives of General Psychiatry* 29 (1973): 276–83.

Krystal, Henry, and Herbert A. Raskin. *Drug Dependence: Aspects of Ego Function.* Detroit: Wayne State University Press, 1970.

Kurtz, P. David, Sara V. Jarvis, and Gail L. Kurtz. "Problems of Homeless Youths: Empirical Findings and Human Services Issues." *Social Work* 36, no. 4 (1991): 309–34.

Kutza, Elizabeth A., and Sharon M. Keigher. "The Elderly 'New Homeless': An Emerging Population at Risk." *Social Work* 36, no. 4 (1991): 288.

Lam, Julie A., and Robert Rosenheck. "Social Support and Service Use Among Homeless Persons with Serious Mental Illness." *International Journal of Social Psychiatry* 45, no. 1 (1999): 3–28.

Lambert, Wade. "EEOC Investigates Law Firm Hiring." *Wall Street Journal*, May 26, 1993, p. B5.

Landström, Björn. *Columbus: The Story of Don Cristobal Colon.* New York: Macmillan, 1967.

LaScala, Michael C. "Coupled Gay Men, Parents, and In-Laws: Intergenerational Disapproval and the Need for a Thick Skin." *Families in Society: The Journal of Contemporary Human Services* 79, no. 6 (November/December 1990: 585–95.

Lauman, Edward O., et al. *The Social Organization of Sexuality: Sexual Practices in the United States.* Chicago: University of Chicago Press, 1994.

Lazarus, Richard, and Susan Folkman. *Stress, Appraisal and Coping.* New York: Springer Publishing Co., 1984.

Legal Marriage Court Cases—A Timeline. Seattle: Partners Task Force for Gay & Lesbian Couples, 1999.

Lemert, Edwin M. *Human Deviance: Social Problems and Social Control.* Englewood Cliffs, N.J.: Prentice-Hall, 1972.

Leo, John. "Homeless Rights, Community Wrongs." *U.S. News and World Report* (July 24, 1989): 56.

Lerner, Stefan. "On the Words 'Mental Illness.'" *American Journal of Psychiatry* 52, no. 11 (November 1995): 62.

Levin, Sue. *In the Pink: The Making of Successful Gay- and Lesbian-Owned Businesses.* Binghamton, N.Y.: Harrington Park Press, 1999.

Levinthal, Charles F. *Drugs, Behavior and Modern Society.* Boston: Allyn and Bacon, 1996.

Lichtenberger, James P. *Divorce: A Social Interpretation.* New York: Arno Press, 1931.

Light, Stephen C. "Assault on Prison Officers: Interactional Themes." *Justice Quarterly* 8 (June 1999): 343.

Lindesmith, Alfred C. *Addiction and Opiate.* Chicago: Aldine Publishing Co., 1968.

Lindsey, Linda L., and Stephen Beach. *Sociology: Social Life and Social Issues.* Upper Saddle River, N.J.: Prentice-Hall, 2000.

Link, Bruce G., et al. "On Stigma and Its Consequences." *Journal of Health and Social Behavior* 38, no. 2 (June 1997): 77–90.

——. "The Social Rejection of Former Mental Patients: Understanding Why Labels Matter." *American Journal of Sociology* 92, no. 6 (May 1987): 1461–1500.

Locklear, Erin M. *Where Race and Politics Collide: The Federal Acknowledgment Process.* Princeton, N.J.: Princeton University Press, 1999.

Longfellow, Henry Wadsworth. *The Song of Hiawatha.* New York: Duell, Sloan and Pearce, 1966.

Lugaila, Terry A. "Marital Status and Living Arrangements: March 1998." *Current Population Reports.* Washington, D.C.: U.S. Department of Commerce, Census Bureau, 1998.

Luken, Paul C. "Social Identity in Late Life: A Situational Approach to Understanding Old Age Stigma." *National Journal of Aging and Social Development* 25, no. 3 (October 1987): 177–93.

Lunsky, Yona, and Susan M. Havercamp. "Distinguishing Low Levels of Social Support and Social Strain: Implications for Dual Diagnosis." *American Journal of Mental Retardation* 94, no. 2 (March 1999): 200–204.

Lupold, Harry Forest. *Forgotten People: The Woodland Erie.* Hicksville, N.Y.: Exposition Press, 1975.

Machan, Dyan. "Free Lunch—No Dishes to Wash." *Forbes* 6, no. 3 (1998): 64.

Macionis, John J. *Sociology.* 7th ed. Upper Saddle River, N.J.: Prentice-Hall, 1999.

MacIver, Robert M. *Social Causation.* New York: Harper Torchbooks, 1964.

MADD. Statistics at http://www.Madd.org/stats/repeat.html.

Maguire, Kathleen, and Ann L. Pastore, eds. *Sourcebook of Criminal Justice Statistics 1998.* Washington, D.C.: Bureau of Justice Statistics, 1998.

Maher, Lisa, and Kathleen Daly. "Women in the Street-Level Drug Economy." *Criminology* 34 (1996).

Mangione, Jerre, and Ben Morreale. *La Storia: Five Centuries of the Italian-American Experience.* New York: HarperCollins, 1992.

Mann, Timothy. "Pride in the Name of Jobs." *Corrections Today* (October 1999): 4–6.

Mannheim, Camryn. *Wake Up! I'm Fat.* New York: Soundelux cassette, 1999.

Mannis, Valerie S. "Single Mothers by Choice." *Family Relations* 48, no. 2 (April 1999): 2–28.

Manson, J. E., et al. "Body Weight and Longevity." *Journal of the American Medical Association* 257 (1987): 353–58.

Markowitz, Fred E. "The Effects of Stigma on the Psychological Well-Being and Life Satisfaction of Persons with Mental Illness." *Journal of Health and Social Behavior* 39, no. 4 (1998): 335–47.

Massimo, Teodori. *The New Left: A Documentary History.* Indianopolis: Bobbs-Merrill, 1969.

McCaffrey, Lawrence J. *Textures of Irish America.* Syracuse, N.Y.: Syracuse University Press, 1992.

McGrath, Claire E., et al. "Academic Achievement in Adolescent Children of Alcoholics." *Journal of Studies on Alcoholism* 60, no. 1 (January 1999): 24.

McGrory, Brian J., David M. McDowell, and Phillip R. Muskin. "Medical Students' Attitudes Toward AIDS, Homosexual, and Intravenous Drug-Abusing Patients: A Reevaluation in New York City." *Psychosomatics* 3, no. 4 (fall 1990): 426–33.

McGuire, Sandra L. "Reduce Ageism in Kids by Screening What They Read." *Childhood Education* 69 (summer 1993): 204–10.

McKeganey, Neil, and Marina Bernard. *Sex Work on the Streets.* Philadelphia: Open University Press, 1996.

McKenna, Neil. "Diary." *New Statesman* 27 (December 4, 1998): 7.

McLeod, Eileen. *Women Working: Prostitution Now.* London: Croom Helm, 1982.

McManamon, Francis P. "Notice of Inventory Completion for Native American Human Remains." *Federal Register Online GPO Access* 64, no. 26 (November 9, 1999).

Mead, George Herbert. *Mind, Self and Society from the Standpoint of a Social Behaviorist.* Chicago: University of Chicago Press, 1934.

Mears, Daniel, Matthew Ploeger, and Mark Warr. "Explaining the Gender Gap in Delinquency: Peer Influence and Moral Evaluations of Behavior." *Journal of Research on Crime and Delinquency* 35 (1998): 251–66.

Mechanic, David. "Establishing Mental Health Priorities." *Milbank Quarterly* 72, no. 3 (1994): 510.

Meil-Hobson, Barbara. *Uneasy Virtue.* New York: BasicBooks, 1987.

"Melting Pot Survives, The." *Economist* 352 (July 3, 1999): 24.

Mendelson, B. K., and D. R. White. "Development of Self-body-esteem in Overweight Youngsters." *Developmental Psychology* 2 (1985): 90–96.

Mercer, Jane R. *Labeling the Mentally Retarded.* Berkeley: University of California Press, 1973.

Michaux, William. *The First Year Out.* Baltimore: Johns Hopkins University Press, 1969.

Mihesuah, Devon A. *American Indians: Stereotypes and Realities.* Atlanta: Clarity Press, 1996.

Miller, Gerald. "An Exploratory Study of Sibling Relationships in Families with Retarded Children." *Dissertation Abstracts International* 35: 21994B–21995B.

Miller, Jody. "Feminist Theory." In Alex Thio and Thomas Calhoun, *Readings in Deviant Behavior.* New York: HarperCollins, 1995.

Mills, Crystal, and Hiro Ota. "Homeless Women with Minor Children in the Detroit Metropolitan Area." *Social Work* 34 (1989): 485.

Mills, Hendrik. "American Indians + Welfare Liberalism = A Deadly Mix." *American Enterprise* 9, no. 6 (November–December 1998): 58.

Moncrieff, John, and D. C. Drummond. "Sexual Abuse in People with Alcohol Problems." *British Journal of Psychiatry* 69 (1996): 355–60.

Morais, Herbert M. *Deism in Eighteenth-Century America.* New York: Russell and Russell, 1960.

Morgan, D. L. "Adjusting to Widowhood: Do Social Networks Really Make It Easier?" *Gerontologist* 29 (1989): 101–107.

Murtagh, John M., and Sara Harris. *Cast the First Stone.* New York: McGraw-Hill, 1957.

Myers, Gustavus. *History of Bigotry in the United States.* New York: Capricorn Books, 1960.

National Coalition for the Homeless. "Why Are People Homeless?" *NCH Fact Sheet*, no. 1(December 29, 1999): 1.

National Institute on Drug Abuse. *Drug Abuse and Drug Abuse Research.* Rockville, Md.: National Institute on Drug Abuse, 1987.

National Law Center on Homelessness and Poverty. *Out of Sight—Out of Mind? A Report on Anti-Homeless Laws, Litigation and Alternatives in Fifty United States Cities, 1999.* Washington, D.C.: National Law Center on Homelessness and Poverty, 1999.

Neuberg, Steven L., et al. "When We Observe Stigmatized and 'Normal'; Individuals Interacting: Stigma by Association." *Personality and Social Psychology Bulletin* 20, no. 2 (April 1994): 196–209.

Newell, Karl M., et al. "Variability of Stereotypic Body-Rocking in Adults With

Mental Retardation." *American Journal of Mental Retardation* 104, no. 3 (May 1999): 279–88.

Nichols, Mark. "The Obesity Epidemic." *Maclean's* 2, no. 2 (January 1999): 55.

Nietzsche, Friedrich. *The Case of Wagner.* Translated by Walter Kaufman. New York: Vintage Books, 1967.

Norton, Sheldon, Albert Wandersman, and C. R. Goldman. "Perceived Costs and Benefits of Membership in a Self-Help Group: Comparisons of Members and Non-members of the Alliance for the Mentally Ill." *Community Mental Health Journal* 29, no. 2 (1993): 43–60.

O'Brien, Gerald Vincent. "Protecting the Social Body: Use of the Organism Metaphor in Fighting 'The Menace of the Feebleminded.'" *Mental Retardation* 37, no. 3 (June 1999): 90.

O'Day, Jennifer A., and Susan Abraham. "Association between Self-Concept and Body Weight." *Adolescence* 34, no. 33 (spring 1999): 69.

O'Hare, Thomas, Cynthia L. Williams, and Alan Ezoviski. "Fear of AIDS and Homophobia: Implications for Direct Practice and Advocacy." *Social Work* 4, no. 1 (January 1996): 5–58.

Ohtake, Yoshi, and Janis G. Chadsey. "Social Disclosure Among Coworkers Without Disabilities in Supported Employment Settings." *Mental Retardation* 37, no. 1 (February 1999): 25–35.

Orbach, Susie. *Fat Is a Feminist Issue.* New York: Berkley Publishing Group, 1988.

Ortega, Tony. "Sky Writer." *Phoenix New Times,* September 25–October 1, 1997.

Palmore, Erdman. "Attiudes Toward Aging as Shown by Humor: A Review." In Lucille Nahemow, Kathleen A. McCluskey-Fawcett, and Paul E. McGhee. *Humor and Aging.* New York: Academic Press, 1986, 101–19.

Parillo, Vincent N. *Strangers to These Shores.* New York: Macmillan Publishing Co., 1990.

Parham, Iris A. *Leonard W. Poon and Irene Siegler.* New York: Springer Publishing Co., 1990.

Park, Robert E., and Ernest W. Burgess. *Introduction to the Science of Sociology.* Chicago: University of Chicago Press, 1924.

Passel, Jeffrey S., and Michael Fix. "Myths About Immigrants." *Foreign Policy* 95 (summer 1994): 51.

Pateman, Carole. "What's Wrong with Prostitution?" *Women's Studies Quarterly* 27 (spring/summer 1999): 53.

Peerman, Dean. "Bare-Bones Imbroglio: Repatriating Indian Remains and Sacred Artifacts." *Christian Century* 107 (October 7, 1990): 935.

Pelka, Fred. "Unequal Justice: Preserving the Rights of the Mentally Retarded in the Criminal Justice System." *Humanist* 57, no. 6 (November–December 1997): 28–32.

Pheterson, Gail. *A Vindication of the Rights of Whores.* Seattle: Free Press, 1989.

Pignitore, Robert, et al. "Bias against Overweight Job Applicants in a Simulated Employment Interview." *Journal of Applied Psychology* 79 (1994): 909–97.

Piner, Kelly E., and Lynn R. Kahle. "Adapting to the Stigmatizing Label of Mental Illness: Foregone But Not Forgotten." *Journal of Personality and Social Psychology* 47, no. 4 (October 1984): 811.

Polk, Nancy. "Homeless Children Find an Advocate." *New York Times*, May 9, 1999, p. C7.

Ponticelli, Charles M. "The Spiritual Warfare of Exodus: A Positivist Research Adventure." *Qualitative Inquiry* 2, no. 2 (1996): 98–129.

Pooley, Eric. "Kiss But Don't Tell." *Time* 5, no. 11 (1998).

Pope, Carl. "Race and Crime Revisited." *Crime and Delinquency* 25 (1979): 347.

Popper, Karl. *The Open Society and Its Enemies.* New York: Harper Torchbooks, 1963.

Post, Diane. "Legalizing Prostitution: A Systematic Rebuttal." *Off Our Backs* 24 (July 1999): 8.

Potter, George. *To the Golden Door: The Story of the Irish in Ireland and America.* Boston: Little Brown & Co., 1960.

Prasad, Monica. "The Morality of Market Exchange: Love Money and Contractual Justice." *Sociological Perspective* 42, no. 2 (summer 1999): 183.

Pratarelli, Marc E., and Jennifer Donaldson. "Immediate Effects of Written Material on Attitudes Toward Homosexuality." *Psychological Reports* 8, no. 3 (December 1997): 1411–45.

Pressley, Sue Ann. "Two Accused of Killing, Burning Gay Man." *Washington Post*, March 5, 1999, p. A24.

Pritchard, Mary E., Sondra L. King, and Dorice M. Czajka-Narins. "Adolescent Body Mass Indices and Self-Perception." *Adolescence* 32, no. 28 (winter 1997): 863–80.

Purdue, Charles W., and Michael B. Gurtman. "Evidence for the Automaticity of Ageism." *Journal of Experimental Social Psychology* 26 (1990): 199–216.

Quinn, M. M. "Attachment between Mothers and Their Down's Syndrome Infants." *Western Journal of Nursing Research* 13 (1991): 382–96.

Rabbinical Assembly's Commission on Human Sexuality. *Pastoral Letter on Human Sexuality.* New York: United Synagogue of Conservative Judaism, 1998.

Rafter, N. H. *White Trash: The Eugenic Family Studies 1877–1927.* Boston: Northeastern University Press, 1988.

Raissman, Bob. "NBC's Gray Wrong to Go After Rose." *Daily News*, October 25, 1999.

Rawls, John. *A Theory of Justice.* Cambridge, Mass.: Harvard University Press, 1997.

Rettig, Richard P., Manuel J. Torres, and Gerald R. Garrett. *Manny: A Criminal Addict's Story.* New York: Houghton Mifflin, 1977.

Rice, Elizabeth. "The Devil, the Body and the Feminine Soul in Puritan New England." *Journal of American History* 82, no. 1 (June 1995): 16.

Rix, Sara E., ed. *The American Woman, 1987–1988: A Report in Depth.* New York: W. W. Norton & Co., 1987.

Roane, Kit. "Gangs Turn to New Trade." *New York Times*, July 11, 1999, p. I23.

Roberts, Nicki. *Whores in History: Prostitution in Western Society.* London: HarperCollins, 1992.

Robinson, Rita. *When Women Choose to Be Single.* North Hollywood, Calif.: Newcastle Publishing Co., 1992.

Rosen, James. "Obesity Stigmatization and Coping." *International Journal of Obesity* 23 (March 1999): 221–30.

Rosenhahn, Daniel L. "On Being Sane in Insane Places." *Science* 79 (1973): 250–58.

Ross, Catherine E. "Overweight and Depression." *Journal of Health and Social Behavior* 35, no. 1 (March 1994): 63–78.

Ross, Stephen D. *The Ring of Representation.* Albany: State University of New York Press, 1992.

Rossi, Peter H. *Down and Out in America.* Chicago: University of Chicago Press, 1989.

Rothblum, Esther. "The Stigma of Women's Weight: Social and Economic Realities." *Feminism and Psychology* 2, no. 1 (1992): 6–73.

Rudolph, John. "The Impact of Contemporary Ideology and AIDS on the Counseling of Gay Clients." *Counseling and Values* 33 (1989): 97–108.

Rumbault, Rubén J. "Origins and Destinies: Immigration to the United States Since World War II." *Sociological Forum* 9, no. 4 (1994): 583–62.

Russell, Jeffrey B. "Concepts of Witchcraft." In *The Encyclopedia of Religion*, edited by Mircea Eliades, pp. 47–423. New York: Macmillan Publishing Co., 1989.

Sabato, Larry J. *Feeding Frenzy: How Attack Journalism Has Transformed American Politics.* New York: Free Press, 1995.

Sachar, Abraham Leon. *A History of the Jews.* New York: Alfred A. Knopf, 1970.

"Same-Sex Marriage Loses in Alaska, Hawaii Elections." *Marantha Christian Journal* (November 4, 1998).

Sanders, Jennings B. *History of the United States.* Evanston, Ill.: Row, Peterson and Co., 1962.

Sandmaier, Marian. *The Invisible Alcoholics: Women and Alcohol Abuse in America.* New York: McGraw-Hill Book Co., 1980.

Sapir, Edward. *Language: An Introduction to the Study of Speech.* New York: Harcourt, Brace and World, 1949.

Scambler, Graham, and Annette Scambler. *Rethinking Prostitution: Purchasing Sex in the 1990s.* London and New York: Routledge, 1997.

Schaefer, Richard T. *Racial and Ethnic Groups.* New York: HarperCollins, 1993.

Schaie, K. Warner. "Ageist Language in Psychological Research." *American Psychologist* 58, no. 1 (January 1993): 49–51.

Schaler, Jeffrey A. "Drugs and Free Will." *Society* 28 (September 1991): 42.

Scheff, Thomas. *Being Mentally Ill: A Sociological Theory.* Chicago: Aldine Publishing Co., 1987.

Schlesinger, Arthur, Jr. *The Age of Roosevelt: The Crisis of the Old Order.* Boston: Houghton-Mifflin Co., 1957.

Schlosser, Eric. "The Prison-Industrial Complex." *Atlantic Monthly* (December 1998).

Schreiber, Elliott S., and Douglas A. Boyd. "How the Elderly Perceive Television Commercials." *Journal of Communication* 30, no. 1 (winter 1980): 52.

Schur, Edwin M. *Labeling Women Deviant: Gender, Stigma and Social Control.* New York: Random House, 1983.

Schwanberg, Sandra L. "Attitudes Towards Homosexuality in American Health Care Literature 1983–1987." *Journal of Homosexuality* 9, no. 3 (1990): 7–36.

Schwartz, Hillel. *Never Satisfied.* New York: Free Press, 1986.

Seligman, Milton, and Rosalyn Darling. *Ordinary Families, Special Children: A Systems Approach to Childhood Disabilities.* New York: Guilford Press, 1989.

Seltzer, Richard. "AIDS, Homosexuality, Public Opinion, and Changing Correlates Over Time." *Journal of Homosexuality* 26, no. 1 (1993): 85–97.

Sengupta, Somini. "Despite Cold, Some Homeless Devise Strategies to Avoid Shelters." *New York Times,* January 4, 1999, p. B5.

Shane, Paul G. *The State of America's Children.* Washington, D.C.: Children's Defense Fund, 1992.

——. *What About America's Homeless Children?* Thousand Oaks, Calif.: Sage Publications, 1996.

Sheaffer, Robert. *Resentment Against Achievement.* Amherst, N.Y.: Prometheus Books, 1988.

Shenck, Joshuah. "Doctors Given Federal Threat on Marijuana." *New York Times,* December 3, 1996, p. A1.

Shenon, Phillip. "Administration Offers a Tough New Drug Bill." *New York Times,* May 7, 1990, p. A2.

Sher, Kenneth J., et al. "Characteristics of Children of Alcoholics." *Journal of Abnormal Psychology* 100 (1991): 427–48.

Shover, Neal, and David Honaker. "The Socially-bounded Decision Making of Persistent Property Offenders." *Howard Journal of Criminal Justice* 3 (1992): 283.

Shuman, Todd. "Misanthropy or No—Where Does It Go?" *Earth First Journal* (May 1, 1999): 9.

Siegel, Larry J. *Criminology.* Belmont, Calif.: Wadsworth/Thompson Learning, 1999.

Simon, Barbara L. *Never Married Women.* Philadelphia: Temple University, 1987.

Simon, Bennett. *Mind and Madness in Ancient Greece.* Ithaca, N.Y.: Cornell University Press, 1978.

Smart C., and B. Smart. *Women, Sexuality and Social Control.* London: Routledge and Kegan Paul, 1978.

Smith, M. B. *The Single Woman Today: Her Problems and Adjustment.* London: Watts Publishing Co., 1995.

Smith, Wanda J., and K. Vernard Harrington. "Younger Supervisor-Older Subordinate Dyads: A Relationship of Cooperation or Resistance." *Psychological Reports* 47, no. 3 (June 1994): 803–82.

Snyder, Catherine Jorgensen, and Gerald V. Barrett. "The Age Discrimination in Employment Act: A Review of Court Decisions." *Experimental Age Research* 4 (spring 1988): 3.

Sobal, John, Victor Nicolopoulos, and J. Lee. "Attitudes about Weight and Dating among Secondary School Students." *International Journal of Obesity* 9 (1995): 376–81.

Sobal, Jeffrey, Barbara S. Rauschenbach, and Edward A. Frongillo Jr. "Marital Status, Fatness and Obesity." *Social Science and Medicine* 35, no. 7 (October 1992): 915–23.

Sobal, Jeffrey, Richard T. Tropiano, and Edward A. Frongillo Jr. "Rural-Urban Differences in Obesity." *Rural Sociology* 6, no. 2 (summer 1996): 289–305.

Spectrum 46, no. 4 (December 1996): 4.

Spicer, Edward H. "The Nations of a State." *Boundary* 9, no. 2 (1992): 26–48.

Starkey, Marion L. *The Devil in Massachusetts.* New York: Alfred A. Knopf, 1949.

Status Report on Hunger and Homelessness in American Cities. Washington, D.C.: U.S. Conference of Mayors, 1999.

Steigerwald, Fran, and David Stone. "Cognitive Restructuring and the 12-Step Program of Alcoholics Anonymous." *Journal of Substance Abuse Treatment* 6, no. 4 (1999): 321.

Stolley, Kathy Shepherd, and Archie E. Hill. "Presentation of the Elderly in Textbooks on Marriage and the Family." *Teaching Sociology* 24, no. 1 (January 1996): 34–35.

Stouffer, Samuel A. *The American Soldier: Adjustment during Army Life.* Princeton, N.J.: Princeton University Press, 1949.

Sutherland, Edwin H., and Donald R. Cressey. *Criminology.* 10th ed. Philadelphia: J. B. Lippincott, 1978.

Sykes, Gresham M., and David Matza. "Techniques of Neutralization: A Theory of Delinquency." *American Sociological Review* 22 (December 1957): 664–70.

Szacz, Thomas S. *The Myth of Mental Illness.* New York: Dell Publishing Co., 1996.

Szivos, S. E., and Edward Griffiths. "Group Processes Involved in Coming to Terms with a Mentally Retarded Identity." *Mental Retardation* 28, no. 6 (December 1990): 338–41.

Taubes, Tanaquil. "Healthy Avenues of the Mind: Psychological Theory Building and the Influence of Religion During the Era of Moral Treatment." *American Journal of Psychiatry* 55, no. 8 (1998): 1003–1008.

Taylor, S. E., J. V. Wood, and R. R. Lichtman. "It Could Be Worse: Selective Evaluation as a Response to Victimization." *Journal of Social Issues* 39 (1983): 1940.

Terkel, Studs. *Working.* New York: Pantheon Books, 1974.

Terkelson, Kathleen G. "Schizophrenia and the Family: Adverse Effects of Family Therapy." *Family Process* 22 (1983): 191–200.

Thickstun, Margaret O. *Fictions of the Feminine: Puritan Doctrine and the Representation of Women.* Ithaca, N.Y.: Cornell University Press, 1988.

Thio, Alex. *Sociology.* New York: Longman, 1998.

"Thirty-seven Percent Say AIDS Altered Their Attitude to Homosexuals." *New York Times*, December 5, 1985, p. A41.

"This Is What You Thought: Is Society Biased against Single Women?" *Glamour* 95, no. 4 (April 1999): 229.

Thomas, William I. *The Child in America.* New York: Alfred Knopf & Co., 1928.

Thompson, Mark. "Why Do People Have to Push Me Like That?" *Time* 54 (December 3, 1999): 56.

Thornton, Russell. "American Indian Fertility Patterns." *American Indian Quarterly* 5 (summer 1991): 359–67.

Toch, Hans. *Peacekeeping: Police, Prisons and Violence.* Lexington, Mass.: Lexington Books, 1976.

Toth, Jennifer. *The Mole People; Life in the Tunnels beneath New York City.* Chicago: Chicago Review Press, 1993.

Tuke, D. Hack. *A Dictionary of Psychological Medicine.* New York: Arno Press, 1976.

Turner, Patricia A. *I Heard It Through the Grapevine: Rumor in African-American Culture.* Berkeley: University of California Press, 1993.

Twain, Mark. "Concerning the Jews." *Harper's New Monthly Magazine* 199, no. 592 (1899): 527–35.

U.S. Bureau of the Census. Washington, D.C.: Census Bureau On Line Service, 1996.

———. *Poverty in the United States.* Washington, D.C.: U.S. Department of Commerce, July 24, 1997.

———. *Statistical Abstracts of the U.S.* 6th ed. Washington, D.C.: U.S. Government Printing Office, 1996.

U.S. Congress, 101st Session, Anti-Drug Abuse Act of 1988, Public Law No. 00-690; Sub-Title A-Death Penalty, Sec. 700 (June 1, 1989).

U.S. Department of Education. *Seventeenth Annual Report to Congress on the Implementation of the Individuals with Disabilities Education Act.* Washington, D.C.: U.S. Government Printing Office, 1995.

———. *Twentieth Annual Report to Congress on the Implementation of the Individuals with Disabilities Education Act.* Washington, D.C.: U.S. Government Printing Office, 1999.

U.S. Department of Health and Human Services. *The Household Survey of Drug Abuse.* Washington, D.C.: U.S. Government Printing Office, 1998.

U.S. Department of Health and Human Services, National Center for Health Statistics. DHHS Publication No. PHS 85–232. Washington, D.C., 1985.

U.S. Department of Justice, Office of Juvenile Justice and Delinquency Prevention. *Juvenile Offenders and Victims: 1997 Update on Violence.* Washington D.C.: U.S. Government Printing Office, 1998.

U.S. Public Health Service. *1988 Surgeon General's Report on Nutrition and Health.* Washington, D.C.: U.S. Department of Health and Human Services, 1988.

Van Voorhis, Patricia, Sandra Lee Browning, and Marilyn Simon. "The Meaning of Punishment: Inmates Orientation to the Prison Experience." *Prison Journal* 77 (1997): 73.

Vissing, Yvonne M. *Out of Sight—Out of Mind.* Lexington: University of Kentucky Press, 1996.

Von Krafft-Ebing, Richard. *Textbook of Insanity.* Philadelphia: F. A. Davis, 1904.

Voysey, Margaret. *A Constant Burden: The Reconstitution of Family Life.* Boston: Routledge and Kegan Paul, 1975.

Wadsworth, Nancy D. "Reconciliation Politics: Conservative Evangelicals and the New Race Discourse." *Politics and Society* 25, no. 3 (September 1997): 350–52.

Wagner, David. *Checkerboard Square; Culture and Resistance in a Homeless Community.* Boulder, Colo.: Westview Press, 1993.

Warner, W. Lloyd, and Leo Srole. *The Social Systems of American Ethnic Groups.* New Haven, Conn.: Yale University Press, 1945.

Warnick, Mark S. "Feeling Free, Wrongly Jailed for Two Years, Randall Adams Is Having His Say." *Chicago Tribune,* June 28, 1991, Tempo section, p. 14.

Weber, Adna Ferrin. *The Growth of Cities in the Nineteenth Century.* Ithaca, N.Y.: Cornell University Press, 1963.

Weber, Max. *The Protestant Ethic and the Spirit of Capitalism.* New York: Scribner's Sons, 1974.

"Weighty Problem, A." *American Institute for Cancer Research Science News* (March 1999): 11.

Weinstein, Raymond M. "Goffman's Asylums and the Total Institution Model of Mental Hospitals." *Psychiatry* 57, no. 4 (November 1994): 348–67.

Weisberg, D. Kelly. *Children of the Night: A Study of Adolescent Prostitution.* Lexington, Mass.: Lexington Books, 1985.

Weisse, Allen B. *Conversations in Medicine: The Story of Twentieth-Century American Medicine in the Words of Those Who Created It.* New York: New York University Press, 1984.

Whitam, Frederick L., and Ronin M. Mathay. *Male Homosexuality in Four Societies: Brazil, Guatemala, the Philippines and the United States.* New York: Praeger, 1986.

Whitbourne, Susan K., and Irene M. Hulicka. "Ageism in Undergraduate Psychology Texts." *American Psychologist* 45, no. 10 (October 1990): 27–36.

Wickens, Barbara. "Extreme Acts: Drastic Shortcuts to Slimness Carry Their Own Risks." *Maclean's* 2, no. 2 (January 11, 1999): 11, 60–66.

Wistrich, Robert S. "Once Again, Anti-Semitism Without Jews." *Commentary* 94 (August 1992): 45–49.

Witkin, Gordon. "Why This Country Is Losing the Drug War." *U.S. News & World Report* (September 6, 1996): 60.

Wittke, Carl. *The Irish in America.* Baton Rouge: Louisiana State University Press, 1950.

Wolf, Naomi. *The Beauty Myth: How Images of Beauty Are Used Against Women.* New York: Murrow, 1990.

Wright, John W., ed. *The New York Times Almanac.* New York: Penguin Books, 1998.

Wright, Richard T., and Scott H. Decker. *Armed Robbers in Action.* Boston: Northeastern University Press, 1997.

Yang, Alan S. "Attitudes Toward Homosexuality." *Public Opinion Quarterly* 6, no. 3 (fall 1997): 477–88.

Yedidia, Michael J., Carolyn A. Berry, and Judith K. Barr. "Changes in Physicians' Attitudes Toward AIDS During Residency Training: A Longitudinal Study of Medical School Graduates." *Journal of Health and Social Behavior* 37, no. 2 (June 1996): 179–91.

Yip, Andrew K. T. "The Politics of Counter-Rejection: Gay Christians and the Church." *Journal of Homosexuality* 37, no. 2 (1999): 51.

Zaitzow, Barbara H. "Treatment Needs of Women in Prison." In *Turnstile Justice: Issues in American Corrections*, edited by Ted Alleman and Rosemary Gido. Upper Saddle River, N.J.: Prentice-Hall, 1998.

Zborowski, Mark, and Elizabeth Herzog. *Life Is with People: The Culture of the Shtetl.* New York: Schocken Books, 1952.

Zdrodowski, Dawn. "Eating Out: The Experience of Eating in Public for the Overweight Woman." *Women's Studies International Forum* 9, no. 6 (November–December 1996): 665–66.

Zeitlin, Marilyn. "Too Old for Hollywood." *Progressive* 56, no. 1 (January 1992): 33–34.

Zilboorg, Gregory. *A History of Medical Psychology.* New York: W. W. Norton & Co., 1994.

GLOSSARY

Achieved status. A position or rank that is earned through the efforts of the individual.

Age cohort. A group of people born the same year.

Ageism. An ideology which justifies prejudice based on age.

Alienation. Feeling powerless to control one's own destiny.

Ascribed status. A rank assigned at birth.

Assimilation. The merging of two or more cultures.

Behavioral assimilation. The situation in which the minority adopts the conduct of the majority.

Behaviorism. A theory which holds that all behavior is learned.

Class. A social stratum defined by economic considerations.

Crime. An act or failure to act that is prohibited by law.

Culture lag. The time required to adopt to a major technological change.

Culture. The man-made environment.

Deviance. Behavior that violates the norms of any **reference group.**

Differential association. A theory which explains deviance as learned behavior.

Discrimination. Unfair treatment based on group membership.

Education. The transmission of knowledge from one generation to the next.

Endogamy. Marriage within a specified group.

Ethnic group. A group which shares a common culture.

Exogamy. Marriage outside a specified group.

Folkways. Weakly sanctioned norms.

Function. Anticipated consequence.

Functionalism. A sociological theory which explains how all social structures contribute to social order.

Gender. The culturally defined role played by each sex.

Genocide. The mass murder of an entire people by another people.

Heterosexuality. Sexual orientation toward the opposite sex.

Homosexuality. Sexual orientation toward the same sex.

Hypothesis. A statement concerning the relationship of two or more variables testable through empirical obeservation.

In-group. A group to which an individual owes allegiance or to which he refers his conduct.

Institution. A structure of statuses and roles which meets the needs of society.

Labeling. A theory that explains deviance as a societal reaction.

Life expectancy. The average number of years members of a given group can expect to live.

Master status. A status that takes precedence over any other status a person may have.

Metropolitan area. An area including a city and those suburbs which constitute an economic unit.

Minority group. Any group singled out for unequal treatment.

Mores. Strongly sanctioned norms.

Norms. Specific rules of behavior.

Nuclear family. Two or more people related by blood, marriage, or adoption who share a household.

Out-group. Any group of people who are viewed as outsiders and to whom one has no allegiance.

Patriarchy. The dominance of men over women.

Prejudice. A prejudgment (an opinion based on hearsay, not observation) concerning the characteristics of a group.

Primary group. A group in face-to-face association such as a family.

Race. A subdivision of the human species who have several physical characteristics in common.

Racism. The belief that acquired characteristics are inherited.

Reference group. A group whose opinions determine our conduct.

Role. The manner in which each individual in any group must behave.

Sample. A set of respondents selected from a specific population.

Secularization. The reduction of religious dominance by objective analysis.

Sexism. An ideology that justifies discrimination based on sex.

Significant other. Any person important to another.

Social control. A set of rules, either formal or informal, which seek to limit the behavior of anyone in the group.

Social mobility. Movement by an individual or a group from a higher to a lower or a lower to a higher status.

Social stratification. The process by which members of a society are sorted into different statuses.

Sociology. The scientific study of the situation in which any human act occurs.

Status. Any position in any social arrangement such as husband and wife; the sum of one's rights and privileges.

Stigma. An attribute in a person or group which is viewed as setting that person or group apart from the rest of society.

Structural assimilation. A situation in which the minority is accepted on equal terms by the majority.

Subculture. A culture within a larger culture.

Survey. A research method that involves asking questions about opinions, beliefs, or behavior.

Technology. The use of knowledge and tools to manipulate the natural environment.

Total institution. An institution isolated from the outside world and used to control inmates.

Urbanization. A process whereby an increasing segment of the population settles in cities.

Values. The preferences for any line of action.

INDEX